Microsoft® VBScript
Step by Step

Ed Wilson

PUBLISHED BY
Microsoft Press
A Division of Microsoft Corporation
One Microsoft Way
Redmond, Washington 98052-6399

Library of Congress Control Number: 2006934395

Printed and bound in the United States of America.

1 2 3 4 5 6 7 8 9 QWT 1 0 9 8 7 6

Distributed in Canada by H.B. Fenn and Company Ltd.

A CIP catalogue record for this book is available from the British Library.

Microsoft Press books are available through booksellers and distributors worldwide. For further information about international editions, contact your local Microsoft Corporation office or contact Microsoft Press International directly at fax (425) 936-7329. Visit our Web site at www.microsoft.com/mspress. Send comments to mspinput@microsoft.com.

Acquisitions Editor: Martin DelRe
Project Editor: Maureen Williams Zimmerman
Copy Editor: Sarah Wales-McGrath
Technical Reviewer: David Holder
Indexer: Jeanne Busemeyer

Body Part No. X13-24158

Dedication

This book is dedicated to my best friend, Teresa.

Contents at a Glance

Part I   **Starting from Scratch**

  1   Covering the Basics 3

  2   Looping Through the Script 25

  3   Adding Intelligence 55

  4   Working with Arrays 81

  5   More Arrays 113

Part II   **Basic Windows Administration**

  6   Working with the File System 139

  7   Working with Folders 165

  8   Using WMI 187

  9   WMI Continued 207

 10   Querying WMI 227

Part III   **Advanced Windows Administration**

 11   Introduction to Active Directory Service Interfaces 251

 12   Writing for ADSI 269

 13   Using ADO to Perform Searches 293

 14   Configuring Network Components 315

 15   Using Subroutines and Functions 329

 16   Logon Scripts 349

 17   Working with the Registry 367

 18   Working with Printers 381

Part IV Scripting Other Applications

20   Working with Exchange 2003 407

21   Troubleshooting WMI Scripting 419

Part V Appendices

A   VBScript Documentation 443

B   ADSI Documentation... 449

C   WMI Documentation... 457

D   Documentation Standards 463

E   Special Folder Constants..................................... 467

Index 469

Table of Contents

Acknowledgments. xvii

Introduction xix

Part I   Starting from Scratch

1   Covering the Basics 3

Running Your First Script 3

Header Information 5

Reference Information. 8

Worker Information 9

Output Information 12

Enhancing Your Script 13

Modifying an Existing Script. 14

Modifying the Header Information. 15

Modifying the Reference Information. 16

Modifying the Worker Information. 18

Modifying the Output Information. 19

Exploring a Script: Step-by-Step Exercises 22

One Step Further: Customizing an Existing Script. 22

2   Looping Through the Script. 25

Adding Power to Scripts 25

For Each...Next 26

Header Information 27

Reference Information. 30

Worker Information 30

For...Next 31

Header Information 32

Reference Information. 33

Worker and Output Information 34

Do While...Loop 37

    Header Information. 38

    Reference Information 39

    Worker and Output Information 40

Do Until...Loop 43

    Worker and Output Information 45

Do...Loop 47

While...Wend 47

Creating Additional Objects 48

Using the *For Each...Next* Command Step-by-Step Exercises 51

One Step Further: Modifying the Ping Script 52

3   Adding Intelligence **55**

If...Then 55

    Header Information. 57

    Reference Information 57

    Worker and Output Information 58

If...Then...ElseIf 62

    Header Information. 64

    Reference Information 65

    Worker and Output Information 65

If...Then...Else 67

Select Case 69

    Header Information. 71

    Reference Information 71

    Worker and Output Information. 72

Modifying CPUType.vbs Step-by-Step Exercises 74

One Step Further: Modifying ComputerRoles.vbs 76

4   Working with Arrays **81**

Passing Arguments 81

Command-Line Arguments 81

    Making the Change. 82

    Running the Command Prompt 83

    No Arguments? 84

    Creating a Useful Error Message 84

Using Multiple Arguments 86

    Header Information. 88

    Reference Information 88

Worker and Output Information 89
Tell Me Your Name 89
    Reasons for Named Arguments 90
    Making the Change to Named Arguments 90
    Running a Script with Named Arguments 92
Working with Arrays. 93
Moving Past Dull Arrays 95
    Header Information 96
    Reference Information. 96
    Worker and Output Information 96
    What Does UBound Mean? 97
Two-Dimensional Arrays 101
    Mechanics of Two-Dimensional Arrays. 101
    Header Information 102
    Reference Information. 102
    Worker and Output Information 102
Passing Arguments Step-by-Step Exercises 103
One Step Further: Building Arrays. 107

5   More Arrays **113**
Strings and Arrays. 113
Parsing Passed Text into an Array 114
    Header Information 115
    Reference Information. 116
    Worker Information 117
    Output Information 118
Parsing Passed Text. 121
    Header Information 123
    Reference Information. 123
    Worker Information 124
    Output Information 124
Working with Dictionaries. 125
    Understanding the Dictionary Object. 125
    Adding Items to the Dictionary 126
Using Basic InStr Step-by-Step Exercises. 132
One Step Further: Creating a Dictionary 133

Part II   Basic Windows Administration

6   Working with the File System **139**

Creating the File System Object 139

File It Under Files 140

Header Information.. 140

Reference Information 141

Worker and Output Information.. 142

File Properties... 144

File Attributes 145

Implementing the Attributes Property............................... 146

Setting File Attributes 148

Creating Files 149

Writing to a Text File... 149

Determining the Best Way to Write to a File....................... 150

Overwriting a File 150

Verifying a File Exists... 156

Creating Files Step-by-Step Exercises 161

One Step Further: Creating a Log File 162

7   Working with Folders **165**

Working with Folders 165

Creating the Basic Folder 165

Creating Multiple Folders... 166

Header Information.. 167

Reference Information 167

Worker Information.. 167

Output Information... 168

Automatic Cleanup 172

Deleting a Folder.. 172

Deleting Multiple Folders... 173

Binding to Folders 174

Does the Folder Exist?.. 175

Copying Folders.. 176

Moving Folders 178

Creating Folders Step-by-Step Exercises 182

One Step Further: Deleting Folders 184

8   Using WMI **187**

   Leveraging WMI 187

   Understanding the WMI Model 188

   Working with Objects and Namespaces 189

   Digging Deeper 191

   Listing WMI Providers 192

   Working with WMI Classes 194

      Viewing Properties 197

      Working with WMI Methods 199

   Querying WMI 201

      Header Information 202

      Reference Information 202

      Worker and Output Information 203

   Retrieving Hotfix Information Step-by-Step Exercises 204

   One Step Further: Echoing the Time Zone 205

9   WMI Continued **207**

   Alternate Ways of Configuring the WMI Moniker 207

   Accepting Defaults 208

      Reference Information 208

      Worker and Output Information 208

   Moniker Security Settings 214

      WbemPrivilege Has Its Privileges 215

   Using the Default WMI Moniker Step-by-Step Exercises 220

   Invoking the WMI Moniker to Display the Machine Boot Configuration 221

   Including Additional Security Permissions 222

   One Step Further: Using *Win32_Environment* and VBScript to Learn About WMI   224

10   Querying WMI **227**

   Tell Me Everything About Everything! 227

      Header Information 228

      Reference Information 229

      Worker and Output Information 229

   Selective Data from All Instances 230

   Selecting Multiple Properties 231

   Choosing Specific Instances 237

   Using an Operator 238

   Where Is the Where Clause? 241

Writing an Informative WMI Script Step-by-Step Exercises 244

One Step Further: Obtaining More Direct Information 245

Part III Advanced Windows Administration

11 Introduction to Active Directory Service Interfaces 251

Working with ADSI 251

Reference Information 253

LDAP Names 255

Worker Information 255

Output Information 257

Creating Users 258

Reference Information 259

Worker Information 259

Output Information 259

Creating OUs Step-by-Step Exercises 263

One Step Further: Creating Multi-Valued Users 265

12 Writing for ADSI 269

Working with Users 269

General User Information 270

Reference Information 272

Worker Information 272

Output Information 273

Modifying the Address Tab Information 274

Reference Information 275

Worker Information 275

Output Information 277

Modifying Terminal Server Settings 283

Deleting Users 287

Deleting Users Step-by-Step Exercises 289

One Step Further: Using the Event Log 290

13 Using ADO to Perform Searches 293

Connecting to Active Directory to Perform a Search 293

Header Information 295

Reference Information 295

Worker and Output Information 296

Creating More Effective Queries 297

Searching for Specific Types of Objects 299

    Reference Information. 301

    Output Information 301

What Is Global Catalog? 303

Creating an ADO Query into Active Directory Step-by-Step Exercises 311

One Step Further: Controlling Script Execution While
Querying Active Directory 312

14   Configuring Network Components. 315

WMI and the Network. 315

    Making the Connection. 316

    Header Information 317

    Reference Information. 318

    Worker and Output Information 318

Changing the TCP/IP Settings 320

    Header Information 321

    Reference Information. 321

    Worker and Output Information 321

Merging WMI and ADSI 322

Win32_NetworkAdapterConfiguration. 323

Using WMI to Assign Network Settings Step-by-Step Exercises. 325

One Step Further: Combining WMI and ADSI in a Script 326

15   Using Subroutines and Functions 329

Working with Subroutines. 329

    Calling the Subroutine. 331

    Creating the Subroutine 332

Creating Users and Logging Results 332

    Header Information 335

    Reference Information. 335

    Worker Information 336

    Output Information 336

Working with Functions. 341

Using ADSI and Subs, and Creating Users Step-by-Step Exercises. 343

One Step Further: Adding a Logging Subroutine. 345

16   Logon Scripts **349**

    Working with *IADsADSystemInfo* 349

    Using Logon Scripts. 351

    Deploying Logon Scripts. 352

        Header Information. 354

        Reference Information 355

        Worker Information. 357

        Output Information. 358

    Adding a Group to a Logon Script Step-by-Step Exercises. 360

    One Step Further: Adding Logging to a Logon Script. 362

17   Working with the Registry **367**

    First You Back Up. 367

    Creating the *WshShell* Object 368

        Setting the *comspec* Variable. 368

        Defining the Command 369

    Connecting to the Registry 370

        Header Information. 371

        Reference Information 371

        Worker and Output Information. 372

    Unleashing the Power of the *StdRegProv* Class. 372

    Creating Registry Keys. 373

        Header Information. 374

        Reference Information 374

        Worker and Output Information. 375

    Writing to the Registry 375

    Deleting Registry Information 376

    Reading the Registry Using WMI Step-by-Step Exercises 377

    One Step Further: Creating Registry Keys 378

18   Working with Printers **381**

    Working with Win32_Printer 381

    Obtaining the Status of Printers 382

        Header Information. 383

        Reference Information 384

        Worker Information. 384

        Output Information. 385

Creating a Filtered Print Monitor. 386

    Reference Information. 387

    Output Information 387

Monitoring Print Queues. 388

    Worker and Output Information 389

Monitoring Print Jobs Step-by-Step Exercises 389

One Step Further: Checking the Status of a Print Server 391

Part IV   Scripting Other Applications

19   Managing IIS 6.0 395

Locating the WMI Classes for IIS 6.0. 395

    CIM_ManagedSystemElement 395

    CIM_Setting 395

    IisStructuredDataClass. 396

    CIM_Component. 396

    CIM_ElementSetting 396

    Using *MicrosoftIISv2* 396

Making the Connection. 397

    Header Information 397

    Reference Information. 398

    Worker and Output Information 399

Creating a Web Site 399

    Header Information 400

    Reference Information. 401

    Worker and Output Information 402

Backing Up the Metabase Step-by-Step Exercises 403

One Step Further: Importing the Metabase. 404

20   Working with Exchange 2003 407

Working with the Exchange Provider 407

Connecting to MicrosoftExchangeV2 408

The *Exchange_QueueSMTPVirtualServer* Class 409

    Header Information 409

    Reference Information. 410

    Worker Information 410

    Output Information 410

Exchange Public Folders 411

Exchange_FolderTree 413

Using the *Exchange_Logon* Class Step-by-Step Exercises 414

One Step Further: Using the *Exchange_Mailbox* Class 416

21   Troubleshooting WMI Scripting **419**

Identifying the Problem 419

Spotting Common Sources of Errors 419

Testing the Local WMI Service 420

Using the WMI Control Tool 420

Using the Scriptomatic 422

Examining the Status of the WMI Service 422

Using WBEMtest.exe 423

Testing Remote WMI Service 424

Remotely Using the WMI Control Tool. 424

Testing Scripting Interface 425

Obtaining Diagnostic Information 426

Enabling Verbose WMI Logging 427

Examining the WMI Log Files 428

Using the Err Tool 429

Using MofComp.exe 430

Using WMIcheck 431

General WMI Troubleshooting Steps 432

Working with Logging Step-by-Step Exercises 433

One Step Further: Compiling MOF Files 437

Part V   Appendices

Appendix A: VBScript Documentation 443

Appendix B: ADSI Documentation 449

Appendix C: WMI Documentation 457

Appendix D: Documentation Standards. 463

Appendix E: Special Folder Constants. 467

Index 469

Acknowledgments

The process of writing a technical book is more a matter of collaboration, support, and team work, than a single wordsmith sitting under a shade tree with parchment and pen. It is amazing how many people know about your subject after you begin the process.

I am very fortunate to have assembled a team of friends and well wishers over the past few years to assist, cajole, exhort, and inspire the words to appear. First and foremost is my wife Teresa. She has had the great fortune of reading 10 technical books in the past 11 years, while at the same time putting up with the inevitable encroachment of deadlines on our otherwise well timed vacation schedule. Claudette Moore of the Moore Literary Agency has done an awesome job of keeping me busy through all her work with the publishers. Martin DelRe at Microsoft Press has been a great supporter of scripting technology, and is a great person to talk to. Maureen Zimmerman, also of Microsoft Press, has done a great job of keeping me on schedule, and has made numerous suggestions to the improvement of the manuscript.

Introduction

Network administrators and consultants are confronted with numerous mundane and time-consuming activities on a daily basis. Whether it is going through thousands of users in Active Directory Users and Computers to grant dial-in permissions to a select group, or changing profile storage locations to point to a newly added network server, these everyday tasks must be completed. In the enterprise space, the ability to quickly write and deploy a Microsoft Visual Basic Script (VBScript) will make the difference between a task that takes a few hours and one that takes a few weeks.

As an Enterprise Consultant for Microsoft Corporation, I am in constant contact with some of the world's largest companies that run Microsoft software. The one recurring theme I hear is, "How can we effectively manage thousands of servers and tens of thousands of users?" In some instances, the solution lies in the employment of specialized software packages—but in the vast majority of the cases, the solution is a simple VBScript.

In Microsoft Windows Server 2003, enterprise manageability was one of the design goals, and VBScript is one path to unlocking the rich storehouse of newly added features. Using the techniques outlined in *Microsoft VBScript Step by Step*, anyone can begin crafting custom scripts within minutes of opening these pages. I'm not talking about the traditional Hello World script—I'm talking about truly useful scripts that save time and help to ensure accurate and predictable results.

Whereas in the past scripting was somewhat hard to do, required special installations of various implementations, and was rather limited in its effect, with the release of Microsoft Windows XP, Windows Server 2003, and Windows Vista, scripting is coming into its own. This is really as it should be. However, most administrators and IT professionals do not have an understanding of scripting because in the past scripting was not a powerful alternative for platform management.

However, in a large enterprise, it is a vital reality that one simply cannot perform management from the GUI applications because it is too time-constraining, too error prone, and, after a while, too irritating. Clearly there needs to be a better way, and there is. Scripting is the answer.

A Practical Approach to Scripting

Microsoft VBScript Step by Step will equip you with the tools to automate setup, deployment, and management of Microsoft Windows 2003 networks via the various scripting interfaces contained within the product. In addition, it will provide you with an understanding of a select number of VBScripts adaptable to your own unique environments. This will lead you into an awareness of the basics of programming through modeling of fundamental techniques.

The approach I take to teaching you how to use VBScript to automate your Windows 2003 servers is similar to the approach used in some executive foreign language schools. You'll learn by using the language. In addition, concepts are presented not in a dry academic fashion, but in a dynamic, real-life manner. When a concept is needed to accomplish something, it is presented. If a topic is not useful for automating network management, I don't bring it forward.

This is a practical, application-oriented book, so the coverage of VBScript, Windows Scripting Host, Active Directory Service Interfaces (ADSI), and Windows Management Instrumentation (WMI) is not exceedingly deep. This is not a reference book; it is a tutorial, a guide—a springboard for ideas, perhaps—but not an encyclopedia.

Is This Book for Me?

Microsoft VBScript Step by Step is aimed at several audiences, including:

- **Windows networking consultants**   Anyone desiring to standardize and automate the installation and configuration of .NET networking components.
- **Windows network administrators**   Anyone desiring to automate the day-to-day management of Windows .NET networks.
- **Windows Help Desk staff**   Anyone desiring to verify configuration of remotely connected desktops.
- **Microsoft Certified Systems Engineers (MCSEs) and Microsoft Certified Trainers (MCTs)**   Although scripting is not a strategic core competency within the MCP program, a few questions about scripting do crop up from time to time on various exams.
- **General technical staff**   Anyone desiring to collect information, configure settings on Windows XP machines, or implement management via WMI, WSH, or WBEM.
- **Power users**   Anyone wishing to obtain maximum power and configurability of their Windows XP machines either at home or in an unmanaged desktop workplace environment.

Outline of This Book

This book is divided into four parts, each covering a major facet of scripting. The following sections describe these parts.

Part I: Covering the Basics

Okay, so you've decided you need to learn scripting. Where do you begin? Start here in Part I! In Chapter 1, "Starting From Scratch," you learn the basics: what a script is, how to read it, and how to write it. Once you move beyond using a script to figure out what your IP address is and print it to a file, you need to introduce some logic into the script, which you do in Chapter 2 through Chapter 5. You'll learn how to introduce conditions and add some intelligence to allow the script to check some stuff, and then based upon what it finds, do some other stuff. This section concludes by looking at troubleshooting scripts. I've made some mistakes that you don't need to repeat! Here are the chapters in Part I:

- Chapter 1, "Starting from Scratch"
- Chapter 2, "Looping Through The Script"
- Chapter 3, "Adding Intelligence"
- Chapter 4, "Working with Arrays"
- Chapter 5, "More Arrays"

Part II: Basic Windows Administration

In Part II, you dig deep into VBScript and WMI and really begin to see the power you can bring to your automation tasks. In working with the file system, you see how to use the file system object to create files, delete files, and verify the existence of files. All these basic tasks provide loads of flexibility for your scripts. Next, you move on to working with folders, learning how to use VBScript to completely automate the creation of folders and files on your servers and users' workstations. In the last half of Part II, you get an in-depth look at the power of WMI when it is combined with the simplicity and flexibility of VBScript. Here are the chapters in Part II:

- Chapter 6, "Working with the File System"
- Chapter 7, "Working with Folders"
- Chapter 8, "Using WMI"
- Chapter 9, "WMI Continued"
- Chapter 10, "Querying WMI"

Part III: Advanced Windows Administration

This section will shave at least four points off your golf handicap because you'll get to play an extra 18 holes a week due to the time you'll save! At least three things are really painful when it comes to administering Windows servers: all those click, click, and save motions; all the time spent waiting for the screen to refresh; and loosing your place in a long list of users. Guess what? In this section, some of that pain is relieved. When Human Resources hires 100 people, you tell them to send you a spreadsheet with the new users, and then use a script to create those users. It takes 2 minutes instead of 2 hours. (Dude, that's the front nine!) In addition to saving time, scripting your administrative tasks reduces the likelihood of errors. If you have to set a particular set of access control lists on dozens of folders, a script is the only way to ensure all the flags are set correctly. Here are the chapters in Part III:

- Chapter 11, "Introduction to Active Directory Service Interfaces"
- Chapter 12, "Writing for ADSI"

- Chapter 13, "Using ADO to Perform Searches"
- Chapter 14, "Configuring Networking Components"
- Chapter 15, "Using Subroutines and Functions"
- Chapter 16, "Logon Scripts"
- Chapter 17, "Working with the Registry"
- Chapter 18, "Working with Printers"

Part IV: Scripting Other Applications

Once you learn how to use WMI and VBScript to automate Windows Server 2003, the logical question is, "What else can I do?" Well, with the latest version of Microsoft Exchange and Internet Information Services (IIS), the answer is, "Quite a lot." So in this part of the book, you look at using WMI and VBScript to automate other applications.

In IIS 6.0, nearly everything that can be configured via GUI tools can also be scripted. This enables the Web administrator to simplify management and to also ensure repeatable configuration of the Web sites from a security perspective.

In Exchange administration, many routine tasks can be simplified by using VBScript. In Part IV, you look at how to leverage the power of VBScript to simplify user management, to configure and administer Exchange, and to troubleshoot some of the common issues confronting the enterprise Exchange administrator. The chapters in Part IV are as follows:

- Chapter 19, "Managing IIS 6.0"
- Chapter 20, "Working with Exchange 2003"
- Chapter 21, "Troubleshooting WMI Scripting"

Part V: Appendices

The appendices in this book are not the normal "never read" stuff. Indeed, you will find yourself referring again and again to these five crucial documents. In Appendix A you will find lots of ideas for further work in developing your mastery of VBScript. Appendix B will save you many hours of searching for the "special names" that unlock the power of ADSI scripting. Appendix C helps you find the special WMI namespaces that enable you to perform many cool "tricks" in your scripting. And last but certainly not least is Appendix D, which contains my documentation "cheat sheet." Actually, you will want to read it rather early in your scripting career. Appendix E contains the Special Folder Constants, which, as you will see in the very first script in the book, can provide easy access to some of the most vital folders on your workstation!

- Appendix A, "VBScript Documentation"
- Appendix B, "ADSI Documentation"

- Appendix C, "WMI Documentation"

- Appendix D, "Documentation Standards"

- Appendix E, "Special Folder Constants"

Finding Your Best Starting Point

This book will help you add essential skills for using VBScript to automate your Windows environment. You can use this book if you are new to scripting, new to programming, or switching from another scripting language. The following table will assist you in picking the best starting point in the book.

If you are	Follow these steps
New to programming	Install the practice files as described in the section "Installing the Practice Files on Your Computer" later in this Introduction.
	Learn the basic skills for using VBScript by working through Chapters 1-7 in order.
New to VBScript	Install the practice files as described in the section "Installing the Practice Files on Your Computer" later in this Introduction.
	Skim through Chapter 1, making sure you pay attention to the section on creating objects.
	Skim Chapter 2 and Chapter 3.
	Complete Chapter 4 through Chapter 7 in order.
Experienced with VBScript but are interested in using WMI	Install the practice files as described in the section "Installing the Practice Files on Your Computer" later in this Introduction.
	Skim Chapter 4, paying attention to handling arrays.
	Work through Chapters 8-10 in order. Complete Chapter 14.

About the Companion CD

The CD accompanying this book contains additional information and software components, including the following files:

- **Sample Files**   The chapter folders contain starter scripts, some text files, and completed solutions for each of the procedures contained in this book. In addition, each of the scripts discussed in the book is contained in the folder corresponding to the chapter number. For instance, in Chapter 1 we talk about enumerating disk drives on a computer system. The script that makes up the bulk of our discussion around that topic is contained in the \My Documents\Microsoft Press\VBScriptSBS\ch01 folder. You'll also find many bonus scripts in the chapter folders. In addition to the sample files in the chapter folders, the CD includes a Templates folder, a Resources folder, a Supplemental folder, and a Utilities folder. These folders contain dozens of my favorite scripts and utilities I have written over the last several years to solve literally hundreds of problems. You will enjoy playing around with these and incorporating them into daily scripting tasks. For example, in the Templates folder you will find my WMITemplate.vbs script. By using it as a starter, you can write a custom WMI script in less than five seconds. By using the ADOSearchTemplate.vbs script as a starter, you can write a script that returns all the users in a particular OU in less than three seconds. In the Utilities folder you will find, for example, a script that converts bytes into kilobytes, megabytes, or gigabytes depending on the largest whole number that can be so created.

- **eBook**   You can view an electronic version of this book on screen using Adobe Acrobat Reader. For more information, see the Readme.txt file included in the root folder of the Companion CD.

- **Tools and Resources**   Additional tools and resources to make scripting faster and easier: Scriptomatic 2.0, Tweakomatic, EZADScriptomatic, WMI Admin Tools, WMI CodeCreator, WMI Diag.

Installing the Practice Files on Your Computer

Follow these steps to install the practice files on your computer so that you can use them with the exercises in this book.

1. Remove the companion CD from the package inside this book and insert it into your CD-ROM drive.

> **Note**   An end user license agreement should open automatically. If this agreement does not appear, open My Computer on the desktop or Start menu, double-click the icon for your CD-ROM drive, and then double-click StartCD.exe.

2. Review the end user license agreement. If you accept the terms, select the accept option and then click Next.

    A menu will appear with options related to the book.

3. Click Install Code Samples.

4. Follow the instructions that appear.

The code samples are installed to the following location on your computer:

My Documents\Microsoft Press\VBScriptSBS

Uninstalling the Practice Files

Follow these steps to remove the practice files from your computer.

1. In the Control Panel, open Add Or Remove Programs.

2. From the list of Currently Installed Programs, select Microsoft VBScript Step by Step.

3. Click Remove.

4. Follow the instructions that appear to remove the code samples.

System Requirements

- Special Folder Constants

- Minimum 233 MHz in the Intel Pentium/Celeron family or the AMD k6/Atholon/Duron family

- 64 MB memory

- 1.5 GB available hard disk space

- Display monitor capable of 800 x 600 resolution or higher

- CD-ROM drive or DVD drive

- Microsoft Mouse or compatible pointing device

- Windows Server 2003,Windows XP, or Windows Vista

- The MSI Provider installed on Windows Server 2003 (required for some of the WMI procedures)

- Microsoft Office Excel or Excel Viewer

Technical Support

Every effort has been made to ensure the accuracy of this book and the contents of the companion CD-ROM. Microsoft Press provides corrections for books through the World Wide Web at *http:// www.microsoft.com/learning/support.*

To connect directly with the Microsoft Press Knowledge Base and enter a query regarding a question or an issue that you might have, go to *http://www.microsoft.com/learning/support /search.asp.*

If you have comments, questions, or ideas regarding this book or the companion CD-ROM, please send them to Microsoft Press using either of the following methods:

E-mail:

msinput@microsoft.com

Postal Mail:

Microsoft Press

Attn: Editor, *Microsoft VBScript Step by Step*

One Microsoft Way

Redmond, WA 980526399

Please note that product support is not offered through the preceding addresses.

For additional support information regarding this book and the CD-ROM (including answers to commonly asked questions about installation and use), visit the Microsoft Press Technical Support Web site at *www.microsoft.com/learning/support/books/*. For support information regarding Microsoft software, please connect to *http://support.microsoft.com*.

Part I
Covering the Basics

In this part:

Chapter 1: Starting from Scratch 3

Chapter 2: Looping Through the Script 25

Chapter 3: Adding Intelligence 55

Chapter 4: Working with Arrays 81

Chapter 5: More Arrays 113

Chapter 1

Starting from Scratch

After completing this chapter, you will be able to:

- Read from the registry to obtain configuration information
- Use *Option Explicit* to identify typing and spelling errors
- Declare variables to identify which variables you intend to use
- Use basic error handling to control execution of a script
- Identify the four parts of a script
- Produce output from your script for documentation purposes
- Run scripts in six different ways

In this chapter, you begin your journey down the winding road that leads to the automation of Microsoft Windows Server 2003, Windows XP, and Windows Vista. Your first step will be to examine several scripts written in Microsoft Visual Basic, Scripting Edition (VBScript). On the next part of your journey, you'll dissect a few scripts so that you can see what elements make up a script. Many of the concepts covered in this chapter will come up throughout this book, as well as in your day-to-day life as a network administrator, so be sure you understand the material here before moving on.

Running Your First Script

It is late at night and the cold air conditioning is drying out your eyes, making it impossible to keep them open. You have drunk nearly a dozen cups of coffee, and you try to steady your hands. The last item on your migration check-off list stares out at you eerily from the page: "Ensure all servers have the administrator tools installed." Slowly your predicament begins to sink in, through the caffeine cloud surrounding your eyes. "I should have been doing this hours ago." The hum of the equipment room seems to grow louder, and the rows of servers stretch for miles and miles. Supper is a distant memory and sleep a fleeting dream. "How in the world am I supposed to check a thousand servers for administrator tools?"

The darkness of foreboding doom begins to envelop you but then suddenly vanishes with a single fulgurant idea: I bet we can script this! Within five minutes, the following script is tested on a single server and works like a charm:

DisplayAdminTools.vbs
```
Set objshell = CreateObject("Shell.Application")
Set objNS = objshell.namespace(&h2f)
Set colitems = objNS.items
For Each objitem In colitems
WScript.Echo objitem.name
Next
```

> **Just the Steps**   To run an existing script
>
> 1. Open a command prompt. (From the Start menu, select Run\CMD.)
> 2. Change the directory to My Documents\Microsoft Press\VBScriptSBS\ch01.
> 3. Type **CScript DisplayAdminTools.vbs** and press Enter.

A good way to learn how to write scripts is to read scripts. So what is a script? For our purposes, a script is nothing more than a collection of commands that we include in a text file. In this regard, scripts are like batch files that many network administrators have used since DOS days. Just like batch files, scripts can be written using nothing more sophisticated than Microsoft Notepad. An important difference between a batch file and a script is that a script has greater flexibility and its language is more powerful. In this section, you'll look at several scripts and learn to identify their common elements. I know some of you probably want to start typing your first script, but be patient. In the long run, you'll benefit from taking the time now to understand the elements common to most enterprise ready scripts.

> **Just the Steps**   To open an existing script
>
> 1. Open Notepad.
> 2. From the File menu, choose Open. In the Files Of Type box, choose All Files from the drop-down list.
> 3. Navigate to VBScriptSBS\Ch01\.
> 4. Select DisplayComputerNames.vbs, and choose Open from the Action menu.

After you open the script, the following text appears. We'll be referring to it again in the next few sections.

> **Note**   DisplayComputerNames.vbs, seen in the following text, uses line continuation and concatenation to fit the printed style. Line continuation is specified by a single underscore. Line concatenation (glues two things together) is an ampersand character. They are often seen together as &_, or as & _ the spacing between the ampersand and the underscore character is a matter of personal preference. This is covered in more detail in the next section.

DisplayComputerNames.vbs

```
Option Explicit
On Error Resume Next
Dim objShell
Dim regActiveComputerName, regComputerName, regHostname
Dim ActiveComputerName, ComputerName, Hostname

regActiveComputerName = "HKLM\SYSTEM\CurrentControlSet\Control\" & _
    "ComputerName\ActiveComputerName\ComputerName"
regComputerName = "HKLM\SYSTEM\CurrentControlSet\Control\" & _
    "ComputerName\ComputerName\ComputerName"
regHostname = _
    "HKLM\SYSTEM\CurrentControlSet\Services\Tcpip\Parameters\Hostname"

Set objShell = CreateObject("WScript.Shell")
ActiveComputerName = objShell.RegRead(regActiveComputerName)
ComputerName = objShell.RegRead(regComputerName)
Hostname = objShell.RegRead(regHostname)

WScript.Echo ActiveComputerName & " is active computer name"
WScript.Echo ComputerName & " is computer name"
WScript.Echo Hostname & " is host name"
```

As you can see, this script contains a lot of information. Let's break it down piece by piece so that it's not too overwhelming. For the purposes of our discussion, you can think of the script as being made up of four main parts:

- Header information
- Reference information
- Worker information
- Output information

Header Information

You can think of the header information as administrative overhead for your script. For most scripts, you can leave out the Header information section and lose none of the functionality. In fact, the preceding script would run just fine if the Header information section were deleted. (And it just so happens that you'll get a chance to prove this assertion during the step-by-step exercises at the end of this chapter.) If this information is so unrelated to the script's functionality, why should you include it? The header information should be a standard part of your script for two reasons: It makes the script easier to read and maintain, and it controls the way the script runs (as opposed to the way it might run by default). You'll learn more about how it controls the script later in the chapter when we look at the *Option Explicit* command and the *On Error Resume Next* command.

In the DisplayComputerNames.vbs script, the header information consists of the following lines of code:

```
Option Explicit
On Error Resume Next
Dim objShell
Dim regActiveComputerName, regComputerName, regHostname
Dim ActiveComputerName, ComputerName, Hostname
```

Although this code might look complicated, in reality, only three different commands are being used: *Option Explicit*, *On Error Resume Next*, and *Dim*. Each of these commands is covered in detail in the following sections, but before we dive into the nuts and bolts, let's do a quick reality check.

> Quick Check
>
> **Q.** **What is one way to run a script written in the VBScript language?**
>
> **A.** Type **CScript** before the name of the .vbs file at the command prompt.
>
> **Q.** **What is one tool you can use to read the text of a .vbs file?**
>
> **A.** Notepad.
>
> **Q.** **What are three commands found in the Header information section of a script written using the VBScript language?**
>
> **A.** *Option Explicit, On Error Resume Next,* and *Dim*.

Option Explicit and Dim

The *Option Explicit* statement tells the script that each variable used in the script is going to be listed before it is actually used.

> **Note**   Not sure what a variable is? The official definition of a *variable* is a named storage location capable of containing data that can be modified during program execution. For now, however, it's sufficient to think of a variable as a kind of "nickname" for a piece of information stored in a script.

If you want to use a variable and you specify *Option Explicit* in the Header information section of the script, you have to tell the script you're going to use this variable *before you actually use it*. This is called declaring a variable. If you omit *Option Explicit*, VBScript assumes by default that any statement it doesn't recognize is a variable. To declare a variable, you must use the command *Dim*, as illustrated in the preceding code. We do not have to specify what kind of information we are going to store in the variable, as VBScript treats everything as a "varient." In VB.NET, we would use the following command: *Dim j as int*. In VBScript, we just Dim j and it is a varient, which means it can be anything from a string to a date. By treating everything as a varient, VBScript is very easy to use. One problem that "scripters" have when transitioning their VBScript code to VB.NET is the "*as thing*." Dim j as WHAT? J is just a variable many scripters often say because in VBScript we do not normally need to worry about data types.

This code has a whole bunch of *Dim* stuff. As mentioned in the preceding paragraph, you use the word *Dim* to declare a variable. For instance, in the code at the end of this section, *objShell* and all the other words (except for *Dim*) are variable names I made up. I could have just as easily used *a*, *b*, *c*, *d*, and so on as the variables' names (kind of like the variables you used in high school algebra) and saved myself a lot of typing. However, a good variable name makes the code easier to read and to understand. For example, in the following code, you can assume that the variable named *ComputerName* actually holds a computer name. (I think you'd agree that *ComputerName* is much more descriptive than *a*.) And notice how similar *regActiveComputerName*, *regComputerName*, and *regHostname* are (except for the *reg* part) to the following variables: *ActiveComputerName*, *ComputerName*, and *Hostname*. The variables are arranged according to how they will be used. That is, variables used to hold registry keys are on one line, and variables containing the corresponding output values of those registry keys appear on the next line.

```
Dim objShell
Dim regActiveComputerName, regComputerName, regHostname
Dim ActiveComputerName, ComputerName, Hostname
```

On Error Resume Next

What does *On Error Resume Next* sound like it's trying to do? Let's break it down. *On Error* means that you want the computer to do something if it finds an error. *Resume Next* is what you want it to do. But *Next* what? A very good question. The *Next* you want it to resume is the next line of code in the script. So *On Error Resume Next* tells the computer that when something is messed up (causing an error), you want the computer to just skip that line and try the next line in the script. This process is called *error handling*, and it's a very basic task when writing scripts. You should probably consider using *On Error Resume Next* when you're using VBScript for logon scripts so that you don't get lots of phone calls right at 9:00 A.M. when your script has a problem. Of course, you'll test the script prior to deploying it, but we all know that tests don't always catch every eventuality. You'll learn about error handling in more detail later, including some pretty cool tricks, so stay tuned.

> **Note**   Even though we show it here for a complete script, your best practice is to *not* use *On Error Resume Next* while developing scripts; it will prevent you from seeing any errors produced during normal script execution. If you are using it and a script fails to work the way you expect, your first troubleshooting step should be to remove the *On Error Resume Next* statement.

Reference Information

The Reference information section of the script gives you the ability to assign values to the variables you named in the Header information section of the script. Another reason for using a variable is to create a shortened alias for some value. Aliases make the script easier to work with. In the following code, values are assigned to some of the variables created in the Header information section of the script.

```
regActiveComputerName = "HKLM\SYSTEM\CurrentControlSet\Control\" &_
    "ComputerName\ActiveComputerName\ComputerName"
regComputerName = "HKLM\SYSTEM\CurrentControlSet\Control" &_
    "\ComputerName\ComputerName\ComputerName"
regHostname = "HKLM\SYSTEM\CurrentControlSet\Services" &_
    "\Tcpip\Parameters\Hostname"
```

Notice that everything on the right-hand side of the equal sign looks like a registry key. If you caught that, you can probably figure out what the *reg* part of the variable name stands for. You got it—registry! Did you also notice that the three variable names (on the left-hand sides of the equal signs) are the same ones we talked about in the preceding section? What you're doing in this code is tying each of those variables to a registry key. For example, the first line of code shows that *regActiveComputerName* is equal to the very long string *HKLM\SYSTEM\Current-ControlSet\Control\ComputerName\ActiveComputerName\ComputerName*. (By the way, *HKLM* is shorthand for HKEY_LOCAL_MACHINE. Because VBScript understands this abbreviation, using *HKLM* will save you some typing. But keep in mind that HKLM is case sensitive! It must be all caps.) The lines containing the registry keys are using two special characters. The & (ampersand) is the concatenation operator, and it is glue. When you use it you glue two things together. The _ (space underscore) is used to continue the code to the next line. This is necessary to make the code easier to read in the book. We talk about this in more detail in Chapter 2, "Looping Through the Script."

Getting the Proper Registry Key

One easy way to make sure you get the proper registry key for your scripts is to use the Copy Key Name feature of the Registry Editor (Regedit.exe). As shown in Figure 1-1, you select the registry key containing the information you want VBScript to extract, open the Edit menu, and select Copy Key Name from the list. The entire key name is pasted on the clipboard, and from there you paste it into your script.

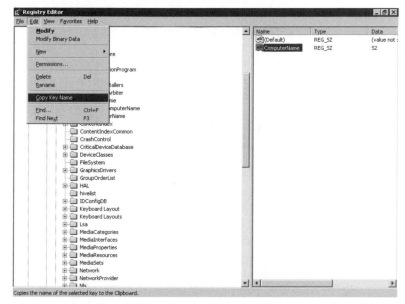

Figure 1-1   Registry Editor Copy Key Name feature

The Reference information section has the following purposes:

- Minimizes typing, and therefore ensures accuracy. You have to type long strings only once.

- Makes the script easier to read. If a variable is used several times in the script, the variable is "referenced" to the actual item only once.

- Makes it easier to change the script later. For example, the sample script you've been examining pulls out computer names. By changing the registry key and nothing else, you can make the script pull out any other information in the registry.

Worker Information

The Worker information section of the script gets its name because it actually does something. The variables are declared in the Header section and referenced in the Reference section; in the Worker information section, the variables get busy.

> **Note**   I haven't yet explained WScript, which can also be used to create objects, or how to create file system objects. These subjects are covered in later chapters. At this point, you should focus on understanding the flow and the functionality of the script.

Let's look at some code.

```
Set objShell = CreateObject("WScript.Shell")
ActiveComputerName = objShell.RegRead(regActiveComputerName)
ComputerName = objShell.RegRead(regComputerName)
Hostname = objShell.RegRead(regHostname)
```

Because you've read through the header information and looked at all the *Dim* statements, you know which names in the preceding code are variables. For instance, *objShell* is a variable; that is, it is shorthand for something. The question is, shorthand for what? Let's walk through the first line of code:

```
Set objShell = CreateObject("WScript.Shell")
```

Notice that the sentence begins with *Set*. *Set* is a command in VBScript that is used to assign an object reference to a variable. For VBScript to be able to read from the registry, it must have a connection to it. This requirement is similar to that for reading from a database—you must first establish a connection to the database. To create an object reference, you use the *Set* keyword to assign the reference to a variable.

VBScript uses *automation objects* as a way to use the capabilities of other programs to provide more power to the system administrator who needs to create powerful scripts to manage today's complex networking environments. For example, instead of dumping output to a black and white, text-only command prompt, you can use an automation object to leverage the display and formatting capabilities of the products in the Microsoft Office system and create multicolor, three-dimensional graphs and charts.

You are setting the variable name *objShell* to the reference you created by using *CreateObject*. Notice the equal sign following *objShell*. It indicates that *objShell* should be equal to something else—in this case, to everything to the right of the equal sign, or *CreateObject("WScript.Shell")*. For now, pay attention to the *CreateObject* part of the expression. The use of the verb *Create* is a tip-off that some action is about to take place. As you'll see in a moment, this line assigns to *objShell* a connection that will enable the script to read the registry.

Objects, Properties, Methods

By itself, VBScript is rather boring. It can print out things, loop through some things, but that is about it. To do anything interesting, VBScript needs to create an object. An object is a thing that gives us the ability to either describe something or to do something. If we are not going to do something, or describe something, then there is no reason to create the object. In programming terms, we use "Methods" to do something. In grammar, we would call these Verbs. We we describe something, we are using a "Property." In grammer, we would call these Adjectives. Depending on the circumstances, there may be times in which we are more interested in the methods, or the properties. As an example, let's consider rental cars. I travel a great deal in my role as a consultant at Microsoft, and I often need to obtain a rental car.

When I get to the airport, I go to the rental car counter, and I use the *CreateObject* command to create the rentalCAR object. When I use this command, I am only interested in the methods available from the rentalCAR object. I will need to use the driveDowntheRoad method, the StopAtaRedLight method, and perhaps the PlayCoolMusic method. I am not, however, interested in the properties of the rentalCAR object.

At home, I have a cute little sports car. It has exactly the same methods as the rentalCAR object, but I created the sportsCar object primarily because of its properties. It is green and has alloy rims, a convertible top, and a 3.5-liter engine. Interestingly enough, it has exactly the same methods as the rentalCAR object. It also has the driveDowntheRoad method, the StopAtaRedLight method, and the PlayCoolMusic method, but the deciding factor in creating the sportsCar object was the properties, not the methods.

Note   You might also see *WScript.CreateObject* used to create objects, instead of VBScript's plain *CreateObject*. For our purposes, and in about 99.9% of the cases, the two statements do exactly the same thing: They create objects. I prefer the plain CreateObject command as it is less typing!

You can now use the variables *ActiveComputerName* and *regActiveComputerName* to read the registry by taking advantage of the newfound power of the variable *objShell*. Remember that earlier you defined *regActiveComputerName* as equal to the registry key that contains the active computer name. You now define *ActiveComputerName* to be equal to the name that comes out of the registry key when you read the registry. You do the same thing for the other two registry keys.

Let's take a moment to recap what you've done so far. You've stored three computer names into memory by using the variables named *ActiveComputerName*, *ComputerName*, and *Hostname*. To get the computer names into those variables, you read the values that are stored in three different registry keys on the computer. To do this, you created three variables named *regActiveComputerName*, *regComputerName*, and *regHostname*. You used the prefix *reg* to denote that the variables contain strings for the actual registry keys. You then used the *RegRead* capability of the *objShell* variable that you assigned to the object reference by using the *CreateObject* command. Now that you have this information stored into three variables, you need to do something with it. In the script you are examining, you will use the output capability of VBScript, described in the next section.

Output Information

Being able to read from the registry, though cool, doesn't do you much good when you can't use the information. That's why it's important for a script to have an Output section. Of course, you can write a script that uses the information to perform tasks other than creating output, such as monitoring the status of a service and restarting it when it fails, but even then most network administrators would want at least a log entry stating that the service was restarted. In our script, output is provided through a series of *Echo* commands. The use of the *WScript.Echo* command is illustrated in the following code:

```
WScript.Echo activecomputername & " is active computer name"
WScript.Echo ComputerName & " is computer name"
WScript.Echo Hostname & " is host name"
```

The *WScript.Echo* command is used to type text inside a command prompt or to produce a pop-up message box, depending on how the script is actually run. When the script is run by using CScript, as detailed in the earlier procedure titled "Just the Steps: To run an existing script," the script writes inside the command shell.

Each variable name that you just set is equal to the registry key information in the last section of our script. So what does *Echo* do? You guessed it—it repeats something. Because the variables are now linked to the strings contained within the registry keys (via the Reference information section), we can use *WScript.Echo* to write the information currently held by the variables. In the code, the ampersand (&), which simply means *and*, is followed by a phrase within quotation marks. The current value of the variable on the left side of the ampersand gets put together with the string value contained inside the quotation marks on the right side of the ampersand. This "putting together" of two things with the ampersand is called *concatenation*. You are echoing what is stored in memory for each of our three variables, and you're also adding some text to explain what each variable is. When you run this script by double-clicking the script, you're rewarded with the results in Figure 1-2.

Figure 1-2   Screen output of DisplayComputerNames.vbs

Dealing with only three dialog boxes is a bit tedious, so imagine the frustration that dealing with a thousand or even just a hundred dialog boxes could cause. Some scripts can easily return a listing of more than a thousand items (for example, a script that queried all the users in a medium-sized domain). Clearly you need a more efficient way to write data. In fact, you have several ways to do this, such as using VBScript's MsgBox to display a pop-up box containing text, but I am going to save that for Chapter 2.

> ## What Is the Windows Scripting Host?
>
> The Windows scripting host is a language independent environment that exists on Windows based machines. It gives us the ability to write administrative scripts in various scripting languages. By default, Windows ships with a development environment for both VBScript and JScript, but you can install other runtime engines if you wish.
>
> Once a runtime engine is installed, the Windows scripting host will choose the appropriate engine for the script that is attempted to run. For VBScript, there are two script hosts: Cscript.exe and Wscript.exe. Cscript.exe provides command line switches that enable you to supply arguments to modify the way your script runs. Wscript.exe is the default scripting host and provides Windows based dialog boxes.

Enhancing Your Script

You've worked your way through your first script, and now let's see how we can modify it to enhance its capabilities. Here is the new functionality you will add to your script:

- Creating documentation that will keep track of what you learned in the previous section
- Obtaining information in addition to the three computer names

Let's first add some documentation to the script so that when you look at it six months from now, you'll know what you're looking at.

To add documentation, you simply type information into the script. To prevent the script from choking, you need to indicate that you are adding the text. You can do this in several ways. Perhaps the most efficient way is to preface each note with a single quotation mark (') followed by explanatory text (often called a *comment*).

If you are wondering what kinds of documentation you might want to include in your script, you can refer to Appendix D, "Documentation Standards," which provides guidance on the kinds of information you may want to include in each of the four sections of the script.

Here's what the script looks like with the added documentation:

DisplayComputerNamesWithComments.vbs

```
'This script displays various Computer Names by reading the registry

Option Explicit     'forces the scripter to declare variables
On Error Resume Next 'tells VBScript to go to the next line
                'instead of exiting when an error occurs
'Dim is used to declare variable names that are used in the script
Dim objShell
Dim regActiveComputerName, regComputerName, regHostname
Dim ActiveComputerName, ComputerName, Hostname
```

```
'When you use a variable name and then an equal sign (=)
'you're saying the variable contains the information on the right.
'The registry keys are quite long, so make them easier to read on
'a single screen by splitting the line in two.

regActiveComputerName = "HKLM\SYSTEM\CurrentControlSet" & _
    "\Control\ComputerName\ActiveComputerName\ComputerName"
regComputerName = "HKLM\SYSTEM\CurrentControlSet\Control" & _
    "\ComputerName\ComputerName\ComputerName"
regHostname = "HKLM\SYSTEM\CurrentControlSet\Services" & _
    "\Tcpip\Parameters\Hostname"


Set objShell = CreateObject("WScript.Shell")
ActiveComputerName = objShell.RegRead(regActiveComputerName)
ComputerName = objShell.RegRead(regComputerName)
Hostname = objShell.RegRead(regHostname)

'To make dialog boxes you can use WScript.Echo
'and then tell it what you want it to say.

WScript.Echo activecomputername & " is active computer name"
WScript.Echo ComputerName & " is computer name"
WScript.Echo Hostname & " is host name"
```

Just the Steps   To add documentation to a script

1.   Open the script in Notepad.

2.   Preface the line with a single quotation mark (').

3.   On the first line of script, after the single quotation mark, type a short description of the script's purpose.

4.   Save the script.

Modifying an Existing Script

Now that your script is fully documented, you can modify it to pull in additional information. Thus far, you have learned to retrieve the active computer name, the host name, and the computer name. (Actually, these names could be different in certain situations, so this script really is useful.) What kind of information could you be interested in retrieving at this juncture? Look at Table 1-1 for some ideas. (Notice in Table 1-1 that the registry keys are spelled out completely—HKEY_LOCAL_MACHINE, for instance—and the script you worked on earlier was abbreviated *HKLM*. VBScript allows you to reference the registry using several forms. These forms are covered in depth in Chapter 17, "Working with the Registry.")

Table 1-1   Useful registry keys for script writers

Information	Location
Service information	HKEY_LOCAL_MACHINE\SYSTEM\CurrentControlSet\Services
User name used to log on to the domain	HKEY_CURRENT_USER\Software\Microsoft\Windows\ CurrentVersion\Explorer\Logon User Name
Microsoft Exchange 2000 domain information	HKEY_CURRENT_USER\Software\Microsoft\Exchange\ LogonDomain
Exchange 2000 domain user information	HKEY_CURRENT_USER\Software\Microsoft\Exchange\UserName
Group Policy server	HKEY_CURRENT_USER\Software\Microsoft\Windows\ CurrentVersion\Group Policy\History\DCName
User's home directory	HKEY_CURRENT_USER\Volatile Environment\HomeShare
The server that authenticated the currently logged-on user	HKEY_CURRENT_USER\Volatile Environment\LOGONSERVER
The DNS domain name of the currently logged-on user	HKEY_CURRENT_USER\Volatile Environment\USERDNSDOMAIN

Note   Much of the information that you can gather via the registry can be obtained by other approaches, such as using Active Directory Service Interface (ADSI) or Windows Management Instrumentation (WMI) (which you'll learn about in later chapters). These are two other ways you can use the power of VBScript to gather information you need to manage your network. You should be aware of this because the registry is a dynamic environment, and keys get moved around from time to time. Thus, the registry is not always consistent among all machines on the network. For instance, there are obviously differences between Microsoft Windows 95 and Microsoft Windows XP, but there are also differences between Microsoft Windows 2000 and Windows XP, and even between Windows XP and a version of Windows XP that has been upgraded from Microsoft Windows Me, for example. Mining information from sources other than the registry can ensure a more consistent result. If at all possible, only try to read the registry for items that cannot be obtained via other methods.

To modify your script to gather some of the information listed in Table 1-1, you need to make a few changes in each of its four sections. Much of your script will be exactly the same, and a few sections will be similar (meaning that you'll need to change a few names to ensure clarity in your documentation). Now you'll look at each section of your script to see what needs to be changed.

Modifying the Header Information

The first three lines of your script can remain exactly the same. You still want to make sure you specify which variables you plan to use in the script, so leave *Option Explicit*. You also don't want the script to blow up when a value is absent or some other problem arises, so leave *On Error Resume Next* in place. In addition, because you're connecting to the registry to read items, you'll need the *objShell* variable in place. There is really no point in renaming these variables or changing them in any other way. By keeping the same name for *objShell*, for example, you'll always know its purpose. In this respect, you are developing your own *naming convention* for your scripts.

```
Option Explicit
On Error Resume Next
Dim objShell
```

The first three lines are in place and working fine, so now you need to create variables that you will use for the new registry values you want to read. For this example, we use some (but not all) of the values identified in Table 1-1. These variables are here:

```
Dim regLogonUserName, regExchangeDomain, regGPServer
Dim regLogonServer, regDNSdomain
Dim LogonUserName, ExchangeDomain, GPServer
Dim LogonServer, DNSdomain
```

Notice that we use our previous naming convention: We preface with *reg* all names of variables that will hold registry keys, and we leave *reg* off the names of all variables that will hold the information contained in the registry keys. (The variable item names are the same except for *reg*.)

> **Just the Steps**   To modify the header information
>
> 1. Open Notepad.
> 2. Ensure *Option Explicit* is listed on the first non-commented line.
> 3. Ensure *On Error Resume Next* is listed.
> 4. Delete variables that are not required.
> 5. Add variables for new information.
> 6. Add comments describing use of the newly added variables.
> 7. Save the script with a new name.

Modifying the Reference Information

Because you are changing the registry keys you will pull information from, you'll need to completely replace the Reference information section. The good news is that the format for the section is exactly the same. The pattern looks like this:

Variable name	=	Registry key in quotation marks
regLogonUserName	=	"HKEY_CURRENT_USER\Software\Microsoft\" & _"Windows\ CurrentVersion\Explorer\Logon User Name"

There are three parts of the script involved in reading a registry key, and all the information we want to obtain can be easily modified by changing the assignment of values to the variable names listed in the preceding syntax example. In addition, because you listed all the variable names we want to use to hold the registry keys in the Header information section of the script, you can simply cut and paste the variables into the Reference information section. In the next listing, you remove the *Dim* portion and the commas and place each variable name on a separate line. You will start with the code listed below:

```
Dim regLogonUserName, regExchangeDomain, regGPServer
Dim regLogonServer, regDNSdomain
```

Once you have finished cleaning up the variable names, your resulting code will look like Figure 1-3.

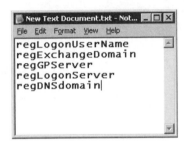

Figure 1-3   Using Notepad to speed script modification

After the variable names and the equal signs are inserted, add each registry key and enclose it in quotation marks. Remember to use the copy key feature of Regedit. Once all the registry keys are pasted into the script, the modified Reference information section looks like the following listing. Remember that the ampersand and underscore are used to indicate line continuation and are included here for readability. I also include them in production scripts to avoid having to scroll to the right while revising code.

```
regLogonUserName = "HKEY_CURRENT_USER\Software\Microsoft\" & _
    "Windows\CurrentVersion\Explorer\Logon User Name"
regExchangeDomain = "HKEY_CURRENT_USER\Software\Microsoft\" & _
    "Exchange\LogonDomain"
regGPServer = "HKEY_CURRENT_USER\Software\Microsoft\Windows\" & _
    "CurrentVersion\Group Policy\History\DCName"
regLogonServer = "HKEY_CURRENT_USER\Volatile Environment\" & _
    "LOGONSERVER"
regDNSdomain = "HKEY_CURRENT_USER\Volatile Environment\" & _
    "USERDNSDOMAIN"
```

Just the Steps   To modify the reference information

1. Open Notepad.
2. Copy the *Dim* section of the header information.
3. Paste the *Dim* section from step 2 into a new Notepad file.

4. From the Edit menu, select Replace to display the Replace dialog box. In the Find What box, type **Dim**. Do not type anything in the Replace With box. This will erase all occurrences of the word *Dim*.

5. Place each variable on a separate line and remove the commas.

6. Open Regedit and locate the desired registry keys.

7. Using the Copy Key Name feature, paste the key after each variable name.

8. Ensure the variable name is separated from the registry key name with an equal sign.

9. Ensure the registry key name is enclosed in quotation marks.

10. Save the script.

Modifying the Worker Information

You are halfway through creating the new script. The first line in the Worker information section of the script is fine and does not need to be changed.

```
Set objShell = CreateObject("WScript.Shell")
```

Notice that same two variables listed in the third line of the Header information section are used here. The challenge now is to modify each line so that it assigns the variables you created *without* the *reg* prefixes to the variables you created *with* the *reg* prefixes. This command has four parts associated with it:

Variable name	=	Worker	Registry variable in ()
LogonUserName	=	*objShell.RegRead*	*(regLogonUserName)*

Here's the entire Worker information section of the new script:

```
LogonUserName = objShell.RegRead(regLogonUserName)
ExchangeDomain = objShell.RegRead(regExchangeDomain)
GPServer = objShell.RegRead(regGPServer)
LogonServer = objShell.RegRead(regLogonServer)
DNSdomain = objShell.RegRead(regDNSdomain)
```

The variables were all listed in the Header information section and were copied and pasted on separate lines in this section of the script without the *Dim* statements—just as we copied and pasted information for the Reference information section of our script. In the next part of the script, insert the equal sign and the same worker component (you always do this), which in this case is *objShell.RegRead*. The last part of the script contains the registry variable created in the Reference section enclosed in parentheses. This again can be a really quick cut and paste job from the Reference information section.

Just the Steps   To modify the Worker information section

1. Open Notepad.

2. Copy the *Dim* section of the header information.

3. Paste the *Dim* section from step 2 into a new Notepad file.

4. From the Edit menu, select Replace to display the Replace dialog box. In the Find What box, type **Dim**. Do not type anything in the Replace With box. This will erase all occurrences of the word *Dim*.

5. Place each variable on a separate line and remove the commas.

6. Paste an equal sign and the worker component *objShell.RegRead* onto each line.

7. Paste the appropriate variable from the Reference information section and enclose it in parentheses.

8. Save the script.

Note   I tend to use the cut and paste feature when working with scripts because some of the variable names I create are a little long. Although the names are typically not case-sensitive, for the most part *spelling counts*, to rephrase something I learned in first grade. The best way I've found to avoid messing up the script is to copy and paste the variable names between my Header information section and my Worker information section.

After you finish modifying the Worker information section of your script, double-check that all declared variables are in place and that everything else is accounted for. Save your script under a different name if you were editing the DisplayComputerNames script. You could try to run it, but it won't do too well because you need to change the last section—the Output information section.

Modifying the Output Information

The Output information section of the script takes what you've learned from the registry and displays it in an easy-to-understand format. This section is what really makes the script usable. It's amazing that we spend a lot of time figuring out how to find information but not too much time formatting the data we get. You'll beef up your knowledge of displaying and writing data quite a bit in later chapters. For now, you'll use *WScript.Echo* to bounce data back.

You can't really salvage much from the old script—the process would be too confusing because you'd have to change every variable that holds information from the registry, as well as all the comments added after the keys. So all you will keep are the *WScript.Echo* lines. Delete everything after *WScript.Echo* and start cutting and pasting. Make sure you include every variable name identified in the Worker information section of the script. The syntax for this section is made up of four parts and looks something like this:

Command	Variable	&	Comment
WScript.Echo	*LogonUserName*	&	*" is currently Logged on"*

Notice that there's a space after the first quotation mark in the comment section. You include the space because the ampersand is used to glue two phrases together, and VBScript does not add spaces when concatenating lines. Our new code section looks like this:

```
WScript.Echo LogonUserName & " is currently Logged on"
WScript.Echo ExchangeDomain & " is the current logon domain"
WScript.Echo GPServer & " is the current Group Policy Server"
WScript.Echo LogonServer & " is the current logon server"
WScript.Echo DNSdomain & " is the current DNS domain"
```

To put this section together, you just cut and paste each variable assigned to a registry key in the Worker information section of the script, add an ampersand, and put quotation marks around whatever text will be echoed out. Later on, you'll use *WScript.Echo* to troubleshoot problems because it's an excellent way to follow progress in a script.

Just the Steps   To modify the Output section

1. Open Notepad.
2. Copy each variable added to the Worker information section.
3. Paste the variables from step 2 into the Output information section.
4. Add an ampersand after each variable.
5. Place quotation marks around any text to be echoed out to the screen.
6. Paste an equal sign and the worker component *objShell.RegRead* onto each line.
7. Preface each line with *WScript.Echo*.
8. Save the script.

How to Run Scripts

You can run scripts in several ways on Windows Server 2003, each of which has advantages and disadvantages. Let's look at some of these approaches now.

Double-Clicking a File with a .vbs Extension

By default, when you double-click a file with a .vbs extension, the file runs within an instance of WScript.exe. Therefore, using *WScript.Echo* in the Output information section of the script results in the cute little pop-up boxes. This might not be a big deal when we're talking about two or three variables, but it can be a real pain when one is listing all the user names in a domain with thousands of users! Perhaps a better alternative is the CScript approach.

CScript

CScript can be thought of as the command-line version of the Windows Scripting Host (Figure 1-4). CScript is nice because you don't have to click any dialog boxes to make the script continue. (Yes—that's right—with the default Windows Scripting Host, the entire script pauses until you click OK in the dialog box, and then the script waits for you to do the same in each dialog box after that.) In addition, you can pretty easily capture output from CScript because you can enable Quick Edit mode from the command window. To do this, click C:\ in the upper left part of the window, and select Properties from the Action menu. Then click the Options tab and select the Quick Edit Mode box. Next, choose Save Properties For Future Windows Of The Same Title, and you're finished. This feature enables you to highlight text and copy it to the clipboard from the CMD window. Once the data is on the clipboard, you can do everything from pasting the data into Notepad to using the text driver for Microsoft Excel and sorting the data into various cells that you can use to produce graphs. You'll learn more about this feature later in the book.

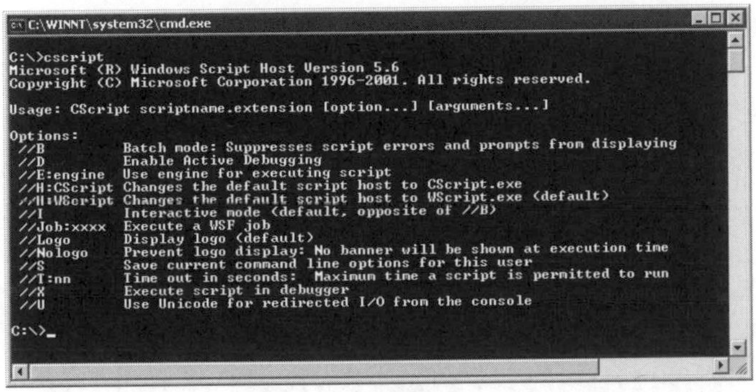

Figure 1-4   CScript offers many options, which can be set from the command line

Embedding Scripts in Web Pages

You can embed scripts inside Web pages. This has some potential use in the enterprise environment in which users who have access to a particular Web site on the intranet can click a button to launch a particular script. This might be a useful and valid use of VBScript for, say, information gathering or troubleshooting. There are some security concerns, however, which you'll learn about later in the book.

Dragging and Dropping a .vbs File to an Open Command Prompt

You can drag and drop a .vbs file to an open command prompt, which launches the script with the default scripting host. The nice thing about this is that you do not have to type the path to the file because Windows Explorer automatically puts it onto the command prompt line.

Dragging and Dropping a .vbs File to Notepad

You can drag and drop the .vbs file to an open Notepad file with a blank page to automatically open the file and display the text.

> ### Adding Notepad to the SendTo Menu
> You can easily edit the script by opening it in Notepad. Just add Notepad to the SendTo menu by going into C:\Documents and Settings\%*USERNAME*%\SendTo and adding a shortcut to Notepad.exe.

Exploring a Script: Step-by-Step Exercises

In this section, you will explore the four parts of a script written in VBScript language. This section also provides practice in using comments to add notes to an existing script.

1. Open ExploringVBS.vbs in Notepad.exe. It is located in the My Documents\Microsoft Press\VBScriptSBS\ch01\StepByStep folder.

2. Add comments that identify each section of the script. (Make sure to include all four parts of the script: header information, reference information, worker information, and output information.)

3. Save the script with a different file name, such as YourNameExploringVBS.vbs.

4. Delete the entire Header information section.

5. Save the script and then try to run it. Does it run?

6. Add the *Option Explicit* command again and save the file. Now does it run?

7. Put a comment mark (') in front of *Option Explicit* and save the file. Does it run?

One Step Further: Customizing an Existing Script

This section will provide addional practice and illustrate the important technique of customizing an existing script. It is common knowledge that when confronted with the task of creating a script, most network administrators often start with a script they found on the Internet. It is, however, important for the administrator to customize the script and ensure that only the most useful portions of the script are left behind prior to deployment.

Scenario

You are a new network administrator at a *Fortune* 500 company. You recently had a server crash, and it did not generate a dump file. Because you have several servers on your network, you don't want to have to "mouse around" very much; rather, you'd like to simply run a script to confirm the crash recovery configuration. Because your company is fortunate to have a college intern working for the summer, and you haven't yet learned how to remotely run the script, you've decided to do the following:

1. Create a script that reads crash recovery information from the registry. Your research has revealed the following keys to be of interest:

```
"HKLM\SYSTEM\CurrentControlSet\Control\CrashControl\AutoReboot"
"HKLM\SYSTEM\CurrentControlSet\Control\CrashControl\MinidumpDir"
"HKLM\SYSTEM\CurrentControlSet\Services\Tcpip\Parameters\Hostname"
"HKLM\SYSTEM\CurrentControlSet\Control\CrashControl\LogEvent"
"HKLM\SYSTEM\CurrentControlSet\Control\CrashControl\DumpFile"
```

2. Copy the script to a share on a local server.

3. Run the script under CScript.

4. Have the intern copy the output from the command prompt and paste it into a Notepad file that has the same name as the server.

Step-by-Step Instructions

1. Open the \My Documents\Microsoft Press\VBScriptSBS\ch01\OneStepFurther\CustomizeExistingScript.vbs file and save it as YourNameCustomizeExistingScript.vbs.

2. Edit the Header information section of the script and include variables for each of the items you are going to read from the registry. (Remember, you'll need two variables for each registry item: one for the registry key itself, and one for the data contained in the registry key.)

3. Edit the Reference information section of the script. (Use the *reg* variable names you created in step 2 of this procedure and assign them to the appropriate registry keys.)

4. Edit the Worker information section of the script. (Assign the non-registry variable names you created in step 2 to the *regRead* Worker part of the script.)

5. Edit the Output information section of the script. (Use the *same* variables you assigned to the *regRead* parts in step 4.)

6. Add any documentation you need to the script. (Make sure you *over*-comment your script. Concepts that are perfectly clear today will be a dull memory within a few days.)

7. Save your script.

8. Open a command prompt.

9. Type **CScript YourNameCustomizeExistingScript.vbs** and press Enter. (If you get a File Not Found comment, change to the directory where you saved your script and repeat the command.)

Chapter 1 Quick Reference

To	Do This
Catch misspelled variable names	Use *Option Explicit* on the first line of your script
Declare a variable	Use the *Dim* command, followed by the variable name
Continue to the next line, following an error	Use *On Error Resume Next*
Produce a pop-up dialog box when you double-click on a script	Use *WScript.Echo*
Produce a line of output when running a script under CScript at a CMD prompt	Use *WScript.Echo*
Create an object	Use the *CreateObject* command followed by the name of the automation object to create
Run a script under the default scripting host	Double-click on the script
Run a script under CScript	Open a CMD prompt and precede the name of the script with the command *CScript*
Add documentation to a script	Precede the comment with a single quotation mark '

Chapter 2
Looping Through the Script

Before You Begin

To work through the material presented in this chapter, you need to be familiar with the following concepts from Chapter 1:

- How to run a script
- How to declare a variable by using the *Dim* command
- How to perform basic error suppression by using *On Error Resume Next*
- How to connect to the file system object
- How to read from the registry

After completing this chapter, you will be able to:

- Use *For Each...Next*
- Define constants
- Implement collections
- Use *For...Next*
- Control script execution by using the *Sleep* command
- Implement line concatenation
- Use *Do While...Loop*
- Use *Do Until...Loop*

Adding Power to Scripts

Reading the registry and echoing the results on the screen are useful tasks. At times, however, you need to perform repetitive operations. Even the most casual observer knows that network administration involves many tasks performed over and over again.

How can you harness the power of Microsoft Visual Basic, Scripting Edition (VBScript) to relieve some of the banality of day-to-day network administration on Microsoft Windows Server 2003? At least six constructs are ideal for the task:

- *For Each...Next*

- *For...Next*

- *Do While...Loop*

- *Do Until...Loop*

- *Do...Loop*

- *While...Wend*

This chapter begins by examining a real script to see how you can use these powerful tools in your daily duties as a network administrator.

For Each...Next

For Each...Next lets you walk through a collection of objects and do something with an individual object from the collection. Once it is done, it goes to the next object in the collection. It is impossible to overemphasize how important this structure is. It is basic to working with information retrieved from Windows Management Instrumentation (WMI, see Chapter 8, "Using WMI"). But there are other common situations where you will be using *For Each...Next* as well: files, and folders are returned as a collection from the fileSystemObject as well. Whenever you hear the word *collection*, think *For Each...Next*.

In the CollectionOfDrives.vbs script, you use *For Each...Next* to examine disk space utilization of fixed drives on a server:

CollectionOfDrives.vbs
```
Option Explicit
On Error Resume Next
Dim colDrives 'the collection that comes from WMI
Dim drive    'an individual drive in the collection
Const DriveType = 3 'Local drives. From the SDK

set colDrives =_
GetObject("winmgmts:").ExecQuery("select size,freespace " &_
 "from Win32_LogicalDisk where DriveType =" & DriveType)

For Each drive in colDrives 'walks through the collection
WScript.Echo "Drive: " & drive.DeviceID
WScript.Echo "Size: " & drive.size
WScript.Echo "Freespace: " & drive.freespace
Next
```

Let's peruse this script and see what it's doing. In your initial reading, you see some common elements you learned about in Chapter 1, "Starting from Scratch": the Header information section of the script (*Option Explicit*, *On Error Resume Next*, and *Dim*); and the Reference section (the part with *Const DriveType*). The Worker section of the script contains the *GetObject* statement. Because Windows Management Instrumentation (WMI) is already running, we do not need to create an instance of the WMI object (by using *CreateObject*); we can simply go get it by using *GetObject*. The Output section consists of the *WScript.Echo* statements. By examining the structure of the script, we get a sense of familarity, even though the script introduces a number of new concepts, such as WMI, collections, and the *For Each...Next* statement.

Just the Steps   To use *For Each...Next*

1. On a new line in a script, type **For Each** and then a variable name.
2. On the next line, enter a command you want repeated.
3. On the line following the command you want repeated, type **Next**.

Header Information

The Header information section of your script contains commands that are rapidly becoming old hat:

```
Option Explicit
'On Error Resume Next
Dim colDrives
Dim drive
```

This script begins by using *Option Explicit*, which says that each variable must be specifically listed (declared) by using the *Dim* command. *On Error Resume Next* is a rudimentary error handling technique that says "when an error occurs, skip the line that caused the problem and go on to the next line in the script."

Defining Constants

The *Const DriveType = 3* line is a new concept. In this line, you define a constant. This line says that the word *DriveType* is equal to the number 3. Why do you do this? You want to use the number 3 later in the script when you build the WMI query. Rather than hard-coding the number 3 into your query (hard-coding a value into a script is called *creating a literal*), you replace it with the constant *DriveType*. Just like a variable, the constant can be called anything you want. But because WMI uses a number to refer to the type of drive, you call the constant *DriveType*. The most important thing to remember about a constant is that the value never changes—it is constant.

Constants vs. Variables

Why did we use a constant instead of a variable in the CollectionOfDrives.vbs script? This is a good question, and the answer is that you could have used a variable in this instance. It would look something like this:

```
Dim colDrives 'holder for what comes back from the WMI query
Dim drive 'holder for name of each logical drive in colDrives
Dim DriveType
DriveType = 3 'Local drives. From the SDK
```

In this particular case, using a variable instead of a constant wouldn't have made any difference. However, variables have a dark secret that will come back to haunt you one day (guaranteed). Their value can change during script execution, whereas the value of a constant is set before execution and cannot change. This is illustrated in the following rather silly script. First is the normal Header information section: *Option Explicit, On Error Resume Next*, and a few *Dim* statements to declare the variables. Next, in the Reference section, you assign values to each variable and echo out the total. So far so good. However, you then reassign the *FirstValue* to be equal to the total, and echo out the total. Because the variable *total* is assigned to *FirstValue* + *SecondValue* before the *FirstValue* is reassigned to the *total*, the script produces illogical results. If you added *Total* = *FirstValue* + *SecondValue* right before the second echo, the script would work as expected.

```
Option Explicit
On Error Resume Next

Dim total
Dim FirstValue
Dim SecondValue

FirstValue = 1
SecondValue = 3
Total = FirstValue + SecondValue

WScript.Echo " the total of " & FirstValue & " and " & _
  SecondValue & " Is " & (total)
FirstValue = Total
WScript.Echo " the total of " & FirstValue & " and " & _
  SecondValue & " Is " & (Total)
```

Shared Benefits of Constants and Variables

You gain several advantages by using either a constant or a variable:

- The script is easier to read. When you read the WMI query, notice that you're filtering by *DriveType*. This makes more sense than filtering out number 3 drive types.

- The script is easier to revise. To change the script to filter out CD-ROMs, simply change the constant to the number 5.

Important   The ease of modifying the value of the constant in the reference section points out the advantage of calling our constant *DriveType* instead of something like *LocalDisk*, or *FixedDisk*. If we did this, then we would need to revise the constant name, and every place in the script that referenced that constant, or else the script would be misleading. Can you imagine the confusion a constant called *LocalDisk* would have if you set the value to 4, which refers to network disks? The script would still run fine, because as William Shakespeare said, "A constant by any other name is still a constant."

- Reusing the value in the script later on is easier. This script does not reuse the constant *DriveType*. However, you'll do this in longer scripts, and using constants is a good habit to get into.

- The script is easier to document. You can easily add a comment or a series of comments such as the following:

```
Const DriveType = 3 'used by WMI for fixed disks
'other drive types are 2 for removable,
'4 for Network, 5 for CD
```

After the constant is defined, you list a couple of variables used by the script. In this case, you declared two. The first one is *colDrives*. Now, why did you call this colDrives? Because the WMI query returns a collection of drives. Let's look at collections and see what they do for you. But before we do, let's stop and see how we are doing.

Quick Check

Q.   Name one advantage of using *For Each...Next*.

A.   Using this construct provides the ability to iterate through a collection without knowing the number of members in advance.

Q.   What is the difference between a variable and a constant?

A.   A variable can change value, whereas a constant retains a constant value.

Q.   List three reasons for using constants.

A.   Using constants makes the script easier to read and easier to revise. Reuse later in the script is also easy.

Collections

When you have the possibility of seeing a group of related items, thinking of them as a *collection* is useful. A collection is a familiar concept. For instance, my wife has a collection of key chains. Although each of the key chains is different (some have city names, some have college names, and others have product names), they are also similar enough to be in her collection called key chains. That is, they all have a ring on which keys are hung—without that common feature, they would not be key chains. In a similar fashion, when you run your script, the script will return all the permanently fixed hard disk drives on the server. These drives might be IDE or SCSI, but they will all be hard disk drives.

What's so great about having a collection of hard disks? Consider the alternative. If you couldn't return a collection of hard drives from a server, you'd need to know which drives are actually installed on the machine. You'd have to connect to the server and list information for each drive—for example, you'd need to connect to drives A, C, D, E, F, and so on. In addition, to keep the script from failing when a drive did not exist, you'd need error handling (such as *On Error Resume Next*), or you'd have to test for the presence of each drive prior to querying information about it. Although that approach would work, it would be kludgy, to say the least. It would also defeat the purpose of using automation to retrieve information related to drives.

There is only one bad thing about collections: You cannot simply perform a *WScript.Echo* of the information returned from a query, because each drive in the collection could have different properties. For example, if I wanted drive.size, which size would be returned from the echo command? To retrieve drive.size, we need to singularize a drive from the collection, so that we are working with only one drive from the collection at a time. To do this, you have to do something like a *For Each...Next* loop and go through the loop as many times as there are items in the collection. If you had five drives in your collection, guess what? We, in our current script, make five passes through the loop and echo each of the drives out. Walking through the loop multiple times, once for each member of the collection, is called *iteration* and is a task routinely performed in administrative scripting.

If you have only one drive, guess what? It's still returned as a collection, and you have to iterate through the collection using *For Each...Next* to get out your single drive. Fortunately, by the end of this chapter, you'll have so much experience doing this, it will seem like a piece of cake (or a piece of celery, if you're on a diet like I am).

Reference Information

In the Reference information section of the script is a new concept mentioned earlier—WMI. We're using it here to look at our drives, but you'll learn more about WMI later in this chapter. To connect to WMI, you have to use a string that looks like *GetObject("winmgmts:")*. Then you simply run a query that selects the desired drives. Remember that in the Reference information section of our script, you say that *colDrives* is equal to all the information on the right side of the equal sign. You are creating an alias for the long *winmgmts* connection string that we call *colDrives*. You can see this in the following code:

```
Set colDrives =_
GetObject("winmgmts:").ExecQuery _
  ("select DeviceID from Win32_LogicalDisk where DriveType =" & _
  DriveType)
```

Worker Information

The Worker information section is really small in this script. In addition, the Output information section is sandwiched inside the *For Each...Next* loop. Let's look at the code:

```
For Each drive In colDrives
  WScript.Echo drive.DeviceID
Next
```

Because you sent a fine-tuned query to WMI in the Reference information section of the script, and the purpose of the script was simply to list drives, the Worker information section has little work to do. All it really needs to do is to walk through the collection of drives returned from WMI. You use *For Each* and then the variable drive that you created to hold each of the drives returned from *colDrives*. Once you have the drive in your hands, you look for the *Device ID* of the drive. But, interestingly enough, you use this in the Output information section of the script, which is the *WScript.Echo* part. After you echo the *DeviceID*, you use the *Next* command to do it again for the next drive in the collection.

For...Next

I know what you're thinking: "We just got finished looking at *For...Next*!" Well, sort of, but not really. An important difference between *For Each...Next* and *For...Next* is that with *For Each...Next*, you don't have to know how many times you want to do something. With the *For...Next* construct, you must know exactly how many times you want to do something.

> **Just the Steps**   To implement *For...Next*
>
> 1. On a new line in the script, type **i** followed by a variable and a count (such as *For i = 1 to 10*).
> 2. On the next line, type the command to be performed.
> 3. On the next line, type *Next*.

Using *For...Next* is not necessarily a bad thing, however, because it gives you a lot of extra control. For example, the DisplayProcessInformation.vbs script checks a number of performance indicators on the server (that is, process thread counts, page faults, working set sizes, and the like).

> **Warning**   Make sure you run the DisplayProcessInformation.vbs script under CScript, or you will find yourself clicking an incredible number of dialogue boxes. To launch it under CScript, remember to go to a CMD prompt, and type **cscript DisplayProcessInformation.vbs**.

The values for these items can change quite often, so you want to check them on a regular basis. However, frequent checking can cause a performance hit on either the server or the network (depending on how the script was utilized), so you want to check the status only at certain times. The solution here is to take measurements of all the running processes, then wait an hour and do it again. You do this for an eight-hour cycle and then quit. You could use this type of script to monitor performance on a server that was heavily used during working hours.

> **Important**   In many of the scripts, you will note that I have On Error Resume Next commented out. This is due to the "best practice" of having it turned off during development. You want to see all errors while you are writing the script, so you can fix any problems that may arise.

DisplayProcessInformation.vbs

```
Option Explicit
'On Error Resume Next
Dim objWMIService
Dim objItem
Dim i
Const MAX_LOOPS = 8, ONE_HOUR = 3600000

For i = 1 To MAX_LOOPS
Set objWMIService = GetObject("winmgmts:").ExecQuery _
  ("SELECT * FROM Win32_Process where processID <> 0")
WScript.Echo "There are " & objWMIService.count &_
 " processes running " & Now
 For Each objItem In objWMIService
    WScript.Echo "Process: " & objItem.Name
    WScript.Echo Space(9) & objItem.commandline
    WScript.Echo "Process ID: " & objItem.ProcessID
    WScript.Echo "Thread Count: " & objItem.ThreadCount
    WScript.Echo "Page File Size: " & objItem.PageFileUsage
    WScript.Echo "Page Faults: " & objItem.PageFaults
    WScript.Echo "Working Set Size: " & objItem.WorkingSetSize
    WScript.Echo vbNewLine
  Next
  WScript.Echo "******PASS COMPLETE**********"
  WScript.Sleep ONE_HOUR
Next
```

Header Information

Our Header information section begins with the *Option Explicit* command that tells VBScript that all our variables will have to be formally announced by using the *Dim* command. One issue to keep in mind about *Option Explicit* is that it must be the first non-commented line in the script. For instance, in the electronic version of the next script (found on the companion CD), notice that several lines have been commented out by using the single quotation mark character ('). These lines are used to tell basic information about the purpose of the script, provide documentation on the use of various variables, and explain some of the syntax peculiarities.

Once all that work is done, the first line without a single quotation mark must be *Option Explicit* if you want *Option Explicit* to work. The reason for this is that when the line without the single quotation mark is not the first line in the script, some variables can sneak in without being declared. *On Error Resume Next* uses the second line in our script. As you no doubt have noticed, *On Error Resume Next* and *Option Explicit* seem to appear in all scripts. If you were going to create a template for script creation, *Option Explicit* and *On Error Resume Next* would be a couple of good lines to include, because more than likely you'll want them in all your scripts. However, you might want to comment out the *On Error Resume Next* line by placing a single quotation mark in front of it. In this way, while you are writing and testing your script, you will be able to catch all the errors, because *On Error Resume Next* is turned off. Once testing is completed, you simply remove the single quotation mark from in front of *On Error Resume Next*, turning it back on. This has the advantage of hiding unexpected errors from the "end user" of the script once it moves from development to "production."

This script has only three variables: *objWMIService*, which is used to hold the connection to WMI, allowing you to query for performance information about the running processes; *objItem*, which is used to hold the name of each process that comes back from *objWMIService*; and lastly *i*, which is one of the weird little variables used to increment the *For...Next* loop. Because *i* is, however, a variable, and you turned on *Option Explicit*, you need to declare it by using the *Dim* command.

Reference Information

The Reference information section of the DisplayProcessInformation.vbs script contains two constants: *MAX_LOOPS* and *ONE_HOUR*. *MAX_LOOPS* is used by the *For...Next* statement to control how many times the script will execute. On this line in the script, we have done something new: We put two constant statements on the same line, just like you can do when you dim variables. This is seen here:

```
Const MAX_LOOPS = 8, ONE_HOUR = 3600000
```

This is the same as doing the following (the advantage is that it saves space):

```
Const MAX_LOOPS = 8
CONST ONE_HOUR = 3600000
```

You define a constant named *ONE_HOUR* and set it equal to 3,600,000. You're going to use this constant in conjunction with the *Sleep* command, which counts in milliseconds. To calculate, you'd multiply 60 minutes by 60 seconds, and then multiply the result by 1,000, which yields 3,600,000. By defining the *ONE_HOUR* constant, you make the script easier to read. In addition, you might want to add several other constants in the script, such as *HALF_HOUR*, *QUARTER_HOUR*, and *FIVE_MINUTES*, and then you could easily change the sleep timeout value later in the script. Defining constants but not using them in the script doesn't adversely affect the running of the script, because you comment them to that effect.

Adding additional constants

1. Open Microsoft Notepad.
2. From the File menu, choose Open. In the Files Of Type box, choose All Files from the drop-down list.
3. Navigate to My Documents\Microsoft Press\VBScriptSBS\Ch02\.
4. Select DisplayProcessInformation.vbs, and choose Open from the Action menu.

5. In the Reference section of the script, locate the following line:

```
Const MAX_LOOPS = 8, ONE_HOUR = 3600000
```

6. Add a new line under the two existing constant definitions.

7. Add a constant for half an hour. It will look like the following:

```
Const HALF_HOUR = 1800000
```

8. At the end of the statement, add a comment such as the following:

```
'30 minutes in milliseconds.
```

9. Do the same thing for fifteen minutes, and for five minutes. The completed section will look like the following:

```
Const QUARTER_HOUR = 900000 'fifteen minutes in milliseconds
Const FIVE_MINUTES = 300000 'five minutes in milliseconds
```

10. Save your work and compare the results with DisplayProcessInformationExtraConstants.vbs.

11. Change the *WScript.sleep* command to use the *FIVE_MINUTES* constant at the bottom of the script. It will look like the following:

```
WScript.Sleep FIVE_MINUTES
```

12. Save and run the script using CScript from a CMD prompt. Time the execution. It should make a second pass after five minutes. Compare it with the DisplayProcessInformationFiveMinutes.vbs script.

13. Use Calc.exe to come up with additional constants to use for this script (such as one minute. The formula is n(minutes) * 60(seconds) * 1000(for milliseconds).

Note Notice the underscore (_) that appears at the end of the first and second lines in the Worker information section. This is used to break up the code into more than one line to make the code easier to read. The important aspect to pay attention to is the placement of the open and close parentheses and the quotation marks (" ") as you break up the lines. Notice also that at times, the ampersand is used, which as you'll recall from Chapter 1 is the concatenation character. This ampersand is used when you're inside of the parentheses, and you need to stick the two lines together. At times, you'll need to embed spaces to ensure commands are not messed up when you break the lines. The line continuation following *ExecQuery* does not include the ampersand because it falls outside of the parentheses.

Worker and Output Information

The Worker section of the script consists of a rather nasty WMI query string and its attendant assignment to the *objWMIService* variable. The nasty code is shown here:

```
Set objWMIService = GetObject("winmgmts:").ExecQuery _
  ("SELECT * FROM Win32_Process where processID <> 0")
```

This line of code connects to WMI and then executes a query that lists all Win32 processes running on the machine. You'll learn about WMI in Chapter 8, but for now, it is important to notice that the query looks exactly like a regular SQL Server query. The code says to select (which means to choose something) from the Win32 process. The "something" that is being chosen is *. As you no doubt recognize, * is the wildcard character and means "everything." So this query chooses everything from the Win32 process, but only if the process ID is not equal to 0 (the system idle process).

As we continue, the Worker and the Output information sections kind of merge together. This section begins with the *For i = 1 To MAX_LOOPS* command, which means that you're going to count to eight and on each pass increment the value of the variable *i*. With each pass, the variable *i* changes its value. In the second line of the Worker information section is a *For Each...Next* command. This tells you that the information returned from the *objWMIService* variable is a collection. Because it is a collection, you need to use *For Each...Next* to walk (*iterate*) through the collection. As the code walks, it echoes out the value of the information you want (such as the process, process ID, and thread count). At the end of the grouping of *WScript.Echo* commands is a *Next* command. The problem with nested *Next* commands is trying to keep track of which *Next* belongs to which *For* or *For Each*. Indenting them a little bit will help you see which *For* command lines up with which *Next* command. This technique makes the script easier to read.

The *Now* command is used to echo out the date and time, providing an easy way to time stamp logs and other output obtained from scripts. In addition, because *Now* is inside the *For Each...Next* loop, it will time stamp each process as it is reported. This enables you to see how long it takes the script to complete its processing—the *Now* command reports down to the second.

The *Space ()* command uses the space function that is built into VBScript. We do not need to define it, or declare it, or anything. It is built into the scripting language. It acts like a variable tab command, in that we can tell it how many spaces we want, and it magically skips over that many spaces.

The *vbNewLine* command is really a constant value that is built into VBScript. It tells the script to print out a new line for us.

Using the *Space* function and the *vbNewLine* constant

1. Open Notepad or the script editor of your choice.

2. On the first line of your script, set *Option Explicit*, as seen below:

```
Option Explicit
```

3. On the next line, use *WScript.Echo* and the *Space()* function at the beginning of the line to jump over 10 spaces. Follow the command with some text indicating the space. It may look like the following:

```
WScript.Echo Space(10) & "this is a 10 space line at the beginning"
```

4. On the next line, *WScript.Echo* some text with the *vbNewLine* constant at the end of your line. Your code could look like the following:

```
WScript.Echo "This line ends with vbNewLine" & vbNewLine
```

5. Now let's end by using the *Space* function embedded in a line of text. Note that we will need to use the *&* concatenation character before and after the function, as seen below:

```
WScript.Echo "This is an embedded 5 spaces" & Space(5) & "in the line"
```

6. Save and run your script. If you have problems, you can compare your code with the SpaceAndVBNewLine.vbs script in My Documents\Microsoft Press\VBScriptSBS\Ch02.

The *WScript.Sleep* command is used to pause the execution of the script for a specified amount of time. As mentioned earlier in this chapter, the *Sleep* command takes its input in the form of milliseconds. To pause the script for one second, you would write the code like this:

```
WScript.Sleep 1000
```

I've been calling this the *Sleep* command, but in programming speak it would be called the *Sleep* method of the *WScript* object. However, if I called it that, this book would sound like a programmer's reference and therefore would be boring. So I'll just call it the *Sleep* command and be done with it.

Pausing the script can have a number of uses. For instance, it enables you to have a very flexible running schedule. If you attempted to pause the script using the scheduler service on Windows Server 2003, you would need eight different schedules, because there is no notion of "pause for an hour, and only do it for eight hours." One other very useful aspect of the *Sleep* command is that it allows for "spin-up time." By using the *Sleep* command, you can cause a script to wait for a slower component to come on line prior to execution. The *Sleep* command is not an atomic clock. Although it's fine for generic pausing of a script, don't think you can use it for scientific timing—it was never designed for that purpose. In general, it's not accurate for periods of time less than a second.

We use *WScript.Echo* to indicate that the script has finished its pass through the processes. Remember that anything inside the quotation marks will be echoed to the screen. By padding the script with a bunch of *****, you can more easily find your information. The other important thing to notice here is that each time we make a loop with the *For...Next* statement, we are re-issuing the WMI query. At first glance, this may seem inneficent. However, if we did not do the query a new time for each loop, then we would just be printing out the results of the first query eight times with no new resulting information, which would be even less efficient!

```
For i = 1 To MAX_LOOPS
Set objWMIService = GetObject("winmgmts:").ExecQuery _
  ("SELECT * FROM Win32_Process where processID <> 0")
WScript.Echo "There are " & objWMIService.count &_
 " processes running " & Now
 For Each objItem In objWMIService
    WScript.Echo "Process: " & objItem.Name
    WScript.Echo Space(9) & objItem.commandline
    WScript.Echo "Process ID: " & objItem.ProcessID
    WScript.Echo "Thread Count: " & objItem.ThreadCount
    WScript.Echo "Page File Size: " & objItem.PageFileUsage
    WScript.Echo "Page Faults: " & objItem.PageFaults
    WScript.Echo "Working Set Size: " & objItem.WorkingSetSize
    WScript.Echo vbNewLine
  Next
  WScript.Echo "******PASS COMPLETE**********"
  WScript.Sleep ONE_HOUR
Next
```

Quick Check

Q. **WScript.Sleep is expressed in what unit?**

A. *WScript.Sleep* is expressed in milliseconds.

Q. **What is an important difference between *For Each...Next* and *For...Next*?**

A. With *For Each...Next*, you don't need to know the number of elements in advance.

Do While...Loop

The *Do While...Loop* command enables you to run a script as long as a certain condition is in effect. If you were in Kauai, the *Do While...Loop* might look like this:

```
Do While sun_is_shining
  Surf
Loop
```

Do While...Loop means that as long as the specified condition remains true, the listed action continues to perform—it just loops around and around. In our silly preceding example, as long as the sun is shining, we surf. (Not a bad way to spend an afternoon.)

> **Just the Steps**   To use the *Do While...Loop*
>
> 1. On a new line in the script, type **Do While** followed by a condition to be tested.
> 2. On the next line, type the command to be performed.
> 3. On the next line, type **Loop**.

In the MonitorForChangedDiskSpace.vbs script, you monitor the disk space on a server. If the free space changes, then a message is echoed to the screen. Read through this script and see which parts you can identify. After you finish reading it, we'll discuss it.

MonitorForChangedDiskSpace.vbs

```
Option Explicit
'On Error Resume Next
Dim colMonitoredDisks
Dim objWMIService
Dim objDiskChange
Dim strComputer
Dim startTime, 'snapTime used for timer Function

Const LOCAL_HARD_DISK = 3 'the driveType value from SDK
Const RUN_TIME = 10 'time to allow the script to run in seconds
strComputer = "."
startTime = Timer

Set objWMIService = GetObject("winmgmts:\\" & strComputer & "\root\cimv2")
Set colMonitoredDisks = objWMIService.ExecNotificationQuery _
    ("Select * from __instancemodificationevent within 10 where " _
      & "TargetInstance ISA 'Win32_LogicalDisk'")
Do While True
snapTime = Timer
 Set objDiskChange = colMonitoredDisks.NextEvent
  If objDiskChange.TargetInstance.DriveType = LOCAL_HARD_DISK Then
  WScript.echo "diskSpace on " &_
  objDiskChange.TargetInstance.deviceID &_
  " has changed. It now has " &_
  objDiskChange.TargetInstance.freespace &_
  " Bytes free."
  End If
  If (snapTime - startTime) > RUN_TIME Then
  Exit Do
  End If
Loop
WScript.Echo FormatNumber(snapTime-startTime) & " seconds elapsed. Exiting now"
WScript.quit
```

Header Information

The Header information section, as shown in the next segment of code, begins with the *Option Explicit* command. You can think of *Option Explicit* as a cheap spelling checker.

Because it forces you to list all your variables, if you later misspell a variable, VBScript gives you an error, such as the one shown in Figure 2-1.

Figure 2-1   The *Option Explicit* command acts like a spelling checker for your scripts

After the *Option Explicit* command, you see *On Error Resume Next.* This is one command you want to comment out during testing of the script. The reason for this is that the On Error Resume Next command suppresses error messages while you're in testing and development mode, and you won't know what's going on with the script. One of the easiest errors to see is failure to declare a variable while using *Option Explicit.* The Header information section of our script is shown here:

```
Option Explicit
'On Error Resume Next
Dim colMonitoredDisks
Dim objWMIService
Dim objDiskChange
Dim strComputer
Dim startTime, snapTime     'used for timer function
```

- **colMonitoredDisks**   Used to hold the collection of disks that is returned by the WMI query.

- **objWMIService**   Used to hold the connection string and query to WMI.

- **objDiskChange**   Used to hold the notification event that comes from WMI, which lets you know you have a change in disk status.

- **strComputer**   Used to hold the target of the WMI query. When set to "." it means to run the WMI query on the local machine.

- **startTime**   Used to hold the number of seconds since midnight. Will be used with the *Timer* function.

- **snapTime**   Used to hold the number of seconds since midnight. It will be subtracted from *startTime* and tell us how long the operation has been running.

Reference Information

In the Reference information section, shown next, you assign values to variables and define the constants. Two constants are used: *LOCAL_HARD_DISK* and *RUN_TIME.* The *LOCAL_HARD_DISK* constant is set to 3, which is a local fixed disk. This value comes from the Platform SDK article on the WMI class WIN32_LogicalDisk. The second constant is

RUN_TIME and it is used to control how long we allow the script to run. It is set in seconds, and 10 is used for testing purposes. To allow the script to run for longer periods of time, you would increase the value of this constant.

StartTime is set equal to *Timer*. The *Timer* function is used see how long a script is running. It counts the number of seconds that have elapsed since midnight. Two or three variables are normally employed when using the *Timer* function. In this script, we use two: *startTime* and *snapTime*. We will compute the difference between the two values and echo out the results. We could also have used a third variable to hold the result of the computation, but in this instance there is little value in doing so.

```
Const LOCAL_HARD_DISK = 3 'the driveType value from SDK
Const RUN_TIME = 10 'time to allow the script to run in seconds
strComputer = "."
startTime = Timer
```

Worker and Output Information

The Worker and Output information section of the script is where you do some pretty cool stuff. The two *Set* commands at the beginning of the Worker section are WMI things. The first makes the connection into the default WMI namespace on the local computer. The second *Set* command executes a notification event query. This sets up a subscription that tells WMI we want to be notified if something changes in relation to our logical disks. We only want to be notified if this occurrs during a 10-second interval. In a production server, do not set the *within* clause to less than 60 and preferably not less than 120. But for testing purposes, within 10 seconds is fine. Let's take a look at what is going on in this section of the script:

```
Set objWMIService = GetObject("winmgmts:\\" & strComputer & "\root\cimv2")
Set colMonitoredDisks = objWMIService.ExecNotificationQuery _
    ("Select * from __instancemodificationevent within 10 where " _
        & "TargetInstance ISA 'Win32_LogicalDisk'")
Do While True
snapTime = Timer
 Set objDiskChange = colMonitoredDisks.NextEvent
  If objDiskChange.TargetInstance.DriveType = LOCAL_HARD_DISK Then
  WScript.echo "diskSpace on " &_
  objDiskChange.TargetInstance.deviceID &_
  " has changed. It now has " &_
  objDiskChange.TargetInstance.freespace &_
  " Bytes free."
  End If
  If (snapTime - startTime) > RUN_TIME Then
  Exit Do
  End If
Loop
```

First let's look at the *Do While...Loop* construction. Notice that the line beginning this section is *Do While True*. This tells VBScript that you want to invoke *Do While...Loop*. Everything between *Do While True* and *Loop* will continue to run as long as the *Do While* statement is true. It will continue to be true forever, because we only say *Do While True*.

After you set up *Do While...Loop*, you assign the *objDiskChange* variable to be equal to the next event that comes out of *colMonitoredDisks*. Because the *Do While True* clause will run forever, we want to have a means of exiting the script (so that it does not run forever). We use an *If Then* construction. We will actually talk about this construction in Chapter 3, "Adding Intelligence," but for now it is sufficient to see that if the script has been running for more than 10 seconds, we use the *Exit Do* command and end the script.

Note   Normally, I do not like using *Exit Do* because I prefer to allow the logic of the script to determine when things are finished. In general, you should be able to handle conditions and allow the script to run through the structure and not have to "bail out" early by calling *Exit Do*. There are much better ways of creating a timer (see the WIN32_LocalTime script in *Microsoft Windows Scripting with WMI: Self-Paced Learning Guide* [Microsoft Press]), but this is a rather cute way to create a simple timer.

Quick Check

Q.   What is the primary function of *Do While...Loop*?

A.   It enables you to run a script as long as a certain condition is in effect.

Q.   What is one reason for turning off *On Error Resume Next* during development and testing?

A.   During development and testing, you want to be presented with error messages to facilitate testing and debug operations.

Note   This script is one you would want to run in CScript. To do so, open up a CMD prompt and type **cscript** and the file name. The complete command line would look something like this: *cscript c:* \Documents and Settings*%username%*\My Documents\Microsoft Press*VBScriptSBS\ch02\ MonitorForChangedDiskSpace.vbs* (of course you would need to substitute your user name for the %username% portion). CScript is nice because when you want to break out of the program, all you do is press Ctrl+C. If the script is run under WScript (which is the default), to end the program, you have to open up Task Manager and kill the wscript.exe process.

Using the *Timer* Function and the *FormatNumber* function

1.   Open Notepad or the script editor of your choice.

2.   On the first line of your script, set *Option Explicit*, as seen below:

```
Option Explicit
```

3. Declare three variables using the *Dim* command. I used *startTime, endTime, totalTime,* as seen below:

```
Dim startTime,endTime,totalTime
```

4. Declare a constant to be used with the *Sleep* command. I used *sleepTime,* as seen below:

```
Const sleepTime = 1000
```

5. Use the *startTime* variable and assign the value that comes back from the *Timer* function to it, as seen below:

```
startTime = Timer
```

6. Now let's evaluate the value of total time. If it is less than five, then we will continue to loop through our code. This is seen below:

```
Do While totalTime < 5
```

7. Let's print out the value of *startTime*. You will see it is a large number of seconds.

```
WScript.Echo startTime
```

8. Now let's assign a snapshot to the end time. We again use *timer*.

```
endTime = timer
```

9. Just for fun, let's print out the value of *endTime* so we can compare results with *startTime*.

```
WScript.Echo endTime
```

10. Compute the value of *totalTime* by subtracting the value of *startTime* from *endTime*.

```
totalTime = endTime - startTime
```

11. So we can monitor progress, let's print out the value of *totalTime*:

```
WScript.Echo totalTime
```

12. Clean up the number that was computed as *totalTime* by using the *formatNumber* function. It will trim everything to two decimal places by default, as seen below:

```
totalTime = formatNumber(totalTime)
```

13. Now let's sleep for a little while and print out some blank lines, and then loop. This is done by the following code:

```
wscript.sleep sleepTime
WScript.Echo vbNewLine
loop
```

14. Save and run your script. If you have problems, you can compare your code with the TimerFormatNumberLoop.vbs script in My Documents\MicrosoftPress\VBScriptSBS\ Ch02.

Do Until...Loop

As you know by now, *Do...Loop* enables the script to continue to perform certain actions until a specific condition occurs. *Do While...Loop* enables your script to continue to perform these actions as long as the specified condition remains true. Once the specified condition is no longer true, *Do While...Loop* exits. In contrast, *Do Until...Loop* has the opposite effect—the script continues to perform the action *until* a certain condition is met.

"So what?" you might ask. In and of itself, *Do Until* is not all that exciting, but you can use it to perform certain tasks. Here are common uses of *Do Until*:

- Read text from a file
- Read through records in a record set
- Create a looping condition for monitoring purposes

Each of these implementations will be used in coming chapters. For now, let's look at a typical use of *Do Until*, which is illustrated in the ReadTextFile.vbs script:

ReadTextFile.vbs

```
Option Explicit
'On Error Resume Next
Dim strError
Dim objFSO
Dim objFile
Dim strLine
Dim intResult

CONST ForReading = 1
strError = "Error"

Set objFSO = CreateObject("Scripting.FileSystemObject")
Set objFile = objFSO.OpenTextFile("C:\windows\setuplog.txt", ForReading)
strLine = objFile.ReadLine

Do Until objFile.AtEndofStream
  strLine = objFile.ReadLine
  intResult = InStr(strLine, strError)
  If intResult <> 0 Then
  WScript.Echo(strLine)
  End if
Loop
WScript.Echo("all done")
objFile.Close
```

In this script, you begin with the Header information section, which is where you declare your variables and turn on error handling. Here is the Header information section:

```
Option Explicit
'On Error Resume Next
Dim strError
Dim objFSO
Dim objFile
Dim strLine
Dim intResult
```

As in other scripts, *Option Explicit* tells VBScript that you're going to tell VBScript about each variable before you use it. If an unnamed item comes up and it's not a command, an error is generated. This helps to save us from misspelled variable names and typos. *On Error Resume Next* tells VBScript to ignore all the errors it can and to go to the next line. You don't want this turned on when you're writing scripts, because scripts will fail and not let you know what's going on, so it is turned off here.

After the two standard lines of the script, it's time to declare some variables. Because you can give variables any name you want (except the names for built-in commands or names already used for constants), it makes sense to use names that are self-explanatory. In addition, as you have already noticed, in VBScript you seem to always be using the same types of connections and commands. For instance, by the end of this book, you will certainly know how to create the file system object, and I tend to use the variable name *objFSO* for this. The *obj* part tells me that the item is associated with an object, and the *FSO* portion is simply shorthand for *file system object*. This object could just as well be named *objFileSystemObject*, but I use it a lot and that name requires way too much typing. For some guidance on variable naming conventions, refer to the "Variable Naming Convention" section of Appendix D.

Anyway, because this section is not about the file system object but rather about using *Do Until*, let's plunge ahead. The next part of the script is the Reference information section. It's here that you tell VBScript that you're going to define things to make it easier to work with them. In the following code, you create several reference assignments:

```
CONST ForReading = 1
strError = "error"
```

The constant *ForReading* is set equal to 1. When you use the *openTextFile* method, it can open a file in one of three ways: to read, to write, or to append. In this instance, we will open it so we can read from the file. The constant *ForReading* makes the script easier to read. We will cover this in detail in Chapter 6, "Basic Windows Administration." The *strError* variable is set equal to the word *error*. This is what you want to search for in the log file you're going to open. The word assigned to *strError* can easily be changed to search the log file for other words such as *failure, failed, cannot,* or even *unable to,* all of which show up in log files from time to time. By using a variable for the text you are searching for, you are facilitating the ability to change the script to search for other words.

Worker and Output Information

You use two *Set* commands to talk to the file system and open a text file. We'll be covering these commands in detail in Chapter 6. For now, it's sufficient to note that the text file you're opening to read is C:\windows\setuplog.txt, which is the file that Windows Server 2003 creates during installation. The file is huge and loaded with needed troubleshooting information if setup were ever to fail. But the installation doesn't have to be a complete failure for the file to be useful. For instance, if you're having problems with Windows Product Activation (WPA), just change *strError* and look for WPA. Error codes found in this section of the setuplog.txt are standard HTTP 1.1 messages (for example, 403 is access denied, 404 is file or directory not found, and 407 is initial proxy authentication required by the Web server). Armed with this information and the script, you can search setuplog.txt, parse the return information, and match it with standard HTTP 1.1 messages.

The line *strLine = objFile.ReadLine* tells VBScript to read one line from the text file referenced by *objFile*. *StrLine* holds the line of text that comes out of the file via the *ReadLine* command. If you printed *strLine* by using the *WScript.Echo* command, the line of text would be echoed to the screen. You can also use the *strLine* variable to hold the line of text so that you can search it for our keyword *error*.

Notice that *Do Until* is in effect until we are at *objFile.AtEndofStream*. Think of the *ReadLine* command as a pump—you're going to pump text into *Do Until...Loop* until you reach the end of the text stream. This means that you read lines of text, one line at a time, until you reach the end of the file. You can see this process in the first two lines.

```
Do Until objFile.AtEndofStream
  strLine = objFile.ReadLine
  intResult = InStr(strLine, strError)
  If intResult <>0 Then
  WScript.Echo(strLine)
  End if
Loop
```

Once the text pump is set up and you have a nice steady stream of letters coming across, you use the next command in the Worker and Output information section of the script. You now use the *intResult* variable that you declared earlier. You assign *intResult* to the result of using the *InStr* command (think of it as "in string"), which looks through a string of text and tries to find a match. The command is put together like this:

Command	String 1	String 2
InStr	String to be searched	String being searched for

In this script, you look through each line of text that comes from the Setuplog.txt file to find the word *error*, which you assigned to the variable named *strError*. This part of the script looks like the following:

```
SearchResult = InStr(strLine, strError)
```

Now the situation gets a little complicated, because the *InStr* command is rather peculiar in the way it hands back information, as detailed in Table 2-1.

Table 2-1   Use of the *InStr* function

Condition	Result Returned
String 1 is zero in length	*0*
String 1 is null	*Null*
String 2 is zero in length	*Start*
String 2 is null	*Null*
String 2 is not found	*0*
String 2 is found in string 1	Position at which the match is found

In Table 2-1, the only value we're interested in is the one that is not equal to zero. (Although a null value contains no valid data, it is not the same as zero or as the empty string "", often referred to as a *null string*. You'll learn more about that when we talk about data types in Chapter 8.) To evaluate the results of the *InStr* function, use *If...Then* to make sure that what came back from *InStr* is not equal to zero—which tells us that *InStr* is indicating where in the line the word *error* was found. We really don't care where in the line the word occurs, only that the word is present. You use *WScript.Echo* to echo out the value of *strLine*. Note that you print out *strLine*, which is the variable that contains the line of text that you read from the log file. You don't echo out *intResult* because it contains only a number, as explained in Table 2-1.

After you print out the line containing the error message from the Setuplog.txt file, you end your *If* statement by using the *End If* command, and you *Loop* (which sends us right back to the *Do Until* command). You continue to *Loop Until* until you reach the end of the file, at which time you echo out *all done* and close your file. Echoing *all done* just lets you know (while you watch stuff scroll on the screen) that you've completed running the script (otherwise, there is no indication that the script completed).

Quick Check

Q.   **What is the difference between *Do Until* and *Do While*?**

A.   *Do Until* does not run once a condition becomes true, whereas *Do While* runs as long as a condition is true.

Q.   **What is the *InStr* command used for?**

A.   *InStr* is used to look through a string of text to find a specific sequence of characters.

Do...Loop

The *Do...Loop* statement is used to put a script into a loop for an undetermined number of loops. It causes the script to simply loop and loop and loop. In the DoLoopMonitorForProcessDeletion.vbs script, we use an additional event driven script. Here we use the *Do...Loop* structure, rather than using *Do While True* as in the MonitorForChangedDiskSpace.vbs script.

To use the DoLoopMonitorForProcessDeletion.vbs script, you will want to start up Notepad. Then you run the script. While the script is running, you can close out Notepad. Within 10 seconds, you will get a printed message that lists the name of the process, the process ID, and the amount of user mode time that was consumed. Because the script is a *Do...Loop* script, it will continue to run until you manually exit the script (by using Ctrl+C if you are running under CScript in a CMD prompt, or by killing the wscript.exe process in TaskManager if you are running the script in WScript). This means that if you open another instance of Notepad, wait for a few seconds, and then exit Notepad again, you will once again trigger an alert. You can obviously use this script to monitor more important processes than Notepad.exe. If you did not have the *Do...Loop*, the script would only alert you one time when a process exited— not a very tenable situation for a monitoring script.

DoLoopMonitorForProcessDeletion.vbs

```
Option Explicit
'On Error Resume Next
dim strComputer 'computer to run the script upon.
dim wmiNS 'the wmi namespace. Here it is the default namespace
dim wmiQuery 'the wmi event query
dim objWMIService 'SWbemServicesEx object
dim colItems 'SWbemEventSource object
dim objItem 'individual item in the collection
Dim objName ' monitored item. Any Process.
Dim objTGT 'monitored class. A win32_process.

strComputer = "."
objName = "'Notepad.exe'" 'the single quotes inside the double quotes required
objTGT = "'win32_Process'"
wmiNS = "\root\cimv2"
wmiQuery = "SELECT * FROM __InstanceDeletionEvent WITHIN 10 WHERE " _
    & "TargetInstance ISA " & objTGT & " AND " _
      & "TargetInstance.Name=" & objName

Set objWMIService = GetObject("winmgmts:\\" & strComputer & wmiNS)
Set colItems = objWMIService.ExecNotificationQuery(wmiQuery)
Do
  Set objItem = colItems.NextEvent
  Wscript.Echo "Name: " & objItem.TargetInstance.Name & " " & now
  Wscript.Echo "ProcessID: " & objItem.TargetInstance.ProcessId
  WScript.Echo "user mode time: " & objItem.TargetInstance.UserModeTime
Loop
```

While...Wend

One more kind of looping technology is the *While...Wend* statement. It is read as follows: "While statement A is true, we will continue to loop through the code. Once it is met, then we will exit at the *Wend* statement." It is very similar to a *Do...Until* loop statement. The following script, WhileWendLoop.vbs, illustrates using this construction.

The WhileWendLoop.vbs script is a timer script. We create a time stamp by using the *timeserial* function. If you look up *timeserial* in the My Documents\Microsoft Press\VBScriptSBS\Resources\Scripts56.chm file, it will tell you that it takes three numbers (hour, minute, second) and turns them into a date variant—which means it will turn them into a time stamp we can use.

In the subBeep subroutine, we use the *Run* method to create a beep. Subroutines are discussed in chapter 15 (Using Subs and Functions). For now, you can think of a subroutine as a special part of the script we can access by name. In this script, we use the subroutine to keep the details of creating a beep from the main script. Later, we may want to change the beep to something else ... which could be done by replacing the subroutine with some other code. If it was embedded in the worker section of the script, we would have to make many more changes. We do this once the time has been reached that was specified in the *dtmTime* variable.

To use the WhileWendLoop.vbs script, you will need to pick a time (in 24-hour time format) that is about a minute in the future; make sure you supply that time to the *dteTime* variable in the Reference section of the script. Then run the script. Once the time is reached, the script will beep and print a message indicating that the time has been reached.

WhileWendLoop.vbs

```
Option Explicit
'On Error Resume Next
dim dtmTime

Const hideWindow = 0
Const sleepyTime = 1000
dtmTime = timeSerial(19,25,00) <;$QS>Modify this value with desired time

while dtmTime > Time
WScript.Echo "current time is: " & Time &_
" counting to " & dtmTime
WScript.Sleep sleepyTime
Wend
subBeep
WScript.Echo dtmTime & " was reached."

Sub subBeep
Dim objShell
Set objShell = CreateObject("WScript.Shell")
objShell.Run "%comspec% /c echo " & Chr(07),hideWindow
End Sub
```

Creating Additional Objects

In Chapter 1, we looked at creating objects and we discussed objects, properties, and methods. Recall that to perform anything useful, we need to create an object. In the Script56.chm file on the CD-ROM, we have the scripting SDK documentation. If you look up wshShell.object, you will find the properties and objects provided by this object. WshShell is the actual name of the object, and will result in faster results in the SDK. Of course, we never use the name wshShell in a script, we use *wscript.shell*. We create the *wshShell* object by using the following command:

```
Set objShell = createObject("wscript.shell")
```

Once we create the *wscript.shell* object, we have access to the following methods:

Method	Purpose
Run	Runs an external command
Exec	Runs an external command, but provides access to the datastream
appActivate	Brings a specified window to the foreground
sendKeys	Enables you to send keystrokes to the foreground application
CreateShortCut	Creates shortcuts
LogEvent	Writes to the application Event log
RegRead	Reads from the registry
RegWrite	Writes to the registry
RegDelete	Deletes from the registry
PopUp	Displays a pop-up dialog box
ExpandEnvironmentStrings	Parses environmental variables (these variables can be displayed by using the *Set* command from a CMD prompt)

In the WhileWendLoop.vbs script, we used the *Run* method to run the command prompt (CMD.exe), to have the computer produce a beep. The *echo* command tells the CMD program to print out something. Chr(07) tells the script we want to use an ASCII value. ASCII values less than 31 are all non-printing characters, and 07, as you saw in the script, makes a beep. In the CreateAddRemoveShortCut.vbs script, we are going to use the *CreateShortCut* method to create a shortcut on the desktop. We will also use the specialFolders property to pick up the path to the desktop so we can create a shortcut there. The thing that is special about this particular script is that it supplies values for command line arguments. In this way, we run the control.exe program, which provides access to control panel applets. We then use the arguments property of the shortcut object to supply the command line argument, which then launches the specific control panel applet. Microsoft Knowledge Base article KB192806 (available on support.Microsoft.com) details the names of the control panel applets that can be launched in this manner. Figure 2-2 illustrates the properties that can be set on a shortcut.

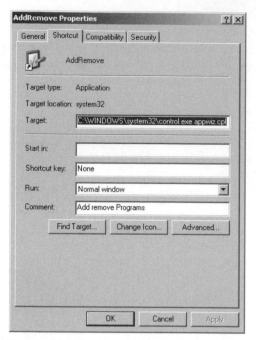

Figure 2-2   Shortcut properties assigned via script

CreateAddRemoveShortCut.vbs

```
Option Explicit
Dim objShell
Dim strDesktop 'pointer to desktop special folder
Dim objShortCut 'used to set properties of the shortcut. Comes from using createShortCut
Dim strTarget
strTarget = "control.exe"
set objShell = CreateObject("WScript.Shell")
strDesktop = objShell.SpecialFolders("Desktop")

set objShortCut = objShell.CreateShortcut(strDesktop & "\AddRemove.lnk")
objShortCut.TargetPath = strTarget
objShortCut.Arguments = "appwiz.cpl"
objShortCut.IconLocation = "%SystemRoot%\system32\SHELL32.dll,21"
objShortCut.description = "addRemove"
objShortCut.Save
```

If we need to run an external script that provides a capability that is not native in VBScript, then we have two choices: We can use the *Run* method, or we can use the *Exec* method. The *Run* method runs a program when we only need to access the program. The *Exec* method gives us access to the text stream that is produced by running the command. When we run command line utilities, we will nearly always want to capture the text stream. The RunNet-Stat.vbs script runs the netstat.exe utility. Netstat.exe -? provides help on using this command, and Microsoft Knowledge base article KB281336 supplies lots of examples for using this awesome tool. The great thing about using Netstat is that it will tell you the process ID of programs on your machine that are listening to Transmission Control Protocol (TCP) ports. It will also tell you the Internet Protocol (IP) address of any connections your machine may have made as well. Try the program below. The script is set up so that you can easily change and run any other command line utility as well. All you do is edit the command variable.

RunNetStat.vbs

```
Option Explicit    'is used to force the scripter to declare variables
'On Error Resume Next 'is used to tell vbscript to go to the next line if it encounters an
Error
Dim objShell'holds WshShell object
Dim objExecObject'holds what comes back from executing the command
Dim strText'holds the text stream from the exec command.
Dim command 'the command to run

command = "cmd /c netstat -ano"
WScript.Echo "starting program " & Now 'used to mark when program begins
Set objShell = CreateObject("WScript.Shell")
Set objExecObject = objShell.Exec(command)

Do Until objExecObject.StdOut.AtEndOfStream
  strText = objExecObject.StdOut.ReadAll()
  WScript.Echo strText
Loop
WScript.echo "complete" 'lets me know program is done running
```

Using the *For Each...Next* Command Step-by-Step Exercises

In this section, you'll explore using the *For Each...Next* command and the *For...Next* command.

1. Open up the ping.vbs script in Notepad. It is located in the My Documents\Microsoft Press\VBScriptSBS\Ch02\StepByStep folder.

2. Change the values *strMachines* = "*s1;s2*" to one or more computers reachable on your network. (If you are not networked, you can do something like this: *strMachines* = "*127.0.0.1;localhost;127.0.0.2*").

3. Save the script with a different name, such as YourNamePing.vbs.

4. Open a CMD prompt and switch to the directory where you saved the script.

5. Type **cscript YourNamePing.vbs** and see whether the script runs. If it does not, use the *PING* command from the CMD prompt to test your networked machine and ensure it is reachable. If you get a reply, make sure you have the quotation marks and the semicolon, as shown in step 2.

6. Set *Option Explicit*.

7. *Dim* each variable that is used in the script.

8. Set *On Error Resume Next*, but comment it out.

9. Add comments to identify each section of the script.

10. Examine the construct of the *For Each...Next* statement.

11. In the Worker and Output sections of the script, put in a *For...Next* statement that makes the script send three pings. Hint: Consider placing the *For* portion after the line that reads *For each machine in aMachines.*

12. Save the script and test.

13. If it runs properly, turn the *On Error Resume Next* statement back on by removing the comment.

14. Save the script. If it does not run, compare it with pingSolution.vbs in the ch02\StepByStep folder.

15. Extra: Play around with the script and see what optimizations you can add, such as reporting on different properties of the *Ping* command. Look up the WIN32_PingStatus WMI class in the Platform SDK for this information. Compare your results with pingSolutionExtra.vbs.

16. Extra, Extra: Add additional comments to the script that explain why certain items are required.

17. More Extras: Configure the script to ping a range of IP addresses (for testing, use 127.0.0.1–127.0.0.255). Compare your results with pingSolutionMoreExtras.vbs.

18. Even more: Have it ping only every fifth computer inside the range. Compare your results with pingSolutionEvenMore.vbs.

19. More more extras: Configure the script to only return computers that do not respond to the ping. Compare your results with pingSolutionMoreMoreExtras.vbs.

One Step Further: Modifying the Ping Script

In this section, you will modify the ping script so that it can be used to monitor your servers.

1. Open pingSolution.vbs and save it as YourNamePingModification.vbs.

2. Comment out *On Error Resume Next* so that you can test the script.

3. Define a constant called *ONE_HOUR* and set it equal to 100 for testing purposes. The *WScript.Sleep* command takes an argument in milliseconds. So normally you would set *ONE_HOUR* to 3600000, which is one hour in milliseconds.

4. Declare a variable to be used to count to eight, such as *ihours*.

5. Add a *For ihours = 1 To 8* command to the beginning of the Worker section. It will go under *aMachines = Split(strMachines, ";")*.

6. Add the *WScript.Sleep(ONE_HOUR)* command to the bottom of the script (after all those *Next* commands). When you define a constant as you did in step 3, testing your script is a lot nicer.

7. Save the script. Try to run the script. (You should get an error.)

8. Add another *Next* command after the *WScript.Sleep* command.

9. Save the script and run it. (It should work now.)

10. Add a *WScript.Echo* command to the bottom of the script with a message letting you know when the script is finished.

Chapter 2 Quick Reference

To	Do This
Walk through a collection of items such as is often returned by WMI	Use *For Each...Next*
Define numbers that could be confusing if they were embedded within a script	Use a constant
Make a script easier to read, and easier to modify in the future	Use a constant
Modify a value during script execution	Use a variable
Perform an operation a certain number of times	Use *For...Next*
Create a looping condition that occurs only as long as a particular condition is true	Use *Do While...Loop*
Create a looping condition that occurs until a particular condition becomes true	Use *Do Until...Loop*
Pause script execution	Use *WScript.Sleep*
Pause script execution for five seconds	Use *WScript.Sleep(5000)*

Chapter 3
Adding Intelligence

Before You Begin

To successfully complete this chapter, you need to be familiar with the following concepts, which were presented in Chapters 1 and 2:

- Declaring variables
- Basic error handling
- Connecting to the file system object
- Using *For Each...Next*
- Using *Do While*

After completing this chapter, you will be able to:

- Use *If...Then*
- Use *If...Then...ElseIf*
- Use *If...Then...Else*
- Use *Select Case*
- Use intrinsic constants

If...Then

If...Then is one of those programming staples (like fried chicken and mashed potatoes are staples in the southern United States). What's nice about *If...Then* is that it makes sense. We use this kind of logic all the time.

The basic operation is diagrammed here:

If	condition	Then	action
If	store is open	Then	buy chicken

The real power of *If...Then* comes into play when combined with tools such as those we looked at in Chapter 2, "Looping Through the Script." *If...Then* is rarely used by itself. Although you could have a script such as IfThen.vbs, you wouldn't find it very valuable.

IfThen.vbs

```
On Error Resume Next
Const a = 2
Const b = 3
Const c = 5
If a + b = c Then
WScript.Echo(c)
End If
```

In this script three constants are defined: *a*, *b*, and *c*. We then sum the numbers and evaluate the result by using the *If...Then* statement. There are three important elements to pay attention to in implementing the *If...Then* construct:

- The *If* and the *Then must* be on the *same* line
- The action to be taken must be on the *next* line
- You must end your *If...Then* statement by using *End If*

If any of these elements are missing or misplaced, your *If...Then* statement generates an error. Make sure you remember that *End If* is two words, and not one word as in some other programming languages. If you do not see an error and one of these elements is missing, make sure you have commented out *On Error Resume Next*.

Now that you have the basic syntax down pat, let's look at the following more respectable and useful script, named GetComments.vbs, which is in the folder \My Documents\Microsoft Press\VBScriptSBS\ch03. *If* you put lots of descriptive comments in your Microsoft Visual Basic, Scripting Edition (VBScript) scripts, *Then* GetComments.vbs pulls them out and writes them into a separate file. This file can be used to create a book of documentation about the most essential scripts you use in your network. In addition, *If* you standardize your documentation procedures, *Then* the created book will require very little touch-up work when you are finished. (OK, I'll quit playing *If...Then* with you. Let's look at that code, which is described in the next few sections.)

GetComments.vbs

```
Option Explicit
On Error Resume Next
Dim scriptFile
Dim commentFile
Dim objScriptFile
Dim objFSO
Dim objCommentFile
Dim strCurrentLine
Dim intIsComment
Const ForReading = 1
Const ForWriting = 2
scriptFile = "displayComputerNames.vbs"
commentFile = "comments.txt"
Set objFSO = CreateObject("Scripting.FileSystemObject")
Set objScriptFile = objFSO.OpenTextFile _
  (scriptFile, ForReading)
```

```
Set objCommentFile = objFSO.OpenTextFile(commentFile, _
  ForWriting, TRUE)
Do While objScriptFile.AtEndOfStream <> TRUE
  strCurrentLine = objScriptFile.ReadLine
  intIsComment = Instr(1,strCurrentLine,"'")
  If intIsComment > 0 Then
    objCommentFile.Write strCurrentLine & VbCrLf
  End If
Loop
WScript.Echo("script complete")
objScriptFile.Close
objCommentFile.Close
```

> **Just the Steps**   To implement *If...Then*
>
> 1. On a new line in the script, type **If** *some condition* **Then**.
> 2. On the next line, enter the command you want to invoke.
> 3. On the next line, type **End If**.

Header Information

The first few lines of the GetComments.vbs script contain the header information. We use *Option Explicit* to force us to declare all the variables used in the script. This helps to ensure that you spell the variables correctly as well as understand the logic. *On Error Resume Next* is rudimentary error handling. It tells VBScript to go to the next line in the script when there is an error. There are times, however, when you do not want this behavior, such as when you copy a file to another location prior to performing a delete operation. It would be disastrous if the copy operation failed but the delete worked.

After you define the two constants, you define the variables. Listing variables on individual lines makes commenting the lines in the script easier, and the commenting lets readers of the script know why the variables are being used. In reality, it doesn't matter where you define variables, because the compiler reads the entire script prior to executing it. This means you can spread constant and variable declarations all over the script any way you want—such an approach would be hard for humans to read, but it would make no difference to VBScript.

Reference Information

In the Reference information section of the script, you define constants and assign values to several of the variables previously declared.

The lines beginning with Const of the GetComments.vbs script define two constants, *ForReading* and *ForWriting*, which make the script easier to read. (You learned about constants in Chapter 2.) You'll use them when you open the DisplayComputerNames.vbs file and the comments.txt file from the ch03 folder on the CD. You could have just used the numbers 1 and 2 in your command and skipped the two constants; however, someone reading the script needs to know what the numbers are doing. Because these values will never change, it is more efficient to define a constant instead of using a variable. This is because the computer knows that you will only store two small numbers in these two constants. On the other hand, if we declared these two as variables, then the operating system would need to reserve enough memory to hold anything from a small number to an entire object. These varients (as they are called) are easy on programmers, but are wasteful of memory resources. But it is, after all, just a scripting language. If we were really concerned about efficiency, and conservation of resources, we would be writing in C++.

The name of the file you are extracting comments from is stored in the variable *scriptFile*. By using the variable in this way it becomes easy to modify the script later so that you can either point it to another file or make the script read all the scripts in an entire folder. In addition, you could make the script use a command-line option that specifies the name of the script to parse for comments. However, by assigning a variable to the script file name, you make all those options possible without a whole lot of rewriting. This is also where you name the file used to write the comments into—the aptly named comments.txt file.

Quick Check

Q.   Is it permissible to have *If* on one line and *Then* on a separate line?

A.   No. Both *If* and *Then* must be on the same logical line. They can be on separate physical lines if the line continuation character (_) is used. Typically, *If* is the first word and *Then* is the last command on the line.

Q.   If the *Then* clause is on a separate logical line from the *If...Then* statement, what command do you use?

A.   *End If*. The key here is that *End If* consists of two words, not one.

Q.   What is the main reason for using constants?

A.   Constants have their value set prior to script execution, and therefore their value does not change during the running of the script.

Q.   What are two pieces of information required by the *OpenTextFile* command?

A.   *OpenTextFile* requires both the name of the file and whether you want to read or write.

Worker and Output Information

The Worker and Output information section is the core engine of the script, where the actual work is being done. You use the *Set* command three times, as shown here:

```
Set objFSO = CreateObject("Scripting.FileSystemObject")
Set objScriptFile = objFSO.OpenTextFile _
  (scriptFile, ForReading)
Set objCommentFile = objFSO.OpenTextFile(commentFile, _
  ForWriting, TRUE)
```

Regarding the first *Set* command, you've seen *objFSO* used several times already in Chapter 2. *objFSO* is a variable name, which we routinely assign to our connection to the file system, that allows us to read and write to files. You have to create the file system object object (as it is technically called) to be able to open text files.

The second *Set* command uses our *objScriptFile* variable name to allow us to read the DisplayComputerNames.vbs file. Note that the *OpenTextFile* command requires only one piece of information: the name of the file. VBScript will assume you are opening the file for reading if you don't include the optional file mode information. We are going to specify two bits of information so that the script is easier to understand:

■ The name of the file

■ How you want to use the file—that is, read or write to it

By using variables for these two parts of the *OpenTextFile* command, you make the script much more flexible and readable.

The third *Set* command follows the same pattern. You assign the *objCommentFile* variable to whatever comes back from the *openTextFile* command. In this instance, however, you write to the file instead of read from it. You also use variables for the name of the comment file and for the option used to specify writing to the file.

The GetComments.vbs script reads each line of the DisplayComputerNames.vbs file and checks for the presence of a single quotation mark ('). When the single quotation mark is present, the script writes the line that contains that character out to the comments.txt file.

A closer examination of the Worker and Output information section of the GetComments.vbs script reveals that it begins with *Do While...Loop*, as shown here:

```
Do While objScriptFile.AtEndOfStream <> TRUE
  strCurrentLine = objScriptFile.ReadLine
  intIsComment = InStr(1,strCurrentLine,"'")
  If intIsComment > 0 Then
    objCommentFile.Write strCurrentLine & vbCrLf
  End If
Loop
WScript.Echo("script complete")
objScriptFile.Close
objCommentFile.Close
```

You first heard about the *Do While* statement in Chapter 2. *ObjScriptFile* contains a *textStream Object*. This object was created when we used the *openTextFile* method from the *fileSystem Object*. The *textStreamObject* has a property that is called *atEndOfStream*. As long as you aren't at the end of the text stream, the script reads the line of text and sees whether it contains a single quotation mark. *AtEndOfStream* is a property. It describes a physical location. Of course, we do not know where *AtEndOfStream* is located, so we use *Do While* to loop around until it finds the end of the stream.

To check for the presence of the <'> character, you use the *InStr* function, just as discussed in Chapter 2. The *InStr* function returns a zero when it does not find the character; when it does find the character, it returns a number representing the location in the line of text that the character was found.

If *InStr* finds the <'> character within the line of text, the variable *intIsComment* holds a number that is larger than zero. Therefore, you use the *If...Then* construct, as shown in the following code, to write out the line to the comments.txt file:

```
If intIsComment > 0 Then
  objCommentFile.Write strCurrentLine & vbCrLf
End If
```

Notice that the condition to be evaluated is contained within *If...Then*. If the variable *intIsComment* is larger than zero, you take the action on the next line. Here you use the *Write* command to write out the current line of the DisplayComputerNames.vbs file.

Use the *Timer* function to see how long the script runs

1. Open the GetComments.vbs script in Microsoft Notepad or the script editor of your choice.

2. Save the script as YourNameGetCommentsTimed.vbs.

3. Declare two new variables: *startTime* and *endTime*. Put these variables at the bottom of your list of variables, and before the constants. It will look like:

   ```
   Dim startTime, endTime
   ```

4. Right before the line where you create the FilesystemObject and set it to the *objFSO* variable, assign the value of the *Timer* function to the *startTime* variable. It will look like the following:

   ```
   startTime = Timer
   ```

5. Right before the script complete line, assign the value of timer to the *endTime* variable. It will look like:

   ```
   endTime = Timer
   ```

6. Now edit the *script complete* line to include the time it took to run. Use the *ROUND* function to round off the time to two decimal places. The line will look like the following:

   ```
   WScript.Echo "script complete. " & round(endTime-startTime, 2)
   ```

7. Save and run your script. Compare your script with GetCommentsTimed.vbs in \My Documents\Microsoft Press\VBScriptSBS\ch03 if desired.

Intrinsic Constants

You use the *vbCrLf* command to perform what is called a *carriage return* and *line feed*. *vbCrLf* is an *intrinsic constant*, which means that it is a constant that is built into VBScript. Because intrinsic constants are built into VBScript, you don't need to define them as you do regular constants. You'll use other intrinsic constants as you continue to develop scripts in VBScript language in later chapters.

vbCrLf has its roots in the old-fashioned manual typewriter. Those things had a handle on the end that rolled the plate up one or two lines (the line feed) and then repositioned the type head (the carriage return). Like the typewriter handle, the *vbCrLf* command positions the text to the first position on the following line. It's a very useful command for formatting text in both dialog boxes and text files. The last line in our *If...Then* construct is the *End If* command. *End If* tells VBScript that we're finished using the *If...Then* command. If you don't include *End If*, VBScript complains with an error.

The Platform SDK documents many other intrinsic constants that we can use with VBScript. Besides *vbCrLf*, the one I use the most is *vbTab*, which will tab over the default tab stop. It is helpful for indenting output. You can look up others in the Scripts56.chm file included in the Resources folder on the CD-ROM by searching for "intrinsic constants."

After using *End If*, you have the *Loop* command on a line by itself. The *Loop* command belongs to the *Do While* construct that began the Worker and Output information section. *Loop* sends the script execution back to the *Do While* line. VBScript continues to loop through, reading the text file and looking for ' marks, as long as it doesn't reach the end of the text stream. When VBScript reaches the end of the text stream from the DisplayComputerNames script, a message displays saying that you're finished processing the script. This is important, because otherwise there would be no indication that the script has concluded running. You then close your two files and the script is done. In reality, you don't need to close the files because they will automatically close once the script exits memory, but closing the files is good practice and could help to avoid problems if the script hangs.

Making a decision using *If...Then*

1. Open Notepad or the script editor of your choice. Navigate to the blankTemplate.vbs template in the \My Documents\Microsoft Press\VBScriptSBS\Templates directory.

2. Save the template as YourNameConvertToGig.vbs.

3. On the first non-commented line, type **Option Explicit**.

4. On the next line, declare the variable *intMemory*.

5. The next line begins the Reference section. Assign the value 120,000 to the *intMemory* variable. It will look like the following:

```
intMemory = 120000
```

6. Use the *formatNumber* function to remove all but the last two digits after the decimal place. It will look like the following:

    ```
    intMemory = formatNumber(intMemory/1024)
    ```

7. If the value of *intMemory* is greater than 1024, then we want to convert it to gigabytes, print out the value, and then exit the script. We will use *formatNumber* to clean up the trailing decimal places. Your code will look like the following:

    ```
    If intMemory > 1024 Then
    intMemory = formatNumber(intMemory/1024) & " Gigabytes"
    WScript.Echo intMemory
    WScript.quit
    End If
    ```

8. Under the *If...Then End If* construction, we assign the value to *intMemory*, as seen below.

    ```
    intMemory = intMemory & " Megabytes"
    ```

9. Then we echo out the value of *intMemory*, as seen below:

    ```
    WScript.Echo intMemory
    ```

10. Save and run the script. Compare your results to ConvertToGig.vbs in the folder \My Documents\Microsoft Press\VBScriptSBS\ch03.

If...Then...ElseIf

If...Then...ElseIf adds some flexibility to your ability to make decisions by using VBScript. *If...Then* enables you to evaluate *one* condition and take action based on that condition. By adding *ElseIf* to the mixture, you can make multiple decisions. You do this in the same way you did it using the *If...Then* command. You start out with an *If...Then* on the first line in the Worker information section, and when you are finished, you end the *If...Then* section with *End If*. If you need to make additional evaluations, add a line with *ElseIf* and the condition.

Just the Steps   To Use *If...Then...ElseIf*

1. On a new line in the script, type **If *some condition* Then**.
2. On the next line, enter the command you want to invoke.
3. On the next line, type **ElseIf** and the new condition to check, and end the line with **Then**.
4. On the next line, enter the command you want to invoke when the condition on the *ElseIf* line is true.
5. Repeat steps 3 and 4 as required.
6. On the next line, type **End If**.

You can have as many *ElseIf* lines as you need; however, if you use more than one or two, the script can get long and confusing. A better solution to avoid a long script is to convert to a *Select Case* type of structure, which is covered later in this chapter in the "Select Case" section.

Using the message box msgBox.vbs

1. Open Notepad or the script editor of your choice.

2. Define four variables that will hold the following: the title of the message box, the prompt for the message box, the button configuration, and the return code from the message box. The variables I used are *strPrompt, strTitle, intBTN, intRTN*. They are declared as follows:

   ```
   Dim strPrompt
   Dim strTitle
   Dim intBTN
   Dim intRTN
   ```

3. Assign values to the first three variables. *strPrompt* is what you want to display to the user. The title will appear at the top of the message box. The value contained in *strTitle* will appear at the top of the message box. The variable *intBTN* is used to control the style of the buttons you want displayed.

   ```
   strPrompt = "Do you want to run the script?"
   strTitle = "MsgBOX DEMO"
   intBTN = 3 '4 is yes/no 3 is yes/no/cancel
   ```

4. Now write the code to display the message box. To do this, we will use *intRTN* to capture the return code from pressing the button. We will use each of our three message box variables as well and the *msgBox* function. The line of code looks like the following:

   ```
   intRTN = MsgBox(strprompt,intBTN,strTitle)
   ```

5. If you run the script right now, it will run and display a message box, but you are not evaluating the outcome. To do that, we will use *If...Then...Else* to evaluate the return code. It will look like the following:

   ```
   If intRTN = vbYes Then
   WScript.Echo "yes was pressed"
   ElseIf intRTN = vbNo Then
   WScript.Echo "no was pressed"
   ElseIf intRTN = vbCancel Then
   WScript.Echo "cancel was pressed"
   Else
   WScript.Echo intRTN & " was pressed"
   End If
   ```

6. Save the script as YourNameMsgBox.vbs and run it. It should tell you which button was pressed from the message box. You would then tie in the code to the appropriate button instead of just echoing the return values. Compare your code with msgBox.vbs in the folder \My Documents\Microsoft Press\VBScriptSBS\ch03 if required.

Let's examine a script that uses *If...Then...ElseIf* to detect the type of central processing unit (CPU) that is installed in a computer. Here is the CPUType.vbs script from the ch03 folder on the CD.

CPUType.vbs

```
Option Explicit
On Error Resume Next
Dim strComputer
Dim cpu
Dim wmiRoot
Dim objWMIService
Dim ObjProcessor
strComputer = "."
cpu = "win32_Processor='CPU0'"
wmiRoot = "winmgmts:\\" & strComputer & "\root\cimv2"
Set objWMIService = GetObject(wmiRoot)
Set objProcessor = objWMIService.Get(cpu)
If objProcessor.Architecture = 0 Then
  WScript.Echo "This is an x86 cpu."
ElseIf objProcessor.Architecture = 1 Then
  WScript.Echo "This is a MIPS cpu."
ElseIf objProcessor.Architecture = 2 Then
  WScript.Echo "This is an Alpha cpu."
ElseIf objProcessor.Architecture = 3 Then
  WScript.Echo "This is a PowerPC cpu."
ElseIf objProcessor.Architecture = 6 Then
  WScript.Echo "This is an ia64 cpu."
Else
  WScript.Echo "Cannot determine cpu type."
End If
```

Header Information

The Header information section contains the usual information (discussed in Chapters 1 and 2), as shown here:

```
Option Explicit
On Error Resume Next
Dim strComputer
Dim cpu
Dim wmiRoot
Dim objWMIService
Dim objProcessor
```

Option Explicit tells VBScript that you'll name all the variables used in the script by using the *Dim* command. *On Error Resume Next* turns on basic error handling. The *strComputer* variable holds the name of the computer from which we will perform the Windows Management Instrumentation (WMI) query. The *cpu* variable tells VBScript where in WMI we will go to read the information.

The *wmiRoot* variable enables you to perform a task you haven't performed before in previous scripts: split out the connection portion of WMI to make it easier to change and more readable. The variables *objWMIService* and *objProcessor* hold information that comes back from the Reference information section.

Reference Information

The Reference information section is the place where you assign values to the variables you named earlier in the script. The CPUType.vbs script contains these assignments:

```
strComputer = "."
cpu = "win32_Processor.deviceID='CPU0'"
wmiRoot = "winmgmts:\\" & strComputer & "\root\cimv2"
```

strComputer is equal to ".", which is a shorthand notation for the local computer that the script is currently executing on. With the *cpu* variable, you define the place in WMI that contains information about processors, which is *win32_Processor*. Because there can be more than one processor on a machine, you further limit your query to *CPU0*. It is necessary to use *CPU0* instead of *CPU1* because *win32_Processor* begins counting CPUs with 0, and although a computer always has a CPU0, it does not always have a CPU1. *DeviceID* is the key value for the WIN32_Processor WMI class. To connect to an individual instance of a processor, it is necessary to use the key value. The key of a WMI class can be discovered using wmisdk_book.chm from \My Documents\Microsoft Press\VBScriptSBS\resources, or by using the wbemTest.exe utility from a CMD prompt. In this script, you're only trying to determine the type of CPU running on the machine, so it isn't necessary to identify all CPUs on the machine.

Worker and Output Information

The first part of the script declared the variables to be used in the script, and the second part of the script assigned values to some of the variables. In the next section, you use those variables in an *If...Then...ElseIf* construction to make a decision about the type of CPU installed on the computer.

The Worker and Output information section of the CPUType.vbs script is listed here:

```
Set objWMIService = GetObject(wmiRoot)
Set objProcessor = objWMIService.Get(cpu)

If objProcessor.Architecture = 0 Then
  WScript.Echo "This is an x86 cpu."
ElseIf objProcessor.Architecture = 1 Then
  WScript.Echo "This is a MIPS cpu."
ElseIf objProcessor.Architecture = 2 Then
  WScript.Echo "This is an Alpha cpu."
ElseIf objProcessor.Architecture = 3 Then
  WScript.Echo "This is a PowerPC cpu."
ElseIf objProcessor.Architecture = 6 Then
  WScript.Echo "This is an ia64 cpu."
Else
  WScript.Echo "Cannot determine cpu type."
End If
```

To write a script like this, you need to know how *win32_Processor* hands back information so that you can determine what a 0, 1, 2, 3, or 6 means. By detailing that information in an *If...Then...ElseIf* construct, you can translate the data into useful information.

The first two lines listed in the preceding script work just like a normal *If...Then* statement. The line begins with *If* and ends with *Then*. In the middle of the *If...Then* language is the statement you want to evaluate. If *objProcessor* returns a zero when asked about the architecture, you know the CPU is an x86, and you use *WScript.Echo* to print out that data.

If, on the other hand, *objProcessor* returns a one, you know that the CPU type is a millions of instructions per second (MIPS). By adding into the *ElseIf* statements the results of your research into return codes for WMI CPU types, you enable the script to handle the work of finding out what kind of CPU your servers are running. After you've used all the *ElseIf* statements required to parse all the possible return codes, you add one more line to cover the potential of an unexplained code, and you use *Else* for that purpose.

Combine msgBox and CPU information

1. Open Notepad or the script editor of your choice.

2. Open the msgBox.vbs script and save it as YourNamePromptCPU.vbs.

3. At the very bottom of the newly renamed msgBox.vbs script, type **Sub subCPU**, as seen below:

```
Sub subCPU
```

4. Open the CPUType.vbs script and copy the entire script to the clipboard.

5. Paste the entire CPUType.vbs script under the words *Sub subCPU*.

6. The first and second lines (from the CPUType.vbs script) that are pasted below the words *Sub subCPU* are not required in our subroutine. The two lines can be deleted. They are listed below:

```
Option Explicit
On Error Resume Next
```

7. Go to the bottom of the script you pasted under the words *Sub subCPU* and type **End sub**. We have now moved the CPU-type script into a subroutine. We will only enter this subroutine if the user presses the Yes button.

8. Under the code that evaluates the *vbYes* intrinsic constant, we want to add the line to call the subroutine. To do this, we simply type the name of the subroutine. That name is *subCPU*. The code to launch the script is seen below. Notice the only new code here is the word *subCPU*, everything else was already in the msgBox script.

```
If intRTN = vbYes Then
WScript.Echo "yes was pressed"
subCPU
```

9. For every other button selection, we want to end the script. The command to do that is *WScript.quit*. We will need to type this command in three different places, as seen below:

```
ElseIf intRTN = vbNo Then
WScript.Echo "no was pressed"
WScript.quit
ElseIf intRTN = vbCancel Then
WScript.Echo "cancel was pressed"
WScript.quit
Else
WScript.Echo intRTN & " was pressed"
WScript.quit
End If
```

10. Save and run the script. Press the Yes button, and the results from CPUType should be displayed. Run the script two more times: Press No, and then press Cancel. On each successive running, the script should exit instead of running the script. If these are not your results, compare the script with the PromptCPU.vbs script in the folder \My Documents\Microsoft Press\VBScriptSBS\ch03.

Quick Check

Q. How many *ElseIf* lines can be used in a script?

A. As many *ElseIf* lines as are needed.

Q. If more than one or two *ElseIf* lines are necessary, is there another construct that would be easier to use?

A. Yes. Use a *Select Case* type of structure.

Q. What is the effect of using *strComputer* = "." in a script?

A. The code *strComputer* is shorthand that means the local computer the script is executing on. It is used with WMI.

If...Then...Else

It is important to point out here that you can use *If...Then...Else* without the intervening *ElseIf* commands. In such a construction, you give the script the ability to make a choice between two options.

Just the Steps   To use *If...Then...Else*

1. On a new line in the script, type **If *some condition* Then**.
2. On the next line, enter the command you want to invoke.
3. On the next line, type **Else**.

4.   On the next line, type the alternate command you want to execute when the condition is not true.

5.   On the next line, type **End If**.

The use of *If...Then...Else* is illustrated in the following code:

ifThenElse.vbs

```
Option Explicit
On Error Resume Next
Dim a,b,c,d
a = 1
b = 2
c = 3
d = 4
If a + b = d Then
   WScript.Echo (a & " + " & b & " is equal to " & d)
Else
   WScript.Echo (a & " + " & b & " is equal to " & c)
End If
```

In the preceding ifThenElse.vbs script, you declare your four variables on one line. You can do this for simple scripts such as this one. It can also be done for routine variables that are associated with one another, such as *objWMIService* and *objProcessor* from your earlier script. The advantage of putting multiple declarations on the same line is that it makes the script shorter. Although this does not really have an impact on performance, it can at times make the script easier to read. You'll need to make that call–does making the script shorter make the script easier to read, or does having each variable on a separate line with individual comments make the script easier to read?

When you do the *WScript.Echo* command, you're using a feature called *concatenation*, which puts together an output line by using a combination of variables and string text. Notice that everything is placed inside the parentheses and that the variables do not go inside quotation marks. To concatenate the text into one line, you can use the ampersand character (&). Because concatenation does not automatically include spaces, you have to put in the appropriate spaces inside the quotation marks. By doing this, you can include a lot of information in the output. This is one area that requires special attention when you're modifying existing scripts. You might need to change only one or two variables in the script, but modifying the accompanying text strings often requires the most work.

Using *If...Then...Else* to fix the syntax of output

1.   Open the QueryAllProcessors.vbs script in the folder \My Documents\Microsoft Press\VBScriptSBS\ch03 using Notepad or the script editor of your choice. Save it as YourNameQueryAllProcessorsSyntax.vbs.

2. Put a new function definition at the end of the script. (We will discuss user defined functions in just a few pages.) Use the word *Function* and give it the name *funIS*. Assign the input parameter the name *intIN*. The syntax for this line will look like the following:

```
Function funIS(intIN)
```

3. Space down a few lines and end the function with the words *End Function*. This command will look like the following:

```
End Function
```

4. Use *If...Then* to see if the *intIN* parameter is less than two. This line will look like:

```
If intIN <2 Then
```

5. If the *intIN* parameter is less than two, then we want to assign the string "is a" the numeric value of *intIN* and the word *Processor*. The result will be that the script will use the singular form of the verb *to be*. This is seen in the line below:

```
funIS = " is a " & intIN & " Processor "
```

6. If this is not the case, we will assign the string "are" and the number of processors to the name of the function. Finally we close out the *If...Then* construction by using *End If*. This is seen below:

```
Else
funIS = " are " & intIN & " Processors "
End If
```

7. Right after we assign the *colItems* variable to contain the object that comes back from using the *execQuery* method, we want to retrieve the count of the number of items in *colItems*. We also want to build an output string that prints out a string stating how many processors are on the machine. We will use the *funIS* function to build up the remainder of the output line. It will look like the following:

```
WScript.Echo "There" & funIS(colItems.count) & _
"on this computer"
```

8. Save and run the script. You may want to compare your results with the QueryAllProcessorsSyntax.vbs script in the folder \My Documents\Microsoft Press\VBScriptSBS\ch03.

Select Case

When I see a *Select Case* statement in a script written in the VBScript language, my respect for the script writer goes up at least one notch. Most beginning script writers can figure out the *If...Then* statement, and some even get the *If...Then...Else* construction down. However, few master the *Select Case* construction. This is really a shame, because *Select Case* is both elegant and powerful. Luckily for you, I love *Select Case* and you will be masters of this construction by the end of this chapter!

> **Just the Steps**   To use *Select Case*
>
> 1. On a new line in the script, type **Select Case** and a variable to evaluate.
> 2. On the second line, type **Case 0**.
> 3. On the third line, assign a value to a variable.
> 4. On the next line, type **Case 1**.
> 5. On a new line, assign a value to a variable.
> 6. On the next line, type **End Select**.

In the following script, you again use WMI to obtain information about your computer. This script is used to tell us the role that the computer plays on a network (that is, whether it's a domain controller, a member server, or a member workstation). You need to use *Select Case* to parse the results that come back from WMI, because the answer is returned in the form of 0, 1, 2, 3, 4, or 5. Six options would be too messy for an *If...Then...ElseIf* construction. The text of ComputerRoles.vbs is listed here:

ComputerRoles.vbs

```
Option Explicit
'On Error Resume Next
Dim strComputer
Dim wmiRoot
Dim wmiQuery
Dim objWMIService
Dim colItems
Dim objItem

strComputer = "."
wmiRoot = "winmgmts:\\" & strComputer & "\root\cimv2"
wmiQuery = "Select DomainRole from Win32_ComputerSystem"

Set objWMIService = GetObject(wmiRoot)
Set colItems = objWMIService.ExecQuery _
  (wmiQuery)
For Each objItem in colItems
  WScript.Echo funComputerRole(objItem.DomainRole)
Next

Function funComputerRole(intIN)
 Select Case intIN
  Case 0
    funComputerRole = "Standalone Workstation"
  Case 1
    funComputerRole = "Member Workstation"
  Case 2
    funComputerRole = "Standalone Server"
```

```
    Case 3
      funComputerRole = "Member Server"
    Case 4
      funComputerRole = "Backup Domain Controller"
    Case 5
      funComputerRole = "Primary Domain Controller"
    Case Else
    funComputerRole = "Look this one up in SDK"
  End Select
End Function
```

Header Information

The Header information section of ComputerRoles.vbs is listed in the next bit of code. Notice that you start with the *Option Explicit* and *On Error Resume Next* statements, which are explained earlier in this chapter and in detail in Chapter 1, "Starting from Scratch." Next, you declare six variables. *wmiQuery* is, however, a different variable. You'll use it in the Reference information section, where you"ll assign a WMI query string to it. By declaring a variable and listing it separately, you can change the WMI query without having to rewrite the entire script.

objWMIService is used to hold your connection to WMI, and the variable *colItems* holds a collection of items that comes back from the WMI query. *objItem* is used to obtain an individual item from the collection. This was discussed in Chapter 2. The complete Header information section is listed below:

```
Option Explicit
On Error Resume Next
Dim strComputer
Dim wmiRoot
Dim wmiQuery
Dim objWMIService
Dim colItems
Dim objItem
```

Reference Information

The Reference information section assigns values to many of the variables named in the Header information part of ComputerRoles.vbs. The Reference information section of the script is listed here:

```
strComputer = "."
wmiRoot = "winmgmts:\\" & strComputer & "\root\cimv2"
wmiQuery = "Select DomainRole from Win32_ComputerSystem"
```

Two variables are unique to this script, the first of which is *wmiQuery*. In the Collection-OfDrives.vbs script discussed in Chapter 2, you embedded the WMI query in the *GetObject* command, which makes for a long line. By bringing the query out of the *GetObject* command and assigning it to the *wmiQuery* variable, you make the script easier to read and modify in the future. Next, you use the *colItems* variable and assign it to hold the object that is returned when you actually execute the WMI query.

> **Quick Check**
>
> Q.   **How is *Select Case* implemented?**
>
> A.   *Select Case* begins with the *Select Case* command and a variable to be evaluated. However, it is often preceded by a *For Each* statement.
>
> Q.   **How does *Select Case* work?**
>
> A.   *Select Case* evaluates the test expression following the *Select Case* statement. If the result from this matches a value in any of the *Case* statements, it executes the code following that *Case* statement.
>
> Q.   **What is the advantage of assigning a WMI query to a variable?**
>
> A.   It provides the ability to easily use the script to query additional information from WMI.

Worker and Output Information

As mentioned earlier, WMI often returns information in the form of a collection (we talked about this in Chapter 2), and to work your way through a collection, you need to use the *For Each...Next* command structure to pull out specific information. In the Worker information section of ComputerRoles.vbs, you begin with making a connection into WMI. We do this by using *GetObject* to obtain a hook into WMI. Once we have made the connection into WMI, we then execute a WMI query and assign the resulting collection of items to a variable called *colItems*. We then use *For Each...Next* to pull one instance of an item from the collection so we can examine it. This is illustrated in code below. The interesting thing is the way we moved the *Select Case* statement from the middle of the script into a function called *funComputerRole*.

```
Set objWMIService = GetObject(wmiRoot)
Set colItems = objWMIService.ExecQuery _
  (wmiQuery)
For Each objItem in colItems
  WScript.Echo funComputerRole(objItem.DomainRole)
Next
```

funComputerRole function

To simplify the reading of the script, and to make it easier to maintain the script, we move the *Select Case* structure into a function we include at the bottom of the script. This moves the decision matrix out of the middle of the Worker section. It vastly simplifies the code (once, of course, you understand how a function works). In Figure 3-1, you can see that when we call the function, we use the name of the function. In parentheses, we include the parameter we wish to supply to the function. In the ComputerRoles.vbs script, we are retrieving a numeric value that corresponds to the role the computer plays in the network. If you look up the

WIN32_computerSystem class in the WMI Platform SDK (\My Documents\Microsoft Press\VBScriptSBS\Resources\WMI_SDKBook.chm), you will see an article that lists all the valuable properties this class can supply. I have copied the values for domain role into Table 3-1. Based on the chart that translates the values for computer role, I created the *funComputerRole* function.

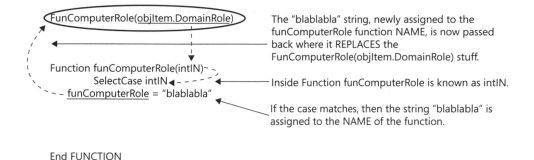

End FUNCTION

Figure 3-1   Assign value to name of the function

In Figure 3-1, you see how the numeric value of the computer role is passed to the *funComputerRole* function. Once the number is inside the function, it is stored in the variable *intIN*. The *Select Case* statement evaluates the value of *intIN* and assigns the appropriate string to the name of the function itself. As you can see in Figure 3-1, the value that is assigned to the name of the function is passed back to the line of code that called the function in the first place. The *funComputerRole* function is listed below.

```
Function funComputerRole(intIN)
 Select Case intIN
  Case 0
    funComputerRole = "Standalone Workstation"
  Case 1
    funComputerRole = "Member Workstation"
  Case 2
    funComputerRole = "Standalone Server"
  Case 3
    funComputerRole = "Member Server"
  Case 4
    funComputerRole = "Backup Domain Controller"
  Case 5
    funComputerRole = "Primary Domain Controller"
  Case Else
  funComputerRole = "Look this one up in SDK"
 End Select
End Function
```

To find out how the *DomainRole* field is structured, you need to reference the Platform SDK for Microsoft Windows Server 2003. You will also be able to find other properties you can use to expand upon the ComputerRoles.vbs script. The value descriptions for domain roles are shown in Table 3-1.

Table 3-1   WMI Domain Roles from *Win32_ComputerSystem*

Value	Meaning
0	Standalone workstation
1	Member workstation
2	Standalone server
3	Member server
4	Backup domain controller
5	Primary domain controller

The first line of the *Select Case* statement contains the test expression—the number representing the role of the computer on the network. Each successive *Case* statement is used to evaluate the test expression, and to identify the correct computer role. The first of these statements is seen here:

```
Case 0
  strComputerRole = "Standalone Workstation"
```

The *strComputerRole* variable will be assigned the phrase "Standalone Workstation" if the text expression (intIN) is equal to 0. You will then use *strComputerRole* to echo out the role of the computer in the domain when we exit the *Select Case* construction.

You end the *Select Case* construction with *End Select*, similarly to the way you ended the *If...Then* statement with *End If*. After you use *End Select*, you use the *WScript.Echo* command to send the value of *strComputerRole* out to the user. Remember that the entire purpose of the *Select Case* construction in ComputerRoles.vbs is to find and assign the *DomainRole* value to the *strComputerRole* variable. After this is accomplished, you use the *Next* command to feed back into the *For Each* loop used to begin the script.

Modifying CPUType.vbs Step-by-Step Exercises

In this section, you will modify CPUType.vbs so that it uses a *Select Case* format instead of multiple *If...Then...ElseIf* statements. This is a valuable skill, because many of the scripts you will find have a tendency to use multiple *If...Then...ElseIf* statements. As you will see, it is relatively easy to make the modification to using *Select Case*. The key to success is to remove as little of the original code as possible.

1. Open CPUTypeStarter.vbs and save it as YourNameCPUType.vbs. It is located in the \My Documents\Microsoft Press\VBScriptSBS\Ch03\StepByStep folder.

2. Turn off *On Error Resume Next* by commenting out the line.

3. Turn the *If...Then* line into a *Select Case* statement. The only element you must keep from this line is *objProcessor.Architecture,* because it is hard to type. When you are finished, your *Select Case* line looks like the following:

```
Select Case objProcessor.Architecture
```

4. Start your case evaluation. If *objProcessor.Architecture = 0*, you know that the processor is an x86. So your first case is *Case 0*. That is all you put on the next line. It looks like this:

```
Case 0
```

5. Leave the *WScript.Echo* line alone.

6. *ElseIf objProcessor.Architecture = 1* becomes *Case 1*, which is a MIPS CPU. Delete the entire *ElseIf* line and enter **Case 1**.

7. Leave the *WScript.Echo* line alone.

   ElseIf objProcessor.Architecture = 2 becomes simply *Case 2*, as you can see here:

```
Case 2
```

   Up to this point, your *Select Case* configuration looks like the following:

```
Select Case objProcessor.Architecture
Case 0
  WScript.Echo "This is an x86 cpu."
Case 1
  WScript.Echo "This is a MIPS cpu."
Case 2
  WScript.Echo "This is an Alpha cpu."
```

8. Modify the "*ElseIf objProcessor.Architecture = 3 Then*" line so that it becomes *Case 3*.

9. Leave the *WScript.Echo* line alone.

   The next case is *not* Case 4, but rather Case 6, because you modify the following line: "*ElseIf objProcessor.Architecture = 6 Then*". The *Select Case* construction now looks like the following:

```
Select Case objProcessor.Architecture
  Case 0
    WScript.Echo "This is an x86 cpu."
  Case 1
    WScript.Echo "This is a MIPS cpu."
  Case 2
    WScript.Echo "This is an Alpha cpu."
  Case 3
    WScript.Echo "This is a PowerPC cpu."
  Case 6
    WScript.Echo "This is an ia64 cpu."
```

10. You have one more case to evaluate, and it will take the place of the *Else* command, which encompasses everything else that has not yet been listed. You implement *Case Else* by changing the *Else* to *Case Else*.

11. Leave the line *WScript.Echo "Cannot determine cpu type"* alone.

12. Change *End If* to *End Select*. Now you're finished with the conversion of *If...Then...ElseIf* to *Select Case*.

13. Save the file and run the script. If you need assistance, refer to the CPUTypeSolution.vbs script in the same folder you found the starter script.

One Step Further: Modifying ComputerRoles.vbs

In this lab, you'll modify ComputerRoles.vbs so that you can use it to turn on Dynamic Host Configuration Protocol (DHCP) on various workstations. This is the first script we use that calls a WMI method.

Scenario

Your company's network was set up by someone who really did not understand DHCP. In fact, the person who set up the network probably could not even spell DHCP, and as a result every workstation on the network is configured with a static IP address. This was bad enough when the network only had a hundred workstations, but the network has grown to more than three hundred workstations within the past couple of years. The Microsoft Excel spreadsheet that used to keep track of the mappings between computer names and IP addresses is woefully out of date, which in the past month alone has resulted in nearly 30 calls to the help desk that were traced back to addressing conflicts. To make matters worse, some of the helpful administrative assistants have learned to change the last octet in Transmission Control Protocol/Internet Protocol (TCP/IP) properties, which basically negates any hope of ever regaining a managed network. Your task, if you should choose to accept it, is to create a script (or scripts) that will do the following:

■ Use WMI to determine the computer's role on the network and to print out the name of the computer, the domain name (if it is a member of a domain), and the user that belongs to the computer

■ Use WMI to enable DHCP on all network adapters installed on the computer that use TCP/IP

Your research has revealed that you can use *Win32_ComputerSystem* WMI class to obtain the information required in the first part of the assignment.

 Warning   Keep in mind, this script will change network settings on the machine that this script runs on. Also, when run, it will need administrator rights to make the configuration changes. If you do not wish to change your TCP/IP settings, then do not run this script on your machine.

Part A

1. Open up the ComputerRoles.vbs file from \My Documents\Microsoft PressVB ScriptSBS\Ch03\OneStepFurther and save it as YourNameComputerRoles Solution.vbs.

2. Comment out *On Error Resume Next* so that you will receive some meaningful feedback from the Windows Script Host (WSH) run time.

3. *Dim* new variables to hold the following items:

   ❑ *strcomputerName*

   ❑ *strDomainName*

   ❑ *strUserName*

4. Modify *wmiQuery* so that it returns more than just *DomainRole* from *Win32_ComputerSystem*. Hint: Change *DomainRole* to a wildcard such as *. The original wmiQuery line is seen below:

   ```
   wmiQuery = "Select DomainRole from Win32_ComputerSystem"
   ```

   The new line looks like this:

   ```
   "Select * from Win32_ComputerSystem"
   ```

5. Because *colComputers* is a collection, you can't directly query it. You'll need to use *For Each...Next* to give yourself a single instance to work with. Therefore, the assignment of your new variables to actual items will take place inside the *For Each...Next* loop. Assign each of your new variables in the following manner:

   ❑ *strComputerName = objComputer.name*

   ❑ *strDomainName = objComputer.Domain*

   ❑ *strUserName = objComputer.UserName*

6. After the completion of the *Select Case* statement (*End Select*) but before the *Next* command at the bottom of the file, use *WScript.Echo* to return the four items required by the first part of the lab scenario. Use concatenation (by using the ampersand) to put the four variables on a single line. Those four items are declared as follows:

   ❑ *Dim strComputerRole*

   ❑ *Dim strcomputerName*

   ❑ *Dim strDomainName*

   ❑ *Dim strUserName*

7. Save the file and run it.

8. Modify the script so that each variable is returned on a separate line. Hint: Use the intrinsic constant *vbCrLf* and the ampersand to concatenate the line. It will look something like this:

```
strComputerRole & vbCrLf & strComputerName
```

9. Save and run the file.

10. Use *WScript.Echo* to add and run a complete message similar to the following:

```
WScript.Echo("all done")
```

11. Save and run your script. If it does not run properly, compare it with \My Documents\Microsoft PressVBScriptSBS\ch03\StepByStep\ComputerRoles Solution.vbs.

Part B

1. Open the YourNameComputerRolesSolution.vbs file and save it as YourNameEnableDHCPSolution.vbs.

2. Comment out *On Error Resume Next* so that you will receive some meaningful feedback from the WSH run time.

3. *Dim* new variables to hold the new items required for this script. Hint: You can rename the following items:

   ❑ *Dim colComputers*

   ❑ *Dim objComputer*

   ❑ *Dim strComputerRole*

4. The new variables are listed here:

   ❑ *colNetAdapters*

   ❑ *objNetAdapter*

   ❑ *DHCPEnabled*

5. Modify the *wmiQuery* so that it looks like the following:

```
wmiQuery = "Select * from Win32_NetworkAdapterConfiguration where IPEnabled=TRUE"
```

6. Change the following *Set* statement:

```
Set colComputers = objWMIService.ExecQuery (wmiQuery)
```

   Now, instead of using *colComputers*, the statement uses *colNetAdapters*. The line will look like the following:

```
Set colNetAdapters = objWMIService.ExecQuery (wmiQuery)
```

7. Delete the *Select Case* construction. It begins with the following line:

```
Select Case objComputer.DomainRole
```

   And it ends with *End Select*.

8. You should now have the following:

```
For Each objComputer In colComputers
  WScript.Echo strComputerRole
Next
```

9. Change the *For Each* line so that it reads as follows:

```
For Each objNetAdapter In colNetAdapters
```

10. Assign *DHCPEnabled* to *objNetAdapter.EnableDHCP()*. You can do it with the following:

```
DHCPEnabled = objNetAdapter.EnableDHCP()
```

11. Use *If...Then...Else* to decide whether the operation was successful. If DHCP is enabled, *DHCPEnabled* will be *0*, and you want to use *WScript.Echo* to echo out that the DHCP is enabled. The code looks like the following:

```
If DHCPEnabled = 0 Then
  WScript.Echo "DHCP has been enabled."
```

12. If *DHCPEnabled* is not set to *0*, the procedure does not work. So you have your *Else* condition. It looks like the following:

```
Else
  WScript.Echo "DHCP could not be enabled."
End If
```

13. Conclude the script by using the *Next* command to complete the *If...Then...Next* construction. You don't have to put in a closing echo command, because you're getting feedback from the *DHCPEnabled* commands.

14. Save and run the script. Compare your script with the EnableDHCPSolution.vbs script in the \My Documents\Microsoft Press\VBScriptSBS\ch03\OneStepFurther folder.

Chapter 3 Quick Reference

To	Do This
Evaluate a condition using *If...Then*	Place the condition to be evaluated between the words *If* and *Then*
Evaluate one condition with two outcomes	Use *If...Then...Else*
End an *If...Then...Else* statement	Use *End If*
Use an intrinsic constant in a script	Type it into the code (it does not need to be declared, or otherwise defined)
Evaluate one condition with three outcomes	Use *If...Then...ElseIf*, or use *Select Case*
Evaluate one condition with four potential outcomes	Use *Select Case*

Chapter 4
Working with Arrays

Before You Begin

To work through the material presented in this chapter, you need to be familiar with the following concepts from earlier chapters:

- The *For Each* command
- The *Do Until* command
- The *For...Next* command

After completing this chapter, you will be able to:

- Use command-line arguments to control code execution at run time
- Use a text file in place of arguments to run a program against multiple machines
- Create a useful error message when arguments are missing
- Use named arguments to control the way multiple arguments are processed
- Create an array to supply multiple values to a single variable

Passing Arguments

Passing arguments might sound like a technique to help people get along, but in reality it's a way to get additional information into a script. *Command-line arguments* are words or phrases that follow the name of the script when it is run from the command line. In this section, you'll look at two methods for obtaining run time information: command-line arguments and text file data. You can use these two sources of information to modify the way a script runs. Let's first look at command-line arguments and see how to change the behavior of a script.

Command-Line Arguments

Command-line arguments provide you with the ability to modify the execution of a script prior to running it.

> **Just the Steps** To implement command-line arguments
>
> 1. On a new line, create a variable to hold *WScript.Arguments.Item(0)*.
> 2. Use the variable holding *WScript.Arguments.Item(0)* as a normal variable.

In the Ping.vbs script, which you examined in Chapter 2, "Looping Through the Script," and which appears in the next code listing (minus the comments), you use the variable *strMachines* to hold the target of the ping command. To ping other computers on the network, you have to modify the values within the quotation marks (*"loopback;127.0.0.1;localhost"* in this instance).

> **Note** In this and in other scripts, we leave out the Header information section (*Option Explicit, On Error Resume Next*, and the *DIM* for the variables.) This is done so we can focus on learning about command-line arguments and arrays (both rather complicated concepts). As indicated in Chapter 1, "Starting from Scratch;" before moving a script into "production," you really should make sure it is fully documented and that it runs without error (which will mean turning off *On Error Resume Next* by remarking it out), because this will save you much work if you need to modify the script at a later date.

Modifying the values might be an acceptable solution when you always ping the same computers, but when you want the flexibility of the normal command-line ping, a better script is clearly called for—the command-line argument.

Ping.vbs

```
strMachines = "loopback;127.0.0.1;localhost"
aMachines = Split(strMachines, ";")
For Each machine In aMachines
  Set objPing = GetObject("winmgmts:")._
  ExecQuery("select * from Win32_PingStatus where address = '" _
    & machine & "'")
  For Each objStatus In objPing
    If IsNull(objStatus.StatusCode) Or objStatus.StatusCode<>0 Then
      WScript.Echo("machine " & machine & " is not reachable")
    Else
      WScript.Echo("reply from " & machine)
    End If
  Next
Next
```

Making the Change

To modify the Ping.vbs script to accept multiple computer names prior to running, you need to make two modifications:

- In the first non-commented line, delete *"loopback;127.0.0.1;localhost"*.
- Delete the addresses following *strMachines* = and add *WScript.Arguments.Item(0)*.

That's all you need to do. The new script, named PingMultipleComputers.vbs, is shown here:

PingMultipleComputers.vbs

```
strMachines = WScript.Arguments.Item(0)
aMachines = Split(strMachines, ";")
For Each machine In aMachines
  Set objPing = GetObject("winmgmts:")._
  ExecQuery("select * from Win32_PingStatus where address = '"_
    & machine & "'")
  For Each objStatus In objPing
    If IsNull(objStatus.StatusCode) Or objStatus.StatusCode<>0 Then
      WScript.Echo("machine " & machine & " is not reachable")
    Else
      WScript.Echo("reply from " & machine)
    End If
  Next
Next
```

Running from the Command Prompt

To run the script, you go to the command prompt in the directory containing your script and type the following:

```
Cscript pingMultipleComputers.vbs localHost;127.0.0.1;loopback
```

You use this syntax because of the *Split* function you used on the second line, which expects a ";" to separate the computer names. If you change the ";" on the second line into a ";" as seen in the next code line, you can use the comma character to separate the machine names and have a slightly more orthodox command.

```
aMachines = Split(strMachines, ",")
```

Once this modification is made, the command-line syntax looks like the following:

```
Cscript pingMultipleComputers.vbs localHost,127.0.0.1,loopback
```

Quick Check

Q. **To implement command-line arguments, what action needs to be performed?**

A. Assign a variable to the command *WScript.Arguments.Item(0)*.

Q. **What is the function of the *Split* command?**

A. The *Split* command can be used to parse a line of text based on a delimiter of your choosing.

No Arguments?

If a script tries to read command-line arguments not provided by the user, you get a Microsoft Visual Basic, Scripting Edition (VBScript) runtime error that makes a rather vague reference to "subscript out of range." This error is illustrated in Figure 4-1.

Figure 4-1 When a Visual Basic script tries to read a command-line argument that was not supplied, you get a "subscript out of range" error message

If another administrator is running your script and gets the "subscript out of range" error, that administrator will have a hard time determining the cause of the message. A quick search at http://support.microsoft.com returns dozens of support articles referencing "subscript out of range," but none of them tell you that VBScript requires command-line arguments. It behooves you to make sure users of your Visual Basic scripts are not presented with such unfriendly error messages. Let's look at handling that now.

Creating a Useful Error Message

When you supply command-line arguments for your scripts, the VBScript run time (called the Windows Scripting Host, or WSH for short) stores the arguments in an area of memory that is referenced by the *WshArguments* collection. This is nice because this storage location allows you to see how many command-line arguments are in there. Why is this important? It's important because when you know where the arguments are stored, and you know that they're kept in a collection, you can count the contents of that collection. For your script to run properly, there must be at least one argument supplied on the command line. You can make sure there is at least one argument by using the *WScript.Arguments.Count* method and putting it in an *If...Then* construction. To make the script easy to read, we place this logic in a subroutine. We call the subroutine first thing. If the value of the count is equal to zero, use *WScript.Echo* to send a message to the user that at least one argument is required. Once you make these modifications, CheckArgsPingMultipleComputers.vbs looks like the following:

CheckArgsPingMultipleComputers.vbs

```
Option Explicit
On Error Resume Next
Dim strMachines
Dim aMachines, machine
Dim objPing, objStatus
subCheckArgs 'uses the count method for WshArguments

strMachines = WScript.Arguments.Item(0)
```

```
aMachines = Split(strMachines, ";")
For Each machine in aMachines
Set objPing = GetObject("winmgmts:{impersonationLevel=impersonate}")._
ExecQuery("select * from Win32_PingStatus where address = '"_
& machine & "'")
For Each objStatus in objPing
   If IsNull(objStatus.StatusCode) or objStatus.StatusCode<>0 Then
   WScript.Echo("machine " & machine & " is not reachable")
   Else
   WScript.Echo("reply from " & machine)
   End If
Next
Next

Sub subCheckArgs
If WScript.Arguments.count = 0 Then
 WScript.Echo "You must enter a computer to ping" & VbCrLf & _
   "Try this: Cscript CheckArgsPingMultipleComputers.vbs " _
     & "127.0.0.1;localhost"
 WScript.Quit
End If
End sub
```

Quick Check

Q. **What is a possible cause of the "subscript out of range" error message when running scripts that are configured to use command-line arguments?**

A. The error message could be caused by trying to run a Visual Basic script that requires command-line arguments without supplying them.

Q. **List one method of creating useful error messages to trap the "subscript out of range" error.**

A. You can use an *If…Then…Else* construct to test *WScript.Arguments.Count* for the presence of a command-line argument. If none is present, you can then use the *Else* part to display a meaningful error to the user. In addition, it is important to note that you cannot always rely on the user putting in meaningful data. To solve this problem, you must check the input data to ensure it meets the criteria for correct input.

Note   There are two kinds of *arguments*: *unnamed* and *named*. With unnamed arguments when you supply a value to the script, the argument is interpreted according to its position on the command line. With named arguments, you supply a name for each argument. Each item in the collection of arguments has a name and is retrieved from the collection by name. Unnamed arguments are retrieved by index number.

Supply value for missing argument

1. Open CheckArgsPingMultipleComputers.vbs from \My Documents\Microsoft Press\VBScriptSBS\ch04 in Microsoft Notepad or the script editor of your choice.

2. Save the file as YourNameSupplyMissingArgument.vbs.

3. Declare a variable *colArgs* to hold a collection of unnamed arguments.

4. Set *colArgs* to hold a collection of unnamed arguments. This command will go right under the Header section of the script. The line of code will look like the following:

```
Set colArgs = WScript.Arguments.UnNamed
```

5. In the *subCheckArgs* subroutine, modify *If WScript.Arguments.count = 0 Then* so that it uses the *colArgs* variable instead. The modified line of code will look like the following:

```
If colArgs.count = 0 Then
```

6. Leave the remaining prompt the same.

7. Delete the *WScript.Quit* line of code. We are not going to exit the script if no argument is supplied, rather we are going to supply a default value.

8. On a new line, under the *WScript.Echo* command, assign the loopback adapter and local host to *strMachines*. The line will look like the following:

```
strMachines = "127.0.0.1;ocalhost"
```

9. If the value of *colArgs.count* is greater than 0, then we want to use *item(0)* to assign to *strMachines*. This clause will look like the following:

```
Else
 strMachines = colArgs(0)
```

10. Save and run the script. Supply a value at the command line; it should ping those machines.

11. Run the script a second time. This time, do not supply a value for the command-line argument. The script should echo help that illustrates usage and then ping both the loopback and the localhost. If this is not the case, compare your script with CheckArgsPingMultipleComputersSupplyValue.vbs in the Chapter 4 folder.

> **Note** The *Arguments* collection is read-only. This is the reason for checking the number of arguments in the collection and then assigning a value to the variable that would have held the value if the argument had been present. This makes for more work in the script (as illustrated in the "Supply Value for Missing Argument" procedure), but the increased usability of the script is worth the effort. If the collection were not read-only, then we could have simply assigned the desired value directly to the argument once we detected that it was missing.

Using Multiple Arguments

In PingMultipleComputers.vbs, you use only one argument, which you assigned to the variable *strMachines* by using this command:

```
strMachines = WScript.Arguments.Item(0)
```

When you look at the command, you see that it's made up of several parts:

Variable	=	WScript.Arguments.Item	Item #
strMachines	=	WScript.Arguments.Item	(0)

If you need to use multiple arguments, you add another line and increment the item number contained within the parentheses.

> **Just the Steps**   To implement multiple command-line arguments
>
> 1. On a new line, assign a variable to *WScript.Arguments.Item(0)*.
> 2. On a new line, assign a variable to *WScript.Arguments.Item(1)*.
> 3. Use the variable from step 1 as you would any variable.
> 4. Use the variable from step 2 as you would any variable.

Remember that the index values for the *WScript.Arguments* collection are *zero-based*, which means that the first item counted will be zero, as used in the PingMultipleComputers.vbs script. The following script (ArgComputerService.vbs) illustrates how you handle zero-based index values. In ArgComputerService.vbs, you use two arguments. The first one is a computer name, and the second argument is the name of a service. To run this script, change to the directory containing your script at a command prompt and use the following command:

```
Cscript argComputerService.vbs localhost lanmanserver
```

By using this command, the status of the lanmanserver server service on the localhost is returned to you. Lanmanserver is the name of the server service when it is registered in the registry. If you have access to a different machine, then supply the name or Internet Protocol (IP) address in place of localhost and use that name when running the following script, Arg-ComputerService.vbs.

ArgComputerService.vbs
```
Option Explicit
On Error Resume Next
Dim computerName
Dim serviceName
Dim wmiRoot
Dim wmiQuery
Dim objWMIService
Dim colServices
Dim oservice

computerName = WScript.Arguments(0)
serviceName = WScript.Arguments(1)
wmiRoot = "winmgmts:\\" & computerName & "\root\cimv2"
Set objWMIService = GetObject(wmiRoot)
wmiQuery = "Select state from win32_Service" &_
    " where name = " & "'" & serviceName & "'"
```

```
Set colServices = objWMIService.ExecQuery _
   (wmiQuery)
For Each oservice In colServices
   WScript.Echo (serviceName) & " Is: "&_
   oservice.state & (" on: ") & computerName
Next
```

Header Information

The standard header information is in the ArgComputerService.vbs script. It begins with *Option Explicit*, which tells VBScript that you're going to specifically name all the variables you'll be using. If you fail to list a variable in this section, you get an error from VBScript. The variables used in ArgComputerService.vbs are listed in Table 4-1.

Table 4-1   Variables used in ArgComputerService.vbs

Variable Name	Use
computerName	Holds the first command-line argument
serviceName	Holds the second command-line argument
wmiRoot	Holds the namespace of WMI
wmiQuery	Holds the query issued to WMI
objWMIService	Holds the connection into WMI
colServices	Holds the result of the WMI query
oservice	Holds each service in colServices as you walk through the collection

Reference Information

In the Reference information section, you assign specific values to variable names to make the script work properly. By changing reference assignments, you can modify the script to perform other actions. The variable *computerName* is used to hold the first command-line argument. If the first item entered on the command line is not the name of a valid computer on the network, the script fails. In this particular script, you haven't taken steps to ensure the script will end normally. The variable *serviceName* is used to hold the value of the second item from the command line. In the same way that *computerName* must be the name of a valid computer on the network, *serviceName* must be the name of a valid installed service on the target computer. The service name is not the same as the display name that is used in the services application, rather it is the name assigned within the registry when the service is created. The script could be modified to provide a list of installed services on the target machine and then to allow the user to pick one of those services.

Tip   Select only information you intend to use from WMI. The *wmiQuery* variable used in ArgComputerService.vbs only selects the state of the service. The name is automatically selected and does not have to appear in the select statement here. If we had used *Select **, then we would have returned all 25 properties of the service...a real waste when we are only using two of the properties in the Output section of the script.

Worker and Output Information

Once again, the Worker and Output information section of the script is quite simple:

```
For Each oservice In colServices
  WScript.Echo (serviceName) & " Is: " & _
  oservice.State & (" on: ") & computerName
Next
```

Because WMI returns service information in a collection (even when the collection has only a single value), you must use a *For Each...Next* loop to walk through each item in the collection to obtain your information. A *For Each...Next* loop is the engine that drives your script. The variable *colServices* contains every service that was returned by *wmiQuery*. The variable *oservice* holds each individual service and is used as the "hook" for asking for certain information through WMI. In this instance, you're interested only in the status information, and so you echo out the *oservice.status* information. If you modified the query contained in the *wmiQuery* variable, you'd be able to echo any of the information that is held within the *Win32_Service* part of WMI.

To find out more information about Win32_Service, search in the WMI Platform SDK in the Resources directory of the CD, or on www.microsoft.com.

The only other interesting aspect of the Worker and Output information section of the script is the use of concatenation, which was talked about in Chapter 3, "Adding Intelligence." Notice how the ampersand character (&) is used to glue two parts of the output line together. The other use of the ampersand is in conjunction with the underscore character (_). The underscore character signals to VBScript that the line is continued onto the next line. The ampersand character is often used with the line continuation character because the underscore breaks up the long line, and the ampersand is used to glue pieces together. Because a line might be in parts anyway, the line continuation character is a convenient place for breaking the script. The continuation character is primarily used to make a script more readable (both on screen and on paper).

Earlier in this section, you learned that ArgComputerService.vbs requires two command-line arguments: The first must be the name of a target computer, and the second must be the name of a valid service on the target computer. How would the user of the ArgComputerService.vbs script know about this requirement? If the script failed, the user could open the script in Notepad to see which argument is required. A second solution might be to modify the script so that when it failed, it would echo the correct usage to the user. There is, however, a third choice—the use of named arguments—which is the subject of the next section.

Tell Me Your Name

One of the rules I learned as a network administrator and as a consultant was to keep things simple. I'd therefore use short computer names and basic network designs as much as possible, because at some point, I'd be using ping.exe, tracert.exe, nslookup.exe, and so forth from the command line. As you know, I hate to type, so "the shorter the better" is my motto. This being the case, I am in somewhat of a quandary with this next section, because the methodology will require more typing on the command line.

Reasons for Named Arguments

Despite additional typing, there are valid reasons to use named arguments. One of the biggest reasons is the way VBScript handles unnamed arguments. For instance, in the ArgComputerService.vbs script, you must use command-line syntax such as this:

```
Cscript argComputerService.vbs computer1 lanmanserver
```

Suppose you happen to forget in which order the commands get entered, and you type the following:

```
Cscript argComputerService.vbs lanmanserver computer1
```

The script would fail unless you happen to have a server named lanmanserver on your network *and* a service named computer1 is running on lanmanserver. Don't laugh! I've seen stranger happenings. (For example, static Domain Name System [DNS] entries can point to the wrong machine. A ping would in fact work—it would just go to the wrong computer. Those kind of errors are always fun.) Therefore, in keeping with my philosophy of trying to make things simple, let's explore how to create named arguments. You'll thank me, your boss will thank me, and even your mom will thank me (because stuff will run so well, and you'll be able to make it home for the holidays).

Named arguments can be used to make the order of command-line arguments irrelevant. This can make correct usage of running the script easier, especially when three or more distinct arguments are being used with a script that does not intuitively suggest a particular order.

> **Just the Steps**   To implement named arguments
>
> 1. On a new line, use the *Set* command to assign *WScript.Arguments.Named* to a variable.
> 2. On the next line, create a name for the argument and assign it to a variable.
> 3. On the next line, assign create a second name for the second argument and assign it to a variable as well.
> 4. Use the variables defined in steps 2 and 3 as you would regular variables. Their values will be assigned when you run the script.

Making the Change to Named Arguments

To modify the previous script to require named arguments instead of unnamed arguments, you need to modify only four lines of code. The first change is to add an additional variable that will be used to hold the named arguments from the command line. The second modification will take place in the Reference section, in which you will assign the new variable to the named arguments collection. The last two changes will take place as you assign the variables to hold the server name and the service names in the script. The revised script, NamedArgCS.vbs follows:

NamedArgCS.vbs

```
Option Explicit
'On Error Resume Next
Dim computerName
Dim serviceName
Dim wmiRoot
Dim wmiQuery
Dim objWMIService
Dim colServices
Dim oservice
Dim colNamedArguments

Set colNamedArguments = WScript.Arguments.Named
computerName = colNamedArguments("computer")
serviceName = colNamedArguments("service")
wmiRoot = "winmgmts:\\" & computerName & "\root\cimv2"
wmiQuery = "Select state from Win32_Service" &_
    " where name = " & "'" & serviceName & "'"

Set objWMIService = GetObject(wmiRoot)
Set colServices = objWMIService.ExecQuery _
  (wmiQuery)
For Each oservice In colServices
    WScript.Echo serviceName & " Is: " &_
    oservice.state & " on: " & computerName
Next
```

The four lines that were changed in the preceding script are listed here:

```
Dim colNamedArguments
Set colNamedArguments = WScript.Arguments.Named
computerName = colNamedArguments("computer")
serviceName = colNamedArguments("service")
```

Because you added a variable for named arguments in the Reference section, you'll need to *Dim* that variable in the Header section. Declare *colNamedArguments* in the Header information section of the script. In the next line, you make *colNamedArguments* equal to the named arguments by using the *Set* command. You now assign each of the named arguments to variables of the same name: *computerName* and *serviceName*. This time, instead of simply referencing the *WScript.Arguments* element by index number, you are referencing the *WScript.Arguments* element using their names. Instead of simply using a *0* or a *1* (like we do when working with the unnamed arguments), you use the name from the command line.

Running a Script with Named Arguments

To supply data to a script with named arguments, you type the name of the script at the command prompt and use a forward slash (/) with the name of the argument you are providing, separated by a colon and the value you assign to the argument. The preceding script is named NamedArgCS.vbs, and it takes two arguments: *computer* and *service*. The command to launch this script is run against a computer named S2 and queries the lanmanserver service on that machine:

```
Cscript namedargcs.vbs /computer:127.0.0.1 /service:lanmanserver
```

> **Quick Check**
>
> **Q.** **What is one reason for using named arguments?**
>
> **A.** With named arguments, when you have multiple command-line arguments, you don't need to remember in which order to type the arguments.
>
> **Q.** **How do you run a script with named arguments?**
>
> **A.** To run a script with named arguments, you use a forward slash and then enter the name of the argument. You follow this with a colon and the value you want to use.

Check and supply named arguments

1. Open NamedArgCS.vbs from \My Documents\Microsoft Press\VBScriptSBS\ch04 in Notepad or your script editor of choice. Save it as YourNameCheckNamedArgCS.vbs.

2. After you create the named arguments collection and assign arguments for both *service* and *computer*, call the *subCheckArgs* subroutine. To do this, place the name of the subroutine on a line by itself, as seen below:

   ```
   subCheckArgs
   ```

3. At the bottom of your script, begin the subroutine section with the word *Sub* followed by the name of the subroutine. This is seen below:

   ```
   Sub subCheckArgs
   ```

4. Skip down a few lines and end the subroutine section with the words *End Sub*.

5. Now develop the logic that will check for the presence of two command-line arguments and supply a default value if one of the arguments is missing. Use an *If...Then* construction.

   ```
   If colNamedArguments.Count < 2 Then
   ```

6. Nest another *If...Then* block to test for the presence of the computer argument. Use the *Exists* method. If the argument does exist, this means that the service argument was omitted. Assign the spooler service to the *serviceName* variable and let the user know you are using the default service for the check. It will look like the following:

```
If colNamedArguments.exists("computer") Then
        serviceName = "spooler"
        WScript.Echo "using default service: spooler"
```

7. If the service argument was supplied, and you are in this code block, then it means they omitted the computer argument. Assign the value *localhost* to the *computerName* variable and let the user know you are using the default computer. This code looks like the following:

```
Else If colNamedArguments.Exists("Service") Then
        computerName = "localHost"
        WScript.Echo "using default computer: localhost"
```

8. If you are inside the *If...Then* statement, and it was not either the service or the computer that was missing, then it means the user completely munged the input to the command-line argument. Let's print out a friendly help message and end the script. This will look like the following:

```
Else
        WScript.Echo "you must supply two arguments" _
            & " to this script." & VbCrLf & "Try this: " _
            & "Cscript checkNamedArgCS.vbs /computer:" _
            & "localhost /service:spooler"
        WScript.Quit
```

9. You will need three *End If* statements before *End Sub*.

10. Save and run the script. Test each condition: no aruguments, one argument, two arguments. The script should run fine. If it does not, then compare it with the Check-NamedArgCS.vbs script in the Chapter 4 folder.

Working with Arrays

Because we have discussed collections, you might find it easy at this point to think of *arrays* as collections that you create and can control—and you would be right. Arrays are like collections you can create and control yourself. There are several nice aspects of arrays; for example, you can populate them with information for later use in the script. In addition, you can create an array dynamically during the execution of the script. You'll explore each of these concepts in this section.

Just the Steps   To create an array

1. On a new line, use the *Dim* command to declare the name to use for the array.

2. Populate the array by assigning values to the name declared in the first line by using the *Array* command and enclosing the values in parentheses.

One way to create an array is to use the *Dim* command to declare a regular, or normal, variable. You then use the variable to populate the array with computer names and use a *For Each...Next* loop to walk through the array. Remember, an array is basically a collection, and you therefore need to use a *For Each...Next* loop to walk through it. The following script creates an array with the names of three computers. The variable *i* is used as a counter to track your progress through the collection. Because an array is zero-based (that is, it begins counting at zero), you set *i* to an initial value of zero. Next, you populate the array with your computer names, making sure to enclose the names in quotation marks; and you use a comma to separate the values. The collection of computer names is placed inside the parentheses. You use a *For Each...Next* loop to walk through and echo the computer names to the screen. You then increment the counter *i* to the next number and go back into the *For Each...Next* loop. Because *For Each...Next* already knows how to retrieve an item from a collection, we do not need to point to a specific element in the array. Using *For Each...Next* in this manner is a great way to walk through an array when you do not know how many items are in the array. This script, BasicArrayForEachNext.vbs, follows.

BasicArrayForEachNext.vbs

```
Option Explicit
On Error Resume Next
Dim myTab 'Holds custom tab of two places
Dim aryComputer 'Holds array of computer names
Dim computer     'Individual computer from the array
Dim I            'Simple counter variable. Used to retrieve by
                 'Element number in the array.
myTab = Space(2)
i = 0            'The first element in an array is 0.
aryComputer = array("s1","s2","s3")

WScript.Echo "Retrieve via for each next"
For Each computer In aryComputer
        WScript.Echo myTab & "computer # " & i & _
        " is " & computer
    i = i+1
Next
```

Another approach to dealing with elements in an array is to use the *For...Next* statement. As you may recall from Chapter 2, *For...Next* enables you to walk through a collection if you know how many times you want to do something. Because you may not always know how many items you have in the array, it is helpful to use the function *UBound*. *UBound* acts just like the *Count* method we used with the command-line arguments. It tells us how many items are in the array. Armed with this information, we can use *For...Next*. This is seen in the BasicArrayForNext.vbs script below.

BasicArrayForNext.vbs

```
Option Explicit
On Error Resume Next
Dim myTab 'Holds custom tab of two places
Dim aryComputer 'Holds array of computer names
Dim computer     'Individual computer from the array
```

```
Dim i                'Simple counter variable. Used to retrieve by
                     'Element number in the array.
myTab = Space(2)
i = 0                'The first element in an array is 0.
aryComputer = array("s1","s2","s3")


WScript.Echo "Retrieve via for next"
i = 0
For i = 0 To UBound(aryComputer)
   WScript.Echo myTab & "computer # " & i & _
         " is " & aryComputer(i)
Next
```

Moving Past Dull Arrays

I will admit the previous two scripts were pretty dull. But because the construction of an array is very finicky, I wanted you to have a reference for the basic array (you will need it for your labs).

In the next script (ArrayReadTxtFile.vbs), you open up a text file, parse it line by line, and write the results into an array. You can use this line-parsing tactic later as a way to feed information into a more useful script. Right now, all you're doing with the array after it is built is echoing its contents out to the screen.

ArrayReadTxtFile.vbs

```
Option Explicit
'On Error Resume Next
Dim objFSO
Dim objTextFile
Dim arrServiceList
Dim strNextLine
Dim i
Dim TxtFile

TxtFile = "ServersAndServices.txt"
Const ForReading = 1

Set objFSO = CreateObject("Scripting.FileSystemObject")
Set objTextFile = objFSO.OpenTextFile _
  (TxtFile, ForReading)
Do Until objTextFile.AtEndOfStream
  strNextLine = objTextFile.Readline
  arrServiceList = Split(strNextLine , ",")
  WScript.Echo "Server name: " & arrServiceList(0)
  For i = 1 to UBound(arrServiceList)
    WScript.Echo vbTab & "Service: " & arrServiceList(i)
  Next
Loop
WScript.Echo("all done")
```

Header Information

The Header information section of your script incorporates the standard bill of fare. You use *Option Explicit* to ensure all variables are specifically declared, which prevents the misspelling of variable names during the development phase of the script. *On Error Resume Next* is a rudimentary error suppression command that tells VBScript to skip a line containing an error and proceed to the next line in the script. This is best turned off during development. After using *On Error Resume Next*, you declare six variables. The first variable, *objFSO*, is used to hook the file system object (which allows you to access files and folders from the script). The next variable, *objTextFile*, is used as the connection to the text file itself. The variable *arrServiceList* is used to refer to the array of services and servers that you build from the text file. The variable *strNextLine* holds the text of the next line in the text file. The *i* variable is simply a counter that gets incremented on each loop through the text file. The last variable is *TxtFile*. It holds the location inside the file system that points to the specific text file with which you will work.

```
Option Explicit
'On Error Resume Next
Dim objFSO
Dim objTextFile
Dim arrServiceList
Dim strNextLine
Dim i
Dim TxtFile
```

Reference Information

The Reference information section of the script is used to point certain variables to their required values. These will be a listing of servers in column 0 and service names in the remaining columns. The text file used as input into the array is defined with the variable *TxtFile*. By using a variable for input into ArrayReadTxtFile.vbs, you make changing the location of the file easy. The ServersAndServices text file needs only to be defined in this location, and the variable *TxtFile* is left untouched—wherever it might be used within the script. The constant *ForReading* is set to *1*, which tells VBScript that you are going to read a text file (as opposed to write to the file).

```
TxtFile = "ServersAndServices.txt"
const ForReading = 1
```

Worker and Output Information

In the Worker and Output information section of ArrayReadTxtFile.vbs, you're finally going to settle down and do something worthwhile. You must first connect to *FileSystemObject* to be able to read the text file. You do this by using the variable *objFSO*. You set *objFSO* to be equal to the object *Scripting.FileSystemObject*. Once you have created the file system object, you define the variable *objTextFile* to be the result of opening *TxtFile* so that you can read it. *ObjTextFile* will contain *textStreamObject* at this point.

To work with the array, you need to implement some type of looping construction. This is where *Do Until...Next* excels. You defined *objTextFile* to hold the text stream object that came back from opening the ServersAndServices text file so that you could read the file. Because you can look inside and read the file by using *objTextFile*, you now say that you'll continue to read the file *until* you reach the end of the stream of text. This is a most excellent use of *Do Until...Next*. What is the script going to do until it reaches the end of the text file? It's going to read each line and assign that line of text to the variable *strNextLine*. After it's made that assignment, it will look for commas and then split the text up into pieces that are separated by those commas. Each piece of text will then be assigned to your array. You're still using a single dimension array. (A *single dimension array* is an array that is like a single column from a Microsoft Excel spreadsheet.) Interestingly enough, you're actually creating a new array every time you use the *Split* function.. The nice part is that you can include as many services as you need to use by adding a comma and the service *on the same line*. Once you go to another line in the text file, you have a new array.

The array portion of ArrayReadTxtFile.vbs is not really created until you get to the Worker and Output information section of the script. In the Header information section, when you declared the variable *arrServiceList*, you really didn't know whether it was a regular variable or something else. This is why it was given the prefix *arr*–it sort of looks like *array* (and requires less typing). You could have just as easily called it *arrayServiceList*, but doing so would have made your script longer. When you use the suffixes *(0)* and *(i)* in the *WScript.Echo* statement, VBScript knows you want to refer to elements in the array. The Worker and Output information section of the script follows:

```
Do Until objTextFile.AtEndofStream
  strNextLine = objTextFile.Readline
  arrServiceList = Split(strNextLine , ",")
  WScript.Echo "Server name: " & arrServiceList(0)
  For i = 1 To UBound(arrServiceList)
    WScript.Echo "Service: " & arrServiceList(i)
  Next
Loop
```

What Does *UBound* Mean?

Did you notice that I didn't explain the *For...Next* construction embedded in the *Do Until* loop? The goal was to make ArrayReadTxtFile.vbs as flexible as possible, and therefore I didn't want to limit the number of services that could be input from the text file. To make sure you echo through all the services that could be listed in the ServersAndServices text file, you need to use the *For...Next* loop to walk through the array. You can find out how many times you need to do *For...Next* by using *UBound*. Think of *UBound* as standing for the upper boundary of the array. As you might suspect, because there is an upper boundary, there is also a lower boundary in the array, but because the lower boundary is always zero, *LBound* isn't needed in this particular script.

When you run ArrayReadTxtFile.vbs, the *i* counter in *For i = 1 To UBound(arrServiceList)* changes with each pass through the list of services. To track this progress, and to illustrate how *UBound* works, I've modified the ArrayReadTxtFile.vbs script to echo out the value of *UBound* each time you read a new line from the ServersAndServices text file. The modified script is called ArrayReadTxtFileUBound.vbs and is located in the Chapter 4 folder. Its Worker section follows:

```
Do Until objTextFile.AtEndofStream
  boundary = UBound(arrServiceList)
  WScript.Echo "upper boundary = " & boundary
  strNextLine = objTextFile.Readline
  arrServiceList = Split(strNextLine , ",")
  WScript.Echo "Server name: " & arrServiceList(0)
  For i = 1 To UBound(arrServiceList)
    WScript.Echo "Service: " & arrServiceList(i)
  Next
Loop
```

To track changes in the size of the upper boundary of the array by looking at the value of *UBound*, it was necessary to assign the value of our new variable *boundary* after the *Do Until* command but prior to entry into the *For...Next* construction. At this location in the script, the new line of text has been read from the ServersAndServices text file, and the script will continue to track changes until it reaches the end of the file.

> ### Quick Check
>
> **Q. How did we declare an array in the previous example?**
>
> A. We declared a regular variable, using the *Dim* command.
>
> **Q. How can the population of an array be automated?**
>
> A. You can automate the population of an array by using the *For...Next* command.
>
> **Q. If you do not know in advance how many elements are going to be in the array, how can you automate the population of an array?**
>
> A. You can automate the population of an array with an unknown number of elements by using the *For...Next* command in conjunction with *UBound*.

Combine text file array and WMI

1. Open the \My Documents\Microsoft Press\VBScriptSBS\ch04\ArrayReadTxtFile.vbs script in Notepad or your preferred script editor. Save the script as YourNameArrayReadTxtFileCheckServices.vbs.

2. In the Reference section of the script, change the value of *TxtFile* to point to "*RealServers AndServices.txt*". It will look like the following:

   ```
   TxtFile = "RealServersAndServices.txt"
   ```

3. Declare a new variable, *boundary*, in the Header section of the script.

4. In the Worker section, *arrServiceList* is an array that is created by using the *Split* function on *strNextLine*. Assign *boundary* to be equal to *UBound(arrServiceList)*. This goes on the line following the *Split* function, and it looks like the following:

```
boundary = UBound(arrServiceList)
```

5. Following the assignment of *boundary*, assign *strComputer* to be equal to element 0 of the *arrServiceList*.

```
strComputer = arrServiceList(0)
```

6. Modify the *WScript.Echo* line so that it informs users the output is a listing of service status messages on the computer. My *Echo* command looks like the following:

```
WScript.Echo "Status of services on " & strComputer
```

7. Define a new subroutine called *subCheckWMI*. Do this at the bottom of your script. Begin the construction with the word *Sub* followed by the name of the subroutine, as seen below:

```
Sub subCheckWMI
```

8. Skip a few lines and end the subroutine with the *End Sub* command, as seen below:

```
End Sub
```

9. Open the CheckServiceStatus.vbs script from the Chapter 4 folder and copy everything but the variable declarations between the *Sub subCheckWMI* and *End sub* lines. It will look like the following when you are done:

```
Sub subCheckWMI
strComputer = "."
serviceName = "spooler"
wmiRoot = "winmgmts:\\" & strComputer & "\root\cimv2"
wmiQuery = "win32_service.name=" & funFIX(serviceName)

Set objWMIService = GetObject(wmiRoot)
Set objItem = objWMIService.get(wmiQuery)
        WScript.Echo vbTab & (serviceName) & " Is: " _
        & objItem.state & " startup mode is: " & objItem.StartMode
End sub
```

10. Clean up the subroutine. Delete the *strComputer = "."* line because the value of *strComputer* is assigned via the text file.

11. Delete the *serviceName = "spooler"* line because it will be assigned via the text file as well.

12. Move the *Set objWMIService = GetObject(wmiRoot)* line under the *wmiRoot* line and above the *wmiQuery* line.

13. The subroutine now looks like the following:

```
Sub subCheckWMI
wmiRoot = "winmgmts:\\" & strComputer & "\root\cimv2"
Set objWMIService = GetObject(wmiRoot)
wmiQuery = "win32_service.name=" & funFIX(serviceName)

Set objItem = objWMIService.get(wmiQuery)
        WScript.Echo vbTab & (serviceName) & " Is: " _
        & objItem.state & " startup mode is: " & objItem.StartMode
End sub
```

14. Use *For...Next* to walk through the array that contains the service names to inspect. Place it on the next line after Set *objWMIService = GetObject(wmiRoot)* The line of code will look like the following

```
For i = 1 to boundary
```

15. On the last line before the *End sub* line, add the *Next* statement to close out the *For...Next* loop.

16. As we walk through the array, we want to pick up the names of the services. Under the *For i = 1 to boundary* line, assign the element from the array to the variable *serviceName*, as seen below:

```
serviceName = arrServiceList(i)
```

17. Now that the subroutine is complete, go back to the main script and add the line to call the subroutine. It goes on the line after we print out the status of services on *strComputer*, as seen below:

```
WScript.echo "Status of services on " & strComputer
        SubcheckWMI
```

18. On the line after the one that calls the subroutine, add a command to print out a blank line. I used the following code:

```
WScript.Echo vbNewLine
```

19. Go back to the CheckServiceStatus.vbs script. Copy the function from the bottom of that script and paste it into the bottom of your script. The function looks like the following:

```
Function funFIX(strIN)
    funFIX = "'" & strIN & "'"
End Function
```

20. Save and run the script. It should work without error. If there is a problem, compare your script with the \My Documents\Microsoft Press\VBScriptSBS\ch04\ArrayRead-TextFileCheckServices.vbs script.

Two-Dimensional Arrays

A *two-dimensional array* gives you the ability to store related information in much the same way you would store it in an Excel spreadsheet. To visualize a two-dimensional array, it is helpful to think of a spreadsheet that contains both rows and columns.

> **Just the Steps**   To create a two-dimensional array
>
> 1. On a new line, use the *Dim* command to declare the name to use for the array, followed by parentheses and the number of elements to be used for each dimension, separated by a comma.
> 2. Populate the array by assigning values to the name declared in line 1 by using the array name and assigning a value with each element.

To create a two-dimensional array, include both dimensions when you declare the variable used for the array, as illustrated here:

```
Dim a (3,3)
```

All you've really done is include the extra dimension inside the parentheses. The array just listed contains two dimensions, each holding four elements for a total of 16 elements. Each dimension of the array is separated by a comma within the parentheses. Remember that the array begins numbering with a zero, and thus *Dim a (3,3)* states that the array *a* has four rows numbered from zero to 3, and four columns numbered from zero to 3.

The key points to remember about an array are that it resides in memory and can be used to hold information that will be used by the script. With a two-dimensional array, you have a matrix (not *The* Matrix—but a matrix nonetheless). *Dim a (3,3)* would look like the matrix in Table 4-2.

Table 4-2   Two-dimensional array

0,0	0,1	0,2	0,3
1,0	1,1	1,2	1,3
2,0	2,1	2,2	2,3
3,0	3,1	3,2	3,3

Each square in the array in Table 4-2 can hold a single piece of information. However, by using concatenation (putting strings together by using the ampersand) or by manipulating the string in other ways, you can get quite creative with the array.

Mechanics of Two-Dimensional Arrays

In the next script (WorkWith2DArray.vbs), a two-dimensional array is created. The script then populates each of the 16 elements with the string "Loop" concatenated with the loop number. In this way, you can keep track of where you are within the matrix as you echo out the value contained within the elements.

WorkWith2DArray.vbs

```
Option Explicit
Dim i
Dim j
Dim numLoop
Dim a (3,3)
numLoop = 0
For i = 0 To 3
  For j = 0 To 3
    numLoop = numLoop+1
    WScript.Echo "i = " & i & " j = " & j
    a(i, j) = "loop " & numLoop
    WScript.Echo "Value stored In a(i,j) is: " & a(i,j)
  Next
Next
```

Let's look at the script in a little more detail.

Header Information

The Header information section of the script follows the normal procedure of beginning with *Option Explicit* (which forces the declaration of each variable used in the script by using the *Dim* command). Next, two variables (*i* and *j*) are declared that will each be used to count from 0 to 3 within a *For...Next* construction. The variable *numLoop* is used to keep track of the 16 passes that are required to work through all 16 elements contained in the array. The last item in the Header information section of the WorkWith2DArray.vbs script specifically declares our two-dimensional array: *Dim a (3,3)*.

Reference Information

The Reference information section of our script consists of one line: *numLoop = 0*. Because you use *numLoop* to keep track of how many loops are made through the array, it is important to set it to zero. Later, you'll reassign the value of *numLoop* to be equal to its current value in the loop plus 1. By incrementing the *numLoop* counter, you can easily know exactly where you are within the array.

Worker and Output Information

The Worker and Output information section of the script (shown in the next code listing) begins immediately with a pair of nested *For...Next* constructions. The reason for nesting the *For...Next* loop in this section of the script is to have a separate value for both the variable *i* and the variable *j*.

Using the *For...Next* Construction

Because the array was declared as *Dim a (3,3)* and you happen to know that the array is zero-based, you use *i = 0 to 3* in the *For...Next* loop, as shown in the first line of the following script. You next increment the *numLoop* counter and echo the current values contained in the variables *i* and *j*. Once you know your location in the array, you assign the word *loop* concatenated with the current value held in the *numLoop* counter to the particular array element that is currently described by *a(i,j)*. If, for instance, the script is in its first loop, the value of *i* is *0* and the value of *j* is *0*, and when you get down to the *WScript.Echo* commands, the value of *numLoop* has already been incremented. So, you would echo "*i = 0 j = 0*". Look closely at the following script portion to make sure you understand what is happening in the first four lines:

```
For i = 0 To 3
  For j = 0 To 3
    numLoop = numLoop+1
    WScript.Echo "i = " & i & " j = " & j
    a(i, j) = "loop " & numLoop
    WScript.Echo "Value stored In a(i,j) is: " & a(i,j)
  Next
Next
```

Assigning Values to Each Element

Once the loop counter (*numLoop*) is incremented, it's time to assign a value to each element within the array. Rather than typing a whole series of *a(0,0) = "loop" & numLoop* lines, you instead dynamically build the value of *a(i,j)* by using the two *For...Next* loops. Thus, prior to assigning the value "*loop*" and *numLoop* to the array element, the element is empty.

> **Tip**   To assign a value to an element within an array, you specify the element number, followed by the equal sign, and then specify the value. If, however, you use a *For...Next* loop, you can in many instances automate the process.

After you assign values to the array, you use one final *WScript.Echo* command to echo out the values that are contained within the array. This is where you'd do the actual work if this were a real script. You close out the script with a pair of *Next* commands: one for each *For* introduced earlier in the script.

Passing Arguments Step-by-Step Exercises

In this section, you'll work with passing arguments by modifying a script that uses WMI to list all the services associated with a particular process on the machine. This is in fact a very useful script. While we are at it, we will simplify the script a little to make it easier to read.

1. Open the \My Documents\Microsoft Press\VBScriptSBS\ch04\StepByStep\Services ProcessStarter.vbs script and save it as YourNameServicesProcess.vbs.

2. Add the *Option Explicit* command at the top of the script.

3. Declare each variable used in the script. This would include the following:

```
Dim objIdDictionary
Dim strComputer
Dim objWMIService
Dim colServices
Dim objService
Dim colProcessIDs
Dim i
```

4. Save the script and run it to ensure you have all the variables defined. If you missed a variable, *Option Explicit* will cause the "variable is undefined" error and list the line number containing the undefined variable.

5. Add a declaration for *wmiRoot* by adding *Dim wmiRoot* under the line that says *Dim colProcessIDs*.

6. Under the line that says *strComputer* = ".", add the following:

```
wmiRoot = "winmgmts:\\" & strComputer & "\root\cimv2"
```

7. The preceding line allows you to shorten the following line to read:

```
Set objWMIService = GetObject("winmgmts:" _
  & "\\" & strComputer & "\root\cimv2")
```

8. Edit the *Set objWMIService = GetObject* line by deleting everything after the *GetObject* command. Inside the open parenthesis, type **wmiRoot** and add a close parenthesis. The line should now look like the following:

```
Set objWMIService = GetObject(wmiRoot)
```

What you have done is created shorthand for the long *winmgmts* string. In addition, you deleted some commands you didn't need (which we'll discuss in detail when we talk about WMI in Chapter 8, "Using WMI"). The script is now much easier to read.

9. Run the script—it should work fine to this point. If it does not, compare it with \My Documents\Microsoft Press\VBScriptSBS\ch04\StepByStep\ServicesProcessPT1.vbs and see where your code needs tweaking. Your script must run correctly at this point to complete the lab.

10. If everything is working, examine closely the following line:

```
Set colServices = objWMIService.ExecQuery _
  ("Select * from Win32_Service Where State <> 'Stopped'")
```

You'll make this line easier to read by placing the "*Select * from Win32_Service Where State <> *"Stopped"* line into a variable, which we unceremoniously call *wmiQuery*. To do this, you must adjust the code in two ways. First, you must declare the variable *wmiQuery* by typing the following after the *wmiRoot* declaration in the header section of the script:

```
Dim wmiQuery
```

Your second adjustment is much trickier and therefore much more critical. You must define *wmiQuery* to be equal to the *Select* statement. You place this code under the following line:

```
Set objWMIService = GetObject(wmiRoot)
```

To define *wmiQuery*, copy the *Select* statement from the *Set colServices* line, making sure to include the quotation marks with your copy. The *wmiQuery* line now looks like the following:

```
wmiQuery = "Select * from Win32_Service Where State <> 'Stopped'"
```

After you add the *wmiQuery* line above the *Set colServices* line, you delete the *Select* statement from the *Set colServices* line. In place of the *Select* statement, you use the variable *wmiQuery*. The modified line looks like this:

```
Set colServices = objWMIService.ExecQuery _
  (wmiQuery)
```

11. Save the file and run the script. It should still work properly. If it does not, compare it with the \My Documents\Microsoft Press\VBScriptSBS\ch04\StepByStep\ ServicesProcessPT2.vbs file to see where changes need to be made.

12. Now you will perform the same kind of adjustments to the second half of the script. Look at the following code (which starts around line 44):

```
For i = 0 To objIdDictionary.Count - 1
  Set colServices = objWMIService.ExecQuery _
    ("Select * from Win32_Service Where ProcessID = '" & _
      colProcessIDs(i) & "'")
```

You want to put the *Select* statement into a *wmiQuery* variable. Recall from our discussion in Chapter 1 that you can reuse variables whenever you want to. To illustrate this point, you will reuse the variable name *wmiQuery*. You define *wmiQuery* to be equal to the *Select* statement. To do this, you must define it prior to the line where you'll need to use it. This will be below the *For i = 0* line and above the *Set colServices* line. After you do this, you replace the *Select* statement with the variable *wmiQuery*. The modified code looks like the following:

```
For i = 0 To objIdDictionary.Count - 1
  wmiQuery = "Select * from Win32_Service Where ProcessID = '" & _
    colProcessIDs(i) & "'"
  Set colServices = objWMIService.ExecQuery _
    (wmiQuery)
```

13. Run your script. If it does not run, compare it with   \My Documents\Microsoft Press\VBScriptSBS\ch04\StepByStep\ServicesProcessPT3.vbs.

14. One aspect of your script that you might find annoying is that it doesn't indicate when it is finished running. Let's fix this by adding a *WScript.Echo* command to let us know the script is done. At the bottom of the script, you just do something like the following:

```
WScript.Echo "all done"
```

15. To modify the script to accept a command-line argument, simply edit *strComputer* = "." so that the variable *strComputer* is assigned to be whatever comes in from the command line, not ".", which means this local computer. The revised line looks like the following:

```
strComputer = WScript.Arguments(0)
```

By doing this, you now will run the script against any computer whose name is placed on the command line at the time you run the script.

16. Save your script. You can compare it with \My Documents\Microsoft Press\VBScriptSBS\Ch04\StepByStep\ServicesProcessPT4.vbs. To run the script, open a command prompt and go to the directory where you have been saving your work. You will want to run the script under CScript, and you will need to include the name of a reachable computer on your network. The command line for mine looks like this:

```
\My Documents\Microsoft Press\VBScriptSBS\ch04\StepByStep>Cscript ServicesProcessPT4.vbs
 localhost
```

17. What happens when you try to include two server names? What happens when you try to run the script without a command-line argument? Let's now modify the script so that it will provide a little bit of help when it is run. As it stands now, when the script is run without a command-line argument, you simply get a "subscript out of range" error. In addition, when you try to include several computer names from the command line, the first one is used and the others are ignored.

18. To add some help, check to ensure that the person running the script added a command-line argument when they executed the script. To do this, check *WScript.Arguments.UnNamed.Count* and make sure it is not zero. Use an *If...Then* construction to perform this check. Put this code in a subroutine called *subCheckArgs*. The subroutine will go at the bottom of the script, but you will call the subroutine just after the Header section. The code for the subroutine looks like the following:

```
Sub subCheckARGS
If WScript.Arguments.count = 0 Then
WScript.Echo("You must enter a computer name")
WScript.quit
End If
End Sub
```

19. Because you're using an *If...Then* construction, you must end the *If* statement. The script to this point is saved as \My Documents\Microsoft Press\VBScriptSBS\ch04\Step-ByStep\ServicesProcessPT5.vbs and you can use it to check your work.

20. Now use the *Split* function so that you can enter more than one computer name from the command line. Doing this will be a little tricky. First you must declare two new variables, listed here:

```
Dim colComputers
Dim strComputers
```

Because *strComputer* is used to hold the command-line arguments, and you want to be able to run the script against multiple computers, you'll need to be able to hold a collection of names. *colComputers* is used to hold the collection of computer names you get after you parse the command-line input and "split" out the computer names that are separated by commas. Because you now have a collection, you have to be able to iterate through the collection. Each iterated item will be stored in the variable computer.

21. Under the *strComputer* = *WScript.Arguments (0)* line, add the *colComputers* line in which you use the *Split* command to parse the command-line input. Then use a *For Each* line to iterate through the collection. The two new lines of code are listed here:

```
strComputer = WScript.Arguments(0)
colComputers = Split(strComputer, ",")

For Each computer In colComputers
```

22. Because you're modifying the input into the script, you need to change your *wmiRoot* statement so that it points to the parsed line that comes from the *Split* command. To do this, you use the following line of code just after the *For Each* command in the *colComputers* line:

```
wmiRoot = "winmgmts:\\" & Computer & "\root\cimv2"
```

23. Add an additional *Next* statement near the end of the script. Because you are doing a *For Each...Next* construction, you need to add another *Next* command. The bottom section of the script now looks like the following:

```
        For Each objService In colServices
            WScript.Echo VbTab & objService.DisplayName
        Next
      Next
  Next

    WScript.Echo "all done"
```

The script starts to get confusing when you wind up with a stack of *Next* commands. You might also notice that in the \My Documents\Microsoft Press\VBScriptSBS\ ch04\StepByStep\ServicesProcessPT6.vbs script, I indented several of the lines to make the script easier to read. If you're careful, you can use the Tab key to line up each *For Each* command with its corresponding *Next* command.

24. Save your script and try to run it by separating several computer names with a comma on the command line. Compare your script with mine, which is saved as ServicesProcessPT6.vbs.

One Step Further: Building Arrays

In this section, you explore building arrays. To help in the process, you'll take a few ideas from the script in the "Passing Arguments" section and use them in a starter file.

1. Open the \My Documents\Microsoft Press\VBScriptSBS\ch04\OneStepFurther\OneStepFurtherStarter.vbs file and save it as YourNameOneStepFurther.vbs. Note that OneStepFurtherStarter.vbs will not run. It is provided to save you some typing so that you can spend more time working with arrays.

2. You first need to declare your arrays. The first array you need to declare is *array1*. It is initialized without a specific number of elements, and so you use the format *Dim array1()*.

3. Declare the second array, *array2*. Because *array2* is created automatically when you use the *Filter* command, you just simply use the format *Dim array2*.

4. Initialize the variables *a* and *i*, which are used for counting the elements in the array. In fact, in this script you'll be creating two arrays. The code goes under the series of *Dim* statements, which are used to declare the variables used in this script.

```
a - 0
i = 0
```

5. Now you come to the first of the *For Each* statements in this script. This will come on the line after you use *set colServices* to make the connection into WMI.

```
For Each objService In colServices
  ReDim Preserve array1(i)
  array1(i) = objService.ProcessID
  i = i + 1
Next
```

Here you are creating a *For Each...Next* loop that you'll use to *add* elements into the first array, which is called *array1*. Recall our discussion about arrays: Because you wanted to add information to the array and keep the existing data, and because you didn't know how many elements you'd have in the array, you used the format *array1()* when you declared it. Now you want to keep the information you put into the array, so you must use the *ReDim Preserve* command. Then you add items to each element of the array by using the following command:

```
array1(i) = objService.ProcessID
```

Once you add the process ID into the array, you increment the counter and go to the beginning of the *For Each* loop.

6. Save the script. Compare your script with the \My Documents\Microsoft Press\VBScriptSBS\ch04\OneStepFurther\OneStepFurtherPT1.vbs file. If you try to run your script, you will still get an error.

7. Now you populate *array2*, once again using a *For Each...Next* loop. The significant item in the code in this step is the *Filter* command. If you didn't create a second array, when you ran the script, you'd get pages of junk because the looping would create duplicate process IDs. (Remember, you're performing a query for process IDs that are associated with services, so that behavior is to be expected.)

Because there is no unique command or method for arrays, you have to create a second array—named *array2*—by using the *Filter* command, and you also have to use a comparison filter as you add elements into it. The input into the filter is *array1*. You are matching the *ProcessID*s from *objService*. (This is actually rather sloppy coding. Because you used *objService.ProcessID* several times, you could have created an alias for it.) The *false* in the last position of the command tells VBScript that the item is brought into the array only if a match is *not* found, which gets rid of our duplicate problem. You might want to change this value to *true* and see what happens to your script!

```
For Each objService In colServices
  array2 = Filter(array1,objService.processID, false)
  a = a + 1
Next
```

8. Save the script. At this point, the script should run. If yours does not run, then compare it with \My Documents\Microsoft Press\VBScriptSBS\ch04\OneStepFurther\OneStepFurtherPT2.vbs.

9. You need to put a *For...Next* loop around the bottom WMI query. Because you're working with an array, determine the upper element in the array by using the *UBound* command, as shown in the following code:

```
For b = 0 To UBound(array2)
```

This line will be used by the second array. What you are doing now is running a second WMI query against only the unique elements that reside in the second array. Make sure you add the last *Next* command. You just added two statements around six statements already in the file. The completed section of script, called \My Documents\Microsoft Press\VBScriptSBS\ch04\OneStepFurther\OneStepFurtherPT3.vbs, looks like the following:

```
For b = 0 To UBound(array2)
  wmiQuery = "Select * from Win32_Service Where ProcessID = '" & _
    array2(b) & "'"
  Set colServices = objWMIService.ExecQuery _
    (wmiQuery)
  WScript.Echo "Process ID: " & array2(b)
  For Each objService In colServices
    WScript.Echo VbTab & objService.DisplayName
  Next
Next
```

10. Run the script. The script should now run as intended. If it doesn't, compare your script with OneStepFurtherPT3.vbs.

11. Now let's make some further changes to the script, to add functionality. Save your script from step 10 to a new name such as YourNameOneStepFurtherPartOne.vbs.

12. Open the \My Documents\Microsoft Press\VBScriptSBS\ch04\OneStepFurther\OneStepFurtherPartTWOstarter.vbs script and save it as YourNameOneStepFurtherPartTwo.vbs.

13. Because you're going to feed a text file, you won't need the code that references the *Arguments* collection. You will, therefore, also have to remove the following lines of code:

```
If WScript.Arguments.count = 0 Then
  WScript.Echo("You must enter a computer name")
Else
  strComputer = WScript.Arguments(0)
  colComputers = Split(strComputer, ",")
```

Make sure you leave the line that is used to create the dictionary object. In addition, do not forget to get rid of the *End If* line at the bottom of the script. See \My Documents\Microsoft Press\VBScriptSBS\ch04\OneStepFurther\OneStepFurtherPT4.vbs to make sure you removed the correct lines of code.

14. Add code to accept a command-line text file. You'll need to create a variable named *TxtFile* for the text file and then point the variable to a valid text file on your computer. Inside the text file, you need a list of only those computer names reachable on your network, separated by a comma. (Refer to my Servers.txt file for a sample, or simply edit it to your needs.)

   Next you create a constant called *ForReading* and set it equal to *1*. This is a good way to simplify accessing the file. Now create the *FileSystem* object by using the *CreateObject("Scripting.FileSystemObject")* command, which you set equal to the *objFSO* variable.

   After you do that, open the text file by setting the *objTextFile* variable to be equal to *objFSO.OpenTextFile*—we feed this the variable for our text file and also the constant *ForReading*. Code for accomplishing all this follows. You place this code right below the *Dim* commands. This code is saved as \My Documents\Microsoft Press\VBScriptSBS\ch04\OneStepFurther\OneStepFurtherPT5.vbs.

```
TxtFile = "Servers.txt"
Const ForReading = 1
Set objFSO = CreateObject("Scripting.FileSystemObject")
Set objTextFile = objFSO.OpenTextFile _
   (TxtFile, ForReading)
```

15. Look over the text file so that you know where to look for services and processes. To do this, use a *Do Until* loop. The interesting thing about this section of the code is that the loop is rather large, because you want to work with one computer at a time and query its services and processes *prior* to making another round of the loop. Therefore, placement of the outside *Loop* command is vital. In addition, you need to change the variable used in the *For Each* computer line, which follows the outside loop. Change *colComputers* to be *arrServerList*. Also, add a variable for *strNextLine* and *arrServerList* to the Header information section of your script.

```
Do Until objTextFile.AtEndofStream
  strNextLine = objTextFile.Readline
  arrServerList = Split(strNextLine , ",")
```

16. Save your file. You can compare your file with \My Documents\Microsoft Press\VBScriptSBS\ch04\OneStepFurther\OneStepFurtherPT6.vbs. This script now runs.

17. To keep track of how the script runs, add the following line just above the *wmiRoot = "WinMgmts:* line:

```
WScript.Echo" Processes and services on " & (computer)
```

18. To control the creation of the dictionary, move the line *Set objIdDictionary = CreateObject("Scripting.Dictionary")* inside the *For Each computer In arrServerList* line. Save your file and compare it with \My Documents\Microsoft Press\VBScriptSBS\ch04\OneStepFurther\OneStepFurtherPT7.vbs, if you want to.

19. Add a new variable called *j*.

20. Change *i* to *j* in the following line: *For i = 0 To objIdDictionary.Count − 1*. This gives us a new counter the second time the script is run. In addition, edit the other two places where *colProcesses(i)* appears in this section and change *colProcesses(i)* to *j* as well.

21. To make sure you don't reuse dictionary items the second time the script runs, remove all items from the dictionary by employing the *objIdDictionary.RemoveAll* command. You need to do this outside the *For j* loop but inside the *For Each* computer loop. The completed section looks like the following:

```
For j = 0 To objIdDictionary.Count - 1
      wmiQuery = "Select * from Win32_Service Where ProcessID = '" & _
          colProcessIDs(j) & "'"
    Set colServices = objWMIService.ExecQuery _
      (wmiQuery)
    WScript.Echo "Process ID: " & colProcessIDs(j)
    For Each objService In colServices
      WScript.Echo VbTab & objService.DisplayName
    Next
      objIdDictionary.RemoveAll
  Next
 Next
Loop
WScript.Echo "all done"
```

This completes the "One Step Further" exercise. Compare your work to the \My Documents\Microsoft Press\VBScriptSBS\ch04\OneStepFurther\OneStepFurtherPT8.vbs script.

Chapter 4 Quick Reference

To	Do This
Include a command-line argument without using switches	Use unnamed arguments
Use command-line arguments to supply more than one argument	Use named arguments
Ensure that the arguments are not position sensitive	Use named arguments
Avoid typing multiple arguments at the command line	Use a text file for input
Provide convenient storage inside memory to control execution of the script	Use an array
Supply multiple values for a single variable within a script	Use an array
Create an array from a line of text	Use the *Split* function
Create a string value from an array	Use the *Join* Function
Find the upper limit of an array	Use the *UBound* function

Chapter 5
More Arrays

Before You Begin

To work through the material presented in this chapter, you need to be familiar with the following concepts from earlier chapters:

- Creating single dimension arrays
- Creating two-dimensional arrays
- Implementing the *For Next* construction
- Implementing the *Select Case* construction

After completing this chapter, you will be able to:

- Convert text files into arrays to add power to analysis
- Convert delimited strings into arrays to enable analysis of log files
- Work with dictionaries to create on-the-fly storage

Strings and Arrays

In this section, you'll use text files as an input into your script to dynamically create an array that you'll use to do real work. Why is this topic important? Even though we all know about the event log in Microsoft Windows Server 2003, many network administrators and consultants are unaware of the literally hundreds of other log files lying about on the hard disk drives of their networks. Indeed, lying about is an appropriate state for the vast majority of these log files because they contain little in the way of operational guidance for the enlightened network administrator. The following list summarizes uses for converting a text file into an array construction:

- Import existing log files for ease of manipulation
- Import comma-separated value (CSV) lists for ease of script operation
- Import CSV files to control script execution

Just the Steps　To convert a text file into an array

1.　Identify a text file to convert to an array by using the *fileSystemObject* to point to the file.

2. Use the *InStr* function to parse the data.

3. Use the file system object to connect to a data source.

4. Use a dynamic array to hold the data.

5. Use *LBound* and *UBound* to set the limits when we iterate through the array.

Parsing Passed Text into an Array

In this example, you work through a script that creates a dynamic array used to hold information parsed from the Windows 2003 setup log file, Setuplog.txt.

More Info   When we parse text, we are looking through the text to identify word strings, numbers, or even case sensitive letter matches using the *InStr* function. This technique is foundational to working with text files, log files, and even event logs. You can use multiple *InStr* functions in the same script to come up with complex test scenarios. For advanced pattern matching, you can use *Regular Expressions*, which are documented in the Platform SDK (\My Documents\Microsoft Press\VBScriptSBS\Resources\Scripts56.chm).

One issue to note: If you're working on an upgraded version of Windows 2003, your Setuplog.txt file is contained in the WINNT directory. If you're working with a fresh installation, the Setuplog.txt file is contained in the Windows directory. The reason for this is that beginning with Microsoft Windows XP, the name of the default Windows directory was changed from WINNT to Windows. However, in an upgrade, the Windows directory cannot be renamed without potentially breaking applications.

In our script, SearchTXT.vbs, you create a dynamic array and set its initial size to zero. You next make a connection to the file system object and open the Setuplog.txt file, located in the Windows directory (this path may be edited if required), for reading. Once the Setuplog.txt file is opened for reading, you define a search string of "Error" and use the *InStr* command to look through each line. If the string "Error" is found on the line being examined, the line with the error is added to the array. You then increment the next element in the array in case you find another line with the string "Error" in it. After you go through the entire text file, you use a *For...Next* loop and echo out each element of the array. The script concludes with a friendly "all done" message. The code for SearchTXT.vbs follows.

SearchTXT.vbs

```
Option Explicit
On Error Resume Next
Dim arrTxtArray()
Dim myFile
Dim SearchString
Dim objTextFile
Dim strNextLine
```

```
Dim intSize
Dim objFSO
Dim i
intSize = 0
myFile = "c:\windows\setuplog.txt" <'>Modify as required
SearchString = "Error"
Const ForReading = 1
Set objFSO = CreateObject("Scripting.FileSystemObject")
Set objTextFile = objFSO.OpenTextFile _
  (myFile, ForReading)
Do until objTextFile.AtEndOfStream
  strNextLine = objTextFile.ReadLine
  if InStr (strNextLine, SearchString)then
   ReDim Preserve arrTxtArray(intSize)
   arrTxtArray(intSize) = strNextLine
   intSize = intSize + 1
  End If
Loop
objTextFile.close
For i = LBound(arrTxtArray) To UBound(arrTxtArray)
   WScript.Echo arrTxtArray(i)
Next
WScript.Echo("all done")
```

Header Information

The Header information section of SearchTXT.vbs contains few surprises at this juncture. The important aspect in this section is the listing of all the variables contained in SearchTXT.vbs. This declaring of the variables provides a blueprint for understanding the script. Each variable and its use is listed in Table 5-1. The Header information section of the script is listed here:

```
Option Explicit
On Error Resume Next
Dim arrTxtArray()
Dim myFile
Dim SearchString
Dim objTextFile
Dim strNextLine
Dim intSize
Dim objFSO
Dim i
```

Table 5-1   Variables declared in SearchTXT.vbs

Variable	Use
arrTxtArray()	Declares a dynamic array
myFile	Holds the file name of the file to open up
SearchString	Holds the string to search for
objTextFile	Holds the connection to the text file
strNextLine	Holds the next line in the text stream
intSize	Holds the initial size of the array

Table 5-1   Variables declared in SearchTXT.vbs

Variable	Use
objFSO	Holds the connection to the file system object
i	Used to increment *intSize* counter

Reference Information

The Reference information section of the script is used to assign values to many of the variables that are declared in the Header information section. The Reference information section of SearchTXT.vbs follows.

```
intSize = 0
myFile = "c:\windows\setuplog.txt"
SearchString = "Error"
Const ForReading = 1
Set objFSO = CreateObject("Scripting.FileSystemObject")
Set objTextFile = objFSO.OpenTextFile _
   (myFile, ForReading)
```

The variable *intSize* is used to hold the value of the initial size of the dynamic array used in this script. It is set to zero because you do not know how many items you will have in your dynamic array. You start with the value of zero, and then you later increase the array to the required size as you read through the log file. A different approach would be to create an array that is much larger than you think you'd need and then populate the array with the items gathered from the log file. However, there are at least two problems with this approach:

■ Creating an array that is too large wastes memory resources

■ Creating an array that is too large results in too many elements that have a zero value

The *myFile* variable is assigned to the physical location of the log file you want to parse. In this instance, you are looking at the Windows Server 2003 setup log file contained in the Windows directory. This is one modification you will need to make to your script—changing the location and name of the log file you want to parse. By creating a variable called *myFile*, and by assigning it to a log file in the Reference information section of the script, you make it easy to modify the script for future use. By simply changing the file you want to parse, you can use this script to peruse many different log files.

SearchString is the variable that holds the string of letters you want to glean from the log file. As the script currently stands, you are searching for the word "Error" in the Windows Server 2003 setup log file. By searching for "Error," you create an array that holds all the errors that occurred during the installation of the Windows Server 2003 server.

You create a constant called *ForReading* and set it to the value of *1*. Then the next step is to create a *FileSystemObject* and use the *ForReading* constant to open the log file. When you open a text file using a *FileSystemObject*, you must tell VBScript whether you're going to open the file and read from it, or open the file and write to it. In your script, you need only to be able to read from the file to find the lines containing the word *Error*.

> **Note**   For more information about creating and using constants, refer to Chapter 2, "Looping Through the Script."

You now use the *Set* command to assign the variable *objTextFile* to be equal to the command that opens the text file for reading. Here is the syntax for this command:

Set	New variable	Command	File name	Read or write
Set	objTextFile	objFSO.OpentextFile	myFile	ForReading

Worker Information

The Worker information section of the SearchTXT.vbs script, shown in the following code, is where you create a text-processing engine. This engine is made up of the following components:

- *Do Until...Loop*
- *If...Then* loop
- *ReDim Preserve*

```
Do Until objTextFile.AtEndofStream
  strNextLine = objTextFile.ReadLine
  If InStr (strNextLine, SearchString) Then
    ReDim Preserve arrTxtArray(intSize)
    arrTxtArray(intSize) = strNextLine
    intSize = intSize + 1
  End If
Loop
objTextFile.Close
```

Do Until...Loop is used to walk through the text stream that comes from the connection to our setup log file. The *Do Until* structure controls the entire process and will continue working until it comes to the end of the data stream (which incidentally occurs when you reach the bottom of the text file).

The variable *strNextLine* is assigned to the line of text that comes from the text file when you use the *ReadLine* command on *objTextFile*. (Remember that you defined *objTextFile* to be *textStreamObject* you get back from the setup log file. You do this by using the read-only version of the *OpenTextFile* command in the Reference information section of the script.)

You use an *If...Then* structure to look through *strNextLine* for the value contained in the variable you called *SearchString*. In the Reference section, you assigned the value of "Error" to the variable *SearchString*. You use the *InStr* command to search *strNextLine* for the text string "Error." The *InStr* command has the following syntax:

InStr	Starting position (optional)	String being searched	String searched for	Compare mode (op-tional)
InStr		*strNextLine*	*SearchString*	

When using *InStr*, the starting position is the first character in the text string to be searched. It is important to remember that the *InStr* command is not zero-based. A position that is actually 38 spaces away will be reported as 38. The optional starting position field of the *InStr* command is useful when parsing certain log files that begin each line with a time stamp or other information that makes the file difficult to parse. By skipping past the time stamp, you can parse the line more easily.

> **Note**   Many of the commands you use in VBScript are, for whatever reason, zero-based, which means that you start counting at zero. But now you come to *InStr*, which is *not* zero-based. A position that is 12 spaces away will be reported as 12. Forget this fact, and your scripts will act really strange.

If the *InStr* command finds the search text in the search string, you use *ReDim Preserve* to expand the array by one element. *ReDim Preserve* actually performs two tasks. The first is to resize the array, and the second is to make sure you don't lose any data when the array is resized. The *arrTxtArray(intSize) = strNextLine* line adds the value contained in *strNextLine* to the *arrTxtArray* element identified by the *intSize* variable. The *intSize = intSize + 1* construct increases the *intSize* variable by 1. You'll use this variable to add one more element to your array when the *InStr* command finds an additional line containing the word "Error" in the text string.

When you reach the end of the data string, you use *End If* to end the *If* loop and the *objText-File.Close* command to close the text file. This closing step is not really required, because the text file automatically closes when the program quits; however, this step is considered good practice and can prevent potential file-locking problems in the future.

Output Information

After you load the array with the information gathered from the setup log file, you really have accomplished only half of the task. This is because constructing an array and not using it is pretty well useless. In this script, you're going to simply echo out the lines found that contain the word "Error" in them. In many cases, echoing the errors out is sufficient. In later chapters, you'll learn how to save this information to a text file for future manipulation if desired. Because your script is modular in its design, you could easily replace this Output information section with one that saves to a text file or creates a Web page, or one that creates and sends an e-mail.

You use a *For...Next* loop to work through the lower boundary and the upper boundary of your dynamic array. Once you get to each new element in the array, you use the *WScript.Echo* command to print to the screen the data contained in that element of the array. Then use the *Next* command to go back and read the next element in the array. You continue to do this until you reach the upper boundary of the array. Once you reach the end of the array, you use *WScript.Echo* to let yourself know that the script completed successfully. This section of the script is listed here:

```
For i = LBound(arrTxtArray) To UBound(arrTxtArray)
  WScript.Echo arrTxtArray(i)
Next
WScript.Echo("all done")
```

Quick Check

Q.   **What is the advantage of using a dynamic array?**

A.   You can expand a dynamic array when a new element is needed. This saves memory and is more efficient.

Q.   **How is *ReDim Preserve* used?**

A.   *ReDim Preserve* is used to resize a dynamic array while ensuring that the data contained in the array is not lost.

Use the *InputBox* function and separator line function

1.   Open \My Documents\Microsoft Press\VBScriptSBS\ch05\MultiValuesSearch.vbs in Microsoft Notepad or your script editor of choice. Save the script as YourNameSearch1X1MultiValues.vbs.

2.   Declare three new variables to be used for the *InputBox* function. The variables are: *strPrompt*, *strTitle*, and *strDefault*. This is seen below:

```
Dim strPrompt,strTitle,strDefault 'used for input box
```

3.   In the Reference section, assign value to *strPrompt*. The value assigned to *strPrompt* will appear in the gray section of the input box. It should tell the user to enter values to search for, and it should specify the name of the text that will be searched. It will look something like the following:

```
strPrompt = "Enter error words to search for in: " & _
         VbCrLf & myFile
```

4.   Under the entry for *strPrompt*, assign value to the *strTitle* variable. This will appear at the top of the input box and should inform the user of the purpose of the input box. My entry looks like the following:

```
strTitle = "Error locator"
```

5. Under the entry for *strTitle*, assign value to *strDefault*. This will be the multiple strings searched for in the text file if the user just presses Enter and does not edit the input box. Make sure to *not* put spaces between the comma-separated values. Otherwise, when the *Split* function breaks the line into an array, the *InStr* function will search for a space as well as the value. My entry looks like the following:

```
strDefault = "Error,failed,unable to,was NOT"
```

6. Modify the *searchString* variable so that it is equal to what is returned from the *InputBox* function. It will look like the following:

```
SearchString = InputBox(strPrompt,strTitle,strDefault)
```

7. Save and run the script. You should see an input box appear, and when you press Enter, the script should search for the values you entered for *strDefault*. If this does not happen, compare your script to \My Documents\Microsoft Press\VBScriptSBS\ch05 \SearchTXTMultiValues.vbs.

8. Now let's clean up the output just a little to make it easier to read. To do this, we will use the *funLine* function. Copy the function from the \My Documents\Microsoft Press\VBScriptSBS\Utilities\FunLine.vbs file. The function is seen below. You will paste it at the very bottom of your script.

```
Function funLine(lineOfText)
Dim numEQs, separator, i
numEQs = Len(lineOfText)
For i = 1 To numEQs
    separator = separator & "="
Next
 FunLine = VbCrLf & lineOfText & vbcrlf & separator
End Function
```

9. Use the *funLine* function to create a header for the listing of each line that corresponds to a searched value. In this header, list how many matches were found. This header will go just before the *For i = 0 To UBound(arrTxtArray)* line of code in the Output section of your script. My header line looks like the following:

```
WScript.Echo funLine("There are " & ubound(arrTxtArray) &_
    " Lines with " & """" & Item & """" & " in them")
```

10. Save and run the script. It should produce an output that looks similar to the following (abbreviated):

```
There are 58 Lines with "Error" in them
=======================================
07/16/2005 16:28:31.109,d:\xpsprtm\base\ntsetup\ …
```

11. If you look closely, you will notice that the script counts incorrectly. There are actually 59 lines in my log file that have the word "Error" in them. This is due to the array being zero based. To fix this, we need to add 1 to our count. This is seen below:

```
WScript.Echo funLine("There are " & ubound(arrTxtArray)+1 &_
    " Lines with " & """" & Item & """" & " in them")
```

12. If your output does not look like this, or if you receive an error, compare your script to SearchTXTMultiValues.vbs.

Parsing Passed Text

One nice thing you can do with arrays is use them to hold the results of parsing a comma-separated value (CSV) file. With Windows Server 2003, you can easily create a CSV file from the event viewer. Right-click the log you are interested in, select Save As from the menu, and choose CSV File. Now, suppose you have a file such as a CSV (I included an application log, \My Documents\Microsoft Press\VBScriptSBS\ch05\appLog.csv, from one of my test machines) and you're trying to find out about Windows Installer errors on that server. Well, you can try to weed through all those long lines of text, or you can open the file up in Microsoft Office Excel, or you can use a script to do the heavy lifting.

Just the Steps   To convert a CSV file into an array

1. Identify a CSV file to convert into an array by using *fileSystemObject* to point to the file.
2. Use the *InStr* function to parse the data.
3. Use the file system object to connect to a data source.
4. Use a dynamic array to hold the data.
5. Use *LBound* and *UBound* to iterate through the array.
6. Use the *Split* function to break the text line into elements.
7. Add the new elements into a multidimensional array.

The ParseAppLog.vbs script follows. Remember, the script will need to be in the same path as the appLog.csv file.

ParseAppLog.vbs

```
Option Explicit
On Error Resume Next
Dim arrTxtArray()
Dim appLog
Dim SearchString
Dim objTextFile
Dim strNextLine
Dim intSize
Dim objFSO
```

```
Dim i
Dim ErrorString
Dim newArray
intSize = 0
appLog = "applog.csv" <'>Ensure in path
SearchString = ","
ErrorString = "1004"
Const ForReading = 1
Set objFSO = CreateObject("Scripting.FileSystemObject")
Set objTextFile = objFSO.OpenTextFile _
  (appLog, ForReading)
Do until objTextFile.AtEndOfStream
  strNextLine = objTextFile.ReadLine
  if InStr (strNextLine, SearchString)Then
   If InStr (strNextLine, ErrorString) then
        ReDim Preserve arrTxtArray(intSize)
        arrTxtArray(intSize) = strNextLine
        intSize = intSize + 1
     End If
  End If
Loop
   objTextFile.close
For i = LBound(arrTxtArray) To UBound(arrTxtArray)
  If InStr (arrTxtArray(i), ",") Then
  newArray = Split (arrTxtArray(i), ",")
        WScript.Echo "Date: " & newArray(0)
        WScript.Echo "Time: " & newArray(1)
        WScript.Echo "Source: " & newArray(2)& " "& newArray(3)
        WScript.Echo "Server: " & newArray(7)
        WScript.Echo "Message1: " & newArray(8)
        WScript.Echo "Message2: " & newArray(9)
        WScript.Echo "Message3: " & newArray(10)
        WScript.Echo " "
  End If
Next
WScript.Echo("all done")
```

Tip   Why save an event log as a CSV instead of as an .evt file, which is the default for an Event Viewer backup file? Keep in mind that a .evt file is a binary file and it has a dependency to dynamic-link library (.dll) files that reside on the server that hosted the event log file. These .dll files provide the description information to the Event Viewer application. This means that if you export the log file as a .evt file and then open it on your laptop or other personal computer, you may find many of the event log entries report they are missing the description. This is due to the .dll files from the server not residing on your laptop or on your personal computer. One way around this would be to install the server application onto your laptop or personal computer (not a very good idea). For this reason, saving a log file from the server as a CSV file makes the file independent of the installed applications because the CSV file will contain the event descriptions as well as the event ID numbers.

Header Information

The Header information section in ParseAppLog.vbs is similar to the Header section in the previous script. The declared variables are listed in Table 5-2.

Table 5-2   Variables declared in ParseAppLog.vbs

Variable	Use
arrTxtArray()	Declares a dynamic array
appLog	Holds the file name of the file to open
SearchString	Holds the string to search for
objTextFile	Holds the connection to the text file
strNextLine	Holds the next line in the text stream
intSize	Holds the initial size of the array
objFSO	Holds the connection to the file system object
i	Used to increment the intSize counter
ErrorString	Holds the second search string used
newArray	New array created to sort the output

Reference Information

The Reference information section is where you assign values to certain variables and define constants that are used in the script. Here is the Reference information section of the script:

```
intSize = 0
appLog = "appLog.CSV"
SearchString = ","
ErrorString = "1004"
Const ForReading = 1
Set objFSO = CreateObject("Scripting.FileSystemObject")
Set objTextFile = objFSO.OpenTextFile _
  (appLog, ForReading)
```

You use *appLog* is used to point to the CSV file you want to parse. You use *SearchString* to specify that you want to look for commas. The error string you are looking for in this script is 1004, which is an error from MSI installer. By changing the error message ID, you can use the script to look for everything from dropped Internet Protocol (IP) packets from the Microsoft Internet Security and Acceleration Server (ISA) to bad logon attempts from Windows Server 2003.

> **Important**   This technique won't perfectly parse every CSV file in the world. Some are very complex and include commas and even line feeds within single pieces of data.

Although special rules for advanced parsing are beyond the scope of this chapter, you are unlikely to need advanced parsing with normal application setup logs (and you definitely won't see this need in CSV files exported from the Event Viewer).

Worker Information

In the Worker information section of the script, things start to get a little interesting. You begin by using a *Do Until* construction that looks for the end of the read-only text string coming from *objTextFile*. You then define *strNextLine* to be equal to what comes back from the *ReadLine* command that we used on *objTextFile*. The magic begins when you use the *InStr* command to look for commas in the line-by-line streams of text. After you find a comma in a line, you look for the error message ID of 1004, which indicates a problem with an MSI installer package. By nesting a pair of *If...Then* statements and using *InStr*, you easily filter only the desired messages. As a result, the size of the array is smaller and less memory is required. You haven't implemented error handling here, which could easily be accomplished by using the *Else* command.

```
Do Until objTextFile.AtEndofStream
  strNextLine = objTextFile.ReadLine
  If InStr (strNextLine, SearchString) > 0 Then
    If InStr (strNextLine, ErrorString) > 0 Then
      ReDim Preserve arrTxtArray(intSize)
      arrTxtArray(intSize) = strNextLine
      intSize = intSize + 1
    End If
  End If
Loop
objTextFile.Close
```

Output Information

After the array *arrTxtArray* is created, each element of the array contains an entire event message from the event log. You could just print out each line, but a more functional approach is to organize the data so that it is more comprehensible. To this end, you create a multidimensional array that holds specific elements of the event message. You begin the Output information section by using *For...Next* to walk from the lower boundary of the single dimensional array *arrTxtArray* to the upper boundary of *arrTxtArray*. You then look for commas in each line contained in the elements incremented by using the *i* counter. Once this is done, you build the multidimensional array and echo out only the elements that contain information you're interested in seeing. The script ends by echoing out an "all done" message.

```
For i = LBound(arrTxtArray) To UBound(arrTxtArray)
  If InStr (arrTxtArray(i), ",") Then
    newArray = Split (arrTxtArray(i), ",")
    WScript.Echo "Date: " & newArray(0)
    WScript.Echo "Time: " & newArray(1)
    WScript.Echo "Source: " & newArray(2)& " "& newArray(3)
    WScript.Echo "Server: " & newArray(7)
    WScript.Echo "Message1: " & newArray(8)
    WScript.Echo "Message2: " & newArray(9)
    WScript.Echo "Message3: " & newArray(10)
    WScript.Echo " "
  End If
Next
```

> **Quick Check**
>
> **Q.** **What is the simplest way to break up a CSV data stream to populate an array?**
>
> **A.** You need to use the *Split* command and look for commas.
>
> **Q.** **What is the *InStr* command used for?**
>
> **A.** The *InStr* command is used to look for character combinations in a stream of text.
>
> **Q.** **What construct can be used to hold data records that are separated by commas?**
>
> **A.** A multidimensional array can be used to hold this type of data.

Working with Dictionaries

I don't know about you, but I usually think about using a dictionary to check the spelling of a word or to find a definition. In Windows Scripting, however, a dictionary has nothing to do with either of these concepts, although its use is just as important, perhaps more so. So what is a dictionary in our context? Well, a *dictionary* is kind of like an array, only easier to work with. It is a place to hold data. Just like an array can be used to hold data in a convenient place for use within the script, a dictionary also holds data. A dictionary works like a single dimension array. You can store only one column's worth of data in your dictionary.

Because enterprise scripts have to get information from other places (a command-line argument, a text file, or an Active Directory Services Interface [ADSI] query), it is convenient to store the information locally to avoid repeated calls to the outside source. Once the information is local, you can manipulate it into a more manageable form. In Chapter 4, "Working with Arrays," and earlier in this chapter, you looked at using arrays to store information locally. In certain situations, you can use a dictionary to perform the same type of activity—that is, for convenience, you can temporarily store working information in the *Dictionary* object.

As mentioned earlier, the dictionary works like an array in that each item in the dictionary is stored with its associated key. The key is used to identify the value we want to store, or retrieve, from the dictionary. With an array, we used the index number to retrieve the data. In the dictionary, we use the key. In a dictionary, we have a *key* and an *item*. The dictionary offers a couple of advantages over arrays. The first advantage is that you can retrieve any specific item from the dictionary simply by knowing the key, whereas with an array, you need to know the array index number. The second advantage is that a dictionary doesn't require any specific size configuration. With an array, you must either know its exact size or resize it.

Understanding the *Dictionary* Object

To use the VBScript dictionary, you need to first create it. (In technical terms, the dictionary is a Microsoft Component Object Model (COM) object and gets created via the *CreateObject* method.) The basic syntax for this is seen below:

```
Set objDictionary = CreateObject("scripting.dictionary")
```

Compare Mode

The dictionary enables us to configure only one property: the compare mode. This is actually part of what makes the dictionary easy to use (the lack of configurable properties, not the compare mode itself). In reality, most of the time, the default compare mode (which is binary mode) is fine. Compare mode enables you to configure the way in which the dictionary compares items when used to search for previously added items. The other compare mode (besides binary) is text mode. Text mode is case-insensitive. In binary mode, server1 and Server1 are two different computers, whereas in text mode they would be the same machine. It is important to remain aware of these differences.

Note   If you want to change the compare mode from binary to text mode, you must do this before you add any information to the dictionary.

Adding Items to the Dictionary

After you create the dictionary, you add items to it. (It's basically useless without information, just like a printed dictionary containing only blank pages.) So how do you add information to the dictionary? You guessed it—using the *Add* method. In this example, we are using a number for the key. This is perfectly acceptable, and we can easily walk through the dictionary via *For ... Next*. The advantage of the dictionary in the BasicDictionary.vbs script is that it is automatically dynamic.

BasicDictionary.vbs

```
Option Explicit
Dim objDictionary, i
Set objDictionary = CreateObject("scripting.dictionary")
objDictionary.Add 1, "server1"
objDictionary.Add 2, "server2"
objDictionary.Add 3, "server3"
objDictionary.Add 4, "server4"
For i = 1 To 4
WScript.Echo objDictionary.item (i)
next
```

In the BasicDictionary.vbs script, you first create the dictionary and assign it to the variable *objDictionary*. You use this variable because you use the *CreateObject* command to make a dictionary, and the name *objDictionary* tells us that the variable is an object that is a dictionary. You then add one item to the dictionary, called *server1*, which is assigned to a key called *1*. From this code, you can see the syntax is *add key item*, as illustrated here:

Command	Key	Item
objDictionary.Add	1	Server1

Counting with the count

1. Open the BasicDictionary.vbs script in Notepad or your favorite script editor. Save the file as YourNameBasicDictionaryCount.vbs.

2. On the line that reads *For i = 1 To 4*, change the number 4 to be the count of items in the dictionary. To do this, we use the Count property, as seen below:

```
For i = 1 To objDictionary.count
```

3. Save and run the script. You will see it behaves exactly as the BasicDictionary.vbs script. The advantage of this is that we can now add other items to the dictionary and echo out the items in the collection without having to change the for *i = 1 To 4* line of code each time.

4. Under the *For...Next* loop, add server5 to the dictionary. Use 5 for the key value. The line of code *must* be typed exactly:

```
objDictionary.Add "5", "Server5"
```

5. Save and run the script. You will notice server5 is not printed out in the output. This is because we added it after the Output section of the script. To verify the item was added properly to the dictionary, echo out the count of the dictionary, as seen below:

```
WScript.Echo "The count after adding key ""5"" with ""server5""" & _
        " to the dictionary is " & objDictionary.Count
```

6. Add another *For...Next* loop after the *WScript.Echo* line. You can copy the one already used by the script. It looks like the code below.

```
For i = 1 To objDictionary.count
    WScript.Echo objDictionary.item (i)
Next
```

7. Save and run your script. You will notice the output *does not* include server5. The output is seen below:

```
server1
server2
server3
server4
```

```
The count after adding key "5" with "server5" to the dictionary is 5
server1
server2
server3
server4

Exit code: 0 , 0000h
```

8. Notice there is a blank line after the second printout, right before the exit code. (Depending on how your script editor is configured, you may or may not have an exit code printed out at the conclusion of your script.) Query the Count property again to see if you can find any change. My code looks like the following:

```
WScript.Echo "The count after using the second for ... next loop "&_
    "Is " & objDictionary.Count
```

9. The count has now incremented to 6. Let's see what is going on with our new server. Echo out the type name of *objDictionary.item("5")* by using the *TypeName* function.

```
WScript.Echo "Item ""5"" is a " & TypeName(objdictionary.Item("5"))
```

10. Run the script. It reports that the item associated with "5" is a string.

11. Modify the echo line to print out the type name of the item associated with 6. This is seen below:

```
WScript.Echo "Item 6 is a " & TypeName(objdictionary.Item(6))
```

12. Notice that the item associated with key 6 is empty. What happened is that the dictionary added an empty item to the dictionary. The question at this point is why? To find out, we will need to work with the keys. We will do this in the next procedure, "The key to keys."

> **Important**   There are many times when we need to include a quotation mark inside an output string. To do this, we need to "escape" the character. If I use only one quotation mark, then the script runtime engine will think I am done with my string value and interpret the next character as a command, which nearly always results in errors. In the Counting the count procedure, we escape the key value with two sets of quotation marks. What really looks strange is the three quotation marks in a row at the end of the first line. The extra quotation character is required to end the first selection of quotes.

The key to keys

1. Open BasicDictionaryCount.vbs and save it as YourNameBasicDictionaryKEYS.vbs. You can use Notepad or your favorite script editor to do this.

2. To work with the keys, we will need to create an array of keys so we can walk through them. To do this, we need to first create two variables: *aryKeys* and *key*. This is seen below:

```
Dim aryKeys 'holds array of keys from keys method
Dim key 'an individual key in the array
```

3. To get a collection of keys, we use the *Keys* method of the *Dictionary* object. Assign it to the *aryKeys* variable as seen below:

```
aryKeys = objDictionary.Keys
```

4. To confirm we have an array of keys, let's use the *vartype* function to echo out the data type of *aryKeys*. This is seen below:

```
WScript.Echo "aryKeys is " & vartype(aryKeys)
```

5. *vartype* returns a number. The number for *aryKeys* is 8204. Open the \My Documents\Microsoft Press\VBScriptSBS\Resources\Script56.chm file and find the article associated with *vartype*. You will see that these values can be additive. Although these *varitype numbers* are not listed specifically, they can be determined by adding 8192 (which is an array) to 12 (which is a variant). This tells us that *aryKeys* is an array of variants.

6. Now use *vartype* to print out the data type of each key stored in our array of keys. Use *For Each* to do this. My code looks like the following:

```
For Each key in aryKeys
    WScript.Echo "key " & key & " is a " & vartype(key)
Next
```

7. Examine the output produced by this script. Look up the *vartype* of each key in the Script56.chm file. I have copied the output below:

```
server1
server2
server3
server4
The count after adding key "5" with "server5" to the dictionary is 5
server1
server2
server3
server4

The count after using the second for ... next loop Is 6
Item "5" is a String
Item 6 is a Empty
aryKeys is 8204
key 1 is a 2
key 2 is a 2
key 3 is a 2
key 4 is a 2
key 5 is a 8
key 5 is a 3
key 6 is a 2
```

8. Notice we have two keys listed for 5. The first is a string. The second is a long. The first four keys are all integers.

9. Notice there is also a key 6. This one is an integer and not a long. This one was added when we tried to see the data type of the item associated with the newly added item that had increased the count. Because we did not know the key, we assumed it would be 6. However, because there was not a number five in use, that one was added first. Then by querying a key that did not exist for its type name, we created an additional key in the dictionary.

10. Compare your results with \My Documents\Microsoft Press\VBScriptSBS\ch05\Basic-DictionaryKeys.vbs.

Caution   When we added key 5, we enclosed the number 5 with quotation marks. This caused the script engine to interpret it as a string, the letter five, instead of as an integer, the number five. When we used the *For...Next* command to walk through the items in the dictionary, we were specifying the keys that were integers. However, because we went to the count of the dictionary, we printed out five items associated with the keys that were integers. Because the number five did not exist, the *Dictionary* object added it automatically. Please note: It is perfectly acceptable to have a mixture of integers and strings as key items in a dictionary; however, it is very confusing.

Removing items from the dictionary

1. Open the \My Documents\Microsoft Press\VBScriptSBS\ch05\Basic DictionaryKeys.vbs script in Notepad or your favorite editor and save it as YourNameBasicDictionaryRemoveKeys.vbs.

2. At the bottom of the script, echo out the count of the dictionary, so we know what we are working with. My code looks like the following:

```
WScript.Echo "before we remove key 6, the count is: " & objDictionary.Count
```

3. Now use the *Remove* method to remove key 6. Echo out a message telling the user you are going to remove the key. Concatenate the lines with *&* and call the *Remove* method. This code looks like the following:

```
WScript.Echo "removing key 6 ..." & objDictionary.Remove(6)
```

4. Confirm the removal of key 6 by using the count again. This line of code looks like the following:

```
WScript.Echo "After removal of 6, the count is: " & objDictionary.Count
```

5. Now we want to add "server5" to the item of key 5 (the integer) and remove key 5 (the string). To do this, however, we want keep the data stored in *item("5")*. Declare a variable *strItem* to hold the data in *item("5")*. It looks like this:

```
Dim strItem 'holds data stored in key "5"
```

6. At the bottom of your script, use *strItem* to hold the data stored in *item("5")*. The code for this looks like:

```
strItem = objDictionary.Item("5")
```

7. Now remove both *key("5")* and *key(5)*. Use the following code to remove these keys:

```
objDictionary.Remove("5")
objDictionary.Remove(5)
```

8. Verify the two keys were removed by checking the count. My code looks like the following:

```
WScript.Echo "after removing two keys, count is: " & objDictionary.Count
```

Adding items back to the dictionary

1. Open \My Documents\Microsoft Press\VBScriptSBS\ch05\BasicDictionaryRemoveKeys.vbs and save it as YourNameBasicDictionaryAddKeys.vbs. Use Notepad or your favorite script editor.

2. To add data back to the dictionary, we use the *Add* method. However, because we have removed several items and added back some other items, we may not be sure of what the last key in the dictionary is. To avoid creating an error, let's use the count to create the proper key. We get the count, which tells us how many items are in the dictionary, then we add one to it. This gives us the next number in the dictionary. To do this, use the following code:

```
objDictionary.Add objdictionary.Count + 1,strItem
```

3. Verify the data was added by checking the count. I used the following code to do this:

```
WScript.Echo "after adding back, the count is: " & objDictionary.count
```

4. Print out each item in the dictionary. Use *For...Next* and go to the count of the dictionary. Use *i* to indicate the key value and use it with the *Item* method to retrieve the item associated with the key. This code is seen below:

```
For i = 1 To objDictionary.Count
    WScript.Echo objDictionary.Item(i)
Next
```

5. To avoid adding empty key values to the dictionary, as we did in the original script, use the *Exists* method of the *Dictionary* object to verify the existence of the key prior to echoing it out. Use an *If...Then* statement to do this. The following code shows the completed structure—including the *For...Next* loop added in step 4.

```
For i = 1 To objDictionary.Count
    If objDictionary.exists(i) Then
        WScript.Echo objDictionary.Item(i)
    End If
Next
```

6. You should see all five servers printed out at the bottom of the output. If you do not, compare your script with BasicDictionaryAddKeys.vbs.

Using Basic *InStr* Step-by-Step Exercises

In this section, you play with the *InStr* function to become familiar with the basic features of its implementation. Because this is a short script, you don't need to implement a full Header information section.

1. Open the \My Documents\Microsoft Press\VBScriptSBS\Templates \blankTemplate.vbs template in Notepad or your favorite script editor and save the file as YourNameInstr1.vbs.

2. Create a variable called *searchString* and set it equal to 5. Your line will look like the following:

```
searchString = "5"
```

3. Create another variable called *textSearched* and set it equal to *123456789*. Your second line will look like this:

```
textSearched = "123456789"
```

4. Create a third variable called *InStrReturn* and set it equal to the following *InStr* command: *InStr (textSearched, searchString)*. This line will look like the following:

```
InStrReturn = InStr (textSearched, searchString)
```

5. Use the *WScript.Echo* command to print out the results of the *InStr* command. This line will look like the following:

```
WScript.Echo (InStrReturn)
```

6. Save the file.

7. Run the YourNameInstr1.vbs file by double-clicking it. You should see a dialog box with the number 5 printed in it. This indicates that search string 5 was found in the fifth position of the script.

8. Open the \My Documents\Microsoft Press\VBScriptSBS\Templates \BlankTemplate.vbs template in a script editor save it as YourNameInstr2.vbs.

9. Create a variable called *searchString* and set it equal to 5. Your line will look like the following:

```
searchString = "5"
```

10. Create another variable called *textSearched* and set it equal to *123456789*. Your second line will look like this:

```
textSearched = "123456789"
```

11. Create a third variable called *InStrReturn* and set it equal to the following *InStr* command: *InStr (1, textSearched, searchString, 0)*. This line will look like the following:

```
InStrReturn = InStr (1, textSearched, searchString, 0)
```

12. Use the *WScript.Echo* command to print out the results of the *InStr* command. This line will look like the following:

```
WScript.Echo InStrReturn
```

13. Run YourNameInstr2.vbs by double-clicking it. You should see a dialog box with the number 5 printed in it. This indicates that the search string 5 was found in the fifth position of the script when you started looking from the first position of the search string.

14. Change the 1 to a 5 in your *InStrReturn* line. It will look like the following:

```
InStrReturn = InStr(5, textSearched, searchString, 0)
```

15. Save your work.

16. Run YourNameInstr2.vbs by double-clicking it. You should see a dialog box with the number 5 printed in it. This indicates that the search string 5 was found in the fifth position of the script when you started looking from the fifth position of the search string.

17. Change the 5 to a 6 in your *InStrReturn* line. It will look like the following:

```
InStrReturn = InStr(6, textSearched, searchString, 0)
```

18. Save your work.

19. Run YourNameInstr2.vbs by double-clicking it. You should see a dialog box with the number 0 printed in it. This indicates that the search string 5 was not found in the search string when you started looking from the sixth position of the search string.

One Step Further: Creating a Dictionary

In this section, you create a dictionary and then populate it with a list of file names provided by the file system object.

1. Open the \My Documents\Microsoft Press\VBScriptSBS\Templates \BlankTemplate.vbs template in a script editor. Save it as YourNameDictionary.vbs.

2. On the first line, type **Option Explicit**.

3. Declare the following variables by using the *Dim* command:

```
Dim objDictionary    'the dictionary object
Dim objFSO           'the FileSystemObject object
Dim objFolder        'created by GetFolder method
Dim colFiles         'collection of files from Files method
Dim objFile          'individual file
Dim aryKeys          'array of keys
Dim strKey           'individual key from array of keys
Dim strFolder        'the folder to obtain listing of files
```

4. In the Reference section of the script, assign a folder to the *strFolder* variable. I used c:\windows, but you can use any folder you have rights to access. This is illustrated below:

    ```
    strFolder = "c:\windows" <'>Ensure correct path
    ```

5. Use *CreateObject* to create the dictionary. Assign it to the *objDictionary* variable, as seen below:

    ```
    Set objDictionary = CreateObject("scripting.dictionary")
    ```

6. Use *CreateObject* to create the file system object and assign it to the variable *objFSO*:

    ```
    Set objFSO = CreateObject("Scripting.FileSystemObject")
    ```

7. Use the *GetFolder* method to create a folder object. Use *GetFolder* to retrieve the folder represented by the *strFolder* variable. Assign it to the variable *objFolder*:

    ```
    Set objFolder = objFSO.GetFolder(strFolder)
    ```

8. Use the *Files* method of the *Folder* object represented by the *objFolder* variable. Assign it to *colFiles*, as seen below:

    ```
    Set colFiles = objFolder.Files
    ```

9. Use *For Each* to iterate through *colFiles*:

    ```
    For Each objFile In colFiles
    ```

10. Use the *Add* method of the *Dictionary* object to add the file name and the file size to the dictionary. The file name will be the key, and the file size will be the item associated with the key. This is seen below:

    ```
    objDictionary.Add objFile.Name, objFile.Size
    ```

11. Close out the *For Each...Next* loop by using the *Next* statement.

    ```
    Next
    ```

12. Assign *aryKeys* to the *Keys* array of the dictionary that gets created by using the *Keys* method.

    ```
    aryKeys = objDictionary.Keys
    ```

13. Use *For Each* to iterate through the collection of keys:

    ```
    For Each strKey In colKeys
    ```

14. Echo out the file name and the file size:

    ```
    WScript.Echo "The file: " & strKey & " is: " & _
            objDictionary.Item(strKey) & " bytes"
    ```

15. Close out the *For Each...Next* construction by typing **Next**.

16. Add a header to the report of files that are contained in the directory listing. Do this by using the *strFolder* variable, which contains the name of the folder being reported. This line will need to go before the *For Each...Next* construction and is seen below:

    ```
    WScript.Echo "Directory listing of " & strFolder
    ```

17. On the next line, use the Count property of the *Dictionary* object to list the number of files in the folder. This is seen below:

```
WScript.Echo "***there are " & objDictionary.count & " files"
```

18. Save and run your work using Cscript. If it does not run properly, compare your script with \My Documents\Microsoft Press\VBScriptSBS\ch05\OneStepFurther\ Dictionary.vbs.

Chapter 5 Quick Reference

To	Do This
Use a string to populate an array	Use the *Split* function to turn the string into an array
Resize a dynamic array	Use the *ReDim* command
Resize a dynamic array and keep the existing data in it	Use the *ReDim* command with the *Preserve* keyword
Change the way string values are compared in a *Dictionary* object	Change the Compare Mode property of the dictionary object
Create a *Dictionary* object	Use the *createObject* command and specify the scripting.dictionary program ID
Determine how many items are in the dictionary	Use the Count property
Determine if an item exists in the dictionary prior to adding it	Use the *Exists* method
Obtain a collection of keys from the dictionary	Use the *Keys* method

Part II
Basic Windows Administration

In this part:

Chapter 6: Working with the File System 139

Chapter 7: Working with Folders 165

Chapter 8: Using WMI 187

Chapter 9: WMI Continued 207

Chapter 10: Querying WMI 227

Chapter 6
Working with the File System

Before You Begin

To work through the material presented in this chapter, you need to be familiar with the following concepts from earlier chapters:

- Using the *For Each...Next* construction
- Applying *Select Case* constructions
- Adopting constants
- Implementing intrinsic VBScript properties such as *VbTab* and *Now*
- Employing *If...Then...Else*

After completing this chapter, you will be able to:

- Create an instance of the FileSystemObject object
- Obtain a listing of files in a folder
- Create files
- Verify the existence of a file
- Obtain a listing of the properties associated with a file
- Read and write file attributes

Creating the File System Object

To talk to the file system, the script needs to make a connection to it so that it can read files and folders. The tool used with Microsoft Visual Basic, Scripting Edition (VBScript) is called the *file system object*. Once an instance of the file system object is created, you can leverage its power to perform some or all of the following tasks:

- Create files and folders
- Copy files and folders
- Move files and folders
- Delete files and folders
- List properties of files and folders

> **Just the Steps**   To enumerate a list of files
>
> 1. Use *CreateObject* to create the file system object.
> 2. Define the folder to be searched by using *GetFolder*.
> 3. Use the *Files* command to list files.
> 4. Use a *For Each* statement to walk through the folder.

File It Under Files

In your first file system script, ListFiles.vbs, connect to *FileSystemObject*, attach it to a folder defined by the variable *FolderPath*, and then use the *Files* command to enable the *For Each* loop to echo out each file in the folder. This is just the beginning of what can be done with this script. Continue to think of ways to expand this script so that you can perform some really useful network administration tasks.

ListFiles.vbs

```
Option Explicit
On Error Resume Next
Dim FolderPath          'path to the folder to be searched for files
Dim objFSO              'the FileSystemObject
Dim objFolder           'the folder object
Dim colFiles            'collection of files from files method
Dim objFile             'individual file object

FolderPath = "c:\fso"
Set objFSO = CreateObject("Scripting.FileSystemObject")
Set objFolder = objFSO.GetFolder(FolderPath)
Set colFiles = objFolder.Files

For Each objFile in colFiles
  WScript.Echo objFile.Name, objFile.Size & " bytes"
  WScript.Echo VbTab & "created: " & objFile.DateCreated
  WScript.Echo VbTab & "modified: " & objFile.DateLastModified
Next
```

Header Information

In the Header information section of ListFiles.vbs are the normal *Option Explicit* and *On Error Resume Next* commands. These are used to specify the declaration of all variables and to provide rudimentary error suppression. Next, five variables will need to be declared. These variables and the description of their use are listed in Table 6-1.

Table 6-1   Variables used in ListFiles.vbs

Variable name	Use
FolderPath	Defines the folder to be enumerated in the script
objFSO	Creates *FileSystemObject*

Table 6-1   Variables used in ListFiles.vbs

Variable name	Use
objFolder	Holds the connection to the folder whose path is stored in the *FolderPath* variable. The connection is returned by the *GetFolder* method of *FileSystemObject*
colFiles	Holds the collection of files returned by using the *Files* method
objFile	Holds individual files as the script iterates through the collection of files by using the *For Each* construction

For more information about using the Option Explicit *and* On Error Resume Next *commands, see Chapter 1, "Starting from Scratch."*

Reference Information

The Reference information section of the ListFiles.vbs script is similar to other scripts. Assign a value to the *FolderPath* variable created in the Header information section. The *FolderPath* variable is used to make the script easier to modify in the future. By changing the path contained in the *FolderPath* variable, the script can list files on any machine. In addition, *FolderPath* provides a great deal of flexibility.

With just a little work, ListFiles.vbs can be modified to take command-line input or to find the value for *FolderPath* by reading a list of paths from a text file. Perhaps a more intriguing way of obtaining the folder path is to use the *BrowseForFolder* method from the *Shell.Application* object we used in Chapter 1. The graphical tool created by this method is seen in Figure 6-1.

The complete Reference information section follows:

```
FolderPath = "C:\fso"
```

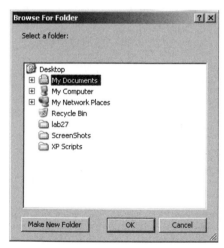

Figure 6-1   Use *BrowseForFolder* to obtain the folder path

Worker and Output Information

The Worker and Output information section of the ListFiles.vbs script first creates the file sytem object and assigns it to the *objFSO* variable. *objFSO* is used to hold the instance of *FileSystemObject* that comes back from the *CreateObject* command. By using the *CreateObject("Scripting.FileSystemObject")* command, you can work with the file system to enumerate all the files in the folder.

The folder from which files are listed is defined by using the *GetFolder* method. The variable *objFolder* is used to hold the copy of the folder object that is created by using the *GetFolder* method of the *FileSystemObject* as seen in the code *objFSO.GetFolder(FolderPath)*. *FolderPath* is the variable that is used to hold the path to the folder whose contents we want to enumerate.

Once connected to the folder, you use the *Files* method to get a list of files contained in the folder. Assign this list of files to the *colFiles* variable by using the following code:

```
Set colFiles = objFolder.Files
```

Next, use a For *Each...Next* loop to walk through the collection of files returned by the File method. The *WScript.Echo* command is used to display the file name and the file size. The complete Worker and Output information is seen below:

```
Set objFSO = CreateObject("Scripting.FileSystemObject")
Set objFolder = objFSO.GetFolder(FolderPath)
Set colFiles = objFolder.Files

For Each objFile in colFiles
  WScript.Echo objFile.Name, objFile.Size & " bytes"
Next
```

Browse for a folder and list file properties

1. Open the \My Documents\Microsoft Press\VBScriptSBS\ch06\ListFiles.vbs script in Microsoft Notepad or your favorite script editor and save it as YourNameBrowseFolder-ListFiles.vbs.

2. Declare a new variable that will be used to hold the output from script. Call it *strOUT*, as seen below:

```
Dim strOUT 'single output variable
```

3. Open CheckForWScript.vbs from the Utilities folder and copy the subroutine to the bottom of your script. The sub looks like the following:

```
Sub subCheckWScript
If UCase(Right(WScript.FullName, 11)) = "CSCRIPT.EXE" Then
  WScript.Echo "This script must be run under WScript."
  WScript.Quit
End If
End Sub
```

4. Open the BrowseFolderSub.vbs script from the Utilities folder and copy the subroutine to the bottom of your script. The sub looks like the following:

```
Sub subGetFolder
Dim objShell, objFolder, objFolderItem, objPath
Const windowHandle = 0
Const folderOnly = 0
const folderAndFiles = &H4000&

Set objShell = CreateObject("Shell.Application")
Set objFolder = objShell.BrowseForFolder(windowHandle, _
   "Select a folder:", folderOnly)
Set objFolderItem = objFolder.Self
objPath = objFolderItem.Path
End Sub
```

5. Call the *subCheckWScript* subroutine, then call the *subGetFolder* subroutine. Place these two calls to the subroutines directly under the variable Declarations in the Header section of the script. This is seen below:

```
subCheckWScript'ensures script is running under WScript
subGetFolder'calls the BrowseForFolder method
```

6. Save your script, but do not run it yet, because it will result in errors.

7. Go back to the *subGetFolder* subroutine and in the line that builds the path, change the *objPath* variable to *FolderPath*. Delete *objPath* from the Declarations section in the subroutine as well. The modified line looks like the following:

```
FolderPath = objFolderItem.Path
```

8. Inside the *For Each...Next* loop in the Worker section of the main script, modify the output so that instead of making a series of WScript.Echo boxes, it will not make any. This will enable you to capture the output into a single variable. This facilitates future modification, by having all the output in a single variable. To do this, set the *strOUT* variable to be equal to itself and the two properties. Add *VbCrLf* at the end of the line to list each file name and size on an individual line. This is seen below:

```
For Each objFile in colFiles
   strOUT = strOUT & objFile.Name & VbTab & objFile.Size _
   & " bytes" & VbCrLf
Next
```

9. After the *For Each...Next* loop, use *WScript.Echo* to print out the *strOUT* variable. This is seen below:

```
WScript.Echo strOUT
```

10. In the Reference section of the script, delete *FolderPath* = "*c:\fso*" because *FolderPath* is assigned its value in the *subGetFolder* subroutine.

11. Save and run the script under *WScript*. It should produce a single output box listing the files and their size. If it does not, compare your script to the \My Documents\Microsoft Press\VBScriptSBS\ch06\BrowseFolderListFiles.vbs script.

Quick Check

Q. **What is required to talk to the file system by using *FileSystemObject*?**

A. You can use *FileSystemObject* by first using the *CreateObject* command, and then assigning to a variable the object that comes back.

Q. **Why do you want an object for *FileSystemObject*?**

A. You want a object for *FileSystemObject* because it enables you to work with files and folders.

File Properties

Name and *Size* are just two file properties that can be obtained by using *FileSystemObject*. A *file property* describes aspects of the file such as when it was created, when it was last accessed, when it was modified, its path, its size, and its type. The intrepid network administrator can enumerate various file properties, which can be used for both security purposes and user data management. For example, as shown in the following code, you can add a couple of lines to the ListFiles.vbs script to retrieve additional data—in this case, the date the file was created and the date it was last modified. The *VbTab* constant is added to make the output easier to read. The completed script is saved as \My Documents\Microsoft Press\VBScriptSBS\ch06\ListFilesExtProperties.vbs. Here are the additional lines:

```
WScript.Echo VbTab & "created: " & objFile.DateCreated
WScript.Echo VbTab & "modified: " & objFile.DateLastModified
```

Additional file object properties can be retrieved in the same manner. All are listed in Table 6-2.

Table 6-2   File properties

Property	Use
Attributes	Bitmask representation of the file attributes such as read-only and hidden.
DateCreated	Date the file was created.
DateLastAccessed	Date the file was last accessed.
DateLastModified	Date the file was last modified.
Drive	The drive letter representing where the file is stored, followed by a colon (for example, C:).
Name	The name of the file, not including the path information (for example, ListFiles.vbs). The name does include the extension.
ParentFolder	The folder in which the file is located (not including subfolders). For example, the parent folder of C:\windows\system32\logfile.txt is Windows.

Table 6-2   File properties

Property	Use
Path	The full path of the file (for example, C:\windows\system32\logfile.txt).
ShortName	8.3 (MS-DOS format) version of the file name. For example, MyLongFileName.txt might become MyLong~1.txt.
ShortPath	8.3 (MS-DOS style) version of the path. For example, C:\MyLongPath \MyLongFileName.txt might become C:\MyLong~1\MyLong~1.txt.
Size	The size of the file in bytes.
Type	The type of file as recorded in the registry. For example, a .doc file is listed as a Microsoft Word document.

File Attributes

File attributes are aspects such as read-only, hidden, system, and archive that are used to configure how a file can be used by the operating system. These are the same attributes you can set via the *attrib.exe* command or the Properties Action menu in Explorer.exe, as seen in Figure 6-2. These attributes are not hidden from ordinary users (they are easily read in Explorer.exe), and they are used to control how backups run and to prevent accidental overwriting of important configuration and system files. This fact makes file attributes of interest to network administrators.

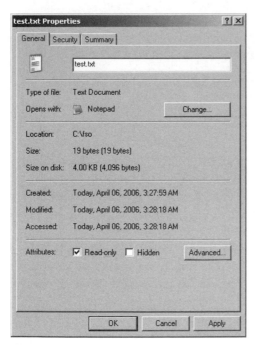

Figure 6-2   File attributes can be read or set via the Attributes property

A file attribute is stored as a bitmask value to conserve space. When you query the file attribute, only a single integer is returned. When a file is hidden, VBScript returns a 2. When a file is a system file, VBScript returns a 4. When, however, a file is both a hidden file and a system file, VBScript return a 6 because the numbers get added together. The numbers are arranged so that each attribute or combination of attributes returns a unique numeric value. There are a number of possible combinations, each of which would need to be tested in a script returning these attributes. The bits representing each attribute value are listed in Table 6-3. A function that inteprets these combinations of integers is FunAttrib.vbs in the Utilities folder on the CD. This function is used in the FileAttributes.vbs script and will be examined shortly.

Table 6-3   File attributes and bitmask values

Attribute	Bitmask value	Meaning
Normal	0	No attributes set
Read-only	1	File can be read but not changed
Hidden	2	File cannot be seen in default view of Microsoft Windows Explorer
System	4	File is used by the operating system (OS)
Archive	32	File changed since last backup
Alias	64	File is a shortcut to another file
Compressed	2048	File has been compressed

Just the Steps   To access file attributes

1. Create an instance of *FileSystemObject*.
2. Use the *GetFile* method to bind to the file.
3. Use the *Attributes* method to return the bitmask value.

Implementing the Attributes Property

In the FileAttributes.vbs script, you first use *CreateObject* to create an instance of *FileSystemObject*. Once the instance is created, you use *GetFile* to provide a reference to a specific file (in this case, C:\fso\test.txt). After you have a reference to the Test.txt file, you echo out the file name and also the attribute number by using the Attributes property in conjunction with the *WScript.Echo* command. Finally, you use a *function* that *AND*'s the different values to build up a string that represents the exact file attributes that are set. When you *AND* two binary numbers, one *AND* one is equal to one. One *AND* zero is equal to zero. Zero *AND* zero is equal to zero. This is a great way to work with bitmask values. By using *AND* we can see if a value is present in a particular location in a bitmask number. This is seen in Figure 6-3.

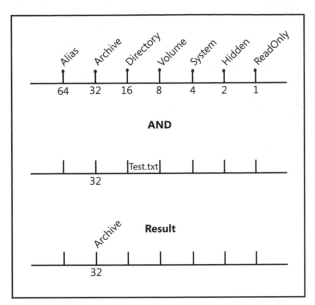

Figure 6-3   Use *AND* to identify file attributes

FileAttributes.vbs

```
Option Explicit
On Error Resume Next
Dim objFSO
Dim objFile
Dim Target

Target = "C:\fso\test.txt"
Set objFSO = CreateObject("Scripting.FileSystemObject")
Set objFile = objFSO.GetFile(Target)

WScript.Echo "The file is: " & target
WScript.Echo "bitmap number is: " & objFile.Attributes & _
    " " & funAttrib(objFile.attributes)


Function funAttrib(intMask)
Dim strAttrib
If IntMask = 0 Then strAttrib = "No attributes"
If intMask And 1 Then strAttrib = strAttrib & "Read Only, "
If intMask And 2 Then strAttrib = strAttrib & "Hidden, "
If intMask And 4 Then strAttrib = strAttrib & "System, "
If intMask And 8 Then strAttrib = strAttrib & "Volume, "
If intMask And 16 Then strAttrib = strAttrib & "Directory, "
If intMask And 32 Then strAttrib = strAttrib & "Archive, "
If intMask And 64 Then strAttrib = strAttrib & "Alias, "
If intMask And 2048 Then strAttrib = strAttrib & "Compressed, "
funAttrib = strAttrib
End Function
```

More Info User defined functions are a great way to write pieces of code that you can copy and paste into other scripts. In the previously mentioned *funAttrib* function, the function translates the value of the file attributes. This is something that VBScript does not know how to do. The function is saved as a file and placed in a directory that makes it easy to find (\My Documents\Microsoft Press\VBScriptSBS\Utilities). The variable *strAttrib* is declared inside the function and is only used within the function. This makes the function self-contained. The result of the *Anding* (stored in the *strAttrib* variable) is assigned to the value of the function name for use within the main body of the script.

Setting File Attributes

You have to assign a numeric value to the Attribute property to set the file attributes for a file. This can be as simple as setting the Attribute property of the file to be equal to an integer value, as seen below:

```
objFile.Attributes = intAttrib
```

In the SetFileAttributes.vbs script, we first create an instance of the file system object and set it equal to the variable *objFSO*, as we have done in other scripts. We next return a file object by using the *GetFile* method from the file system object. Once we have a file object, we query the Attributes property, use the *funAttrib* function to parse the value, and print it out. Next we enter the *subSetAttrib* subroutine, where we assign the desired value for the attribute to the file. Once we have done that, we once again use the *funAttrib* function to translate the new value.

SetFileAttributes.vbs

```
Option Explicit
On Error Resume Next
Dim objFSO       'the file system object
Dim objFile        'the file object
Dim strTarget      'path to target file
Dim intAttrib      'desired file attribute combination

strTarget = "C:\fso\test.txt"
intAttrib = 0
Set objFSO = CreateObject("Scripting.FileSystemObject")
Set objFile = objFSO.GetFile(strTarget)

WScript.Echo "The file is: " & strTarget
WScript.Echo "OLD bitmap number is: " & objFile.Attributes & _
    " " & funAttrib(objFile.attributes) & vbNewLine

subSetAttrib

' *** subs and functions below *****

Function funAttrib(intMask)
Dim strAttrib
If IntMask = 0 Then strAttrib = "No attributes"
```

```
If intMask And 1 Then strAttrib = strAttrib & "Read Only, "
If intMask And 2 Then strAttrib = strAttrib & "Hidden, "
If intMask And 4 Then strAttrib = strAttrib & "System, "
If intMask And 8 Then strAttrib = strAttrib & "Volume, "
If intMask And 16 Then strAttrib = strAttrib & "Directory, "
If intMask And 32 Then strAttrib = strAttrib & "Archive, "
If intMask And 64 Then strAttrib = strAttrib & "Alias, "
If intMask And 2048 Then strAttrib = strAttrib & "Compressed, "
funAttrib = strAttrib
End Function


Sub subSetAttrib
objFile.Attributes = intAttrib
WScript.Echo "The new attibutes are: " & funAttrib(objFile.Attributes)
End Sub
```

Creating Files

There are literally thousands of times when a network administrator needs to create a file. The most common occurrence is when output needs to be captured from a command prompt or from the running of a script. By the time you finish this chapter, you'll have a section of code that you can reuse again and again. Once you know how to create files, you can use this code section instead of the *WScript.Echo* command to direct output to either the command prompt or a dialog box. (Later on, in Chapter 14, "Configuring Networking Components," you'll learn how to automatically invoke Notepad.exe to facilitate reading of the output.) What is involved in creating a file? The following "Just the Steps" section explains the process at a high level.

> **Just the Steps**   To create a file
>
> 1. Use *CreateObject* to create an instance of *FileSystemObject*.
> 2. Use the *CreateTextFile* method.
> 3. Include the full path and the name of the desired file.

As you can see from the preceding steps, the creation of a text file via VBScript is a very easy and straightforward process. In fact, it can be accomplished with just two lines of code, as seen in the listing for CreateTextFile.vbs.

CreateTextFile.vbs
```
Set objFSO = CreateObject("Scripting.FileSystemObject")
Set objFolder = objFSO.CreateTextFile("C:\FSO.txt")
```

Writing to a Text File

Creating text files using VBScript is nice but rather useless unless you can also add information to them. Writing information to a text file gives you a way to save information. In addition, it's a good way to create a log file to track the progress of various automated administrative tasks. You use the *WriteLine* method to write to a text file.

> **Just the Steps**   To write to a text file
>
> 1. Create an instance of *FileSystemObject*.
> 2. Use the appropriate parameter to indicate that you are going to either overwrite the file (*2*) or append data to the file (*8*).
> 3. Use either the *Write*, *WriteLine*, or *WriteBlankLines* method to write to the file.
> 4. Close the text file.

Determining the Best Way to Write to a File

There are actually three different ways you can write to files. These methods are described in Table 6-4.

Table 6-4   Methods used to write to files

Method	Use
Write	Writes to the file without appending the carriage return. (With the carriage return, you might recall, the insertion point is moved to the beginning of the next line.)
WriteLine	Writes to the file and includes a carriage return and a line feed at the end of the line.
WriteBlankLines(n)	Writes blank lines to the file. The placeholder (n) specifies the number of lines to write.

Overwriting a File

You use the constant *ForWriting* in conjunction with the *Write* method to overwrite a file. I use this when I want to track the progress of an operation in a log file. By looking in the file, I can see when the operation last ran, as illustrated in the BasicLog.vbs script. The Header section of this script is left out below for clarity, however BasicLog.vbs does contain this information.

BasicLog.vbs
```
LogFile = "C:\fso\fso.txt"
Const ForWriting = 2
Set objFSO = CreateObject("Scripting.FileSystemObject")
Set objFile = objFSO.OpenTextFile(LogFile, ForWriting)
objFile.WriteLine "beginning process " & Now
objFile.WriteLine "working on process " & Now
objFile.WriteLine "Process completed at " & Now
objFile.Close
```

The script begins by defining the variable *LogFile* and assigning a text file to it. You do this to make it easier to reuse the code and to make it easier to change the file you want to write to.

You then define the constant *ForWriting* and set it equal to 2, which is the number that tells VBScript to overwrite any data found in the text file that might have been previously written to.

> **Tip**   *ForReading, ForWriting, ForAppending* are listed in the VBScript documentation as constants, but they are not intrinisic constants for VBScript. Convention (and readability) dictates using these constant names, but they are always user defined constants.

The variable *objFSO* is then set to be equal to the object returned by the *CreateObject* command that is used to create an instance of *FileSystemObject*. In the next line, the variable *objFile* contains *textStreamObject* that is created when you use the *OpenTextFile* method. All the preceding steps are overhead for the Write operation. Once you have the *ForWriting* handle to the log file, you have completed the Reference information section of the script. You're now ready for the Output information section, which is the section of the script that actually does work. In the Output section, you use the *WriteLine* method.

> Quick Check
>
> **Q.   What are three ways to write to files?**
>
> A.   You can write to files using the *Write*, *WriteLine*, and *WriteBlankLines* methods.
>
> **Q.   If you want to overwrite a file, what do you need to do?**
>
> A.   You need to specify the constant *ForWriting*.

In a logging situation, the dauntless network administrator is looking for two salient pieces of information: what operation completed and when it completed. Armed with this information, a network administrator can judge the success or failure of various procedures. In the BasicLog.vbs script, you can easily glean this information by incorporating the *WriteLine* method inside the *For...Next* loop of any working script. This is exactly the type of thing I do in a lab to estimate how long a certain script will take to complete. If, for instance, a certain Windows Management Instrumentation (WMI) script needs five minutes to complete, you might not want to launch it on 100 servers at the same time because doing so could have an adverse impact on the computing environment.

> ## Using Temporary File Names
>
> One of the problems when logging to a file is the issue of names. Just how many log-file.txt files can you have in the same directory—and what is the most obvious name for a log file? You begin to see the point. Often, we do not really want to perform "actual" logging; rather, we want a better output format. Notepad is almost as powerful a log file reader as it is a script editor. The solution is to use a temporary file name that is randomly created by the file system object. Use the following procedure for doing this.

Creating a temporary file in a temporary directory

1. Create a new script based on the FSOTemplate.vbs script contained in the
   \My Documents\Microsoft Press\VBScriptSBS\Templates directory. Save the new
   script as YourNameCreateTempFileNameAndOpenInNotepad.vbs.

2. Delete the four variables you will not use in this script: *objFolder, strFile, strFolder,*
   and *colFiles.*

3. Delete the line that defines the constants.

4. Declare two new variables: *strPath* and *objShell.*

5. Assign *objShell* to hold the *wshShell* object that comes back from using the *CreateObject* command to create *WScript.shell.* This is seen below:

   ```
   Set objShell = CreateObject("WScript.shell")
   ```

6. Use *strPath* to hold the path that comes back from the *FunTempFile* function. Make
   sure you pass the *objFSO* variable to the function because it contains an instance of
   the file system object (a file system object is required for the *FunTempFile* function
   to work properly). This code is seen below, and must be placed after the *CreateObject* line from step 5.

   ```
   strPath = FunTempFile(objFSO)
   ```

7. Open the FunTempFile.vbs script (\My Documents\Microsoft Press
   \VBScriptSBS\Utilities) in Notepad or your favorite script editor. Copy the function that is defined at the bottom of this script. It looks like the following:

   ```
   Function FunTempFile(objFSO)
   Dim objfolder
   Dim strName

   Const TemporaryFolder = 2

   Set objfolder = objfso.GetSpecialFolder(TemporaryFolder)
       strName = objfso.GetTempName
       strName = objfolder & "\" & strName
       FunTempFile = strName
   End Function
   ```

8. Use the *CreateTextFile* method from the file system object to create the text file that
   is specified in the path statement created by the *FunTempFile* function. You can use
   the *Set objFile* line of code that is remarked out in the file. The only revisions
   required are to change *OpenTextFile* to *CreateTextFile,* and to change *strFile* to *str-
   Path..* This is seen below, and will be placed below the code from the previous step.

   ```
   Set objFile = objFSO.CreateTextFile(strpath)
   ```

9. Use the *Write* method to write to the log file you just created. The code to do this is detailed below:

```
objFile.Write("Writing to a temporary file ") & now
```

10. Use the *Run* command from the *WScript.shell* object to run Notepad and to open the temporary file. Normally you could just use the *Run* method and pass it the name of the text file. The problem is there is no file association between the temporary file name and Notepad, so we need to specifically launch Notepad. This is seen below:

```
objshell.Run("notepad " & strPath)
```

11. Save and run the script. It should produce a Notepad window with a message about a temporary file. If it does not, then compare your results to the \My Documents\Microsoft Press\VBScriptSBS\ch06\CreateTempFileNameAndOpenIn-Notepad.vbs script.

In the DisplayAdminTools_Logged.vbs file, you merge BasicLog.vbs with the Display AdminTools.vbs file from Chapter 1. This script simply checks when the script begins and when it ends. You could add an extra line of code to compute the run time of the script (if you were so inclined). By consulting the log entries, you can estimate how long it will take to obtain the desired information.

DisplayAdminTools_Logged.vbs

```
LogFile = "C:\fso\fso.txt"
Const ForWriting = 2

Set objFSO = CreateObject("Scripting.FileSystemObject")
Set objFile = objFSO.OpenTextFile(LogFile, ForWriting)

Set objshell = CreateObject("Shell.Application")
Set objNS = objshell.namespace(&h2f)
Set colItems = objNS.items

objFile.WriteLine "Process started at " & Now
    For Each objItem In colItems
        WScript.Echo objItem.name
    Next
objFile.WriteLine "Process completed at " & Now
objFile.Close
```

Logging tool names

1. Open the DisplayAdminTools_Logged.vbs script (My Documents\Microsoft Press \VBScriptSBS\ch06) in Notepad or a different script editor. Save the file as YourNameListAdminTools_Logged.vbs.

2. On the first non-commented line of your script, add *Option Explicit*.

```
Option Explicit
```

3. Under *Option Explicit*, add *On Error Resume Next*, but comment it out.

```
'On Error Resume Next
```

4. Declare the seven variables that are used in the DisplayAdminTools_Logged.vbs script. Add comments indicating their use in the DisplayAdminTools_Logged.vbs script. Your list will look like the following:

```
Dim objFSO       'the filesystemobject
Dim objFile      'file object
Dim LogFile      'path to log file
Dim objShell     'shell application object
Dim objNS        'special folder to connect to
Dim colItems     'collection of items in the folder
Dim objItem      'single file in the folder
```

5. Declare two more variables—*strMSG* and *intNS*—that will hold a standard message string and the namespace special folder constant value in hexadecimal from Appendix E. Add comments for these variables as well, as seen below:

```
Dim intNS           'shell special folder constant value
Dim strMSG          'the root message written to log
```

6. In the Reference section of the script, above *LogFile,* assign the string "Enumerating Items: " to the *strMSG* variable, as seen below:

```
strMSG = "Enumerating items: "
```

7. On the next line, assign the value *&h2f* to *intNS*.

```
intNS = &h2f    'hex value of 47 which is admin tools
```

> **Caution**   Make sure you do not enclose *&h2f* with quotation marks, because it would turn this hexadecimal integer into a string and cause your script to fail.

8. Under the *Set objFile = objFSO.OpenTextFile(LogFile, ForWriting)* line, use the *WriteLine* method to write a report header line to the text file. Include the current time stamp, the *intNS* variable, and the *strMSG* variable. The line will look like the following:

```
objFile.WriteLine strMSG & " in folder " & intNS & _
    " Started " & Now
```

9. Delete the old *objFile.WriteLine "Process started at " & Now* line.

10. Instead of just using *WScript.Echo* to list the file names, we want to write to our log file. To do this, you will use the *WriteLine* method. It will go within the *For Each...Next* loop. My line looks like the following:

```
objFile.WriteLine objItem.name
```

11. Edit the *Process Completed* line so that it uses *strMSG*. My line looks like the following:

```
objFile.WriteLine strMSG & "completed " & Now
```

12. Save and run the script. Open your log file, and you should see an output similar to the one in Figure 6-4. If your log does not look similar, compare your script with \My Documents\Microsoft Press\VBScriptSBS\ch06\ListAdminTools_Logged.vbs.

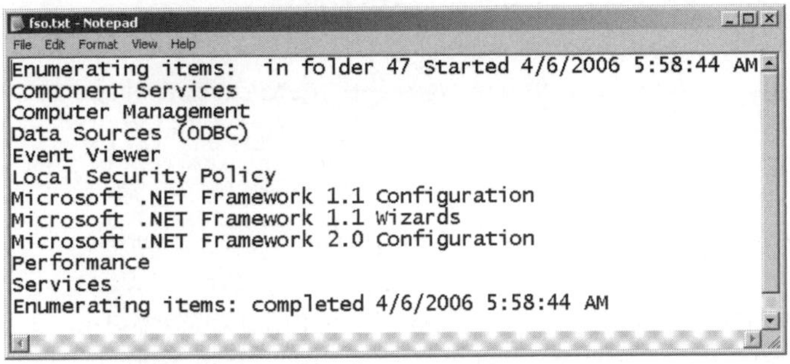

Figure 6-4   Logged output from ListAdminTools_Logged.vbs

Log multiple special folders

1. Open ListAdminTools_Logged.vbs in Notepad or your favorite script editor and save it as YourName_ListMultipleSpecialFolders_logged.vbs.

2. Declare a new variable *aryNS*:

```
Dim aryNS
```

3. In the Reference section of the script, assign some special folders to the array. Make sure you use the *Array* function to turn *aryNS* into a static array.

```
aryNS = array(&ha,&h20,&h6) 'special folder values See Appendix E
```

4. Delete the line containing *intNS* from the Reference section, because we will use this variable to hold an individual namespace from the array.

5. After you have used the *OpenTextFile* method and assigned the file object to *objFile*, use *For Each...Next* to walk through the array. Use *intNS* to hold the individual namespace value, as seen below:

```
For Each intNS In aryNS
```

6. On the line after you write to the log file that the script is completed, close out the *For Each...Next* loop with the word *Next*.

7. Save and run your script. It should run fine. If not, compare it to ListAdminTools_Logged.vbs.

8. Copy the *subOpenLogFile* subroutine from SubOpenLog.vbs in the Utilities folder. Paste it at the bottom of your script.

9. After the final *Next* you entered to close out the *For Each...Next* loop, call your *subOpenLogFile* subroutine.

10. Save and run the script. It should now open the log file for you automatically.

Verifying a File Exists

Although the approach to file management just discussed might seem easy, in many environments, you need to take a more critical approach. In other words, you must first determine whether the file exists, and if it does, you want to append to the file (not overwrite it); if it does not exist, then you want to create it. This ensures that your log file is present on each server running your script.

To check for the existence of a particular file, you use the *FileExists* method of *FileSystemObject*. Although it's true that this method complicates the script a little, it's also true that by checking for and creating a particular file as required, you add an order of magnitude to the flexibility of the script. Without further ado, take a look at the VerifyFileExists.vbs script.

VerifyFileExists.vbs

```
LogFile = "C:\FSO\fso.txt"
Const ForAppending = 8

Set objFSO = CreateObject("Scripting.FileSystemObject")
    If objFSO.FileExists(LogFile) Then
        Set objFile = objFSO.OpenTextFile(LogFile, ForAppending)
        objFile.Write "appending " & Now
    Else
        Set objFile = objFSO.CreateTextFile(LogFile)
            objFile.write "writing to new file " & now
    End If
```

Notice that this script uses code that is very similar to the BasicLog.vbs script presented earlier in this chapter in that you define your *LogFile* and create *FileSystemObject* via the *CreateObject* command. However, that is where the most obvious similarity ends.

In this script, you define two constants, *ForWriting* and *ForAppending*, because you might want to perform one of these operations depending on whether the log file exists. After you create *FileSystemObject*, you move into an *If...Then...Else* loop. Notice the way in which the *FileExists* construct is implemented:

```
If objFSO.FileExists(LogFile) Then
```

To look for the existence of a file, you use the handle to *FileSystemObject* that you obtained and call the *FileExists* method of that object. The only required parameter is the name of the file for which you want to test existence. In this case, it is the file you set equal to the variable called *LogFile*.

If the file does exist, you use the *OpenTextFile* method of *FileSystemObject* and specify *LogFile*, and then add to the file by using the *ForAppending* constant. Remember, when you open a file by using the *OpenTextFile* command, you have to specify whether you are opening it in read-only mode, appending mode, or overwriting mode. After you specify the manner in which you are opening the file, you then use the *Write* command to write a line to the log file. The *Now* function simply writes out the current date and time in a long format.

If the file is not present, you want to create the log file. This is done by using the *CreateTextFile* method of *FileSystemObject*, as shown in the following code:

```
Set objFile = objFSO.CreateTextFile(LogFile)
```

Then you use the *WRITE* command to write out to the file. In reality, you could have specified *ForAppending* and appended to the new file, but by using *ForWriting*, you make it a little easier to know what is actually contained in the file.

> **Tip**   When creating a file, it is not necessary to follow the *CreateTextFile* method with the *OpenTextFile* method because VBScript is smart enough to figure you want to write to the file you just created, and it automatically opens the file for you. If you are not going to be using the file, and depending on the configuration of your script, you may want to use the *Close* method.

Searching ini file for misconfiguration

1. Open the \My Documents\Microsoft Press\VBScriptSBS\Templates\FSOTemplate.vbs script in Notepad or your favorite script editor. Save it as YourNameLookFor3GB.vbs.

2. Delete *objFolder*, *strFolder*, and *colFiles* from the Header section of the script, because they will not be used.

3. Declare a variable to hold the search string. Call it *strSearch*, as seen below:

```
Dim strSearch
```

4. Declare an additional variable to hold the entire text of the TestBoot.ini file. Call it *strText*.

```
Dim strText
```

5. Delete the line of constants from the Reference section of the script.

6. In the Reference section of your script, assign the path to the TestBoot.ini file to the *strFile* variable. You can uncomment the *strFile* line and assign the appropriate path. It will look something like:

```
strFile = "C:\fso\testBoot.ini"
```

7. Assign the value "/3GB" to the *strSearch* variable. It is not critical where you put this, but I put it under the *strFile* line to keep them together. It will look like the following:

```
strSearch = "/3GB"
```

8. Delete the *strFolder* line in the Reference section, because we will not be using it.

9. Uncomment the *Set objFile* line. It will need no modification.

10. Delete the *Set objFolder* and *Set colFiles* lines, because you will not use them.

11. Use the *ReadAll* method from *objFile* and assign the text that comes back to the *strText* variable. It will look like the following:

```
strText = objFile.ReadAll
```

12. Go to the Utilities folder and copy the *funLookup* function from the FunLookup.vbs file. Put it at the bottom of your script. The *funLookup* function takes two input parameters and looks like the code below. No changes are required.

```
Function funLookup(strText,strSearch)
Const blnInsensitive = 1
   If InStr (1,strText, strSearch,blnInsensitive) Then
        funLookup = strSearch & " was found"
   Else
        funLookup = strSearch & " was not found"
   End If
End Function
```

13. Use the *Echo* command to print out the results of the search. Because the *funLookup* function takes two parameters, we will need to supply them when we call the function in the *Echo* command, as seen below. This line of code is placed below the line that uses the *ReadAll* method.

```
WScript.Echo funLookup(strText,strSearch)
```

14. Save and run the script. It should let you know that it found the /3GB switch in the Text-Boot.ini file. If this is not the case, compare your script with the \My Documents\Microsoft Press\VBScriptSBS\ch06\LookFor3GB.vbs script.

Tip   A good way to add functionality to an existing script is to add it within a subroutine. In this way, you have the option to "turn on" or "turn off" the functionality introduced within this set of code. If you mix the new code with the existing code, without keeping it separate, then your new functionality has to be complete the first time you run the script. You risk breaking your script when you do this. In the "Using *SkipLine* to work with malformed ini files" section, we illustrate adding new code in the form of a subroutine.

Using *SkipLine* to work with malformed ini files

1. Open the LookFor3GB.vbs file in Notepad or your script editor of choice and save it as YourNameSkipLineToLookFor3GB.vbs.

2. At the bottom of the script, under the *funLookup* function, add a new subroutine and call it *subLook*. At the same time, end the sub on a separate line. Your code will look like the following:

```
Sub subLook
End sub
```

3. In the subroutine, declare a variable called *strLine*. This variable will hold the results of using the *funLookup* function.

```
Dim strLine
```

4. The beginning of a normal boot.ini file begins with square brackets. Use the existing *strSearch* variable and assign the square bracket to it. This will be your Reference section in this subroutine.

```
strSearch = "["
```

5. Use the *OpenTextFile* method to open *txtFile*. Assign it to the variable *objFile*.

```
Set objFile = objFSO.OpenTextFile(strFile)
```

6. Use *Do Until* to loop through the text file until you get to the end of the text stream. While you are doing this, read a line of text and assign it to the variable *strText*, as seen below:

```
Do Until objFile.AtEndOfStream
strText = objFile.ReadLine
```

7. Use the *funLookup* function to examine the line of text. Pass it two parameters: *strText* and *strSearch*. Hold the results that come back from the function in the variable *strLine*. You code will look like the following:

```
strLine = funLookup(strText,strSearch)
```

8. Use *InStr* to look inside *strLine* for the word *not*. If it finds it, then get the line number and subtract one from that value. Print out a message with the line number by using the Line property. My code to do this looks like the following:

```
If InStr (strLine, "not") Then
   intLine = (objFile.Line -1)
   WScript.Echo intLine & _
   " not at the beginning of the ini"
```

9. If the value is found, then we want to capture the line number and subtract one from it. We will save this number in the variable *intLine*. We then will print out a message that indicates we have found the beginning of the ini file. To do this, we will need to refer to the *intLine* variable outside the subroutine. We need to *DIM* the *intLine* in the Header section of the main script. We will need to close the file and then exit the subroutine.

```
Else
    intLine = (objFile.Line -1)
        WScript.Echo intLine & _
        " is the beginning of the ini"
    objFile.Close
    Exit Sub
```

10. We then need to close out the *Do Until* loop and the *If...Then...Else* statements.

```
End If
    Loop
```

11. Save and run your script. At this point, it should work just like it did before, because we have not yet called the subroutine.

12. Outside of the subroutine, under the line of code where you create the file system object and above the line that uses the *OpenTextFile* method, use *WScript.Echo* to print out a message saying that you are opening the file for a second time. My code looks like the following:

```
WScript.Echo "opening the file a second time ..."
```

13. Delete the *strText = objFile.ReadAll* line. Replace it with a *Do Until...Loop* statement. You will loop until you get to the end of the text stream. This is seen below:

```
Do Until objFile.AtEndOfStream
```

14. Use the Line property of *objFile* and see if the current line is less than the line that was returned by the subroutine you just added to the script. If it is, then we want to use the *SkipLine* method of *objFile* to go to the next line. This is seen in the code below.

```
If objFile.Line < intLine Then
            objFile.SkipLine
```

15. If, however, the Line property of *objFile* is the same as that returned by the subroutine, then you will want to read the line and print out a friendly message. My code to do this looks like the following:

```
ElseIf objFile.Line = intLine Then
            WScript.Echo "The beginning of the ini file is: "_
            & vbNewLine & Space(5)& objFile.readLine
```

16. If the line number is bigger, then you will print out a message saying that the script is over and call the *Quit* method. This is seen below:

```
Else
            WScript.Echo "the script is over"
            WScript.Quit
```

17. Now you will end the *If...Then...Else* statement and the *Do Until...Loop* statement.

```
End If
Loop
```

18. On the line before the one that prints out the message saying that you are reading the file for a second time, call the subroutine by using the word *subLook*.

19. Save and run your script. If your output does not look like the following, then compare it with \My Documents\Microsoft Press\VBScriptSBS\ch06\ SkipLineToLookFor3GB.vbs.

```
1 not at the beginning of the ini
2 not at the beginning of the ini
3 not at the beginning of the ini
4 not at the beginning of the ini
5 not at the beginning of the ini
6 is the beginning of the ini
opening the file a second time ...
The beginning of the ini file is:
   [boot loader]
the script is over
```

Creating Files Step-by-Step Exercises

In this section, you will practice creating files. The result of this practice is essentially a code block that you can employ in other scripts to write information to a file instead of merely echoing it to the screen.

1. Open Notepad or the script editor of your choice. Save a blank file as YourNameStep-ByStep.vbs.

2. Use *Option Explicit* and declare the following variables: *LogFile*, *objFSO*, and *objFile*.

3. Create an assignment for the variable *LogFile* that will hold the name and path of your log file. The code will look like the following:

```
LogFile = "C:\FSO\fso.txt"
```

4. Open Windows Explorer and ensure a folder called FSO and a text file called Fso.txt exist on your C drive.

5. Create a constant called *ForWriting* and set it equal to 2.

6. Use *CreateObject* to create an instance of the *FileSystemObject*. Set it equal to a variable called *objFSO*. Your code will look like the following:

```
Set objFSO = CreateObject("Scripting.FileSystemObject")
```

7. Use the *OpenTextFile* method of *objFSO* to open your log file for writing. Set it equal to a variable called *objFile*. Your code will look like the following:

```
Set objFile = objFSO.OpenTextFile(LogFile, ForWriting)
```

8. Use the *WriteLine* method and the *Now* function to write a line to a text file called Fso.txt that indicates you are beginning your logging. The code will look like the following:

```
objFile.WriteLine "beginning logging " & Now
```

9. Use the *WriteLine* method and the *Now* function to write a line to the text file called Fso.txt that indicates your process is continuing. Your code will look similar to this line:

```
objFile.WriteLine "working on process " & Now
```

10. Use the *WriteLine* method and the *Now* function to indicate the logging is complete. Your code will look like the following:

```
objFile.WriteLine "Logging completed at " & Now
```

11. Use the *Close* command to close out your log file. The code will look like the following:

```
objFile.Close
```

12. Add comments to each of the variables (*LogFile*, *objFSO*, and *objFile*) that were added in step 2 to indicate their use in the script. Here is an example:

```
Dim LogFile 'holds path to the log file
Dim objFSO 'holds connection to the FileSystemObject
Dim objFile 'used by OpenTextFile command to allow writing to file
```

13. Do not delete the folder or the file, because you will use them in the next lab.

One Step Further: Creating a Log File

In this section, you are going to check for the existence of the log file by modifying the script created in the "Creating Files" step-by-step exercise. If the file exists, you will overwrite it. If it does not exist, you will create it.

1. Open Notepad or the script editor of your choice.

2. Use *Option Explicit* and declare the following variables: *LogFile*, *objFSO*, and *objFile*.

3. Create an assignment for the variable *LogFile* that will hold the name and path of your log file. The code will look like the following:

```
LogFile = "C:\FSO\fso.txt"
```

4. Open Windows Explorer and ensure a folder called FSO and a text file called Fso.txt exist on your C drive. (Skip this step if you did this in the step-by-step exercise earlier.)

5. Create a constant called *ForWriting* and set it equal to *2*.

6. Create a constant called *ForAppending* and set it equal to *8*.

7. Use *CreateObject* to create an instance of *FileSystemObject*. Set it equal to a variable called *objFSO*. Your code will look the following:

```
Set objFSO = CreateObject("Scripting.FileSystemObject")
```

8. Use an *If...Then...Else* loop to implement the *FileExists* method of *FileSystemObject*. In this loop, test for the existence of *LogFile*. If the log file exists, append to it a line of text that indicates you appended to it and use the *Now* function so that you know when it ran. Your code will look like the following:

```
If objFSO.FileExists(LogFile) Then
  Set objFile = objFSO.OpenTextFile(LogFile, ForAppending)
  objFile.Write "appending " & Now
Else
```

9. If the file does not exist, use the *CreateTextFile* command to create the log file. Assign the new file to the variable *objFile*. Your code will look like the following:

```
Set objFile = objFSO.CreateTextFile(LogFile)
```

10. Use the *Close* method to close the file you just created. The code will look like the following:

```
objFile.Close
```

11. Use the *OpenTextFile* method to open the *LogFile* variable for writing. Set this equal to *objFile*. The following code illustrates this:

```
Set objFile = objFSO.OpenTextFile(LogFile, ForWriting)
```

12. Use the *Write* method of *objFile* to write to the *LogFile* variable. Use the *Now* function to write the date and time this occurred. Use the following code as an example:

```
objFile.write "writing to new file " & Now
```

13. End the *If* statement. Use *End If* to do this.

14. Close the log file. Use *objFile.Close* for this purpose. Run your script. If you have problems, compare it with \My Documents\Microsoft Press\VBScriptSBS\ch06\OneStepFurther\osfLogIfExistA.vbs in the OneStepFurther folder.

15. Delete lines created in steps 10 and 11.

16. Save and run the script. Notice *you do not* need to close the file before writing–VBScript knows if you created a file to which you want to write. If you have problems when you run this script, then compare it with \My Documents\Microsoft Press\VBScriptSBS\ch06\OneStepFurther\osfLogIfExistB.vbs.

Chapter 6 Quick Reference

To	Do This
Write to a file	Choose either the *Write, WriteLine,* or *WriteBlankLines* methods
Include a carriage return and a line feed when you write to a line	Use the *WriteLine* method
Append to a line when you write to it	Use the *Write* method
Verify the existence of a file prior to writing to it	Use the *FileExists* method
Read file attributes	Use the Attribute property of a *File* object
Obtain a list of all files in a folder	Use the *Files* method once you have connected to a folder
Connect to a folder	Use the *GetFolder* method
Work with a single file from a collection of files	Iterate through the collection of files by using a *For Each...Next* loop

Chapter 7
Working with Folders

Before You Begin

To work through the material presented in this chapter, you need to be familiar with the following concepts from earlier chapters:

- Utilizing the *FileSystemObject*
- Using the *For Each...Next* statement
- Implementing constants
- Applying the *Select Case* statement

After completing this chapter, you will be able to:

- Use the *FileSystemObject* class to create folders
- Use the *FileSystemObject* class to list folders
- Use the *FileSystemObject* class to delete folders
- Use the *FileSystemObject* class to verify the existence of folders

Working with Folders

In your day-to-day life as a network administrator, you must create folders hundreds of times if for no other reason than to hold numerous files. In my life as a consultant, I am constantly creating folders that hold project data for my clients. During the year I wrote this book, I had to create more than two dozen folders to organize the support materials, labs, and scripts so that I could keep track of them and maintain versioning information.

Just the Steps   To create a folder

1. Create a file system object by using *CreateObject*.
2. Use the *CreateFolder* command to create the folder.

Creating the Basic Folder

Creating your basic folder requires only two lines of code. The first line of code creates an instance of the *FileSystemObject* class by using the *CreateObject* method. The second line of code sets the handle returned by *CreateObject* to a variable, which is used to call the *Create-Folder* method. The only parameters required by *CreateFolder* are the path and name of the folder to be created. This process is illustrated in the CreateBasicFolder.vbs script. For simplicity's sake, I am omitting the standard Header section.

CreateBasicFolder.vbs

```
Set objFSO = CreateObject("Scripting.FileSystemObject")
Set objFolder = objFSO.CreateFolder("c:\fso1")
```

Creating Multiple Folders

Suppose you need to create some folders for a number of temporary users. You decide to call the users tempUser1 through tempUser10. It would actually take a while to create these folders for the users, if one had to use the graphical user interface (GUI) tools and perform the operation by hand. However, by making some changes to the CreateBasicFolder.vbs script, you can easily accomplish this task. The revised script, called CreateMultiFolders.vbs, follows.

CreateMultiFolders.vbs

```
Option Explicit
Dim numFolders
Dim folderPath
Dim folderPrefix
Dim objFSO
Dim objFolder
Dim i
Dim objSHell
Dim myDocs

Set objSHell = CreateObject("wscript.shell")
myDocs = objSHell.SpecialFolders("mydocuments")

numFolders = 10
folderPath = myDocs & "\"

folderPrefix = "TempUser"

For i = 1 To numFolders
  Set objFSO = CreateObject("Scripting.FileSystemObject")
  Set objFolder = objFSO.CreateFolder(folderPath & folderPreFix & i)
Next
WScript.Echo(i - 1 & " folders created")
```

Caution   FSO will not create a folder unless its parent folder already exists. Thus, an attempt to create C:\tmp\tmpusers\tmpuser1 will fail unless C:\tmp\tmpusers already exists.

Header Information

The Header information section of CreateMultiFolder.vbs begins with *Option Explicit* to ensure that no variables are misspelled or mistakenly introduced. You then declare six variables that are used in the script. The first variable, *numFolders*, holds the number of folders you want to create. The next variable, *folderPath*, points to the location in which you will create the folders. In this instance, you are going to create 10 folders off the root of the C drive, but these values aren't assigned until the Reference section. The next variable is *folderPrefix*. In this script, you assign a word or a set of characters that Microsoft Visual Basic, Scripting Edition (VBScript) will use to begin the creation of the folders. The beauty of this arrangement is that you can later change the prefix easily. The variable *objFSO* holds the connection to *FileSystemObject*, and *objFolder* holds the handle to the *CreateFolder* command. The last variable declared is *i*, which is used simply as a counter.

As you can see, we did *not* use *On Error Resume Next*. When actually modifying or moving data, it is a good idea to allow errors to cause the script to fail so that data is not harmed if something goes wrong.

Reference Information

The Reference information section of the script assigns values to some of the variables declared in the Header information section. The variable *numFolders* holds the number of folders you want to create. The variable *folderPath* is used by the *CreateFolder* command when it comes time to create the folders. The variable *folderPrefix* is set to *TempUser*, which is the folder prefix you will use for each folder that gets created.

Worker Information

On the first line of the Worker information section, we have a *For...Next* loop. In this section, we use the counter *i* to keep track of how many folders you want to create. The number of folders created is stored in the value *numFolders*. At any given time, you have created *i* number of folders. This counting continues for each number between 1 and *numFolders* (inclusive).

On the second line of the Worker information section of the script, you use the *CreateObject* command to create an instance of the *FileSystemObject*. This exact line was used in all the scripts in Chapter 6, "Working with the File System." In every situation in which you must create an instance of the *FileSystemObject* class, the syntax will be exactly the same: *CreateObject("Scripting.FileSystemObject")*. In most of your scripts, you'll set the handle to *FileSystemObject* equal to *objFSO* (although the variable can be named anything).

The third line of the Worker information section of the CreateMultiFolder.vbs script is used to actually create the folders. Note the syntax of this command:

```
CreateFolder (folderPath)
```

In the script, you concatenate *folderPath* with *folderPrefix* and a counter number. This enables you to reuse the script for a multitude of purposes. In our example, you'll create 10 folders, named TempUser1 through TempUser10. You could just as easily change *folderPrefix* to *ch* and then create folders labeled ch1 through ch10. In a school setting, you might want to change *folderPrefix* to *student*, and thus create folders labeled student1 through student10.

Best Practices   In the CreateMultiFolders.vbs script, we have the *CreateObject* (*"Scripting.FileSystemObject"*) code inside the *For...Next* loop. On my particular laptop, this code executes faster than if it were outside the *For...Next* loop. In the "Discovering the most efficient code" procedure (coming up next), we outline a method to test your machine and see the best place for this code.

If you change the value of *i*, you can create 10,000 or more folders just as easily as you can create 10. As you can see, it is really easy to create folders using the *FileSystemObject* class. It can also shave hours off of lengthy setup procedures. The best thing, however, is that once the script is written and tested, you get repeatable results. Creating folders is done right every single time. The completed Worker section is seen below.

```
For i = 1 To numFolders
  Set objFSO = CreateObject("Scripting.FileSystemObject")
  Set objFolder = objFSO.CreateFolder(folderPath & folderPreFix & i)
Next
```

Output Information

After you create the folders, you want confirmation that the task completed successfully. In this script, you use *WScript.Echo* to let you know that the script completed successfully. The reason you need to use *i – 1* in our count is that the value of *i* gets incremented prior to the *Echo* command. This is shown in the following code:

```
WScript.Echo(i - 1 & " folders created")
```

Quick Check

Q. What is required to create a folder?

A. A connection to *FileSystemObject* is required.

Q. Which method is used to create a folder?

A. The *CreateFolder* method is used to create a folder.

Note   If you ran the CreateMultiFolders.vbs script, you now have 10 temp folders in that folder. In the next procedure, we are going to create 100 temp folders, so you will need to delete the folders created in the previous script. Make sure you are careful not to delete any of your documents while deleting the folders.

Discovering the most efficient code

1. Open \My Documents\Microsoft Press\VBScriptSBS\ch07\CreateMultiFolders.vbs in Microsoft Notepad or your favorite script editor and save the script as YourNameEfficientFolder.vbs.

2. In the Header section of the script, declare three new variables to be used to time the script execution: *startTime, endTime*, and *totalTime*. This is seen here:

```
Dim startTime, endTime, totalTime 'used for timer function
```

3. On the next line, use the *Timer* function to capture the first time stamp for your script. You assign the value from the *Timer* function to the *startTime* variable, as seen here:

```
startTime = Timer
```

4. Change the value of *numFolders* from 10 to 100. This will enable the script to run for a longer period of time and provide you with a better opportunity to monitor the performance of the script.

```
numFolders = 100
```

5. After the *For...Next* loop, assign the *Timer* function to the *endTime* variable to provide an ending time stamp. This will go just before the *WScript.Echo* line at the bottom of your script.

```
endTime = timer
```

6. To figure out how long the script ran, subtract *startTime* from *endTime* and assign the resulting number to *totalTime*, as seen here:

```
totalTime = endTime - startTime
```

7. After your *WScript.Echo* line at the bottom of your script, print out the resulting value. My output line looks like the following:

```
WScript.Echo "It took " & totalTime &" seconds"
```

8. Save and run your script. Remember how long it takes for your script to run.

9. Open up Microsoft Windows Explorer and delete the 100 tempuser folders that were created.

10. Move the create *FileSystemObject* line from inside the *For...Next* loop to the line above the *For...Next* command. This will keep the script from creating 100 different *FileSystemObject* objects. This completed section of code will look like the following:

```
Set objFSO = CreateObject("Scripting.FileSystemObject")
For i = 1 To numFolders
Set objFolder = objFSO.CreateFolder(folderPath & folderPrefix & i)
Next
```

11. Save and run the script. Compare how long it takes to run this time, with how long it took to run earlier.

12. Based upon this test, does it make much difference where the *CreateObject* line is placed? (On my laptop, the script actually runs faster when it creates the file system object 100 times. It seems VBScript is more efficient at creating objects than re-using objects (at least with my laptop). Your results may differ.

13. If your script does not run as expected, then compare your script with the Efficient-Folder.vbs script from the Chapter 7 folder.

Logging test results

1. Open the EfficientFolder.vbs script in Notepad or some other script editor and save the file as YourNameEfficientFolderLogging.vbs.

2. At the very bottom of your script, define a subroutine called *subLogging*. Make sure you also end the subroutine. Your code will look like the following:

```
Sub subLogging
End sub
```

3. Inside the subroutine, you will want to define four variables that will be used for the logging activities. One will be for a *wshShell* object so we can obtain the path to a special folder. Two will be used for the log file, and one will be used to actually create the log file itself. My Header section in the subroutine looks like the following:

```
Dim objShell    'wshShell object
Dim strDir      'directory for log file
Dim strFile     'path to the log file
Dim objFile     'the file object from OpenTextFile method
```

4. To obtain the path for the current desktop, we will use the *wshShell* object. To create this object, we create an instance of *WScript.shell*, as seen below:

```
Set objShell = CreateObject("WScript.shell")
```

5. Use the *strDir* variable to hold the path to the desktop. To obtain this information, we will use the *specialFolders* method from the *WScript.shell* object. This is seen below:

```
strDir = objshell.SpecialFolders("desktop")
```

6. To create the log file, we need to specify the name of the file as well as the path to the file. This is seen in the following code:

```
strFile = strDir & "\myLog.txt"
```

7. In the Reference section of the subroutine, you may want to define some constants. These do not increase functionality; however, they do make the code easier to read. I used the following constants:

```
Const forAppending = 8
Const blnCreate = True 'will create the text file if it does not exist
Const intWindowPos = 4 'use most recent window position
Const blnWait = True 'script will wait until I manually close log file
```

8. The easiest way to create a log file is to use the *OpenTextFile* method of the *FileSystemObject* and specify an optional parameter to create the file if it does not exist. This is a Boolean parameter, which we have assigned to the constant *blnCreate*. Because we are using *tstrFile* for a log file, we will want to append to the file, not overwrite the file. This line of code is seen below:

```
Set objfile = objFSO.OpenTextFile (strFile,ForAppending,blnCreate)
```

9. Once we have opened the text file, it is time to write to the file. You will want to use the *WriteLine* method for your log file, because the entries will be easier to read if they are on separate lines of the file. To do this, I used the following:

```
objFile.WriteLine("Running script" & VbCrLf & Now & " took " & totalTime)
```

10. Having written to the file, it is now time to open the file so it can easily be read. To do this, we need to enclose the path to the file in quotation marks so we can use the *Run* method from *wshShell*. You will need four quotation marks to embed quotation marks inside quotation marks. This strange looking line of code is seen below:

```
strFile = """" & strFile & """"
```

11. Now you can use the *Run* method of the *WScript.shell* object to open the log file. This relies upon the fact there is a file association between txt and Notepad.exe. Use the constant *intWindowPos* to indicate where the program will appear, and the *blnWait* constant to keep the script running until you exit Notepad.

```
objShell.run strFile,intWindowPos,blnWait
```

12. The completed subroutine looks like the following:

```
Sub subLogging 'logs the time the script was run, and how long it took to run
Dim objShell    'wshShell object
Dim strDir            'directory for log file.
Dim strFile           'path to the log file
Dim objFile           'the file object from OpenTextFile method

Set objShell = CreateObject("WScript.shell")
strDir = objShell.SpecialFolders("desktop")
strFile = strDir & "\myLog.txt"
Const forAppending = 8
Const blnCreate = True 'will create the text file if it does not exist
Const intWindowPos = 4 'use most recent window position
Const blnWait = True 'script will wait until I manually close log file.

Set objFile = objFSO.OpenTextFile (strFile,ForAppending,blnCreate)
objFile.WriteLine("Running script" & VbCrLf & Now & " took " & TotalTime)
```

```
strFile = """" & strFile & """"
objShell.run strFile,intWindowPos,blnWait
End sub
```

13. Call the subroutine by placing the name of the subroutine after the line that uses *WScript.Echo* to display the amount of time it takes to run the script. This will look like the following:

```
subLogging
```

14. Save and run the script. It should open up Notepad with a line that indicates how long it took to run the script. If it does not, then compare your script with the EfficientFolderLogging.vbs script from the Chapter 7 folder.

15. Run the script several times while moving the *CreateObject* command in or out of the *For...Next* loop. Remember, you will need to delete the folders prior to each running of the script.

Automatic Cleanup

One nice way to use the script for creating folders is to reuse it and modify it to delete folders. The idea here is that when you use scripts to create folders and then use them to delete folders, you have basically enabled automatic cleanup after your operations are complete.

> **Just the Steps**   To delete a folder
>
> 1. Implement *FileSystemObject* by using *CreateObject*.
> 2. Use the *DeleteFolder* command to delete the folder.

Deleting a Folder

Deleting a folder requires a connection to *FileSystemObject*. Once the connection to *FileSystemObject* is established, you use the *DeleteFolder* method to delete the folder. This is illustrated in the following script, DeleteBasicFolder.vbs. Notice that the big difference between creating a folder and deleting a folder is that the line in which the folder is deleted does not begin with *Set*. Rather than use *Set*, you simply include *objFSO* with the *DeleteFolder* method and then the path to the folder you will delete.

DeleteBasicFolder.vbs
```
Set objFSO = CreateObject("Scripting.FileSystemObject")
objFSO.DeleteFolder("c:\fso")
```

Deleting Multiple Folders

It is just as easy to delete multiple folders as a single folder because the syntax is the same: Make a connection to *FileSystemObject* and then call the *DeleteFolder* method. In the Delete-MultiFolders.vbs script that follows, to make the script clean up after itself, you have to make only three changes to CreateMultiFolders.vbs. Imagine how easy it would be to run Create-MultiFolders.vbs when your school year begins to create individualized student workspace—and then when the school year ends, run DeleteMultiFolders.vbs with three minor modifications to reclaim the storage space used by students during the school year. What are the modifications? There are no modifications in either the Header information or the Reference information section of the script. In the Worker information section of the script, you delete *Set objFolder =* and then change *CreateFolder* to *DeleteFolder*. In the Output information section of the script, you change *folders created* to read *folders deleted*.

DeleteMultiFolders.vbs

```
Option Explicit
Dim numFolders
Dim folderPath
Dim folderPrefix
Dim objFSO
Dim objFolder
Dim i

numFolders = 10
folderPath = "C:\"
folderPrefix = "TempUser"

For i = 1 To numFolders
Set objFSO = CreateObject("Scripting.FileSystemObject")
objFSO.DeleteFolder(folderPath & folderPreFix & i)
Next
WScript.Echo(i - 1 & " folders deleted")
```

Quick Check

Q. **To delete a folder, what two components are required?**

A. You need a connection to *FileSystemObject*, and you need to use the *DeleteFolder* method.

Q. **What is a positive aspect of deleting folders programmatically?**

A. A positive aspect of deleting folders programmatically is that you can do so by easily modifying the script used to create the folders.

Q. **What are two situations in which creating folders and deleting folders programmatically would be useful?**

A. Creating folders programmatically is useful for schools that need to create a lot of student home folders at the beginning of the school year and then delete them at the end of the year. The same technique is useful for companies when they bring in temporary workers.

Automating cleanup

1. Open the \My Documents\Microsoft Press\VBScriptSBS\ch07\EfficientFolderLogging.vbs script and save it as YourNameEfficientFolderLoggingDelete.vbs.

2. Create a new subroutine under the *subLogging* subroutine. Call it *subDelete*. Make sure you close out the subroutine, as seen below:

```
Sub subDelete
End Sub
```

3. Copy everything from the DeleteMultiFolders.vbs script except the *Option Explicit* line. Paste it into the *subDelete* subroutine, as seen below:

```
Sub subDelete
Dim numFolders
Dim folderPath
Dim folderPrefix
Dim objFSO
Dim objFolder
Dim i

numFolders = 10
folderPath = "C:\"
folderPrefix = "TempUser"

For i = 1 To numFolders
Set objFSO = CreateObject("Scripting.FileSystemObject")
objFSO.DeleteFolder(folderPath & folderPreFix & i)
Next

WScript.Echo(i - 1 & " folders deleted")
End Sub
```

4. Change the *numFolders* variable from 10 to 100.

```
numFolders = 100
```

5. Call the *subDelete* subroutine from the last line of the *subLogging* subroutine.

6. Save and run your script. If it does not work, then compare it to the EfficientFolderLoggingDelete.vbs script.

Binding to Folders

To gain information about the properties or attributes of a folder, you must first bind to the folder. Because the file system object represents folders as Component Object Model (COM) objects, you must create a reference to them prior to connecting to them—that is, you must *bind* to them. You already know that to create or delete a folder, you have to create an instance of *FileSystemObject*. After you do that, you use the *GetFolder* method to connect to the folder.

Just the Steps   To bind to a folder

1. Implement the *FileSystemObject* by using *CreateObject*.
2. Specify the path to the folder.
3. Use *Set keyword* to assign the path to a variable.

In the following script, you implement *FileSystemObject* by using *CreateObject*. Next, you use the *GetFolder* method to bind to the folder called fso found in the C drive.

BindFolder.vbs

```
Set objFSO = CreateObject("Scripting.filesystemobject")
Set objFolder = objFSO.getfolder("c:\fso")
WScript.Echo("folder is bound")
```

Does the Folder Exist?

Binding to a folder in and of itself is rather boring, but what if the folder does not exist? If you try to bind to a folder that does not exist, the script generates an error message, and your script might fail. The "path not found" error can be prevented from occurring by using the *FolderExists* method. In the CreateBasicFolder_checkFirst.vbs script, you check for the existence of a folder prior to creating a new one.

By incorporating the *FolderExists* method into the CreateBasicFolder vbs script to create new folders, you gain the ability to delete the existing folder prior to creating a new one. One situation in which this ability would be useful would be when creating a folder for logging onto a workstation. If a previous logging folder were found, that folder could be deleted to make room for a new folder. If you don't want to delete the folder, if that folder exists, you simply omit the *DeleteFolder* command from the script and modify the message displayed to the user. In other situations, the mere presence of a folder is all you need. If you create a folder called RasErrors, when a user fails to make a remote connnection to the network, then the presence of this folder could indicate that the user had a problem connecting remotely.

CreateBasicFolder_checkFirst.vbs

```
Set objFSO = CreateObject("Scripting.FileSystemObject")
If objFSO.FolderExists ("C:\fso1") Then
  WScript.Echo("folder exists and will be deleted")
  objFSO.DeleteFolder ("C:\fso1")
  WScript.Echo("clean folder created")
  Set objFolder = objFSO.CreateFolder("C:\fso1")
Else
  WScript.Echo("folder does not exist and will be created")
  Set objFolder = objFSO.CreateFolder("C:\fso1")
End if
```

Copying Folders

Copying folders is a fundamental task in network administration. It is important for backups and for ease of management. Often the suave network administrator consolidates files and folders prior to backing them up. This allows for both a more accurate backup, and in many instances a quicker backup. In many organizations, the so-called backup window is nearly closed, and getting everything backed up during the time allotted is a constant struggle. Consolidating folders can help with that problem.

You use the *CopyFolder* method of *FileSystemObject* to copy folders. It is important to realize that this method also copies subfolders (even empty ones). The syntax of the *CopyFolder* method follows.

Command	Required	Required	Optional
CopyFolder	Source folder	Destination folder	*overwrite*

Tip   Both the source folder and the destination folder can be specified as either a local path or a Universal Naming Convention (UNC) path. The *overwrite* parameter is optional and will overwrite the destination folder if it is set to *True*.

In the following script, you copy a folder called fso that resides on the C drive to a folder called fso1 on the C drive. It is important to note that the folder does not need to exist in order for the copy process to succeed.

CopyFolder.vbs

```
Set objFSO = CreateObject ("scripting.fileSystemObject")
objFSO.CopyFolder "c:\fso","C:\Myfso"
```

You can make the script a little easier to use by creating variables to hold both the source and the destination folders. In the next script, CopyFolderExtended.vbs, you do exactly that. In ,addition, you create a constant called *overwriteFiles* that you set to *True*. Note that in this next script, the destination folder, called *dFolder*, is located on a network share. The CopyFolderExtended.vbs script could be used by a network administrator to copy user data from the local machine to a network drive for consolidated backup. One negative aspect of the *CopyFolder* command is that it does not indicate that it is working or that it is done. To give yourself a little bit more information, you use the *Now* command and *WScript.Echo* to indicate when the command begins. In addition, after the copy operation is complete, you display another message that the copy ended and the time.

Caution   Depending on how much data you have stored in your Documents and Settings folder, the CopyFolderExtended.vbs script could result in a significant amount of data being copied. Make sure you have sufficient disk space available prior to running the script below, or choose a different folder.

CopyFolderExtended.vbs

```
Const OverWriteFiles = True
startTime = Timer
WScript.Echo " beginning copy ..."
strSource = "c:\Documents and Settings"
strDestination = "\\London\fileBU"

Set objFSO = CreateObject ("scripting.fileSystemObject")
objFSO.CopyFolder strSource, strDestination , OverWriteFiles
endTime = Timer
WScript.Echo "ending copy. It took: " & _
   Round(endtime-startTime) & " seconds to copy"
```

> **Tip**   In the CopyFolderExtended.vbs script, the parentheses were left out when we called the *CopyFolder* method. This is because parentheses are optional when supplying arguments to methods. If you add them in, the script will still work.

Listing folder sizes

1. Open \My Documents\Microsoft Press\VBScriptSBS\Templates\FSOTemplate.vbs in Notepad or some other script editor. Save your file as YourNameListFolderSizes.vbs.

2. Delete two *Dim* statements that will not be used: *strFile* and *colFiles*.

3. Add two new variables: *colFolders* and *strHeader*. The completed Header section of the script looks like the following:

```
Option Explicit
'On Error Resume Next
Dim objFSO      'the fileSystemObject
Dim objFolder   'folder object
Dim strFolder   'individual folder form collection
Dim colFolders  'collection of subFolders
Dim strHeader   'header used for reporting
```

4. In the Reference section of the script, add a constant called *noDecimal* and set it to 0. It will be used in the *formatNumber* function. This is seen below:

```
Const noDecimal = 0
```

5. Assign a folder location to the *strFolder* variable. Use the line that is commented out in the template to save typing. Mine looks like the following:

```
strFolder = "c:\windows"
```

6. Delete the *Const forReading = 1, forWriting = 2, forAppending = 8* line.

7. Delete the three lines in the template that are for use with files. These are listed below:

```
'strFile = "c:\fso\fso.txt"
'Set objFile = objFSO.OpentextFile(strFile)
'Set colFiles = objFolder.files
```

8. Remove the comment from the *Set objFolder = objFSO.GetFolder(strFolder)* line.

9. Assign the path property and the size property of the folder object to the *strHeader* variable. Use *vbTab* to provide spacing between the two properties. Use the *formatNumber* function to add commas to the number and to remove all trailing decimal positions. My code to do this looks like the following:

```
strHeader = objFolder.Path & vbTab & formatNumber(objFolder.size,noDecimal)
```

10. Open the FunLine2.vbs script from the \My Documents\Microsoft Press\VBScriptSBS \Utilities folder and copy the *funLine* function from that file. Paste it at the bottom of your script. The *funLine* function looks like the following:

```
Function funLine(strIn)
funLine = Len(strIN)+1
funLine = strIN & VbCrLf & String(funLine,"=")
End Function
```

11. Use the *funLine* function to underline *strHeader* when you print it out using *WScript.Echo*. The code to do this looks like the following:

```
WScript.Echo funLine(strHeader)
```

12. Create a collection of subfolders and assign it to the *colFolders* variable. This is seen here:

```
Set colFolders = objFolder.SubFolders
```

13. Use *For...Each...Next* to walk through the collection of subfolders. Use *strFolder* as the counter variable. Print out the path and the formatted size of each folder. The code to do this looks like the following:

```
For Each strFolder In colFolders
    WScript.Echo strFolder.path, formatNumber(strFolder.size,noDecimal)
Next
```

14. Save and run your script. You should see a printout of a folder and subfolders. If your code does not perform as expected, compare your script with \My Documents\Microsoft Press\VBScriptSBS\ch07\ListFolderSizes.vbs.

Moving Folders

Copying folders is a very safe operation because nothing happens to the original data. Copy operations are often used to present a consolidated view of data (such as copying log files) or to create redundant data for backup purposes (as in the case of VBScript book manuscripts). Moving folders, on the other hand, can be done to free up disk space, or can be done simply because two copies of the data are neither required nor desired. If a copy operation fails halfway through, you simply end up with an extra copy of half your data. If, on the other hand, a move operation fails halfway through, to have even one complete set of information, you have to go to the destination machine and move your data back. Because of this, with important data, I always copy, verify, and then delete. For files I am not concerned about, I perform a move.

To perform a move operation, use the *MoveFolder* method of *FileSystemObject*. The next script you look at, MoveFolder.vbs, illustrates the *MoveFolder* method. Unlike the *CopyFolder* method, *MoveFolder* has only two parameters: the source and the destination. The *overwrite* parameter, which enables overwriting an existing folder during a move operation, is not implemented. It's common to move folders between drives, but you can also use the *MoveFolder* method to move folders on the same drive, and in effect, you get the ability to rename a folder. This is required, as there is no rename folder method in the *FileSystemObject*. In MoveFolder.vbs, you do exactly that. You begin with a source folder called c:\fso, and the destination folder is c:\fso2.

MoveFolder.vbs

```
Set objFSO = CreateObject ("scripting.fileSystemObject")
objFSO.MoveFolder "c:\fso","c:\fso2"
```

> **Important**   If you run the MoveFolder.vbs script, your c:\fso folder becomes c:\fso2. It is important to rename the c:\fso2 folder back to C:\fso because the following procedure relies upon it being set to c:\fso.

Walking through the directory

1. Open \My Documents\Microsoft Press\VBScriptSBS\Templates\BlankTemplate.vbs. Save your script as YourNameRecursiveListOfFolders.vbs.

2. On the first line of your script that is not commented, add the words *Option Explicit*.

3. Declare two variables: *strTarget* and *objFSO*. The script to this point should look like the following:

    ```
    Option Explicit
    'On Error Resume Next
    Dim strTarget   'the place to begin recursive folder listing
    Dim objFSO             'the file system object
    ```

4. In the Reference section of the script, use *strTarget* to point to a subfolder that does not exist. I used the following folder:

    ```
    strTarget = "c:\fso\mred"
    ```

5. On the next line, create an instance of the *FileSystemObject* and assign it to the *objFSO* variable. It will look like the following:

    ```
    Set objFSO = CreateObject("Scripting.FileSystemObject")
    ```

6. Go to the bottom of your script and create a subroutine called *subCheck*. Make sure you go ahead and close it out as well by using *End sub*.

    ```
    Sub subCheck
    End sub
    ```

7. Inside the subroutine, declare some variables that will be used for a *msgBox* function. I used *strTitle*, *strPrompt*, and *errRTN*. These properties are illustrated in Figure 7-1.

```
Dim strPrompt    'msgBox prompt
Dim strTitle     'title of msgBox
Dim errRTN       'return code from the msgBox function
```

Figure 7-1   Message box title, prompt, and button

8. Build up a string to use for the prompt portion of the *msgBox* function. Include the name of the directory and the fact it does not exist, and ask if the user wants to create the folder. Capture the return from the function in the *errRTN* variable. My code to do this looks like the following:

```
strPrompt = strTarget & " Does not exist." &_
        vbNewLine & "Would you like to Create it?"
```

9. Build up a string to use for the title of the message box. Include the name of the folder and identify that it does not exist.

```
strTitle = strTarget & " not found!"
```

10. If the folder exists, then we want to call the *subRecursiveFolders* subroutine. When we do this, we want to pass the *Folder* object from *GetFolder*. The code to do this is seen below:

```
If objFSO.FolderExists(strTarget) Then
        subRecursiveFolders objFSO.GetFolder(strTarget)
```

11. If the folder does not exist, then we want to display a message box and ask if the user wants to create the missing folder. Use the *strPrompt* variable and the *strTitle* variable for the prompt and the title of the message box. Use the intrinsic button constant *vbYesNo* to display yes and no buttons. Add to this constant the *vbQuestion* constant to cause the message box to display a question mark. Capture the return code in the *errRTN* variable. The code to do this is seen below:

```
errRTN = msgBox(strPrompt,vbYesNo+vbQuestion,strTitle)
```

12. If the *errRTN* code is equal to *vbYes*, then we will create the folder. If not, we do not do anything. This code is seen below:

```
If errRTN = vbYes Then
   objFSO.CreateFolder(strTarget)
End If
```

13. Close out the folder exists *If...Then* loop by using *End If*.

> **Warning**   The coding will actually look a little strange at the end of the *subCheck* sub-routine. You will have *End If*, a new line, *End If*, a new line, and *End sub*. Tab your code over to make it easy to read. Leaving out any of these statements will result in errors.

14. At the bottom of your script, begin a new subroutine called *subRecursiveFolders*. You will pass a value to this subroutine called *folder*. Inside the subroutine, anything that is passed as a parameter to the subroutine will be known as a folder inside the subroutine. Make sure you close out the subroutine. The code to do this looks like the following:

```
Sub subRecursiveFolders(Folder)
End sub
```

15. Dim a variable inside the subroutine called *objFolder*. This variable will be used to hold an individual folder object when iterating through the collection of subfolders. The code to do this looks like the following:

```
Dim objFolder
```

16. Use the *subFolders* method to obtain a collection of subfolders. Use *For...Each...Next* to walk through this collection. Call each individual folder in the collection *objFolder*, as seen below:

```
For Each objFolder In Folder.subFolders
```

17. Print out the path to each folder in the collection and then call the *subRecursiveFolders* subroutine while passing *objFolder* as a parameter. The code to do this looks like the following:

```
  WScript.Echo objFolder.Path
    subRecursiveFolders objFolder
 Next
```

18. Call the *subCheck* subroutine by placing the name of the subroutine on the line after the *FileSystemObject* is created. This is seen below:

```
subCheck
```

19. Save and run the script. It should either produce a listing of folders or offer to create a nonexistent folder. If it does not, then compare your script with the \My Documents\Microsoft Press\VBScriptSBS\ch07\RecursiveListOfFolders.vbs script.

Creating Folders Step-by-Step Exercises

In this section, you are going to practice creating folders. The result of this practice will be a script that can be used for creating multiple folders for a variety of occasions.

1. Open \My Documents\Microsoft Press\VBScriptSBS\Templates\BlankTemplate.vbs in Notepad or some other script editor and save the file as yourNamesbsCreateFolders.vbs.

2. At the top of the script, set *Option Explicit*.

3. Declare variables for the following: *numFolders, folderPath, folderPrefix, objFSO, objFolder, i, objShell,* and *strDocPath*. The Header section of your script will look like the following:

   ```
   Option Explicit
   Dim numFolders
   Dim folderPath
   Dim folderPrefix
   Dim objFSO
   Dim objFolder
   Dim i
   Dim objShell
   Dim strDocPath
   ```

4. Create an instance of the *wshShell* object. Use the variable *objShell* to hold the object that is returned. This line will look like the code below:

   ```
   Set objShell = CreateObject("WScript.Shell")
   ```

5. Use the *strDocPath* variable to hold the path that is obtained by using the *SpecialFolders* property of the *wshShell* object. This is seen below:

   ```
   strDocPath = objShell.SpecialFolders("mydocuments")
   ```

6. Assign a value of 10 to the variable *numFolders*.

7. Use the *folderPath* variable to hold *strDocPath* concatenated with a backslash. This is seen below:

   ```
   folderPath = strDocPath & "\"
   ```

8. Assign *folderPrefix* to be equal to "Student". (The quotation marks are required.) The Reference section of the script will look like the following:

   ```
   Set objShell = CreateObject("WScript.Shell")
   strDocPath = objShell.SpecialFolders("mydocuments")

   numFolders = 10
   folderPath = strDocPath & "\"
   folderPrefix = "Student"
   ```

9. Begin a *For...Next* loop that counts from 1 to *numFolders*. Use *i* for the counter variable, as seen below:

   ```
   For i = 1 To numFolders
   ```

10. Create an instance of the *FileSystemObject* and use the variable *objFSO* to hold the object. The code will look like the following:

```
Set objFSO = CreateObject("Scripting.FileSystemObject")
```

11. Use the *FolderExists* method to check for the existence of the folder prior to creating it. If the folder exists, echo out the path and state that it is not created. The code for this will look like the following:

```
If objFSO.FolderExists(folderPath & folderPrefix & i) Then
  WScript.Echo(folderPath & folderPrefix & i & " exists." _
    & " folder not created")
```

12. If the folder does not exist, you will need to create it. To do this, build the path and the prefix. Then increment the *i* counter. The code will look like the following:

```
Else
    Set objFolder = objFSO.CreateFolder(folderPath & folderPreFix & i)
```

13. Echo out the folder path, prefix, and counter. Then state that the folder was created. The code will look like the following:

```
WScript.Echo(folderPath & folderPrefix & i & " folder created")
```

14. Use *End If* to close out the *If...Then* section.

15. Use *Next* to close out the *For...Next* loop.

The completed code follows:

```
Option Explicit
Dim numFolders
Dim folderPath
Dim folderPrefix
Dim objFSO
Dim objFolder
Dim i
Dim objShell
Dim strDocPath

Set objShell = CreateObject("WScript.Shell")
strDocPath = objShell.SpecialFolders("mydocuments")

numFolders = 10
folderPath = strDocPath & "\"
folderPrefix = "Student"

For i = 1 To numFolders
  Set objFSO = CreateObject("Scripting.FileSystemObject")
  If objFSO.FolderExists(folderPath & folderPrefix & i) Then
    WScript.Echo(folderPath & folderPrefix & i & " exists." _
      & " folder not created")
  Else
    Set objFolder = objFSO.CreateFolder(folderPath & folderPreFix & i)
    WScript.Echo(folderPath & folderPrefix & i & " folder created")
  End If
Next
```

One Step Further: Deleting Folders

In this section, you are going to delete the folders created in the previous step-by-step exercise.

1. Open Notepad or your script editor of choice.

2. Open the \My Documents\Microsoft Press\VBScriptSBS\ch07\OneStepFur-ther\sbsCreateFolders.vbs script and save it as YourNamesbsDeleteFolders.vbs.

3. In the Worker section of the script, inside the *If objFSO.FolderExists* statement, locate the line that says that the folder exists and is not to be created. Delete the portion that says *"folder not created"*. The revised line looks like the following (make sure you remove the line continuation from the end of the revised line):

    ```
    WScript.Echo(folderPath & folderPrefix & i & " exists.")
    ```

4. Use the *DeleteFolder* method from the *fileSystemObject* to delete the *folderPath & folderPrefix & i* folder.

    ```
    objFSO.DeleteFolder(folderPath & folderPrefix & i)
    ```

5. Use *WScript.Echo* to print out that (*folderPath & folderPrefix & i*) was deleted. The code will look like the following:

    ```
    WScript.Echo(folderPath & folderPrefix & i & " was deleted")
    ```

6. In the *Else* portion of the *If* folder exists *Then* ... statement, delete the line that creates the folder. It will look like the following:

    ```
    Set objFolder = objFSO.CreateFolder(folderPath & folderPreFix & i)
    ```

7. Also in the *Else* portion of the *If* folder exists *Then* ... statement, change the line to read that the folder does not exist, rather than saying it was created. The revised line looks like the following:

    ```
    WScript.Echo(folderPath & folderPrefix & i & " folder does not exist")
    ```

Chapter 7 Quick Reference

To	Do This
Prevent errors when creating or deleting folders	Use the *folderExists* method inside of an *If...Then...Else* construction
Bind to a folder	Use the *GetFolder* method
Provide access to the properties of a folder	Bind to the folder using *GetFolder*
Create a folder object	Use the *CreateFolder* method
Delete a folder	Use the *DeleteFolder* method
Obtain a collection of folders	Use the *subFolders* method
Copy a folder	Use the *CopyFolder* method
Move a folder	Use the *MoveFolder* method
Rename a folder	Move the folder to the same location while specifying a new name (use the *MoveFolder* method)

Chapter 8
Using WMI

Before You Begin

To work through the material presented in this chapter, you need to be familiar with the following concepts from earlier chapters:

- Implementing a dictionary
- Implementing the *For...Next* statement
- Implementing the *Select Case* construction

After completing this chapter, you will be able to:

- Connect to the WMI provider
- Navigate the WMI namespace
- Run queries to retrieve information from WMI
- Send the output of a WMI query to a dictionary

Leveraging WMI

The discussion in the first few chapters of this book focused on what you can do with Microsoft Visual Basic, Scripting Edition (VBScript). From a network management perspective, many useful tasks can be accomplished using just VBScript, but to truly begin to unleash the power of scripting, you need to bring in additional tools. This is where Windows Management Instrumentation (WMI) comes into play. WMI was designed to provide access to many powerful ways of managing Microsoft Windows systems. In Windows Server 2003, WMI was expanded to include management of many aspects of server operations, including both configuration and reporting capabilities of nearly every facet of the server. Some of the tasks you can perform with WMI are:

- Report on drive configuration
- Report on available memory, both physical and virtual
- Back up the event log
- Modify the registry
- Schedule tasks
- Share folders

- Switch from a static to a dynamic Internet Protocol (IP) address

Understanding the WMI Model

WMI provides access to information about the managed objects that make up your computer systems. To service information requests, WMI uses a *hierarchical namespace*, in which the layers build upon one another like the folder structure on your hard disk drive. These namespaces are used to organize the objects. For example, there is a RSOP namespace that is used to provide access to Resultant Set of Policy information, and there is a MicrosoftDNS namespace that allows you to work with Domain Name System (DNS). Although it is true that WMI is a hierarchical namespace, the term doesn't really convey the richness of WMI. The WMI model has three sections that you need to be aware of: resources, infrastructure, and consumers (see Figure 8-1). The use of these components is listed below.

- **WMI resources**   Resources include anything that can be accessed by using WMI—the file system, networked components, event logs, files, folders, disks, Microsoft Active Directory directory service, and so on.

- **WMI infrastructure**   The infrastructure comprises three parts: the WMI service, the WMI repository, and the WMI providers. Of these parts, WMI providers are most important to network administrators because they provide the means for WMI to gather needed information. If the provider does not exist, then none of the classes will exist. (This is common on Windows Server 2003, because the MSI Provider is not installed by default. This means the *WIN32_Product* class is not available, because it relies upon the MSI Provider.)

- **WMI consumers**   A consumer "consumes" the data from WMI. A consumer can be a script written in VBScript, an enterprise management software package, or some other tool or utility that executes WMI queries.

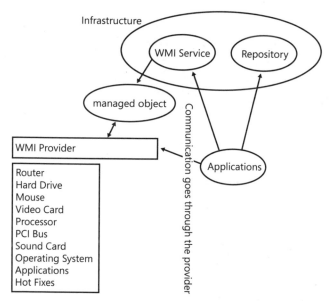

Figure 8-1   Components that make WMI work

Working with Objects and Namespaces

Let's go back to the idea of a namespace introduced earlier in this chapter. You can think of a *namespace* as a way to organize or collect data related to similar items. Visualize an old-fashioned filing cabinet. Each drawer can represent a particular namespace. Inside this drawer are hanging folders that collect information related to a subset of what the drawer holds. For example, at home in my filing cabinet, I have a drawer reserved for information related to my woodworking tools. Inside this particular drawer are hanging folders with information about my table saw, my planer, my joiner, my dust collector, and so on. In the folder for the table saw is information about the motor, the blades, and the various accessories I purchased for the saw (such as an over-arm blade guard).

The WMI namespace is organized in a similar fashion. The namespaces are the file cabinets. The providers are drawers in the file cabinet. The WMI classes are the folders in the drawers of the file cabinet. The namespaces on a Windows XP computer are seen in Figure 8-2.

Figure 8-2   WMI namespaces on Windows XP

Namespaces contain objects, and these objects contain properties you can manipulate. Let's use a WMI script, ListWMINamespaces.vbs, to illustrate just how the WMI namespace is organized.

ListWMINamespaces.vbs

```
strComputer = "."

Set objSwbemServices = GetObject("winmgmts:\\" & strComputer & "\root")
Set colNameSpaces = objSwbemServices.InstancesOf("__NAMESPACE")
```

```
For Each objNameSpace In colNameSpaces
    WScript.Echo objNameSpace.Name
Next
```

On a Windows Server 2003 Server, the results would look like the following when running ListWMINamespaces.vbs from CScript:

```
SECURITY
perfmon
RSOP
Cli
MSCluster
WMI
CIMV2
MicrosoftActiveDirectory
Policy
MicrosoftDNS
MicrosoftNLB
Microsoft
DEFAULT
directory
subscription
```

So what does all this mean, you ask? It means that on a Windows Server 2003 server there are more than a dozen different namespaces from which you could pull information about the server. Understanding that the different namespaces exist is the first step to being able to navigate in WMI to find the information you need. Often, students and people new to VBScript work on a WMI script to make the script perform a certain action, which is a great way to learn scripting. However, what they often do not know is which namespace they need to connect to so that they can accomplish their task. When I tell them which namespace to work with, they sometimes reply, "It is fine for you to tell me this, but how do I know that the such and such namespace even exists?" By using the ListWMINamespaces.vbs script, you can easily generate a list of namespaces installed on a particular machine, and armed with that information, search on Microsoft Developer Network (MSDN) to see what information it is able to provide.

Let's discuss the preceding script, ListWMINamespaces.vbs, because it's similar to many other WMI scripts. The first line sets the variable *strComputer* equal to ".". With this construction (period in quotation marks), the script will operate on this computer only. The dot allows the script to run locally on many computers without you needing to define or change the name included in the script.

The next line of the script is used to define the variable *objSWbemServices* and set it equal to the handle that is returned by using the *GetObject* method to connect to *winmgmts* and access the root namespace on the local computer. (The connection string in WMI is sometimes referred to as a *moniker*. The word *moniker* comes from old Irish and simply means nickname, or familiar name.) We will discuss the WMI moniker in much more detail in Chapter 9, "WMI Continued." These first two lines of the script can be reused time and again in many WMI scripts. In the third line of the script, you use the *Set* command to assign *colNameSpaces* to be equal to a collection represented by the instances of the command that query for the presence of the word __*Namespace*. The Worker information section of the script simply uses a *For Each...Next* loop to iterate through the collection of namespaces returned by the query and to echo them out to the screen.

> **Tip**   Although in the ListWMINamespaces.vbs script I used all lowercase in code for the *winmgmts* name, there really is no requirement for name case with this particular moniker, and in the Microsoft Platform SDK, you will find nearly every possible combination: *winmgmts*, *WinMgmts*, *WINMGMTS*, and I bet even *winMgmts*.
>
> Keep in mind, however, that name case *does* matter with some monikers such as *"WinNT:"*, which is used with Active Directory Service Interfaces (ADSI).

Digging Deeper

Knowing the default namespaces gives some information, and though it's helpful, to better map out the WMI namespace, you'll want information about the child namespaces as well. You'll need to implement a recursive query so that you can gain access to the child namespace data. The next script, RecursiveListWMINamespaces.vbs, is similar to ListWMI Namespaces.vbs, except that it uses a subroutine that calls itself to list the child namespaces. On some computers, this script might seem to perform a little slowly during the first running, so I included a *WScript.Echo (Now)* command at the beginning and at the end of the script. This enables the network administrator to determine how long the script takes to run.

As with the previous script, RecursiveListWMINamespaces.vbs uses *strNamespace* with a "." to indicate the script is run against the local computer. It then calls the subroutine named *EnumNamespaces* and starts with the "root" namespace.

> ## Subroutines
> Basically, a *subroutine* is a section of a script that you can get to from anywhere inside the script. All we need to do is call the subroutine by name to jump to a particular part of the script. You use a subroutine in this script rather than code that is sequential because you need to execute the commands that make up the subroutine as a group. When you are finished, you exit out. You can easily identify a subroutine because it begins with the word *Sub* followed by the name of the subroutine, and it ends with the *End sub* command. When you exit a subroutine (via the *End sub* command), you go back to the line after the one that caused you to enter the subroutine.

Once you enter the subroutine, you echo *strNamespace*, which on the first pass is simply the root. Next you use *GetObject* to make a connection to the WMI namespace that is identified by the subroutine *strNamespace* argument. In the first pass, you are connected to the root. The subroutine then retrieves all namespaces that are immediately below the one it is currently connected to. You then use a *For Each...Next* construction to loop through all the namespaces below the currently connected one. In doing so, you also concatenate the names to provide a fully qualified name to the namespace. You take the newly constructed name, pass it to *Enum-Namespaces*, and work through the namespace one more time.

RecursiveListWMINamespaces.vbs

```
WScript.Echo(Now)
strComputer = "."
Call EnumNamespaces("root")

Sub EnumNamespaces(strNamespace)
    WScript.Echo strNamespace
    Set objSWbemServices = _
        GetObject("winmgmts:\\" & strComputer & "\" & strNamespace)
    Set colNamespaces = objSWbemServices.InstancesOf("__NAMESPACE")
    For Each objNameSpace In colNamespaces
        Call EnumNamespaces(strNamespace & "\" & objNamespace.Name)
    Next
End sub
WScript.Echo("all done " & Now)
```

Listing WMI Providers

Understanding the namespace assists the network administrator with judiciously applying WMI scripting to his or her network duties. However, as mentioned earlier, to access information via WMI, you must have access to a WMI provider. Once the provider is implemented, you can gain access to the information that is made available.

The following script, ListWMIProviders.vbs, enumerates all the WMI providers instrumented on the machine in the *root\cimv2* namespace. In the supplemental folder, there is a series of Microsoft Office Excel spreadsheets that list classes supported by the various providers installed in the different namespaces of a standard Windows build. This information can lead the network administrator to MSDN, the platform SDK, or some other place to find details about the methods supported by the provider.

ListWMIProviders.vbs

```
strComputer = "."

Set objSWbemServices = _
    GetObject("winmgmts:\\" & strComputer & "\root\cimv2")
Set colWin32Providers = objSWbemServices.InstancesOf("__Win32Provider")

For Each objWin32Provider In colWin32Providers
    WScript.Echo objWin32Provider.Name
Next
```

When you run the script on a Windows Server 2003 server, you get the following output:

```
Win32_WIN32_TSLOGONSETTING_Prov
MS_NT_EVENTLOG_PROVIDER
Win32_WIN32_TSENVIRONMENTSETTING_Prov
SCM Event Provider
ProviderSubSystem
VolumeChangeEvents
NamedJobObjectLimitSettingProv
HiPerfCooker_v1
WMIPingProvider
Win32_WIN32_TSNETWORKADAPTERSETTING_Prov
SystemConfigurationChangeEvents
Win32_WIN32_TERMINALSERVICE_Prov
MSVDS__PROVIDER
Win32_WIN32_TSREMOTECONTROLSETTING_Prov
Win32_WIN32_TSNETWORKADAPTERLISTSETTING_Prov
Win32_WIN32_COMPUTERSYSTEMWINDOWSPRODUCTACTIVATIONSETTING_Prov
Win32_WIN32_TSSESSIONDIRECTORY_Prov
CmdTriggerConsumer
Standard Non-COM Event Provider
SessionProvider
WBEMCORE
RouteEventProvider
whqlProvider
Win32_WIN32_TSSESSIONSETTING_Prov
Win32_WIN32_TERMINALTERMINALSETTING_Prov
Win32_WIN32_TSCLIENTSETTING_Prov
Win32_WIN32_TERMINALSERVICESETTING_Prov
WMI Kernel Trace Event Provider
Win32_WIN32_PROXY_Prov
NamedJobObjectProv
MS_Shutdown_Event_Provider
SECRCW32
Win32ClockProvider
MSVSS__PROVIDER
MS_Power_Management_Event_Provider
Win32_WIN32_WINDOWSPRODUCTACTIVATION_Prov
RouteProvider
Cimwin32A
Msft_ProviderSubSystem
Win32_WIN32_TERMINALSERVICETOSETTING_Prov
NamedJobObjectSecLimitSettingProv
Win32_WIN32_TSSESSIONDIRECTORYSETTING_Prov
Win32_WIN32_TSPERMISSIONSSETTING_Prov
Win32_WIN32_TSACCOUNT_Prov
Win32_WIN32_TERMINAL_Prov
DskQuotaProvider
Win32_WIN32_TSGENERALSETTING_Prov
CIMWin32
NamedJobObjectActgInfoProv
NT5_GenericPerfProvider_V1
WMI Self-Instrumentation Event Provider
DFSProvider
MS_NT_EVENTLOG_EVENT_PROVIDER
```

Working with WMI Classes

In addition to working with namespaces, the inquisitive network administrator will also want to explore the concept of classes. In WMI parlance, you have core classes, common classes, and dynamic classes. *Core classes* represent managed objects that apply to all areas of management. These classes provide a basic vocabulary for analyzing and describing managed systems. Two examples of core classes are parameters and the *systemSecurity* class. *Common classes* are extensions of the core classes and represent managed objects that apply to specific management areas. However, common classes are independent from a particular implementation or technology. The *CIM_UnitaryComputerSystem* is an example of a common class. Core and common classes are not used as much by network administrators because they serve as templates from which other classes are derived.

Therefore, many of the classes stored in *root\cimv2* are abstract classes and are used as templates, and their properties and methods are inherited by classes that are derived from them. Abstract classes are not to be queried directly. However, a few classes in *root\cimv2* are dynamic classes used to hold actual information. The important aspect to remember about *dynamic classes* is that instances of a dynamic class are generated by a provider and are therefore more likely to retrieve "live" data from the system.

The following script, ListWMIClasses.vbs, returns a list of classes found in the *root\cimv2* namespace. There are more than 900 classes listed in the *root\cimv2* namespace of most computers. A listing of the WMI classes in each of the namespaces is listed in the spreadsheets in the \My Documents\Microsoft Press\VBScriptSBS\Supplemental folder.

ListWMIClasses.vbs

```
Option Explicit
Dim strComputer        'target computer
Dim wmiNS              'wmi namespace
Dim objwmiService      'SwbemServices object. The connection into WMI
Dim colClasses         'sWbemObject set object. A collection of items
Dim objClass           'sWbemObject. An item in colClasses
Dim strOUT             'output of all items
strComputer = "."
wmiNS = "\root\cimv2" 'must precede namespace with \

Set objwmiService = _
    GetObject("winmgmts:\\" & strComputer & wmiNS)
Set colClasses = objwmiService.SubclassesOf()

For Each objClass In colClasses
    strOUT = strOUT &  objClass.Path_.class & vbcrlf
Next

WScript.Echo funLine("There are " & colClasses.count  & " classes" &_
    " in the " & wmiNS & " namespace")
WScript.Echo strOUT

' *** function below ***
```

```
Function funLine(strIn)
funLine = Len(strIn)+1
funLine = strIN & VbCrLf & String(funLine,"=")
End Function
```

Search for specific WMI classes

1. Open the \My Documents\Microsoft Press\VBScriptSBS\ch08\ListWMIClasses.vbs script in Microsoft Notepad or the script editor of your choosing. Save the file as Your-NameListWMIClassesDictionary.vbs.

2. Delete the line declaring the variable *strOUT*, because it will not be needed in this script.

3. Add a variable to hold the dictionary object that will be created. Call it *objDictionary*, as seen below:

```
Dim objDictionary
```

4. Add a variable to hold an individual key in the dictionary. Call it *strKey*, as seen below:

```
Dim strKey
```

5. Add one more variable. This variable will be used to hold the search string. Call it *strSearch*, as seen below.

```
Dim strSearch
```

6. In the Reference section of your script, assign a string value to the *strSearch* variable. This will be used to locate class names. I used "process" for my initial search.

```
strSearch = "process"
```

7. Now it is time to create the dictionary object. Place the code just before you create the connection into WMI. This will be the first line in your Worker section. Assign the dictionary to the variable *objDictionary*, as seen below:

```
Set objDictionary = CreateObject("Scripting.Dictionary")
```

8. Inside the *For...Each...Next* loop that walks through the *colClasses* collection, delete *strOUT = strOUT* but do not delete the entire line. Instead, prefix the line with the command to add the class name to the dictionary. Because each class name is unique in the WMI namespace, and because we must have both a key and an item in the dictionary, we will use the class name twice, as seen in the code below:

```
objDictionary.Add objClass.Path_.class, objClass.Path_.class
```

9. Delete the Output section of the script, as well as the function. The code to be removed is seen below:

```
WScript.Echo funLine("There are " & colClasses.count  & " classes" &_
   " in the " & wmiNS & " namespace")
WScript.Echo strOUT
```

```
' *** function below ***
Function funLine(strIn)
funLine = Len(strIN)+1
funLine = strIN & VbCrLf & String(funLine,"=")
End Function
```

10. Use *For...Each...Next* to walk through the collection of keys in the dictionary. We can use the *Keys* method to get a collection of dictionary keys. Use the *strKey* variable to singularize an individual dictionary key. Make sure you close out the *For...Each...Next* block with the word *Next*. This is seen below:

```
For Each strKey In objDictionary.Keys
Next
```

11. Use the *InStr* function to look inside the dictionary key represented by the variable *strKey* to see if there is a pattern match with the word specified in the variable *strSearch*. Begin the search at the first position in the word, and make the search case insensitive. Make sure you close out the *If...Then...End If* construction. Echo out the results. This code goes inside the loop and looks like the following:

```
If InStr(1,strKey, strSearch,vbTextCompare) Then
        WScript.Echo strKey
    End If
```

12. Save and run your script. It should produce a listing something like the following when run from CScript. If it does not, then compare your script with the \My Documents\Microsoft Press\VBScriptSBS\ch08\ListWMIClassesDictionary.vbs script.

```
Win32_ProcessTrace
Win32_ProcessStartTrace
Win32_ProcessStopTrace
CIM_Process
Win32_Process
CIM_Processor
Win32_Processor
Win32_PerfRawData_PerfProc_Process
Win32_PerfRawData_PerfOS_Processor
Win32_PerfRawData_PerfProc_ProcessAddressSpace_Costly
Win32_PerfFormattedData_PerfOS_Processor
Win32_PerfFormattedData_PerfProc_Process
Win32_PerfFormattedData_PerfProc_ProcessAddressSpace_Costly
CIM_OSProcess
Win32_SystemProcesses
Win32_ComputerSystemProcessor
CIM_ProcessThread
Win32_SessionProcess
CIM_AssociatedProcessorMemory
Win32_AssociatedProcessorMemory
CIM_ProcessExecutable
Win32_NamedJobObjectProcess
Win32_ProcessStartup
```

13. EXTRA CREDIT: Modify your script to write the results out to a text file. Compare your results to \My Documents\Microsoft Press\VBScriptSBS\ch08\ListWMIClassesText-Search.vbs.

Adding an inputbox search

1. Open the \My Documents\Microsoft Press\VBScriptSBS\ch08\ListWMIClassesDictionary.vbs script and save it as YourNameListWMIClassesDictionarySearch.vbs.

2. Add three variables in the Header section of the script. These variables will be used for the title, prompt, and default value of the *inputbox* function. Call them *strTitle*, *strPrompt*, and *strDefault*, as seen below:

```
Dim strTitle        'title for the inputbox
Dim strPrompt       'prompt for the inputbox
Dim strDefault      'default value for the inputbox
```

3. In the Reference section of the script, assign a string value to indicate the purpose of the script to the *strTitle* variable. My code looks like the following:

```
strTitle = "Search for WMI classes"
```

4. On the next line, assign a prompt to the *strPrompt* variable that tells the user how to use the script. My code looks like the following:

```
strPrompt = "Enter class to search for" &_
        vbNewLine & "No quotes required"
```

5. On the next line in the Reference section, assign the string "Process" to the *strDefault* variable. This is seen below:

```
strDefault = "Process"
```

6. Edit the *strSearch* variable assignment in the Reference section, so it does not have a string literal assigned to it. Instead of "*hardcoding*" our search string, we will use the *inputbox* function to allow the value to be supplied at runtime. This is seen below:

```
strSearch = InputBox(strPrompt,strTitle,strDefault)
```

7. Save and run your script. You should see a dialog box that allows you to change the search string. It should have the value *Process* as the default value.

Viewing Properties

A *property* in WMI is a value that is used to indicate a characteristic (something describable) about a class. A property has a name and a domain that is used to indicate the class that actually owns the property. Properties can be viewed in terms of a pair of functions: one to set the property value and another to retrieve the property value. The ListClassProperties.vbs script lists all the properties of the WIN32_Service class.

ListClassProperties.vbs

```
Option Explicit
'On Error Resume Next
Dim strComputer      'name of target computer
Dim wmiNS            'WMI namespace that contains class
Dim wmiQuery         'simply the name of the class
Dim objWMIService    'connection to WMI namespace AND Class
Dim objItem          'item in the collection of properties

strComputer = "."
wmiNS = "\root\cimv2"
wmiQuery = ":win32_service"
Set objWMIService = GetObject("winmgmts:\\" & strComputer & _
        wmiNS & wmiQuery)

WScript.Echo wmiQuery & vbTab & " has " & _
        objWMIService.Properties_.count & " Properties"

For Each objItem in objWMIService.Properties_
    WScript.Echo "Property: " & objItem.name
Next
```

Detailing service information

1. Open the \My Documents\Microsoft Press\VBScriptSBS\Templates\wmiTemplate.vbs script in Notepad or your favorite script editor. Save the file as YourName ServiceInfo.vbs.

2. Add the word *service* to the end of the *wmiQuery* line, making sure there is no space between the underscore and the word *service*. This will be the WMI class we will query. The completed line looks like the following:

   ```
   wmiQuery = "Select * from win32_Service"
   ```

3. We are going to report on only two properties: *Name* and *Started*. Delete all but two of the *WScript.Echo* commands. On the two remaining echo commands, add the properties Name and Started after the echo. This section of code now looks like the following:

   ```
   WScript.Echo ": " & objItem.Name
   WScript.Echo ": " & objItem.Started
   ```

4. Save and run your script. The output is *not* very user friendly, as seen in the snipped output below:

   ```
   : Alerter
   : False
   : ALG
   : True
   : AppMgmt
   : False
   : aspnet_state
   : False
   ```

5. To improve readability, add the words *Name* and *Started* in front of the colons, as seen below:

```
WScript.Echo "Name: " & objItem.Name
WScript.Echo "Started: " & objItem.Started
```

6. Save and run your script. The output is better but still hard to read, as seen in the snipped output below:

```
Name: Alerter
Started: False
Name: ALG
Started: True
Name: AppMgmt
Started: False
Name: aspnet_state
Started: False
```

7. There are two choices for improving the output. The first is to space over the second line, as seen below:

```
For Each objItem in colItems
    WScript.Echo "Name: " & objItem.Name
    WScript.Echo Space(6) & "Started: " & objItem.Started
Next
```

The second choice is to put the output on the same line:

```
For Each objItem in colItems
    WScript.Echo "Name: " & objItem.Name, _
    "Started: " & objItem.Started
Next
```

8. Choose a method for improving the script output. Save and run the script. If there are problems with the output, compare your script with \My Documents\Microsoft Press\VBScriptSBS\ch08\ServiceINFO.vbs.

Working with WMI Methods

As you've learned in earlier chapters, a *method* answers the question "What does this thing do?" In many cases, the answer is "Well, it does nothing." However, the good thing about WMI is that it's constantly evolving—and in Windows Server 2003, more methods have been added than ever before. Like a property, a method also has a name and a domain. And just like a property, the method's domain refers back to the owning class. To determine if a class has any methods, you can use the ListClassMethods.vbs script. When run in CScript, the List-ClassMethods.vbs script produces the following output:

```
:win32_service  has 10 Methods
Method: StartService
Method: StopService
```

```
Method: PauseService
Method: ResumeService
Method: InterrogateService
Method: UserControlService
Method: Create
Method: Change
Method: ChangeStartMode
Method: Delete
```

The 10 methods from the *WIN32_Service* class can solve a number of problems for the network administrator. Suppose you want to stop the alerter service on all the computers on the network, then you could use the *StopService* method. If you need to change a service account password, then you use the *Change* method.

ListClassMethods.vbs

```
Option Explicit
'On Error Resume Next
dim strComputer         'name of target computer
dim wmiNS               'WMI namespace that contains class
dim wmiQuery            'simply the name of the class
dim objWMIService       'connection to WMI Namespace AND Class
dim objItem             'item in the collection of properties

strComputer = "."
wmiNS = "\root\cimv2"
wmiQuery = ":win32_Service"
Set objWMIService = GetObject("winmgmts:\\" & strComputer & _
        wmiNS & wmiQuery)

WScript.Echo wmiQuery & vbTab & " has " & _
        objWMIService.Methods_.count & " Methods"

For Each objItem in objWMIService.Methods_
    WScript.Echo "Method: " & objItem.name
Next
```

Note Just because a class has a method does not guarantee that the method is implemented. You must verify that the implemented qualifier is attached to the method to ensure the method actually works. This is because methods could be inherited from a parent class and then not implemented in the child class. As an example, WIN32_Processor has a *SetPowerState* method. You cannot use this method because it is not implemented. (The *SetPowerState* method is inheritted from CIM_LogicalDevice, which is an abstract class used to create other WMI classes.) You can do this by looking the method up in the Platform SDK. It will simply say "implemented." Looking up the method is the only way you can ensure that the implementation of the method you wish to use is actually available for the class. I will admit that I have actually wasted several hours trying to make a particular method work, only to find out it was not even implemented.

Querying WMI

In most situations, when you use WMI, you are performing some sort of query. Even when you're going to set a particular property, you still need to execute a query to return a dataset that enables you to perform the modification to the property. (A *dataset* is the data that comes back to you as the result of a query, that is, it is a set of data.) In this section, you'll look at the methods used to query WMI.

> **Just the Steps**   To query WMI
>
> 1. Specify the computer name.
> 2. Define the namespace.
> 3. Connect to the provider using *GetObject*.
> 4. Issue the query.
> 5. Use *For Each…Next* to iterate through collection data.

One of the problems with Windows Server 2003 for the small to medium enterprise is Windows Server 2003 product activation. Although the larger customers have the advantage of "select" keys that automatically activate the product, smaller companies often are not aware of the advantages of volume licensing and as a result do not have access to these keys. In addition, I've seen larger customers use the wrong key—you can easily forget to activate the copy of Windows Server 2003. Many customers like to monitor the newly built machine prior to actual activation because of the problems resulting from multiple activation requests. As is often the case with many information technology (IT) departments, emergencies arise, and it is easy to forget to make the trek back to the server rooms to activate the machines. This is where the power of WMI scripting can come to the rescue. The following script, Display WPAStatus.vbs, uses the new *Win32_WindowsProductActivation* WMI class to determine the status of product activation.

DisplayWPAStatus.vbs

```
Option Explicit      .
'On Error Resume Next
dim strComputer
dim wmiNS
dim wmiQuery
dim objWMIService
dim colItems
Dim objItem

strComputer = "."
wmiNS = "\root\cimv2"
wmiQuery = "Select * from Win32_WindowsProductActivation"
Set objWMIService = GetObject("winmgmts:\\" & strComputer & wmiNS)
Set colItems = objWMIService.ExecQuery(wmiQuery)

For Each objItem In colItems
```

```
        WScript.Echo "ActivationRequired: " & objItem.ActivationRequired
        WScript.Echo "IsNotificationOn: " & objItem.IsNotificationOn
        WScript.Echo "ProductID: " & objItem.ProductID
        WScript.Echo "RemainingEvaluationPeriod: " & _
            objItem.RemainingEvaluationPeriod
        WScript.Echo "RemainingGracePeriod: " & objItem.RemainingGracePeriod
        WScript.Echo "ServerName: " & objItem.ServerName
Next
```

Header Information

The Header information section of DisplayWPAStatus.vbs contains the two normal items, *Option Explicit* and *On Error Resume Next*. (If you are unfamiliar with these commands, refer to Chapter 1, "Starting from Scratch.") Next, you declare six variables to be used in this script. Because you are writing a WMI script, you make up some new variable names. Table 8-1 lists the variables and their intended use in this script.

Table 8-1 Variables used in DisplayWPAStatus.vbs

Variable name	Variable use
strComputer	Holds the name of the computer the query will target at run time
wmiNS	Holds the namespace that the WMI query will target
wmiQuery	Holds the WMI query
objWMIService	Holds the connection to the WMI service
collItems	Holds the collection of items returned by the WMI query
objItem	Holds the individual item from which the properties will be queried

Reference Information

The Reference information section of the script is used to assign value to some of the variables declared in the Header information section. The first variable used in the Reference information section is *strComputer*, whose value is set to ".". In WMI shorthand, "." is used to mean "this computer only." So the WMI query will operate on *localhost*. The second variable assigned a value is *wmiNS*, which is used to hold the value of the WMI namespace you query. You could include the namespace and the query on the same line of the script; however, by breaking the namespace and the query out of the connection string, you make it easier to reuse the script. The next variable is *wmiQuery*, which receives the value of "*Select * from Win32_WindowsProductActivation*". You can easily change the query to ask for other information. You are asking for everything that is contained in the local computer from the *Win32_WindowsProductActivation* namespace.

You use the *Set* command to set *objWMIService* to the handle that is obtained by the *GetObject* command. The syntax for this command is very important because it is seminal to working with WMI. When making a connection using *winmgmts://*, *winmgmts* is called a moniker. A moniker works in the same way that the phrase "abracadabra" used to work in the old movies. It's a shortcut that performs a lot of connection work in the background. Remember the magic phrase *winmgmts* because it will do much of the work for you, including opening the door to the storehouse of valuable WMI data. The last item in the Reference information section is the use of the variable colItems, which is used to object returned by the *ExecQuery* method of the *SWbemServices* object. The Reference information section follows:

```
strComputer = "."
wmiNS = "\root\cimv2"
wmiQuery = "Select * from Win32_WindowsProductActivation"
Set objWMIService = GetObject("winmgmts:\\" & strComputer & wmiNS)
Set colItems = objWMIService.ExecQuery(wmiQuery)
```

Worker and Output Information

The Worker information section is the part of the script that works through the collection of data returned and produces the Windows Product Activation (WPA) information. This section is always going to be customized for each WMI script you write, because each query or each provider used returns customized data.

Because WMI returns data in the form of a collection, you need to use a *For Each...Next* loop to iterate through the items in the collection. This loop is required—even when WMI returns only one item, WMI still returns that item in a collection. Your question at this point is probably "How do I know what to request from WMI?" I looked that up in the Platform SDK. By looking in the SDK for *Win32_WindowsProductActivation*, I learned that several properties of interest to a network administrator will return information. The SDK also told me that the properties are all read-only (which would prevent us from flipping the ActivationRequired field to false. The Worker and Output information section of this script follows:

```
For Each objItem In colItems
    WScript.Echo "ActivationRequired: " & objItem.ActivationRequired
    WScript.Echo "IsNotificationOn: " & objItem.IsNotificationOn
    WScript.Echo "ProductID: " & objItem.ProductID
    WScript.Echo "RemainingEvaluationPeriod: " & _
        objItem.RemainingEvaluationPeriod
    WScript.Echo "RemainingGracePeriod: " & objItem.RemainingGracePeriod
    WScript.Echo "ServerName: " & objItem.ServerName
Next
```

The most interesting information in *Win32_WindowsProductActivation* is listed in Table 8-2.

Table 8-2   Properties of *Win32_WindowsProductActivation*

Property	Meaning
ActivationRequired	If *0*, activation is not required. If *1*, the system must be activated within the number of days indicated by the RemainingGrace Period property.
IsNotificationOn	If *0*, notification reminders and the activation icon are disabled. If not equal to *0* and product activation is required, notification reminders (message balloons) are enabled, and the activation icon appears in the notification tray.

Table 8-2 Properties of *Win32_WindowsProductActivation*

Property	Meaning
ProductID	A string of 20 characters separated by hyphens. This is the same product ID that is displayed on the General tab of the System Properties dialog box in Control Panel.
RemainingEvaluationPeriod	If beta or evaluation media, this returns the number of days remaining before expiration. If retail media, this field is set to the largest possible unsigned value.
RemainingGracePeriod	Number of days remaining before activation is required if *ActivationRequired* is equal to *1*.
ServerName	Name of the system being queried. This could also be the IP address of the system.

Retrieving Hotfix Information Step-by-Step Exercise

In this section, you use the *Win32_QuickFixEngineering* provider to retrieve information about hotfixes installed on your server. This lab incorporates techniques learned in earlier chapters into the information about WMI discussed in this chapter.

1. Open \My Documents\Microsoft Press\VBScriptSBS\Templates\BlankTemplate.vbs in Notepad or your favorite script editor.

2. Turn on *Option Explicit* by typing **Option Explicit** on the first line of the script.

3. Declare variables to be used in the script. There are six variables to be used: *strComputer*, *objWmiService*, *wmiNS*, *wmiQuery*, *objItem*, and *collItems*.

4. Assign the value of "." to the variable *strComputer*. The code will look like the following:

   ```
   strComputer = "."
   ```

5. Assign the value of "*root**cimv2*" to the variable *wmiNS*. The code will look like the following:

   ```
   wmiNS = "\root\cimv2"
   ```

6. Assign the query "*Select * from Win32_QuickFixEngineering*" to the variable *wmiQuery*. The code will look like the following:

   ```
   wmiQuery = "Select * from Win32_QuickFixEngineering"
   ```

7. Use the *winmgmts* moniker and the variable *objWMIService* as well as the *GetObject* method to make a connection to WMI. Use the *strComputer* and the *wmiNS* variables to specify the computer and the namespace to use. The code will look like the following:

   ```
   Set objWMIService = GetObject("winmgmts:\\" & strComputer & wmiNS)
   ```

8. Set the variable *collItems* to be equal to the connection that comes back from WMI when it executes the query defined by *wmiQuery*. Your code should look like the following:

   ```
   Set collItems = objWMIService.ExecQuery(wmiQuery)
   ```

9. Use a *For Each...Next* construction to iterate through the collection called *colItems*. Assign the variable called *objItem* to each of the items returned from *colItems*. Your code should look like this:

```
For Each objItem In colItems
```

10. Use *WScript.Echo* to echo out items such as the caption, *CSName*, and description. You can copy the following items, or use the WMI SDK to look up *Win32_QuickFixEngineering* and choose items of interest to you.

```
WScript.Echo "Caption: " & objItem.Caption
WScript.Echo "CSName: " & objItem.CSName
WScript.Echo "Description: " & objItem.Description
WScript.Echo "FixComments: " & objItem.FixComments
WScript.Echo "HotFixID: " & objItem.HotFixID
WScript.Echo "InstallDate: " & objItem.InstallDate
WScript.Echo "InstalledBy: " & objItem.InstalledBy
WScript.Echo "InstalledOn: " & objItem.InstalledOn
WScript.Echo "Name: " & objItem.Name
WScript.Echo "ServicePackInEffect: " & objItem.ServicePackInEffect
WScript.Echo "Status: " & objItem.Status
```

11. Close out your *For Each...Next* loop with the *Next* command.

12. Save your file as YourNameSBSQueryHotFix.vbs and run it in CScript.exe. If you do not get the expected results, compare your script with \My Documents\Microsoft Press\VBScriptSBS\ch08\StepByStep\SBSQueryHotFix.vbs.

One Step Further: Echoing the Time Zone

In this section, you modify the SBSQueryHotFix.vbs script so that it echoes out the time zone configured on the computer.

1. Open \My Documents\Microsoft Press\VBScriptSBS\ch08\OneStepFurther\SBS QueryHotFix.vbs in Notepad or another script editor and save it as YourName TimeZoneSolution.vbs.

2. Edit the *wmiQuery* line so that it points to *Win32_TimeZone*. The code will look like the following:

```
wmiQuery = "Select * from Win32_TimeZone"
```

3. Inside the *For Each objItem In colItems* loop, delete all but one of the *WScript.Echo* statements so that the code looks like the following:

```
For Each objItem In colItems
    WScript.Echo "Caption: " & objItem.Caption
Next
```

4. Save and run the file. You are now pointing to the Caption property of *Win32_TimeZone* in your script. No further changes are required for this section. If you have a problem, compare your script to the TimeZoneSolution.vbs file in the OneStepFurther folder under Chapter 8.

Chapter 8 Quick Reference

To	Do This
Find the default WMI namespace on a computer	Use the Advanced tab from the WMI Control tool
Find WMI classes on a computer	Use the WMI Object Browser Tool
Make a connection into WMI	Use the WMI moniker in your script
Use a shortcut name for the local computer	Use a "." and assign it to the variable holding the computer name in the script
Find detailed information about all WMI classes on a computer	Use the Platform SDK
Iterate through a collection of objects returned by the *ExecQuery* method of the *SWbemServices* object	Use *For...Each...Next*
List all the namespaces on a computer	Query instances of *__NameSpace*
List all providers installed in a particular namespace	Query instances of *__Win32Provider*
List all the classes in a particular namespace on a computer	Use the *SubclassesOf()* method from the *SwbemServices* object

Chapter 9
WMI Continued

Before You Begin

To work through the material presented in this chapter, you need to be familiar with the following concepts from earlier chapters:

- Connecting to the default WMI namespace
- Accessing properties of dynamic WMI classes
- Implementing the *For...Next* statement
- Implementing a WMI query

After completing this chapter, you will be able to:

- Implement alternate ways of configuring the WMI moniker
- Query WMI
- Set impersonation levels
- Define the WMI object path
- Navigate the WMI namespace

Alternate Ways of Configuring the WMI Moniker

In this section, you are going to look at different ways of constructing the Windows Management Instrumentation (WMI) moniker string. There are essentially three parts to the moniker. Of the three parts, only one is mandatory. These parts are listed here:

- The prefix *winmgmts:* (this is the mandatory part)
- A security settings component
- A WMI object path component

> **Just the Steps**   To construct the WMI moniker
>
> 1. Use the prefix *WinMgmts:*.
> 2. Define the security settings component, if desired.
> 3. Specify the WMI object path component, if desired.

Accepting Defaults

Several fields are optional in constructing a finely tuned WMI moniker, and there are clearly defined defaults for those optional fields. The defaults are stored in the following registry location: HKEY_LOCAL_MACHINE\SOFTWARE\Microsoft\WBEM\Scripting. There are two keys: impersonation level and default namespace. Impersonation level is set to a default of 3, which means that WMI impersonates the logged-on user. The default namespace is set to *root\cimv2*. In reality, these are pretty good defaults. The default computer is the local machine, so you don't need to specify the computer name when you're simply running against the local machine. All this means is that a simple connection string to WMI, using the default moniker, would just be "*winmgmts:*". When using the *GetObject* method, you can use the default connection string as follows:

```
Set objWMIService = GetObject("winmgmts:\\")
```

By using a default moniker and omitting the header information, you come up with a rather lean script. You can shorten it even further, as you'll learn in a bit. The SmallBIOS.vbs script that follows is a shorter script than the DetermineBIOS.vbs script, which is included on the companion CD-ROM. (The header information of SmallBIOS.vbs is omitted.)

SmallBIOS.vbs
```
wmiQuery = "Select * from Win32_BIOS"

Set objWMIService = GetObject("winmgmts:\\")
Set colItems = objWMIService.ExecQuery(wmiQuery)

For Each objItem in colItems
  strBIOSVersion = Join(objItem.BIOSVersion, ",")
  WScript.Echo "BIOSVersion: " & strBIOSVersion
  WScript.Echo ": " & objItem.caption
  WScript.Echo ": " & objItem.releaseDate
Next
```

Reference Information

The Reference information section of the script comprises three lines. Two of the lines are the same as in many other WMI scripts; the first line in the Reference information section changes depending upon what query you want to run. For the script to return information about the basic input/output system (BIOS) on the server, you need to connect to the *Win32_BIOS* namespace. Your WMI query does nothing fancy—it simply tells WMI that you want to select everything contained in the *Win32_BIOS* namespace. The actual query looks like the following:

```
wmiQuery = "Select * from Win32_BIOS"
```

The two standard lines in the Reference section are the connection to WMI that uses the *GetObject* method and the moniker. The short version of the moniker follows:

```
Set objWMIService = GetObject("winmgmts:\\")
```

Once you have the connection into WMI, you can begin to perform tasks with it. In this case, you want to issue a query and hold the results of that query in a variable called *colItems*. So you use the following line:

```
Set colItems = objWMIService.ExecQuery(wmiQuery)
```

By removing the actual WMI query from the ExecQuery string, you won't need to edit this line of the script when you wish to make a change to your WMI query. The same is true for the WMI connection string—as long as you are running the script on your local machine and working in the *root\cimv2* namespace, you don't need to modify that line either when you wish to target a different computer. Now you can see why in our earlier WMI scripts we specified the computer by using *strComputer*—it gave us the ability to modify the value of that variable without having to change the rest of the script.

Worker and Output Information

The Worker and Output information section of the script is used to iterate through the collection that is returned by *wmiQuery*. After that information is loaded into the collection of items (*colItems*), you use a *For Each...Next* construction to walk through the collection and return the desired information. The code for this section of script follows:

```
For Each objItem in colItems
  strBIOSVersion = Join(objItem.BIOSVersion, ",")
  WScript.Echo "BIOSVersion: " & strBIOSVersion
  WScript.Echo ": " & objItem.caption
  WScript.Echo ": " & objItem.releaseDate
Next
```

Each item in the collection is assigned to the variable *objItem*. In this particular situation, only one BIOS can be queried from *Win32_BIOS*; the nature of WMI is to return single items as a collection. Display the requested information by using the *For Each...Next* construction. Only one item is in the collection and only one loop is made.

Working with Multivalue Properties

Most of the items in the Output information section are obvious to readers at this point. You use *WScript.Echo* to output specific values. The first item, *strBIOSVersion*, is unique because you use the Microsoft Visual Basic, Scripting Edition (VBScript) *Join* method to turn an array into a string so you can use *WScript.Echo* to echo out the information. If you tried to use *WScript.Echo* to directly print out the property, you would get a *type mismatch* error. (We talk about the *Join* method later, so for now, let's think of a *Join* as a "black box tool.") This *Join* is necessary because the data contained in the BIOSVersion property is stored as an array. Recall from earlier chapters that you can think of an array as multiple cells in a spreadsheet, each of which can contain a certain amount of data. The BIOSVersion property of *Win32_BIOS* contains several fields of information, but you can't simply use *WScript.Echo objItem.BIOSVersion* because *WScript* won't know which field you want returned and, consequently, the command will fail. As you learned in your previous study of arrays, you could use something like *objItem.BIOSVersion(0)*, and if you knew which field in the array contained the most salient information, this would be a valid approach. Short of running the script multiple times and changing the array value an arbitrary number of times, you need to take a better approach.

> **Note** For more information about arrays, refer to Chapter 4, "Working with Arrays."

One nice way to deal with the multivalue property problem is to use the *Join* function demonstrated in our earlier script. Let's see how that works. First you need to use a new variable that will hold the result of your *Join* statement:

```
strBIOSVersion = Join(objItem.BIOSVersion, ",")
```

The *Join* function should be old hat to readers who are familiar with Transact-SQL (T-SQL). An executed *Join* takes two arguments. It's saying, "I want to join the first thing with the second thing." This is actually quite sophisticated. In the preceding *Join* statement, you join each field from *BIOSVersion* with a comma. You assign the result of the operation to the variable *strBIOSVersion*, and you're ready to echo it out in the next line of your script. Keep in mind that the default query language into WMI is WMI Query Language (WQL). WQL is pronounced "weequil" and SQL (Structured Query Language) is pronounced "seaquil"—they not only sound alike but are alike in that many of the tasks you can perform in SQL can also be accomplished in WQL. The *Join* technique is very important, and you'll use it again when you come across other arrayed properties. Wondering how I knew that *BIOSVersion* was an array? The Platform SDK told me.

> **Important** If you try to print out a data value that is stored as an array, you will receive a message stating: "Microsoft VBScript runtime error: *type mismatch*." You can avoid this error by using the *ISArray* function.

Detecting array properties

1. Open the \My Documents\Microsoft Press\VBScriptSBS\Templates \WMITemplate.vbs script in Microsoft Notepad or some other script editor and save it as YourNameIsArray.vbs.

2. Turn off the *On Error Resume Next* command by remarking out the line.

    ```
    'On Error Resume Next
    ```

3. Modify the *wmiQuery* line so you are choosing everything from the *WIN32_ComputerSystem* class. This is seen below.

    ```
    wmiQuery = "Select * from win32_ComputerSystem"
    ```

4. Inside the *For Each...Next* loop, print out the values for the following properties: Name, Manufacturer, Model, TotalPhysicalMemory, and Username. To do this, edit the *WScript.Echo* lines currently in the loop. This is seen below.

```
WScript.Echo "name: " & objItem.name
WScript.Echo "Manufacturer: " & objItem.Manufacturer
WScript.Echo "model: " & objItem.model
WScript.Echo "totalPhysicalMemory: " & objItem.totalPhysicalMemory
WScript.Echo "username: " & objItem.username
```

5. Save and run your script. It should print out something similar to the output listed below if it is run in CScript. If it does not, compare your script to \My Documents\Microsoft Press\VBScriptSBS\ch09\IsArray.vbs. Your code must be error free prior to going to the next step.

```
name: MREDLAPTOP
Manufacturer: TOSHIBA
model: TECRA M3
totalPhysicalMemory: 2146680832
username: NWTRADERS\iammred
```

6. Add an additional *WScript.Echo* command in your *For Each...Next* loop. You can easily do this by copying one of the existing *Echo* lines and editing both the property name and the associated string message. Modify the line to use the SystemStartupOptions property, as seen below:

```
WScript.Echo "SystemStartupOptions: " & objItem.SystemStartupOptions
```

7. Save and run the script. You will notice it errors out on the line you just added. The error received is listed below:

```
Microsoft VBScript runtime error: Type mismatch
```

8. The easiest way to fix it is to add the *Join* function to the line of code, as seen below:

```
WScript.Echo "SystemStartupOptions: " & join(objItem.SystemStartupOptions)
```

9. Add *join* to the line above the *SystemStartupOptions* line so that you are trying to join the Username property, as seen below:

```
WScript.Echo "username: " & join(objItem.username)
```

10. Save and run the script. You will see it also produces an error:

```
Microsoft VBScript runtime error: Type mismatch: 'join'
```

11. It is therefore impossible to simply try to join everything together. In trying to solve one error, we run into another. Use the *isArray* function to determine if the property is an array and then use the appropriate line of code. Delete *join* from the *objItem.UserName* line of code. Save and run your script. There should be no errors.

12. Add a new line above the *SystemStartUpOptions* line of code. Use the *isArray* function to determine if the property is an array. Encase the code in an *If...Then...End If* loop, as seen below:

```
If IsArray(objItem.SystemStartUpOptions) Then
End If
```

13. Add an *Else* clause that prints out the property without using a *Join* function, as seen below:

```
Else
    WScript.Echo "SystemStartupOptions: " & objItem.SystemStartupOptions
```

14. It is possible that you have multiple startup options specified for your server or workstation in the Boot.ini file. To present a nicer listing from the script, let's add the second parameter for the *Join* function, which is the character to use as a line separator. Here we will use a new line, as seen below:

```
WScript.Echo "SystemStartupOptions: " & join(objItem.SystemStartupOptions, _
        VbCrLf)
```

15. Save and run the script. If there are problems, compare it to IsArray.vbs.

> **Best Practices** In the next procedure, we will illustrate an alternate way to connect to WMI. This can be useful for short, quick scripts. I do not recommend leaving out *Option Explicit*, not declaring variables, or using convuluted monikers as a general course. As they can be difficult to read, hard to modify, and impossible to troubleshoot.

Alternate ways to connect to WMI

1. Open \My Documents\Microsoft Press\VBScriptSBS\Templates\BlankTemplate.vbs in Notepad or your favorite script editor. Save the file as YourNameAlternateWMI.vbs.

2. On the first line, use *Set* to assign the object that comes back from *GetObject* to a variable named *colItems*. Use the *ExecQuery* method to select everything from the WIN32_LogicalDisk class. This can be on a single line. (The line below is wrapped due to publishing style constraints. If you type it on a single line, remove the _ when you put it together.)

```
Set colItems = GetObject("winmgmts:\\").ExecQuery _
    ("Select * from win32_logicaldisk")
```

3. To investigate the type of object that is returned by the command, use the *TypeName* function and print out the name of the object contained in the *colItems* variable, as seen below.

```
WScript.Echo "colitems is: " & TypeName(colItems)
```

4. Save and run the script. You will notice it reports *colItems* is an *SWbemObjectSet* object.

5. On a new line, use *For Each...Next* to walk through the collection of objects returned in the first line of the script. Use the variable *obj* to singularize an item from the collection. Print out the name property from the *WIN32_LogicalDisk* class. This is seen below:

```
For Each obj In colItems
        WScript.Echo "Drive name: " & obj.name
Next
```

6. On the next line, use the *Get* method from *SWbemServices* to connect to a specific drive, drive C. To do this, you must identify the key value of the WMI class and supply a value for the key that represents an individual instance of the class. The WMI object browser can be used to find the key property, as seen in Figure 9-1. Use *objItem* to hold the object that is returned.

```
Set objItem = GetObject("winmgmts:\\").get _
    ("win32_logicaldisk.deviceID='c:'")
```

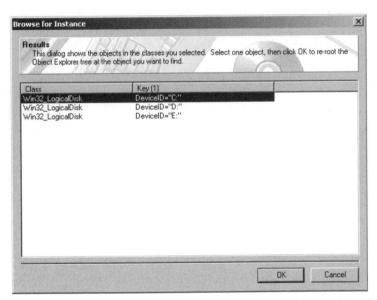

Figure 9-1   The WMI object browser provides an easy way to identify key properties

7. Use the *TypeName* function and echo out the name of the object contained in the *objItem* variable. This is seen below:

```
WScript.Echo "objItem is: " & TypeName(objItem)
```

8. Save and run the script. You will notice *objItem* is reported as *sWbemObjectEx*.

9. Use *WScript.Echo* to print out the size of the C drive. This is seen below.

```
WScript.Echo "Size of drive " & objItem.size
```

10. Save and run the script. If it does not perform as expected, compare your script with AlternateWMI.vbs in the Chapter 9 folder.

Quick Check

Q. **Why do you need a moniker for WMI?**

A. The WMI moniker gives you the ability to easily connect to WMI.

Q. **What construction is required to return property data stored in an array?**

A. You need to either specify the element you're interested in, or simply use the *Join* function to give you a string to work with.

Q. **What part of the WMI moniker is required?**

A. The required part of the WMI moniker is the prefix *WinMgmts:*.

Q. **What are the two optional parts of the WMI moniker?**

A. The two optional parts of the WMI moniker are the security settings and the WMI object path.

Moniker Security Settings

In many cases, the default security settings work just fine for the WMI moniker. In many example scripts, you will see the line *impersonationLevel=impersonate*. This line is often not needed because the default Distributed COM (DCOM) security setting for WMI on Microsoft Windows 2000, Windows XP, and Windows Server 2003 is set so the impersonation level is equal to *impersonate*.

Note   When I first started using WMI in my scripting, I noticed numerous scripts had *impersonationLevel=impersonate* set, and it made me curious. After a lot of searching, I found the other levels. When I tried to change the security settings, the script failed. The reason? You cannot specify security settings when running local. They work only when you are connecting remotely to another computer.

But what does that really mean? Why are there options we would not normally utilize? You can use four levels of impersonation: *Anonymous*, *Identify*, *Impersonate*, and *Delegate*. By default, WMI uses the *Impersonate* permission, which allows a WMI call to use the credentials of the caller. When the person calling the WMI script is a domain administrator, the script runs with domain administrator privileges. You can also use other impersonation levels, as described in Table 9-1.

Table 9-1   Impersonation Levels

Moniker	Meaning	Registry value
Anonymous	Hides the credentials of the caller. Calls to WMI might fail with this impersonation level.	*1*

Table 9-1   Impersonation Levels

Moniker	Meaning	Registry value
Identify	Allows objects to query the credentials of the caller. Calls to WMI might fail with this impersonation level.	2
Impersonate	Allows objects to use the credentials of the caller. This is the recommended impersonation level for Scripting application programming interface (API) for WMI calls.	3
Delegate	Allows objects to permit other objects to use the credentials of the caller. This impersonation will work with Scripting API for WMI calls but might constitute an unnecessary security risk.	4

If you decide to specify the impersonation level of the script, the code would look like the following:

```
Set objWMIService = GetObject("winmgmts:{impersonationLevel=impersonate}")
```

Because Impersonate is the default impersonation level for WMI, the addition of the curly braces and *impersonationLevel=impersonate* code is redundant. If you want to keep your moniker nice and clean, and yet you feel the need to modify the impersonation level, you can do this easily by defining the impersonation level of the *SWbemSecurity* object. In practice, your code might look like the following:

```
Set objWMIService = GetObject("winmgmts:\\" & strComputer & wmiNS)
objWMIService.Security_.impersonationLevel = 4
```

In this code, the first line contains the normal moniker to make the connection to WMI. You use *strComputer* and *wmiNS* to specify target computers and the target namespace, respectively. Because you haven't specified an impersonation level, you're using the default Impersonate security setting. On the next line, you use the handle that came back from the *GetObject* command that was assigned to *objWMIService*, and you define *ImpersonationLevel* to be equal to *4*. (Impersonation values are listed in Table 9-1.) Obviously, you could define a constant and set it to a value of *4* and then substitute the constant value for *4* in the script. ImpersonationLevel is a property of Security_. Security_ is a property of the *SWbemSecurity* object. The *SWbemSecurity* object is used to read or set security settings for other WMI objects such as *SWbemServices*, which is actually the object created when you use *GetObject* and the WMI moniker.

WbemPrivilege Has Its Privileges

To add elevated privileges, you need to add a privilege string in the space immediately following the impersonation level. These privilege strings correspond to the *WbemPrivilegeEnum* constants, which are documented in the Platform SDK. Some of the more useful privilege strings for network administrators are listed in Table 9-2. (There are 26 defined privileges in the Platform SDK, most of which are of interest only to developers writing low-level WMI applications.)

Table 9-2   Privilege Strings

Privilege	Value	Meaning
SeCreateTokenPrivilege	1	Required to create a primary token.
SeLockMemoryPrivilege	3	Required to lock physical pages in memory.
SeMachineAccountPrivilege	5	Required to create a computer account.
SeSecurityPrivilege	7	Required to perform a number of security-related functions, such as controlling and viewing audit messages. This privilege identifies its holder as a security operator.
SeTakeOwnershipPrivilege	8	Required to take ownership of an object without being granted discretionary access. This privilege allows the owner value to be set only to those values that the holder might legitimately assign as the owner of an object.
SeSystemTimePrivilege	11	Required to modify the system time.
SeCreatePagefilePrivilege	14	Required to create a paging file.
SeShutdownPrivilege	18	Required to shut down a local system.
SeRemoteShutdownPrivilege	23	Required to shut down a system using a network request.
SeEnableDelegationPrivilege	26	Required to enable computer and user accounts to be trusted for delegation.

As you can see from Table 9-2, some of these privileges are rather intriguing. This being the case, how do you request them? Well, this is where your work gets a little interesting. If you're requesting the privilege in a moniker string, you use the privilege string listed in Table 9-2, but you have to drop the *Se* part and the *Privilege* part of the string. For example, if you want to request the *SeShutdownPrivilege* privilege in a moniker, you would specify the privilege as *Shutdown*, as illustrated in the following WMI connection string:

```
Set objWMIService = GetObject("winmgmts:{impersonationLevel=impersonate, (Shutdown)}")
```

Querying the security event log

1. Open the \My Documents\Microsoft Press\VBScriptSBS\Templates\WMITemplate.vbs script in Notepad or another script editor and save it as YourNameReadSecurityEventLog.vbs.

2. Declare a variable called *dteDate* to hold the desired date for your event log query. Also declare a variable called *IntEvent* to hold the event ID you wish to query. The two lines of code that do this are seen below:

```
Dim IntEvent 'event code to look for
Dim dteDate    'the date to search from in log
```

3. Use the *dateSerial* function to convert three numbers into a date formatted number. This will be the date you wish to use as the basis of your query into the security event log. To limit the amount of information returned, use yesterday's date for the query. Assign the date that is returned from the function to the variable *dteDate,* as seen below:

```
dteDate = DateSerial(2006,04,22)
```

4. Assign an event ID to the *IntEvent* variable. I used 576, which indicates a privilege escalation. An example of event 576 is seen in Figure 9-2.

```
IntEvent = "576" 'event code
```

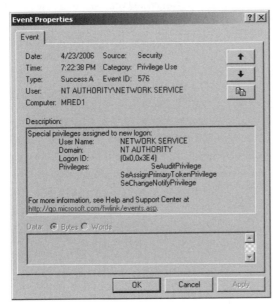

Figure 9-2   Privilege escalation event 576 recorded in event log

5. Edit the WMI query so that you are choosing everything from the *WIN32_ NTLogEvent* class. Use the *IntEvent* variable to assign value to the *EventCode* property in the *Where* clause, and specify the "security" for the *LogFile* property. Use the *funUTC* function to convert the *dteDate* variable into a Coordinated Universal Time (UTC) formatted date type you can use with the TimeGenerated property to reduce the number of records returned from the script. The completed WMI query is listed below:

```
wmiQuery = "SELECT * FROM Win32_NTLogEvent WHERE EventCode = " & _
    IntEvent & " and LogFile = 'security' and timegenerated > " & _
    funUTC(dteDate)
```

Warning   If you do not enclose the name of the log file in the WMI query within a single set of quotation marks, your query will fail.

6. Under the line that connects to WMI by using the moniker, create a security privilege object and use the *addASstring* method to add the *SeSecurityPrivilege* privilege to your script. This is required to allow you to read from the security log. The code below performs this task.

```
objWMIService.security_.Privileges.addASstring "SeSecurityPrivilege"
```

7. In the Output section of the script, edit the existing *WScript.Echo* commands to echo out the TimeGenerated, Message, EventCode, and CategoryString properties from the *WIN32_NTLogEvent* class.

```
WScript.Echo "TimeGenerated: " & objItem.TimeGenerated
WScript.Echo "message: " & objItem.message
WScript.Echo "EventCode: " & objItem.EventCode
WScript.Echo "CategoryString : " & objItem.CategoryString
```

8. Delete the two remaining *WScript.Echo* commands.

9. Turn off *On Error Resume Next*.

10. Copy the function contained in \My Documents\Microsoft Press\VBScriptSBS \Utilities\FunConvertUTC.vbs to the bottom of your script. You will need to modify it just slightly, because the date value needs to be encased in single quotation marks. Add a ""'"& in front of the *dateTime* variable. Also add &"'" at the end of the *dateTime* variable. The completed function is listed below.

```
Function funUTC(mydate)
Dim dateTime
Set dateTime = CreateObject("WbemScripting.SWbemDateTime")
dateTime.SetVarDate(mydate)
funUTC = "'" & dateTime & "'"
End Function
```

11. Save and run the script by using CScript. Your output will probably look something like the following:

```
TimeGenerated: 20060423193754.000000-180
message: Special privileges assigned to new logon:

    User Name:   NETWORK SERVICE

    Domain:      NT AUTHORITY

    Logon ID:    (0x0,0x3E4)

    Privileges:  SeAuditPrivilege
                 SeAssignPrimaryTokenPrivilege
                 SeChangeNotifyPrivilege
```

12. Notice the *TimeGenerated* field is in UTC time format and is therefore difficult to read. To correct this, copy the \My Documents\Microsoft Press\VBScriptSBS\Utilities\Fun-

TimeFunction.vbs script and paste it at the bottom of your script. The function looks like the following:

```
Function FunTime(wmiTime)
Dim objSWbemDateTime 'holds an swbemDateTime object. Used to translate Time
Set objSWbemDateTime = CreateObject("WbemScripting.SWbemDateTime")
 objSWbemDateTime.Value = wmiTime
 FunTime = objSWbemDateTime.GetVarDate
End Function
```

13. To clean up the output from the *TimeGenerated* field in the Output section of your script, modify the existing line to call the function to translate *objItem.TimeGenerated*. This is seen below:

```
WScript.Echo "TimeGenerated: " & FunTime(objItem.TimeGenerated)
```

14. Save and run your script by using CScript. You will notice that the output now has a "normal" date and time format. If your script does not appear to run properly, compare your script with \My Documents\Microsoft Press\VBScriptSBS\ch09\ReadSecurityEventLog.vbs. You may also want to modify the date used in the query by editing the value of *dteDate*.

Adding reporting information

1. Open the YourNameReadSecurityEventLog.vbs script in Notepad or another script editor and save it as YourNameReadSecurityEventLogHeader.vbs.

2. In the Header section of your script, declare two variables, *startTime* and *endTime*, that will be used to hold the return value from the *Timer* function.

```
Dim startTime, endTime 'used with timer Function
```

3. In the Reference section of the script, use the *Timer* function to assign a value to the *startTime* variable, as seen below:

```
startTime = Timer
```

4. Under the *For Each...Next* loop, use the *Timer* function to assign a value to the *endTime* variable. On the following line, echo out the results of subtracting *startTime* from *endTime,* as seen below:

```
endTime = Timer
WScript.Echo "It took " & endTime-startTime
```

5. Copy the function contained in \My Documents\Microsoft Press\VBScriptSBS\Utilities \funLine2.vbs to the bottom of your script. This function will look like the following:

```
Function funLine(strIn)
    funLine = Len(strIN)+1
    funLine = strIN & VbCrLf & String(funLine,"=")
End Function
```

6. Under the *ExecQuery* line in the Worker section of your script, echo out the *wmiQuery* value. Then use the *funLine* function to underline some code that tells how many items are found as a result of your WMI query. The code to do this is seen below:

```
WScript.Echo wmiQuery & VbCrLf & funLine("There are " & _
    colItems.Count & " Events related to eventCode " & IntEvent) & _
    vbNewLine
```

7. Save and run your script in CScript. If it does not run, then compare the results with the \My Documents\Microsoft Press\VBScriptSBS\ch09\ReadSecurityEventLog-Header.vbs. You may also want to modify the date used to perform the query by editing the value of *dteDate*.

Using the Default WMI Moniker Step-by-Step Exercises

In this section, you will practice using the default WMI moniker. To do this, you write a cute little script that enumerates all the programs listed in the Add/Remove Programs dialog box, available from Control Panel.

1. Open Notepad or your favorite script editor.

2. On the first line, type **Option Explicit** to ensure you declare all variables used in the script.

3. Declare the following variables: *objWMIService*, *colItems*, and *objItem*. Add comments following each declaration to specify what each variable is used for.

4. Set *objWMIService* equal to what comes back from the *GetObject* method when used in conjunction with the WMI moniker. Your code will look like the following:

```
Set objWMIService = GetObject("winmgmts:\\")
```

5. Set *colItems* equal to what comes back from issuing the WQL statement "*Select * from WIN32_Product*" as you use the *ExecQuery* method. Your code will look like the following:

```
Set colItems = objWMIService.ExecQuery("SELECT * FROM WIN32_Product")
```

6. Use a *For Each...Next* loop to iterate through *colItems* as you look for the following properties of the *AddRemovePrograms* object: DisplayName, Publisher, and Version. Use the variable *objItem* to assist you in iterating through the collection. Make sure you close out the *For Each...Next* loop with the *Next* command. Your code could will look like the following:

```
For Each objItem In colItems
  WScript.Echo "DisplayName: " & objItem.Name
  WScript.Echo "Publisher: " & objItem.Vendor
  WScript.Echo "Version: " & objItem.Version
  WScript.Echo
Next
```

7. Save your file as YourNameDefaultMoniker.vbs.

8. Make sure you run this program in CScript by going to a command prompt and typing **cscript pathtoyourfile\yourNameDefaultMoniker.vbs**. (More than likely, you have a lot of programs in Add/Remove Programs. If you run the program by double-clicking it, and it runs under WScript, you will have numerous pop-up dialog boxes to close unless you open Task Manager and kill the WScript.exe process.) Depending on how many programs you have installed, it will take several minutes for your script to run.

9. EXTRA CREDIT: Add a message to the beginning of your script letting the user know the script is beginning. Also add a message letting the user know when the script is finished. Then tell the user how long the script ran. Compare your results with \My Documents\Microsoft Press\VBScriptSBS\StepByStep\DefaultMonikerExtra.vbs.

Invoking the WMI Moniker to Display the Machine Boot Configuration

In this section, you explore an alternate method of invoking the WMI moniker. In so doing, you write a WMI script that displays the boot configuration of a machine.

1. Open Notepad or your favorite script editor.

2. On the first line, type **Option Explicit** to ensure you declare all variables used in the script.

3. Declare three variables. The variables are *objWMIService*, *colItems*, and *objItem*.

4. Set *objWMIService* equal to what comes back from the *GetObject* method when used in conjunction with the WMI moniker. In addition, define an impersonation level of Anonymous. Your code will look like the following:

```
Set objWMIService = GetObject("winmgmts:{impersonationLevel=anonymous}")
```

5. Set *colItems* equal to what comes back from issuing the WQL statement *"Select * from Win32_BootConfiguration"* as you use the *ExecQuery* method. Your code will look like the following:

```
Set colItems = objWMIService.ExecQuery("SELECT * FROM Win32_BootConfiguration")
```

6. Use a *For Each...Next* loop to iterate through *colItems* as you look for the following properties of the *Win3_BootConfiguration* object: BootDirectory, Caption, ConfigurationPath, Description, LastDrive, Name, ScratchDirectory, SettingID, and TempDirectory. Use the variable *objItem* to assist you in iterating through the collection. Make sure you close out the *For Each...Next* loop with the *Next* command. Your code will look like the following:

```
For Each objItem In colItems
  WScript.Echo "BootDirectory: " & objItem.BootDirectory
  WScript.Echo "Caption: " & objItem.Caption
  WScript.Echo "ConfigurationPath: " & objItem.ConfigurationPath
  WScript.Echo "Description: " & objItem.Description
```

```
WScript.Echo "LastDrive: " & objItem.LastDrive
WScript.Echo "Name: " & objItem.Name
WScript.Echo "ScratchDirectory: " & objItem.ScratchDirectory
WScript.Echo "SettingID: " & objItem.SettingID
WScript.Echo "TempDirectory: " & objItem.TempDirectory
WScript.Echo
Next
```

7. Save your work as BootConfigA.vbs.

8. Use CScript to run the script. *It will fail!* Why does the script fail? Hint: Check the impersonation level.

9. Change the line containing the WMI moniker. Set the impersonation level to Identify.

10. Save your work as BootConfigB.vbs.

11. Use CScript to run the script. *It will fail!*

12. Why does the script fail? Hint: Check the impersonation level.

13. Change the line containing the WMI moniker. Set the impersonation level to Impersonate.

14. Save your work as BootConfigC.vbs.

15. Use CScript to run the script. It works just fine. Why does the script work?

16. Change the line containing the WMI moniker. Set the impersonation level to Delegate.

17. Save your work as BootConfigD.vbs.

18. Use CScript to run the script. It works just fine. What does this tell you about using the different impersonation levels on Windows Server 2003?

Including Additional Security Permissions

In this section, you will modify the WMI moniker to include the specification of additional security permissions. You will use a script that displays information about the display.

1. Open Notepad or a different script editor.

2. On the first line, type **Option Explicit** to ensure variables are declared and spelled correctly.

3. On the next line, declare the following variables: *objWMIService*, *colItems*, and *objItem*. These are the same variables you used in previous scripts in this chapter.

4. Set *objWMIService* equal to what comes back from the *GetObject* method when used in conjunction with the WMI moniker. In addition, you want to define an impersonation level of Impersonate as well as the special debug privilege. Your code will look like the following:

```
Set objWMIService = GetObject("winmgmts:{impersonationLevel=impersonate, (debug)}")
```

5. Set *colItems* equal to what comes back from issuing the WQL statement *"Select * from Win32_DisplayConfiguration"* as you use the *ExecQuery* method. Your code will look like the following:

```
Set colItems = objWMIService.ExecQuery("SELECT * FROM Win32_DisplayConfiguration")
```

Use a *For Each...Next* loop to iterate through *colItems* as you look for the following properties of the *Win32_DisplayConfiguration* object: BitsPerPel, Caption, Description, DeviceName, DisplayFlags, DisplayFrequency, DriverVersion, LogPixels, PelsHeight, PelsWidth, SettingID, and SpecificationVersion. Use the variable *objItem* to assist you in iterating through the collection. Make sure you close out the *For Each...Next* loop with the *Next* command. Your code will look like the following:

```
For Each objItem in colItems
  WScript.Echo "BitsPerPel: " & objItem.BitsPerPel
  WScript.Echo "Caption: " & objItem.Caption
  WScript.Echo "Description: " & objItem.Description
  WScript.Echo "DeviceName: " & objItem.DeviceName
  WScript.Echo "DisplayFlags: " & objItem.DisplayFlags
  WScript.Echo "DisplayFrequency: " & objItem.DisplayFrequency
  WScript.Echo "DriverVersion: " & objItem.DriverVersion
  WScript.Echo "LogPixels: " & objItem.LogPixels
  WScript.Echo "PelsHeight: " & objItem.PelsHeight
  WScript.Echo "PelsWidth: " & objItem.PelsWidth
  WScript.Echo "SettingID: " & objItem.SettingID
  WScript.Echo "SpecificationVersion: " & objItem.SpecificationVersion
Next
```

6. Save your program as Display.vbs.

7. Modify the WMI connection string to include not only the debug privilege, but also the shutdown privilege. Your code will look like the following:

```
Set objWMIService = GetObject("winmgmts:{impersonationLevel=impersonate, (debug, shutdown) }")
```

8. Modify the WMI connection string to indicate that the WMI connection should attach to the local host machine. This WMI connection string is starting to be rather long, so break the line after you specify the impersonation level. Your code will look like the following:

```
Set objWMIService = GetObject("winmgmts:{impersonationLevel=impersonate," _
& "(debug, shutdown)}\\localhost")
```

9. Save your work.

10. Modify the connection in the preceding string to indicate that you want WMI to make a connection to the *\root\cimv2* namespace on the computer called *localhost*. Your code will look like the following:

```
Set objWMIService = GetObject("winmgmts:{impersonationLevel=impersonate," _
  & "(debug, shutdown)}\\localhost\root\cimv2")
```

11. Save your work and then use CScript to run the script.

One Step Further: Using *Win32_Environment* and VBScript to Learn About WMI

In this section, you use *Win32_Environment* and VBScript to learn about both WMI and the environment settings on your server.

1. Open Notead or some other script editor.

2. On the first line, type **Option Explicit**.

3. Use the *Dim* command to declare the following variables: *objWMIService*, *colItems*, *objItem*, *wmiQuery*, and *strComputer*.

4. Use *WScript.Echo* and the *Now* function to indicate the script is beginning its run.

5. Assign the value of "." to the variable *strComputer*.

6. Assign the query *"Select * from Win32_Environment"* to the variable *wmiQuery*.

7. Set *objWMIService* equal to the handle that comes back from the *GetObject* function with the *winmgmts:* moniker. Incorporate the variable *strComputer* to tell WMI which computer to use to execute the connection.

8. Use the *colItems* variable to hold the object returned from using the *execQuery* method of the *SWbemServicesEx* object. This is seen below:

```
Set colItems = objWMIService.ExecQuery(wmiQuery)
```

9. Use a *For Each...Next* loop to iterate through the collection called *colItems*. For each *objItem* in *colItems*, echo out the following properties: Caption, Description, InstallDate, Name, Status, SystemVariable, UserName, and VariableValue.

10. Close out the *For Each...Next* loop.

11. Echo a line indicating the script is finished and use the *Now* function to print out the time.

12. Save your work as SysEnvironment.vbs.

13. Run the script in CScript.

Chapter 9 Quick Reference

To	Do This
Simplify connecting into WMI, while using default security permissions	Use the WMI moniker
Control security when making a remote connection	Specify the impersonation levels in your script
Allow a script to use the credentials of the person launching the script	Use the Impersonate impersonation level
Allow a script to shut down the server	Use the shutdown privilege

Chapter 10
Querying WMI

Before You Begin

To work through the material presented in this chapter, you need to be familiar with the following concepts from earlier chapters:

- Creating the WMI moniker
- Implementing the *For...Next* construction
- Navigating the WMI namespace
- Implementing *GetObject*
- Implementing the *ExecQuery* method

After completing this chapter, you will be able to:
- Return all properties from all instances of a class
- Return some properties from all instances of a class
- Return all properties from some instances of a class
- Return some properties from some instances of a class

Tell Me Everything About Everything!

When novices first write Windows Management Instrumentation (WMI) scripts, they nearly all begin by asking for every property about all instances of a class that are present on a particular system. (This is also referred to as the infamous *"Select * query"*.) This approach can often return an overwhelming amount of data, particularly when you are querying a class such as installed software, or processes and threads. Rarely would one need to have so much data. Typically, when looking for installed software, you're looking for information about a *particular* software package.

There are, however, several occasions when I want to use the "tell me everything about all instances of a particular class" query:

- During development of a script to see representative data
- When troubleshooting a more directed query (for example, when I'm possibly trying to filter on a field that does not exist)

■ When the returned data is so small that being more precise doesn't make sense

> **Just the Steps**   To return all information from all instances
>
> 1. Make a connection to WMI.
> 2. Use the *Select* statement to choose everything: *Select **.
> 3. Use the *From* statement to indicate the class from which you wish to retrieve data. For example, *From Win32_Share*.

In the next script, you make a connection to the default namespace in WMI and return all the information about all the shares on a local machine. This is actually good practice, because in the past, numerous worms propagated via unsecured shares, and you might have unused shares around—a user might create a share for a friend and then forget to delete it. In the script that follows, called ListShares.vbs, all the information about shares present on the machine is reported.

ListShares.vbs

```
Option Explicit
On Error Resume Next
Dim strComputer
Dim  wmiNS
Dim  wmiQuery
Dim  objWMIService
Dim  colItems
Dim  objItem

strComputer = "."
wmiNS = "\root\cimv2"
wmiQuery = "Select * from Win32_Share"
Set objWMIService = GetObject("winmgmts:\\" & strComputer & wmiNS)
Set colItems = objWMIService.ExecQuery(wmiQuery)

For Each objItem In colItems
  WScript.Echo "AccessMask: " & objItem.AccessMask
  WScript.Echo "AllowMaximum: " & objItem.AllowMaximum
  WScript.Echo "Caption: " & objItem.Caption
  WScript.Echo "Description: " & objItem.Description
  WScript.Echo "InstallDate: " & objItem.InstallDate
  WScript.Echo "MaximumAllowed: " & objItem.MaximumAllowed
  WScript.Echo "Name: " & objItem.Name
  WScript.Echo "Path: " & objItem.Path
  WScript.Echo "Status: " & objItem.Status
  WScript.Echo "Type: " & objItem.Type
  WScript.Echo
Next
```

Header Information

The Header information section of ListShares.vbs contains all the standard information. *Option Explicit* forces the declaration of all variables. This is followed by *On Error Resume Next* to make sure the script goes to the next line of code if it encounters an error.

> **Note**   In Chapter 1, "Starting from Scratch," we talked about the pros and cons of using *On Error Resume Next*. Most of the time, when you are working with WMI, you are displaying property values, which is a harmless activity. Using *On Error Resume Next* helps the script to run, even when the script encounters an error. This is largely a good thing with WMI.

These two standard lines are followed by the same variable names declared in previous WMI scripts: *strComputer*, *wmiNS*, *wmiQuery*, *objWMIService*, *colItems*, and *objItem*. The variable *strComputer* defines the target computer, *wmiNS* specifies the target WMI namespace, *wmiQuery* holds the value of the query to be executed, and *colItems* holds the collection of items that are returned by the query. The variable *objItem* is used by the *For Each...Next* loop to iterate through the collection.

Reference Information

The Reference information section of the script is used to assign values to five of the six variables. The variable *strComputer* is assigned the value of ".", which indicates the script will run against the local computer. The variable *wmiNS* is assigned to *root\cimv2*, which is the default WMI namespace. The variable *wmiQuery* is set to *"Select * from Win32_Share"*. This is the query you want to execute against the default WMI namespace. *Select *** tells WMI that you want to retrieve all properties from the *Win32_Share* object. Note that this query doesn't display all the properties; it simply displays all the properties from the *Win32_Share* object. What you do with the returned data depends on your current needs. Unless you need it, returning all the data might not be a very efficient use of networking resources. It is, however, very easy to construct such a query.

The variable *objWMIService* is used to connect to WMI, and it uses the WMI moniker to do so. Two variables assist in this operation: *strComputer* and *wmiNS*. The *colItems* variable holds the handle that comes back from the *ExecQuery* method that is used to execute your WMI query against the *Win32_Share* class.

Worker and Output Information

The Worker information and Output information sections of the ListShare.vbs script are combined, and the script simply uses *WScript.Echo* to write the various properties and their associated values to the command line (if run in CScript) or to a pop-up dialog box (if run in WScript, which is not a really good idea when you have numerous shares). The most convenient listing of all the available properties for a particular class is contained in the Platform SDK. A quick search for *Win32_Share* reveals the properties listed in Table 10-1.

Table 10-1   Win32_Share Properties

Data type	Property	Meaning
Boolean	AllowMaximum	Allow maximum number of connections? True or False.

Table 10-1   Win32_Share Properties

Data type	Property	Meaning
string	Caption	Short, one-line description.
string	Description	Description.
datetime	InstallDate	When the share was created (optional).
uint32	MaximumAllowed	Number of concurrent connections allowed. Only valid when *AllowMaximum* is set to *False*.
string	Name	Share name.
string	Path	Physical path to the share.
string	Status	Current status of the share: Degraded, OK, or Failed.
uint32	Type	Type of resource shared: disk, file, printer, and so on.

Quick Check

Q. **What is the syntax for a query that returns all properties of a given object?**

A. *Select* * returns all properties of a given object.

Q. **What is one reason for using *Select* * instead of a more directed query?**

A. In troubleshooting, *Select* * is useful because it returns any available data. In addition, *Select* * is useful in trying to characterize the data that might be returned from a query.

Selective Data from All Instances

The next level of sophistication (from using *Select* *) is to return only the properties you are interested in. This is a more efficient strategy. For instance, in the previous example, you did a *Select* * query and returned a lot of data you weren't necessarily interested in. Suppose you wanted to know only which shares are on each machine. With a simple change to the *wmiQuery* variable and by deleting a few *WScript.Echo* commands, you can modify your script to get exactly what you want.

Just the Steps   To select specific data

1. Make a connection to WMI.

2. Use the *Select* statement to choose the specific property you are interested in (for example, *Select name*).

3. Use the *From* statement to indicate the class from which you want to retrieve data (for example, *From Win32_Share*).

Only two small changes in the ListShares.vbs script are required to enable you to garner specific data via the WMI script. In place of the asterisk in the *Select* statement assigned in the Reference information section of the script, you substitute the property you want. In this case, only the name of the shares is required.

The second change is to eliminate all unused properties from the Output section. This is very important because the script *could* fail if you try to echo out a property that is not selected in the *Select* statement. I said it *could* fail as opposed to *would* fail, because if you include *On Error Resume Next*, the script will work. If you don't include this error handling line of code, the script fails with an "Object does not support this property or method" error. Because this error message is rather confusing, you should be able to recognize it! It is important that you select each item for which you want to return information. In this way, WMI Query Language (WQL) acts just like Structured Query Language (SQL). If you don't select a property, you can't do anything with the property, because to the program, the object doesn't exist. Here is the modified ListName_Only_AllShares.vbs script:

ListName_Only_AllShares.vbs

```
Option Explicit
On Error Resume Next
Dim strComputer
Dim wmiNS
Dim wmiQuery
Dim objWMIService
Dim colItems
Dim objItem

strComputer = "."
wmiNS = "\root\cimv2"
wmiQuery = "Select Name from win32_Share"
Set objWMIService = GetObject("winmgmts:\\" & strComputer & wmiNS)
Set colItems = objWMIService.ExecQuery(wmiQuery)

For Each objItem In colItems
  WScript.Echo "Name: " & objItem.Name
Next
```

Selecting Multiple Properties

If you're interested in only a certain number of properties, you can use *Select* to specify that. All you have to do is separate the properties by a comma. Suppose you run the preceding script and find a number of undocumented shares on one of the servers—you might want a little bit more information such as the path to the share and how many people are allowed to connect to it. By default, when a share is created, the "maximum allowed" bit is set. This basically says anyone who has rights to the share can connect. This can be a problem, because if too many people connect to a share, they can degrade the performance of the server. To preclude such an eventuality, I always specify a maximum number of connections to the server.

> **Note**   I occasionally see people asking whether spaces or namecase in the property list matters. In fact, when I first started writing scripts and they failed, I often modified spacing and capitalization in feeble attempts to make the script work. Spacing and capitalization *do not matter* for WMI properties.

The revised script, called ListName_Path_Max_Shares.vbs, now looks like the following:

ListName_Path_Max_Shares.vbs

```
Option Explicit
'On Error Resume Next
Dim strComputer
Dim wmiNS
Dim wmiQuery
Dim objWMIService
Dim colItems
Dim objItem

strComputer = "."
wmiNS = "\root\cimv2"
wmiQuery = "Select path, allowMaximum from win32_Share"
Set objWMIService = GetObject("winmgmts:\\" & strComputer & wmiNS)
Set colItems = objWMIService.ExecQuery(wmiQuery)

For Each objItem in colItems
  WScript.Echo "Name: " & objItem.Name
  WScript.Echo "Path: " & objItem.path
  WScript.Echo "AllowMaximum: " & objItem.AllowMaximum
  WScript.Echo vbNewLine
Next
```

The technique of specifying only the properties you're interested in can be used with any of the supported properties from *Win32_Share* listed in Table 10-1. Interestingly enough, you don't really need to include the Name property on the *Select* line, because for *Win32_Share*, Name is the key property. This is seen in Figure 10-1.

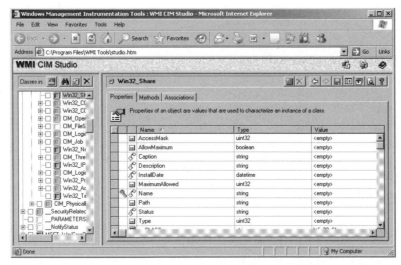

Figure 10-1 Key properties are easily identified via the WMI CIM Studio tool

The key property in WMI works just like the key column in a database: It is used to uniquely identify a row, and it is often the column or property that is indexed to make searching easier. This is just like the key to a house or to a car. The key provides entry into the house or car so that you can access the property inside. The key property is always returned, even when it isn't specifically mentioned on the *Select* line.

To list running processes

1. Open the \My Documents\Microsoft Press\VBScriptSBS\Templates \wmiTemplate.vbs script in Microsoft Notepad or some other script editor and save it as YourNameListRunningProcesses.vbs.

2. Declare two new variables, *strProperties* and *strValues*. One will be used to hold the specific list of properties you will request. The other will hold the values that come back from the query. The code to do this looks like the following:

```
Dim strProperties 'properties to choose
Dim strValues 'string of wmi values
```

3. Look up *WIN32_process* in the Platform SDK and choose some interesting properties. Assign them to the *strProperties* variable as a string. My code to do this looks like the following:

```
strProperties = "name,processID,pageFaults,WorkingSetSize"
```

4. Modify the *wmiQuery* variable so that it selects only the properties specified in the *strProperties* variable from *WIN32_process*, but only if the process is not equal to *0*, which is the system idle process. The code to do this looks like the following:

```
wmiQuery = "Select " & strProperties & " from win32_process" &_
    " where processID <>0"
```

5. Inside the *For Each...Next* loop, delete all the *WScript.Echo* lines. The new *For Each...Next* loop looks like the following:

```
For Each objItem in colItems

Next
```

6. To reduce typing, you can use *With* and *End With* to allow us to refer to a series of properties on the object *objItem* without having to re-qualify the name *objItem* inside the *For Each...Next* loop. This means that every property will now use the qualifier *objItem*. This is seen below:

```
With objItem

End With
```

7. Use the *strValues* variable to hold the output from retrieving the values from each instance in the collection. We are producing a *csv* output, and therefore we will place commas between each property value. The completed code is seen below:

```
strValues = .name & "," & .processID & "," &_
    .PageFaults & "," & .WorkingSetSize
```

8. After the *End With* statement, but before the *Next* command, print out the value of *strValues* by using *WScript.Echo*. This will be a debug statement, and later we will turn it off. The command looks like the following:

```
WScript.Echo strValues
```

9. Save and run your script in CScript. The output will look something like the (trimmed) output listed below. If your script does not work properly, compare it to the \My Documents\Microsoft Press\VBScriptSBS\ch10\ListRunningProcesses.vbs script.

```
System,4,11275,225280
smss.exe,732,211,380928
csrss.exe,932,42425,4616192
winlogon.exe,956,16377,4464640
```

Adding a logging subroutine

1. Open the \My Documents\Microsoft Press\VBScriptSBS\ch10\ListRunningProcesses.vbs script and save it as YourNameLoggedRunningProcesses.vbs.

2. Add a subroutine to be used to write out to a log file. This subroutine will accept one input parameter called *strIN*. The code to do this looks like the following:

```
Sub subText(strIN)
End sub
```

3. At the top of the subroutine, add variables to hold *filesystemobject*, the file object, the *wshShell* object, and the path to the desktop and the name of the log file. I used the variables listed below.

```
Dim objFSO      'the filesystemobject
Dim objFile     'file object
Dim objShell    'wshshell object
Dim strPath     'path to desktop
Dim strFile     'log file name
```

4. Define a constant *ForAppending* and set it to 8. Define an additional constant called *createFile*, and set it equal to *True*. This is seen below:

```
Const ForAppending = 8
Const createFile = True
```

5. Below the *subText* subroutine, define a function called *funfix* that uses an input called *strIN*. Use this function to add a backslash ("\") to the beginning of the *strIN* parameter. Assign it back to the *funfix* function, as seen below:

```
Function funfix (strIN)
funfix = "\" & strIN
End Function
```

6. Under the *createFile* constant in the *subText* subroutine, use the file name *logProps.csv* and assign it to the *strFile* variable. Use the *funfix* function to prepend a backslash to the file name. This is seen below:

```
strFile = funfix("logProps.csv")
```

7. Create an instance of the *wshShell* object and assign the object that comes back from the *CreateObject* command to the variable *objShell*, as seen below:

```
Set objShell = CreateObject("WScript.Shell")
```

8. Create an instance of *FileSystemObject* and assign the object that is returned to the *objFSO* variable, as seen below:

```
Set objFSO = CreateObject("Scripting.FileSystemObject")
```

9. Use the SpecialFolders property of the *wshShell* object to retrieve the path to the desktop. Assign the path to the *strPath* variable. The code to do this is seen below:

```
strPath = objShell.SpecialFolders("desktop")
```

10. Use the *strPath* variable to build up a complete path to the log file. Use *strPath* and concatenate it with the *strFile* variable, as seen below:

```
strFile = strPath & strFile
```

11. Use the *OpenTextFile* method from the file system object to open the *strFile* file and append to it. If the file does not exist, create the file. Assign *testStreamObject*, which is returned to the *objFile* variable, as seen below:

```
Set objFile = objFSO.OpenTextFile(strFile,ForAppending,createFile)
```

12. Once you have a text stream object, you can use the *WriteLine* method to write the data contained in the *strIN* variable to the file, as seen below:

```
objFile.WriteLine (strIN)
```

13. In the main script, just under the line that defines the WMI query, call the *subText* subroutine, and pass it the contents of the *strProperties* variable. This will add a column header to the text output. The code to do this is seen below:

```
subText(strProperties)
```

14. In the main script, just under the *end with* statement, call the *subText* subroutine and pass the contents of the *strValues* variable. This code is seen below:

```
subText(strValues)
```

15. The output will be a .csv file, which when double-clicked will open in Microsoft Excel if you have the Excel application installed. If you do have Excel installed, then the output will look like Figure 10-2.

16. Save and run the script. LogProps.csv should be created on the desktop. If it is not, compare your script with \My Documents\Microsoft Press\VBScriptSBS\ch10\LoggedRunningProcesses.vbs.

	A	B	C	D	E
1	name	processID	pageFaults	WorkingSetSize	
2	System	4	11307	225280	
3	smss.exe	732	211	380928	
4	csrss.exe	932	45432	4841472	
5	winlogon.exe	956	16898	1568768	
6	services.exe	1000	13223	7540736	
7	lsass.exe	1012	82906	2310144	
8	svchost.exe	1180	1686	3674112	
9	svchost.exe	1272	1405	4378624	
10	svchost.exe	1308	649298	38707200	
11	spoolsv.exe	1580	4897	7053312	
12	nvsvc32.exe	1916	3452	2580480	
13	explorer.exe	792	98692	35868672	
14	wmiprvse.exe	1536	5251	5337088	
15	wmiprvse.exe	3288	3566	4689920	
16	WINWORD.EXE	2280	31650	3084288	
17	svchost.exe	3052	1359	4108288	
18	PrimalScript.exe	3056	14786	5009408	
19	wmplayer.exe	4048	175149	9756672	
20	imapi.exe	2968	912	3588096	
21	cscript.exe	2828	1586	6078464	
22	wmiprvse.exe	2168	1378	5529600	

Figure 10-2   By default, a .csv file opens in Microsoft Office Excel

Quick Check

Q. **To select specific properties from an object, what do you need to do on the *Select* line?**

A. You need to separate the specific properties of an object with a comma on the *Select* line of the *ExecQuery* method.

Q. **To avoid error messages, what must be done when selecting individual properties on the *Select* line?**

A. Errors can be avoided if you make sure each property used is specified in the *Select* line. For example, the WMI query is just like a paper bag that gets filled with items that are picked up by using the *Select* statement. If you do not put something in the paper bag, you cannot pull anything out of the bag. In the same manner, if you do not "select" a property, you cannot later print or sort on that property. This is exactly the way that a SQL *Select* statement works.

> **Q.**   **What can you check for in your script if it fails with an "object does not support this method or property" error?**
>
> **A.**   If you are getting "object does not support this method or property" error messages, you might want to ensure you have referenced the property in your *Select* statement prior to trying to work with it in an Output section.

Choosing Specific Instances

In many situations, you will want to limit the data you return to a specific instance of that class in the data set. If you go back to your query and add a *Where* clause to the *Select* statement, you'll be able to greatly reduce the amount of information returned by the query. Notice that in the value associated with the WMI query, you added a dependency that indicated you wanted only information with share name *C$*. This value is not case-sensitive, but it must be surrounded with single quotation marks, as you can see in the wmiQuery string in the following script. These single quotation marks are important because they tell WMI that the value is a string value and not some other programmatic item. Because the addition of the *Where* statement was the only thing you really added to the ListShares.vbs script, we're not going to go into a long discussion of the ListSpecificShares.vbs script.

ListSpecificShares.vbs

```
Option Explicit
'On Error Resume Next
Dim strComputer
Dim wmiNS
Dim wmiQuery
Dim objWMIService
Dim colItems
Dim objItem

strComputer = "."
wmiNS = "\root\cimv2"
wmiQuery = "Select path, allowMaximum from win32_Share" &_
    " where name = 'C$'"
Set objWMIService = GetObject("winmgmts:\\" & strComputer & wmiNS)
Set colItems = objWMIService.ExecQuery(wmiQuery)

For Each objItem in colItems
  WScript.Echo "Name: " & objItem.Name
  WScript.Echo "Path: " & objItem.path
  WScript.Echo "AllowMaximum: " & objItem.AllowMaximum
Next
```

> **Just the Steps**   To limit specific data
>
> **1.**   Make a connection to WMI.

2. Use the *Select* statement to choose the specific property you are interested in (for example, Select name).

3. Use the *From* statement to indicate the class from which you want to retrieve data (for example, *From Win32_Share*).

4. Add a *Where* clause to further limit the data set that is returned. Make sure the properties specified in the *Where* clause are first mentioned in the *Select* statement (for example, *where name*).

5. Add an evaluation operator. You can use the equal sign, or the less than or greater than symbols (for example, *where name = 'C$'*).

Using an Operator

One of the good things you can do is use greater than and less than operators in your evaluation clause. You might wonder what is so good about greater than. It makes working with alphabetic characters and numeric characters easy. If you work on a server that hosts home directories for users (which are often named after their user names), you can easily produce a list of all home directories from the letters *T* through *Z* by using the *> S* expression. This is illustrated in the ListSpecificGreaterThanShares.vbs script.

ListSpecificGreaterThanShares.vbs
```
Option Explicit
'On Error Resume Next
Dim strComputer
Dim wmiNS
Dim wmiQuery
Dim objWMIService
Dim colItems
Dim objItem

strComputer = "."
wmiNS = "\root\cimv2"
wmiQuery = "Select Name, path, allowMaximum from win32_Share where name > 's'"
Set objWMIService = GetObject("winmgmts:\\" & strComputer & wmiNS)
Set colItems = objWMIService.ExecQuery(wmiQuery)

For Each objItem in colItems
  WScript.Echo "Name: " & objItem.Name
  WScript.Echo "Path: " & objItem.path
  WScript.Echo "AllowMaximum: " & objItem.AllowMaximum
  WScript.Echo VbCrLf
Next
```

There are many other available operators in Microsoft Visual Basic, Scripting Edition (VBScript) as well. These operators are listed in Table 10-2.

Table 10-2 VBScript Operators

Operator	Description
=	Equal to

Table 10-2   **VBScript Operators**

Operator	Description
<	Less than
>	Greater than
<=	Less than or equal to
>=	Greater than or equal to
!=	Not equal to
<>	Not equal to (both != and <> mean not equal to)

Identifying service accounts

1. Open the \My Documents\Microsoft Press\VBScriptSBS\Templates\wmiTemplate.vbs script and save it as YourNameServiceAccount.vbs.

2. Modify the WMI query to select the start name and the started status from the *WIN32_service* WMI class. But only do this if the name used to start the service is not equal to *localSystem*. This query is seen below.

```
wmiQuery = "Select StartName, started from win32_service" &_
    " where startName <> 'localSystem'"
```

3. Inside the *For Each...Next* loop, delete all the *WScript.Echo* commands except for one.

4. Modify the output to print out the name of the service, the name used to start the service, and the status of the service. Use the intrinsic constant *VbCrLf* to make a new line. Use intrinsic constant *vbTab* to tab between properties. This code is seen below:

```
WScript.Echo objItem.name, VbCrLf & vbTab &_
    objItem.StartName & vbTab & "Running: " & objItem.Started
```

5. Save and run the script by using CScript. The output will look similar to the following printout.

```
Alerter
    NT AUTHORITY\LocalService      Running: False
ALG
    NT AUTHORITY\LocalService      Running: False
aspnet_state
    NT AUTHORITY\NetworkService  Running: False
```

6. If your script does not run as expected, compare it to the \My Documents\Microsoft Press\VBScriptSBS\ch10\ServiceAccount.vbs script.

Logging the service accounts

1. Open the \My Documents\Microsoft Press\VBScriptSBS\ch10\ServiceAccount.vbs script and save it as YourNameServiceAccountLogged.vbs.

2. Open the \My Documents\Microsoft Press\VBScriptSBS\ch10\LoggedRunning Processes.vbs script and copy the *subText* subroutine, as well as the *funfix* function.

Paste both of these to the bottom of your script. The code you will copy looks like the following:

```
' **** subs below ****
Sub subText(strIN)
Dim objFSO              'the filesystemobject
Dim objFile            'file object
Dim objShell           'wshshell object
Dim strPath            'path to desktop
Dim strFile            'log file name

Const ForAppending = 8
Const CreateFile = True
strFile = funfix("logProps.csv") 'adds \ to file name

Set objShell = CreateObject("WScript.Shell")
Set objFSO = CreateObject("Scripting.FileSystemObject")
strPath = objShell.SpecialFolders("desktop")
strFile = strPath & strFile
Set objFile = objfso.OpenTextFile(strFile,ForAppending,createFile)
objFile.WriteLine (strIN)
End Sub

Function funfix (strIN)
funfix = "\" & strin
End Function
```

3. In the subroutine, locate the line that assigns the file name to the *strFile* variable. Change the name of the file to LogService.csv. This is seen below:

```
strFile = funfix("logService.csv")
```

4. Inside the *For Each...Next* loop of the main script, we need to remove the *WScript.Echo* statement and the *VbCrLf* statements, and intersperse the properties with commas instead. We need to declare a new variable called *strValues* and then assign our Worker section to this variable. The code to be placed in the *For Each...Next* loop is seen here:

```
strValues = objItem.name & "," & objItem.StartName & _
    "," & objItem.started
```

5. On the line below the new line to be placed inside the *For Each...Next* loop, call the subroutine and pass the *strValues* variable as an input parameter to the sub. This is seen here:

```
subText(strValues)
```

6. Save and run the script. A .csv file will appear on the desktop. The results will look like the spreadsheet in Figure 10-3. If they do not, then compare your script with the \My Documents\Microsoft Press\VBScriptSBS\ch10\ServiceAccountLogged.vbs script.

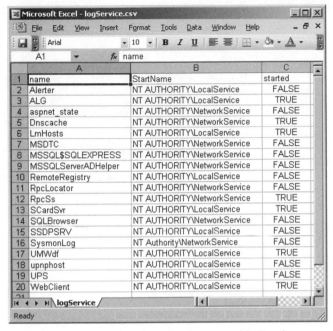

Figure 10-3   To display data that is opened in Excel, use .csv files

Where Is the *Where* Clause?

To more easily modify the *Where* clause in a script, substitute the *Where* clause with a variable. This configuration can be modified to include command-line input as well. This is seen in the ListSpecificWhereVariableShares.vbs script.

ListSpecificWhereVariableShares.vbs

```
Option Explicit
'On Error Resume Next
Dim strComputer
Dim wmiNS
Dim wmiQuery
Dim objWMIService
Dim colItems
Dim objItem
Dim vwhere

strComputer = "."
wmiNS = "\root\cimv2"
vwhere = " name = 'C$'"
wmiQuery = "Select Name, path, allowMaximum from win32_Share where " & vwhere
Set objWMIService = GetObject("winmgmts:\\" & strComputer & wmiNS)
Set colItems = objWMIService.ExecQuery(wmiQuery)

For Each objItem in colItems
  WScript.Echo "Name: " & objItem.Name
  WScript.Echo "Path: " & objItem.path
```

```
WScript.Echo "AllowMaximum: " & objItem.AllowMaximum
WScript.Echo
```

Next

Let's return to our scenario in which you are looking for shares that have not been limited by the number of connections. You can modify the *vWhere* variable to look for *AllowMaximum* = '*true*'. It would look like the following:

```
strComputer = "."
wmiNS = "\root\cimv2"
vWhere = " AllowMaximum = 'true'"
wmiQuery = "Select Name, path, allowMaximum from Win32_Share where " & vWhere
Set objWMIService = GetObject("winmgmts:\\" & strComputer & wmiNS)
Set colItems = objWMIService.ExecQuery(wmiQuery)

For Each objItem In colItems
  WScript.Echo "Name: " & objItem.Name
  WScript.Echo "Path: " & objItem.path
  WScript.Echo "AllowMaximum: " & objItem.AllowMaximum
  WScript.Echo

Next
```

Quick Check

Q. To limit the specific data returned by a query, what WQL statement can be utilized?

A. The *Where* clause is very powerful in limiting the specific data returned by a query.

Q. What are three possible operators that can be employed in creating powerful *Where* clauses?

A. The equal sign and the greater than and less than symbols can be used to evaluate the data prior to returning the data set.

Running against multiple computers

1. Open the wmiTemplate.vbs template in Notepad or your favorite script editor. Save the file as YourNameMultipleComputerMouse.vbs.

2. In the Header section of the script, declare two new variables (*strComputers*, *aryComputers*) that will be used to hold the string of computer names to target, as well as the array that will be created later. This is seen here:

```
Dim strComputers          'string of several computers
Dim aryComputers          'an array of computers
```

3. Assign a few computer names to the *strComputers* variable. Use any computer reachable via your network, or you can use the ones listed here:

```
strComputers = "localhost,127.0.0.1,loopback"
```

4. Use the *Split* function to turn *strComputers* into an array. Assign the array to the variable *aryComputers*, as seen below:

```
aryComputers = Split(strComputers,",")
```

5. Modify the WMI query so that it chooses the Handedness property from the *WIN32_PointingDevice* WMI class. The query will look like the following:

```
wmiQuery = "Select Handedness from win32_pointingdevice"
```

6. Use *WScript.Echo* to print out the WMI query. This will be a header line for the output.

```
WScript.Echo wmiQuery
```

7. Modify the Output section of the script to echo out the Handedness property value. This will be the only line in the *For Each...Next* loop that iterates through *colItems*. Use *vbTab* to space over the output. This is seen below:

```
For Each objItem in colItems
     WScript.Echo vbTab & "handedness: " & objItem.handedness
Next
```

8. Use *For Each...Next* to walk through the array. Use the *strComputer* variable to hold an individual computer from the array. Make sure you close out the loop by putting *Next* as the last line in the script, as seen below:

```
For Each strComputer In aryComputers
   Set objWMIService = GetObject("winmgmts:\\" & strComputer & wmiNS)
   Set colItems = objWMIService.ExecQuery(wmiQuery)

   For Each objItem in colItems
     WScript.Echo vbTab & "handedness: " & objItem.handedness
   Next
Next
```

9. Under the *For Each strComputer In aryComputers* line, use *WScript.Echo* to print out the name of the computer being queried. This value is contained in the *strComputer* variable.

```
WScript.Echo "Computer: " & strComputer
```

10. Save and run the script using CScript. Your output will be similar to the output below. If it is not, then compare your script with \My Documents\Microsoft Press\VBScriptSBS\ch10\MultipleComputerMouse.vbs.

```
Select Handedness from win32_pointingdevice
Computer: localhost
   handedness: 2
   handedness: 2
Computer: 127.0.0.1
   handedness: 2
   handedness: 2
```

```
Computer: loopback
   handedness: 2
   handedness: 2
```

Writing an Informative WMI Script Step-By-Step Instructions

In this section, you are going to write a WMI script that returns a lot of information about processes. This will be used as a starter script later.

1. Open Notepad or your faovirite script editor.

2. On the first line, type **Option Explicit** to ensure you declare all variables used in the script.

3. Declare the following variables: *objWMIService*, *colItems*, *objItem*, and *wmiQuery*. To specify what each variable is used for, add comments following each declaration.

4. Assign *wmiQuery* to be equal to a WQL *Select* statement that returns everything from the *win32_Process* class. Your code will look like the following:

```
wmiQuery = "Select * from Win32_Process"
```

5. Set *objWMIService* equal to the object returned by the *GetObject* method when used in conjunction with the WMI moniker. Your code will look like the following:

```
Set objWMIService = GetObject("winmgmts:\\")
```

6. Set *colItems* equal to object returned by issuing the WQL statement held by the variable *wmiQuery* when you use the *ExecQuery* method. Your code will look like the following:

```
Set colItems = objWMIService.ExecQuery(wmiQuery)
```

7. Use a *For Each...Next* loop to iterate through *colItems*. Instead of typing all the properties in your script, open the student resource CD and copy the *For Each...Next* loop from the StepByStep_Starter_For Each Next Loop.vbs script in \My Documents \Microsoft Press\VBScriptSBS\ch10\StepByStep.

8. Save your work as YourNameInformativeWMI.vbs.

9. Run your script in CScript. Your completed script will look like the following:

```
Option Explicit
On Error Resume Next
Dim wmiQuery
Dim objWMIService
Dim colItems
Dim objItem

wmiQuery = "Select * from Win32_Process"
Set objWMIService = GetObject("winmgmts:\\")
Set colItems = objWMIService.ExecQuery(wmiQuery)

For Each objItem In colItems
  WScript.Echo "Caption: " & objItem.Caption
```

```
    WScript.Echo "CommandLine: " & objItem.CommandLine
    WScript.Echo "CreationClassName: " & objItem.CreationClassName
    WScript.Echo "CreationDate: " & objItem.CreationDate
    WScript.Echo "CSCreationClassName: " & objItem.CSCreationClassName
    WScript.Echo "CSName: " & objItem.CSName
    WScript.Echo "Description: " & objItem.Description
    WScript.Echo "ExecutablePath: " & objItem.ExecutablePath
    WScript.Echo "ExecutionState: " & objItem.ExecutionState
    WScript.Echo "Handle: " & objItem.Handle
    WScript.Echo "HandleCount: " & objItem.HandleCount
    WScript.Echo "InstallDate: " & objItem.InstallDate
    WScript.Echo "KernelModeTime: " & objItem.KernelModeTime
    WScript.Echo "MaximumWorkingSetSize: " & objItem.MaximumWorkingSetSize
    WScript.Echo "MinimumWorkingSetSize: " & objItem.MinimumWorkingSetSize
    WScript.Echo "Name: " & objItem.Name
    WScript.Echo "OSCreationClassName: " & objItem.OSCreationClassName
    WScript.Echo "OSName: " & objItem.OSName
    WScript.Echo "OtherOperationCount: " & objItem.OtherOperationCount
    WScript.Echo "OtherTransferCount: " & objItem.OtherTransferCount
    WScript.Echo "PageFaults: " & objItem.PageFaults
    WScript.Echo "PageFileUsage: " & objItem.PageFileUsage
    WScript.Echo "ParentProcessId: " & objItem.ParentProcessId
    WScript.Echo "PeakPageFileUsage: " & objItem.PeakPageFileUsage
    WScript.Echo "PeakVirtualSize: " & objItem.PeakVirtualSize
    WScript.Echo "PeakWorkingSetSize: " & objItem.PeakWorkingSetSize
    WScript.Echo "Priority: " & objItem.Priority
    WScript.Echo "PrivatePageCount: " & objItem.PrivatePageCount
    WScript.Echo "ProcessId: " & objItem.ProcessId
    WScript.Echo "QuotaNonPagedPoolUsage: " & objItem.QuotaNonPagedPoolUsage
    WScript.Echo "QuotaPagedPoolUsage: " & objItem.QuotaPagedPoolUsage
    WScript.Echo "QuotaPeakNonPagedPoolUsage: " & _
       objItem.QuotaPeakNonPagedPoolUsage
     WScript.Echo "QuotaPeakPagedPoolUsage: " & objItem.QuotaPeakPagedPoolUsage
    WScript.Echo "ReadOperationCount: " & objItem.ReadOperationCount
    WScript.Echo "ReadTransferCount: " & objItem.ReadTransferCount
    WScript.Echo "SessionId: " & objItem.SessionId
    WScript.Echo "Status: " & objItem.Status
    WScript.Echo "TerminationDate: " & objItem.TerminationDate
    WScript.Echo "ThreadCount: " & objItem.ThreadCount
    WScript.Echo "UserModeTime: " & objItem.UserModeTime
    WScript.Echo "VirtualSize: " & objItem.VirtualSize
    WScript.Echo "WindowsVersion: " & objItem.WindowsVersion
    WScript.Echo "WorkingSetSize: " & objItem.WorkingSetSize
    WScript.Echo "WriteOperationCount: " & objItem.WriteOperationCount
    WScript.Echo "WriteTransferCount: " & objItem.WriteTransferCount
    WScript.Echo " **********************************"

Next
```

One-Step-Further: Obtaining More Direct Information

In this section, you modify the \My Documents\Microsoft Press\VBScriptSBS\ch10\
OneStepFurther\InformativeWMI.vbs script to return a bit more directed information.

1. Open Notepad or some other editor.

2. Open the InformativeWMI.vbs script and save it as YourNameDirectedWMI.vbs.

3. Under the list of declared variables, add a new declaration for a variable called *vWhere*.

4. Insert a new line above the line defining the WMI query.

5. Save and run the script from a command line using CScript.

6. Identify no more than five or six "interesting properties" for inclusion in your new script. I decided to use the following: *Name*, *CommandLine*, *MaximumWorkingSetSize*, *QuotaPeakNonPagedPoolUsage*, *ProcessID*, and *ThreadCount*. I chose *CommandLine* rather than the executable path because many times, programs will launch with a command-line parameter (or switch), which does not show up in the executable path variable. In addition, when something is running in the svcHost, the command-line parameter enables you to see what is actually running in that service host. Your *For Each...Next* loop might look something like this code:

```
For Each objItem In colItems
  WScript.Echo "CommandLine: " & objItem.CommandLine
  WScript.Echo "PID: " & objItem.ProcessID
  WScript.Echo "MaximumWorkingSetSize: " & objItem.MaximumWorkingSetSize
  WScript.Echo "QuotaPeakNonPagedPoolUsage: " & _
    objItem.QuotaPeakNonPagedPoolUsage
  WScript.Echo "ThreadCount: " & objItem.ThreadCount
  WScript.Echo " *********************************"
Next
```

7. Save your work.

8. Above the *wmiQuery* line, define the *vWhere* variable to be equal to a *Where* clause that specifies the number of threads as greater than 10. Make sure you encase the entire *Where* clause in a set of double quotation marks. In addition, make sure that the number is also encased in single quotation marks. That will entail a *'10'''* at the end of your *Where* clause. Your code might look like the following:

```
vWhere = " where threadCount > '10'"
```

9. Save your work.

10. Modify the WMI query to utilize the *vWhere* variable. This is rather simple in that all you need to do is insert a space at the end of the query inside the double quotation marks and then use the ampersand and type the *vWhere* variable name. The code will look like the following:

```
wmiQuery = "Select * from Win32_Process " & vWhere
```

11. Save and run your script in CScript. If it does not run properly, compare your script with the \My Documents\Microsoft Press\VBScriptSBS\ch10\OneStepFurther\Directed-WMI.vbs script.

Using a More Complicated *Where* Clause Step-by-Step InstructionsIn this section, you modify the \My Documents\Microsoft Press\VBScriptSBS\ch10\OneStepFurther\Directed-WMI.vbs file to use a more complicated *Where* clause.

1. Open Notpad or your favorite script editor.

2. Open the \DirectedWMI.vbs file and save it as YourNameDirectedWMI_Where.vbs.

3. Modify the *vWhere* clause to include the requirement that the Process ID (PID) is greater than 100. Your completed *vWhere* line might look like the following:

    ```
    vwhere = " where threadCount > '10' and ProcessID >100"
    ```

4. Save your script and run it in CScript. Notice how many lines of data are returned.

5. Modify the *vWhere* clause so that the PID must be greater than 1,000. Your code will look like the following:

    ```
    vwhere = " where threadCount > '10' and ProcessID >1000"
    ```

6. Save the script and run it in CScript. Notice how the data set has been trimmed.

7. Now change the thread count so that it is 50. Your code will look like the following:

    ```
    vwhere = " where threadCount > '50' and ProcessID >1000"
    ```

8. How many lines of data are returned now? On my machine there are none.

9. Now you are going to switch operators. Change the *and* to an *or*. The line will now look like the following:

    ```
    vwhere = " where threadCount > '50' or ProcessID >1000"
    ```

10. Look through the data that is returned. You will see data in which the thread count is greater than 50, and you will see data in which the process ID is greater than 1,000, but you will probably not see both in a single data set (that is what we did in step 7).

11. Save and run your script. If there are problems, compare your script with the DirectedWMI_Where.vbs script in the One Step Further folder.

Chapter 10 Quick Reference

To	Do This
Execute a WMI query	Use the *ExecQuery* method
Limit the number of instances returned in response to a query	Use a *Where* clause
Limit the number of properties returned from the object	Specify individual properties in the *Select* statement
Return only specific data about a specific item	Use a query that chooses individual properties in the *Select* statement, and identify an individual instance via the *Where* clause

Part III
Advanced Windows Administration

In this part:

Chapter 11: Introduction to Active Directory Service Interfaces 251

Chapter 12: Writing for ADSI 269

Chapter 13: Using ADO to Perform Searches 293

Chapter 14: Configuring Networking Components 315

Chapter 15: Using Subroutines and Functions 329

Chapter 16: Logon Scripts 349

Chapter 17: Working with the Registry 367

Chapter 18: Working with Printers 381

Chapter 11

Introduction to Active Directory Service Interfaces

Before You Begin

To work through the material presented in this chapter, you need to be familiar with the following concepts from earlier chapters:

- Creating arrays
- Outputting data to text files
- Reading information contained in text files
- Implementing the *For...Next* construction
- Implementing the *Select Case* construction

After completing this chapter, you will be able to:

- Connect to Microsoft Active Directory Service Interfaces (ADSI) providers
- Work with Microsoft Active Directory directory service namespaces
- Create organizational units (OUs) in Active Directory
- Create users in Active Directory

Working with ADSI

In this section, you use ADSI and Microsoft Visual Basic, Scripting Edition (VBScript) to perform basic network administration tasks. The following list summarizes some high-level uses of ADSI and VBScript:

- Importing a list of names and creating user accounts
- Importing a list and changing user passwords
- Importing a list and creating an entire organizational unit structure following an upgrade to Microsoft Windows Server 2003
- Reading the Microsoft Exchange 5.x directory and setting the display name in Active Directory with the value from Exchange 5.x

- Reading the Exchange 5.x directory for a default personalized Simple Mail Transfer Protocol (SMTP) address and setting it in Active Directory

- Reading the computer name or Internet Protocol (IP) address and mapping local printers to users

- Creating personalized shortcuts for users at logon time based on group memberships

- Mapping drives based on OU membership

> **Just the Steps**   To connect to Active Directory
>
> 1. Implement a connection to Active Directory.
> 2. Use the appropriate provider.
> 3. Specify the path to the appropriate object in Active Directory.
> 4. Use *SetInfo* to write changes to Active Directory.

In a basic fashion, the following script, CreateOU.vbs, uses each of the four steps in the preceding Just the Steps feature. CreateOU.vbs uses variables for each of the four main steps to maintain portability.

> **Note**   When running the CreateOU.vbs script to create an OU, ensure you have access to a Windows Server 2003 running Active Directory, and make sure you change the name of the *strDomain*, *strOU*, and *strOUname* variables to reflect your actual configuration.

CreateOU.vbs

```
Option Explicit
On Error Resume Next
Dim strProvider 'defines how will talk to Active Directory
Dim strOU 'path to where new object will be created
Dim strDomain 'name of Domain connecting to
Dim strClass 'the class of object we are creating
Dim strOUname 'name of object are creating
Dim objDomain 'holds connection to adsi
Dim objOU 'holds handle to create method

strProvider = "LDAP://"
strOU = "" 'When supplying a value here, a trailing comma is required.
strDomain = "dc=nwtraders,dc=msft"
strClass = "organizationalunit"
strOUname = "OU=mred"

Set objDomain = GetObject(strProvider & strOU & strDomain)
WScript.Echo strProvider & strOU & strDomain 'debug
Set objOU = objDomain.create(strClass, strOUname)
WScript.Echo strClass & "," & strOUname 'debug
objOU.SetInfo
```

```
If Err.number = 0 Then
WScript.Echo(strOUname & " was created")
Else If Err.number = "-2147019886" Then
WScript.Echo strOUname & " already exists"
Else
WScript.Echo " error on the play " & Err.Number
End If
End If
```

Reference Information

The Reference information section of the script configures the connection to Active Directory and specifies the path and target of the operation. The first decision to make is which provider to use. Let's talk about ADSI providers prior to looking at the remainder of the Reference information section.

ADSI Providers

Table 11-1 lists four providers available to users of ADSI. Connecting to a Microsoft Windows NT 4 system requires using the special WinNT provider. During Active Directory migrations, consultants often write a script that copies users from a Windows NT 4 domain to a Microsoft Windows Server 2003 Active Directory OU or domain. In some situations (such as with customized naming schemes), writing a script is easier than using the Active Directory Migration Tool (ADMT).

Table 11-1   ADSI Supported Providers

Provider	Purpose
WinNT:	To communicate with Windows NT 4.0 Primary Domain Controllers (PDCs) and Backup Domain Controllers (BDCs), and with local account databases for Windows 2000 and newer workstations
LDAP:	To communicate with Lightweight Directory Access Protocol (LDAP) servers, including Exchange 5.x directory and Windows 2000 Active Directory
NDS:	To communicate with Novell Directory Services servers
NWCOMPAT:	To communicate with Novell NetWare servers

The first time I tried using ADSI to connect to a machine running Windows NT, I had a very frustrating experience because of the way the provider was implemented. Type the WinNT provider name *exactly* as shown in Table 11-1. It cannot be typed using all lowercase letters or all uppercase letters. All other provider names must be all uppercase letters, but the WinNT name is Pascal-cased, that is, it is partially uppercase and partially lowercase. Remembering this will save a lot of grief later. In addition, if you don't type this in the correct case, you don't get an error message telling you that your provider name is "spelled wrong"—rather, the bind operation simply fails to connect.

> **Warning**   The ADSI provider names are case-sensitive. LDAP, NWCOMPAT, and NDS are all caps. WinNT is Pascal-cased and must not be typed in all caps. Keep this in mind to save time in troubleshooting.

Once the ADSI provider is specified, you need to identify the path to the directory target. This is where a little knowledge of Active Directory comes in handy because of the way the hierarchical naming space is structured. When connecting to an LDAP service provider, you must specify where in the LDAP directory hierarchy to make the connection, because the hierarchy is a structure of the directory itself and not the protocol or the provider. For instance, in the CreateOU.vbs script, you create an OU that resides off the root of the domain, which is called the *MrEd* OU. This can get confusing, until you realize that the *MrEd* OU is contained in a domain that is called *nwtraders.msft*. It is vital, therefore, that you understand the hierarchy with which you are working. One tool you can use to make sure you understand the hierarchy of your domain is ADSI Edit.

> **Note** Perhaps the hardest part of using ADSI is finding out what things are called in the directory. This is because the names defined in the Active Directory schema often bear no relationship to the display names you see in tools such as Active Directory Users And Computers. To see an example of this, refer to Appendix B, "ADSI Documentation."

ADSI Edit is included in the support tools on the Windows Server 2003 disk. It is in the support\tools directory and is installed by clicking Suptools.msi. Installation requires Help and other programs to be closed. The installation takes only a couple of minutes and does not require a reboot. After the support tools are installed, you open a blank Microsoft Management Console (MMC) and add the ADSI Edit snap-in. After you install the snap-in, right-click the ADSI Edit icon, select Connect To, and specify your domain using the drop-down box, as illustrated in Figure 11-1.

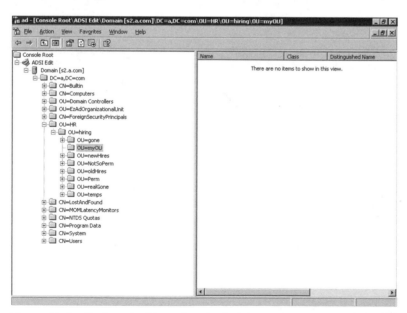

Figure 11-1 Explore the hierarchy of a forest to ensure correct path information for your script

LDAP Names

When specifying the OU and the domain name, you have to use the LDAP naming convention, in which the namespace is described as a series of naming parts called *relative distinguished names (RDNs)*. The relative distinguished name will always be a name part that assigns a value by using the equal sign. When you put together all the relative distinguished names, and the RDNs of each of the ancestors all the way back to the root, you end up with a single globally unique distinguished name.

The relative distinguished names are usually made up of an attribute, an equal sign, and a string value. Table 11-2 lists some of the attribute types you will see when working with Active Directory.

Table 11-2   Common Relative Distinguished Name Attribute Types

Attribute	Description
DC	Domain Component
CN	Common Name
OU	Organizational Unit
O	Organization Name
Street	Street Address
C	Country Name
UID	User ID

Worker Information

The Worker information section of the script includes two lines of code: The first line performs the binding (we talk about binding later in this section), and the second creates the OU. To perform these tasks, you need to build the distinguished name, which entails creating the OU after connecting to the appropriate level in the Active Directory hierarchy.

In the CreateOU.vbs script, the distinguished name is a concatenation of two separate variables. The variables and their associated values are listed here:

```
strOU = ""
strDomain = "dc=nwtraders,dc=msft"
```

You can verify that you are connecting to the correct OU by using ADSI Edit. To do this, right-click the target OU, select Properties, and choose Distinguished Name from the list of available properties. A dialog box like the one shown in Figure 11-2 appears.

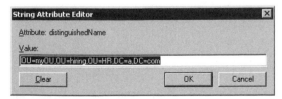

Figure 11-2   Use the String Attribute Editor in ADSI Edit to quickly verify the distinguished name of a potential target for ADSI scripting

The next line in the Reference information section specifies the object class with which you are working. When you get to the Worker section and you use the *Create* method, you will need to specify what type of object you are creating. In CreateOU.vbs, you use code that looks like the following line:

```
strClass = "organizationalUnit"
```

IADsContainer

In your script, you are actually using the *Create* method of a well-known interface called *IADsContainer*. It is used to enable an ADSI container object to create, delete, or otherwise manage ADSI objects. All container objects in Active Directory implement *IADsContainer*. *IADsContainer* supports five methods, listed in Table 11-3, that can be used on any ADSI container object in Active Directory. Each of these methods is used in scripts later in this book.

Table 11-3   *IADsContainer* Methods

Method	Meaning
GetObject	Binds the directory item with the specified ADsPath to a named variable.
Create	Creates a new object of a specified class in the current container.
Delete	Removes an object of the specified class from the current container.
CopyHere	Creates a copy of the object with a specified ADsPath in the current container. Be aware that the object must be in the same directory namespace. For example, you cannot copy an object from an *LDAP:* namespace to a *WinNT:* namespace.
MoveHere	Moves the object with a specified ADsPath from its original location to the current container. The same namespace restrictions that apply to the *CopyHere* method also apply to the *MoveHere* method.

In the CreateOU.vbs script, you implement the *IADsContainer Create* method to create the OU. Two variables do this. The first variable is called *oOU*, which holds the class of the object you want to create. This time, *oOU* is set to equal *OU*. The second variable used is called *oOUname*. It looks like it could hold the name of the OU because it does. The variable *objOU* holds the connection to the *Create* method once you implement the connection using the *Set* command, as shown in this line of code:

```
Set objOU = objDomain.create(strClass, strOUname)
```

Binding

Whenever you want to do anything with ADSI, you must connect to an object in Active Directory, a process also known as *binding*. Think of binding as being like tying a rope around an object to enable you to work with it. (In Texas, they'd call it lassoing.) Before you can do any work with an object in Active Directory, you must supply binding information. The *binding string* enables you to use various ADSI elements, including methods and properties. The target of the proposed action is specified as a computer, a domain controller, a user, or another element that resides within the directory structure. A binding string consists of five parts. These parts are illustrated in the following binding string from a sample script:

Keyword	Variable	Command	Provider	ADsPath
Set	objDomain	GetObject	LDAP://	OU=hr, dc=a, dc=com

> **Note**   Avoid a mistake I made early on: Make sure that when you finish connecting and creating, you actually commit your changes to Active Directory. Changes to Active Directory are transactional in nature, so your change will roll back if you don't commit it. Committing the change requires you to use the *SetInfo* method, as illustrated in the following line from the CreateOU.vbs script: *objOU.SetInfo*.

Output Information

By default, this script would not have any output information. However, to illustrate that the script is actually doing something, I implemented a simple *WScript.Echo* command to echo out the name of the container that was created. Because the OU to be created is held in the variable named *oOUname*, it was a simple proposition to echo out the contents of the variable, as illustrated in the following code snippet—the problem is the line of code could "lie" to you. If an error occurred, it would still say the OU was created.

```
WScript.Echo("OU " & oOUname & " was created")
```

To forestall this inexactitude, check the *err* object. If there are no errors, print out the line. If, however, an error occurs, then trap the message. The error line *Err.number = "-2147019886"* was developed by printing out the error numbers. When it was noticed that *-2147019886* always appeared when a duplicate object existed, it was trivial to report this information. This is seen below:

```
If Err.number = 0 Then
WScript.Echo(strOUname & " was created")
Else If Err.number = "-2147019886" Then
WScript.Echo strOUname & " already exists"
Else
WScript.Echo " error on the play " & Err.Number
End If
End If
```

Quick Check

Q.   What is the process of connecting to Active Directory called?

A.   The process of connecting to Active Directory is called binding.

Q.   When specifying the target of an ADSI operation, what is the target called?

A.   The target of the ADSI operation is called the *ADsPath*.

> **Q.** An LDAP name is made up of several parts. What do you call each part separated by a comma?
>
> **A.** An LDAP name is made up of multiple parts that are called relative distinguished names.

Creating Users

One trick you can do using ADSI is create users. Although using the graphical user interface (GUI) to create a single user is easy, using the GUI to create a dozen or more users would certainly not be. In addition, as you'll see, because there is a lot of similarity among ADSI scripts, deleting a dozen or more users is just as simple as creating them. And because you can use the same input text file for all the scripts, ADSI makes creating temporary accounts for use in a lab or school easy.

Just the Steps   To create users

1. Use the appropriate provider for your network.
2. Connect to the container for your users.
3. Specify the domain.
4. Specify the *User* class of the object.
5. Bind to Active Directory.
6. Use the *Create* Method to create the user.
7. Use the *Put* method to at least specify the sAMAccountName property.
8. Use *SetInfo* to commit the user to Active Directory.

The CreateUser.vbs script, which follows, is very similar to the CreateOU.vbs script. In fact, CreateUser.vbs was created from CreateOU.vbs, so a detailed analysis of the script is unnecessary. The only difference is that *oClass* is equal to the "*User*" class instead of to an "*organizationalUnit*" class.

CreateUser.vbs

```
Option Explicit
On Error Resume Next
Dim strProvider 'defines how will talk to Active Directory
Dim strOU 'path to where new object will be created
Dim strDomain 'name of Domain connecting to
Dim strClass 'the class of object we are creating
Dim strOUname 'name of object are creating
Dim objDomain 'holds connection to adsi
Dim objOU 'holds handle to create method

strProvider = "LDAP://"
strOU = "OU=mred," 'when using is OU=mred, THE , would be required.
strDomain = "dc=nwtraders,dc=msft"
```

```
strClass = "User"
strOUname = "CN=MyNewUser"

Set objDomain = GetObject(strProvider & strOU & strDomain)
WScript.Echo strProvider & strOU & strDomain 'debug
Set objOU = objDomain.create(strClass, strOUname)
WScript.Echo strClass & "," & strOUname 'debug
objOU.Put "SAMAccountName", funfix(strOUname)
objOU.SetInfo

If Err.number = 0 Then
WScript.Echo(strOUname & " was created")
Else If Err.number = "-2147019886" Then
WScript.Echo strOUname & " already exists"
Else
WScript.Echo " error on the play " & Err.Number
End If
End If

Function funfix (strin)
funfix = Mid(strin,4) 'removes cn= from username
End function
```

Reference Information

The Reference information section is where you assign values to the variables that would normally be declared in a script of this type. The provider in this case is *LDAP://*. Remember that the provider name is case-sensitive—all caps is a requirement for the LDAP provider. You next specify the OU you'll use in the *ADsPath* portion of the binding string. You are targeting an OU called *mred* (which will exist if you ran the CreateOU.vbs script from the earlier section). The domain name is made up of two *domain components*, or DCs, separated by commas. The domain name is *nwtraders.msft*, so the first component is *dc=nwtraders*, and the second is *dc=msft*.

You must specify the user class when creating user accounts. When creating a user account, the user name is specified by a *"cn="* prefix. In Table 11-2, you learned that *cn* actually stands for *common name*. For users, you must specify the common name property of the user object.

The user will at least need a *sAMAccountName* to be able to log on to the network. The *sAMAccountName* can be the same as the common name property, and in many cases it is. You are taking the defaults for everything else, including leaving the account disabled. In the Step-by-Step exercises, you'll create a user and assign values to more attributes, but for illustrative purposes, this suffices.

Worker Information

In the Worker information section of the script, the script starts to depart from other scripts you have looked at thus far. In this script are four lines of code, which follow:

```
Set objDomain = GetObject(strProvider & strOU & strDomain)
WScript.Echo strProvider & strOU & strDomain 'debug
Set objOU = objDomain.create(strClass, strOUname)
WScript.Echo strClass & "," & strOUname 'debug
objOU.Put "SAMAccountName", funfix(strOUname)
objOU.SetInfo
```

The binding to ADSI is exactly the same as in the previous script. You even use the same variable name. In the next line, however, when you call the *Create* method, you use different variables because you create a *User* instead of an *OU*. The *strClass* variable is equal to *User*, *strOUName* is equal to "*CN=MyNewUser*". You now utilize the *Put* method to specify the sAMAccountName property. In this script, you use *funfix* to trim the name, and you feed it the *strOUname* variable. Once all that work is done, you call *SetInfo* and write the data to Active Directory.

Output Information

After creating the user, it would be nice to have some type of feedback. You use the same methodology as in the previous script by evaluating the error object and printing out the approriate message. This is seen below:

```
If Err.number = 0 Then
WScript.Echo(strOUname & " was created")
Else If Err.number = "-2147019886" Then
WScript.Echo strOUname & " already exists"
Else
WScript.Echo " error on the play " & Err.Number
End If
End If
```

> **Quick Check**
>
> **Q.   To create a user, which class must be specified?**
>
> A.   You need to specify the *User* class to create a user.
>
> **Q.   What is the *Put* method used for?**
>
> A.   The *Put* method is used to write additional property data to the object that it is bound to.

Creating groups

1. Open the \My Documents\Microsoft Press\VBScriptSBS\ch11\CreateUser.vbs script in Microsoft Notepad or some other script editor and save it as YourNameCreate-Group.vbs.

2. In the Header section of the script, declare a variable called *intGroupType*. This variable will be used to control the type of group to create. This is seen below.

   ```
   Dim intGroupType 'controls type of group to create
   ```

3. In the Reference section of the script, change the value of *strClass* from user to group. This variable is used to control the type of object that gets created in Active Directory. This is seen below.

```
strClass = "Group"
```

4. In the Reference section of the script, change the value of *strOUname* from "CN=*MyNewUser*" to "CN=*MyNewGroup*". The value of this variable is used to set several attributes on the new object. The code to do this is seen below.

```
strOUname = "CN=MyNewGroup"
```

5. Under the *strOUname* line in the Reference section of the script, add a new line to assign the value to *intGroupType*. Use the number *-2147483646* to create a security group.

```
intGroupType = -2147483646 '2= distribution Group
```

6. Save and run the script. It should create a new group in your OU. If it does not, then compare the script to the \My Documents\Microsoft Press\VBScriptSBS\ch11\Create-Group.vbs script.

Creating a computer account

1. Open the \My Documents\Microsoft Press\VBScriptSBS\ch11\CreateUser.vbs script in Notepad or another script editor and save it as YourNameCreateComputer.vbs.

2. Delete the value assigned to the *strOU* variable, "OU=*mred*" but keep the empty double quotation marks, as seen below:

```
strOU = ""
```

3. Modify the value of *strDomain* to include the OU where the computer account will be created. To do this, append *OU=mred* to *dc=nwtraders,dc=msft*. This is seen below:

```
strDomain = "OU=mred,dc=nwtraders,dc=msft"
```

4. Change the class assignment to the *strClass* variable from "User" to "*Computer*", as seen below:

```
strClass = "Computer"
```

5. Change the name supplied to the *strOUname* variable to the name of the computer account. Prefix it with "CN=". I used "CN=*MyMredComputer*", as seen below:

```
strOUname = "CN=MyMredComputer"
```

6. After you call *SetInfo* to write the account to Active Directory, you will need to activate the account. To do this, put a special value in the *userAccountControl* attribute; *4128* will

activate the account. Once again, call *SetInfo* to write it to Active Directory. This is seen below:

```
objOU.put "userAccountControl",4128 'enables the computer account
objOU.SetInfo
```

7. Save and run the script. If an enabled computer account is not created in the target OU, check your script against \My Documents\Microsoft Press\VBScriptSBS\ch11\Create-Computer.vbs.

What Is *UserAccountControl*?

UserAccountControl is an attribute stored in Active Directory that is used to enable or disable a user account, computer account, or other object defined in Active Directory. It is not a single string attribute, rather it is a series of flags that gets computed from the values listed in the following table, Table 11-4. Because of the way the *UserAccountControl* attribute gets created, simply examining the numerical value is of little help unless you can decipher the individual numbers that make up the large number. These flags, when added together, control the behavior of the user account on the system. In the script CreateComputer.vbs, we set two user account control flags: the ADS_UF_PASSWD_NOTREQD flag and the ADS_UF_WORKSTATION_TRUST_ACCOUNT flag. The password not required flag has a hex value of 0x20, and the the trusted workstation flag has a hex value of 0x1000. When added together and turned into decimal value, they equal 4,128, which is the value actually seen in ADSI Edit. The use of these user account control values is seen in Figure 11-3.

Table 11-4   User Account Control Values

Ads Constant	Value
ADS_UF_SCRIPT	0x0001
ADS_UF_ACCOUNTDISABLE	0x0002
ADS_UF_HOMEDIR_REQUIRED	0x0008
ADS_UF_LOCKOUT	0x0010
ADS_UF_PASSWD_NOTREQD	0x0020
ADS_UF_PASSWD_CANT_CHANGE	0x0040
ADS_UF_ENCRYPTED_TEXT_PASSWORD_ALLOWED	0x0080
ADS_UF_TEMP_DUPLICATE_ACCOUNT	0x0100
ADS_UF_NORMAL_ACCOUNT	0x0200
ADS_UF_INTERDOMAIN_TRUST_ACCOUNT	0x0800
ADS_UF_WORKSTATION_TRUST_ACCOUNT	0x1000
ADS_UF_SERVER_TRUST_ACCOUNT	0x2000
ADS_UF_DONT_EXPIRE_PASSWD	0x10000
ADS_UF_MNS_LOGON_ACCOUNT	0x20000

Table 11-4   User Account Control Values

Ads Constant	Value
ADS_UF_SMARTCARD_REQUIRED	0x40000
ADS_UF_TRUSTED_FOR_DELEGATION	0x80000
ADS_UF_NOT_DELEGATED	0x100000
ADS_UF_USE_DES_KEY_ONLY	0x200000
ADS_UF_DONT_REQUIRE_PREAUTH	0x400000
ADS_UF_PASSWORD_EXPIRED	0x800000
ADS_UF_TRUSTED_TO_AUTHENTICATE_FOR_DELEGATION	0x1000000

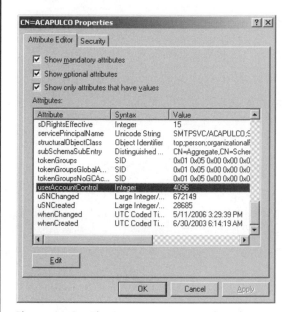

Figure 11-3   The *UserAccountControl* attribute

Creating OUs Step-by-Step Exercises

In this section, you are going to practice creating OUs. The result will eventually become a subroutine that can be employed in other scripts to create OUs.

Important   To successfully complete this section, you must have access to a Microsoft Windows Server 2003 or later Active Directory Domain Controller. You must know the name of the domain, and you must have rights to create objects in that domain.

These step-by-step instructions do not apply to Microsoft Windows Vista or Microsoft Windows XP workstations.

1. Open Notepad or your favorite script editor.

2. On the first line, type **Option Explicit**.

3. Declare the following variables: *provider*, *domain*, *oClass*, *oOU*, *objDomain*, *objOU*, *oOUname*, and *oDescription*.

4. Assign the LDAP provider to the variable called *provider*. Your code will look like the following:

   ```
   provider = "LDAP://"
   ```

5. Assign the name of a domain that is accessible on your network, such as *nwtraders.msft*, to the *domain* variable. Split each section of the domain name into domain components. This will look like the following:

   ```
   domain = "dc=nwtraders,dc=msft"
   ```

6. Assign the variable to the *organizationalUnit* class. Make sure you encase the class name in quotation marks, as shown here:

   ```
   oClass = "organizationalUnit"
   ```

7. Assign the value *ou=* to the variable *oOU*, as seen below:

   ```
   oOU = "ou="
   ```

8. Assign a value to the variable used to hold the *OU* name. In this case, the variable is *oOUname* and the value is *Lab22*. The code will look like the following:

   ```
   oOUname = "Lab22"
   ```

9. Assign an appropriate description to the *oDescription* variable. It will look something like the following:

   ```
   oDescription = "For Lab 22 Use"
   ```

10. Use the *Set* command to set the variable *objDomain* equal to the handle that comes back from using the *GetObject* method when using the provider variable and the domain variable. The code will look like the following:

    ```
    Set objDomain = GetObject(provider & domain)
    ```

11. Use the *Set* command to set the variable *objOU* equal to the handle that comes back from using the *Create* method when given the *oClass*, *oOU*, and *oOUname* variables. The code will look like the following:

    ```
    Set objOU = objDomain.create(oClass, oOU & oOUname)
    ```

12. Use the *Put* method to put the data contained in the *oDescription* variable into the field designated as *Description*. Separate the variable from the field name with a comma. The code will look like the following:

    ```
    objOU.Put "description", oDescription
    ```

13. Use the *SetInfo* method to commit the changes to Active Directory. The code will look like the following:

```
objOU.SetInfo
```

14. Conclude your script by using *WScript.Echo* to echo out the name of *oOUname* and an appropriate description of the action that was taken. I used the following code to do this:

```
WScript.Echo("OU " & oOUname & " was created")
```

15. Save the script as YourNameCreateOU.vbs.

16. Run the script. For this script, it doesn't matter whether you run it in CScript or from WScript. It's probably easier to just double-click the script and let it run in WScript.

17. Open Active Directory Users And Computers to verify the presence of the Lab22 OU.

18. Right-click the Lab22 OU and choose Properties from the Action menu. On the General tab, verify that the description you assigned in step 11 is present in the *Description* field.

19. Close everything out. Do not delete the Lab22 OU because you'll use it in the next exercise.

One Step Further: Creating Multi-Valued Users

In this section, you are going to practice creating users. You'll place the user in the OU created in the previous step-by-step exercise.

> **Important**   To successfully complete this section, you must have access to a Microsoft Windows Server 2003 or later Active Directory Domain Controller. You must know the name of the domain, and you must have rights to create objects in that domain.

The result of this One Step Further exercise will eventually become a subroutine that you can employ in other scripts when you need to use *Users*.

1. Open Notepad or your favorite script editor.

2. On the first line, type **Option Explicit**.

3. Declare the following variables: *provider*, *ou*, *domain*, *oClass*, *oCN*, *objDomain*, *objUser*, *oUname*, and *oDescription*.

4. Assign the LDAP provider to the variable provider. It will look like the following:

```
provider = "LDAP://"
```

5. Assign the Lab22 OU to the *OU* variable. It will look like the following:

```
OU = "ou=lab22,"
```

6. Assign the domain used in step 5 of the Step-by-Step exercise to the domain variable. This domain should be the one on your local network. Your code will look something like the following:

```
domain = "dc=nwtraders,dc=msft"
```

7. Assign the *User* class to the *oClass* variable. It will look like the following:

```
oClass = "User"
```

8. Assign the "*CN=*" value to the *oCN* variable, as shown here:

```
oCN = "CN="
```

9. Assign to the *oUname* variable the name of the user to be created. For this exercise, we will call the user labUser.

```
oUname = "labUser"
```

10. Assign an appropriate description for the new user. This entails assigning a value to the *oDescription* variable:

```
oDescription = "created for lab22 use"
```

11. Use the *Set* command to set the variable *objDomain* equal to the handle that comes back from using the *GetObject* function when fed the provider variable, *OU* variable, and *domain* variable. The code looks like the following:

```
Set objDomain = GetObject(provider & OU & domain)
```

12. Use the *Set* command to set the variable *objUser* equal to the handle that comes back from using the *Create* method when fed the *oClass*, *oCN*, and *oUname* variables. The code will look like the following:

```
Set objUser = objDomain.Create(oClass, oCN & oUname)
```

13. Use the *Put* method to put the data contained in the *oUname* variable into the field designated as *sAMAccountName*. Separate the variable from the field name with a comma. The code looks like the following:

```
objUser.Put "sAMAccountName", oUname
```

14. Use the *Put* method to put the data contained in the *oUname* variable into the field designated as *DisplayName*. Separate the variable from the field name with a comma. The code looks like the following:

```
objUser.Put "DisplayName", oUname
```

15. Use the *Put* method to put the data contained in the *oDescription* variable into the field designated as *description*. Separate the variable from the field name with a comma. The code looks like the following:

```
objUser.Put "description", oDescription
```

16. Use the *SetInfo* method to commit the changes to Active Directory. The code will look like the following:

```
objUser.SetInfo
```

17. Conclude your script by using *WScript.Echo* to echo out the name of *oUname* and an appropriate description of the action that was taken. I used the following code to do this:

```
WScript.Echo("User " & oUname & " was created")
```

18. Save the script as YourNameCreateMultiValuedUser.vbs.

19. Run the script. It doesn't matter whether you run this script in CScript or from WScript. It's probably easier to just double-click the script and let it run in WScript.

20. Open Active Directory Users And Computers to verify the presence of the new user. The user will be contained in the Lab22 OU.

21. Right-click the new user and choose Properties from the Action menu. On the General tab, verify that the display name and description you assigned earlier are present.

22. Close everything out.

Chapter 11 Quick Reference

To	Do This
Talk to Active Directory, without having to specify the complexity of the specific directory	Use the ADSI provider
Talk to a NT 4.0 based directory	Use the WinNT provider
Talk to Active Directory	Use the LDAP provider
Talk to a NDS directory	Use the NDS provider
Talk to a bindery based directory	Use the NWCOMPAT provider
Refer to the common name in a LDAP relative distinguished name attribute	Specify the *CN* attribute
Bind to a directory object with the specified ADsPath to a named variable	Use the *GetObject* Method of the *IADsContainer* object

Chapter 12

Writing for ADSI

Before You Begin

To work through the material presented in this chapter, you need to be familiar with the following concepts from earlier chapters:

- Binding to Microsoft Active Directory directory service
- Creating users in Active Directory
- Creating organizational units (OUs) in Active Directory
- Implementing Active Directory Service Interfaces (ADSI) providers
- Working with Active Directory namespaces
- Implementing constants

After completing this chapter, you will be able to:

- Modify user profile information in Active Directory
- Modify Terminal Server settings in Active Directory
- Modify direct reporting information in Active Directory
- Delete users in Active Directory
- Delete organizational units in Active Directory

Working with Users

In this section, you will use Active Directory Service Interfaces (ADSI) to modify user properties stored in Active Directory. The following list summarizes a few of the items you can change or configure:

- Office and telephone contact information
- Mailing address information
- Department, title, manager, and direct reports (people who report to the user inside the "chain of command")

User information that is stored in Active Directory can easily replace several pieces of disparate information in a single swoop. For instance, you might have an internal Web site that contains a telephone directory; you can put the phone number into Active Directory as an attribute of the *User* object. You might also have a Web site containing a social roster that includes employees and their hobbies; you can put hobby information in Active Directory as a custom attribute. By having the information stored in a single location (Active Directory), then updating the attributes in Active Directory would also update the Web sites. You can also add to Active Directory information such as an organizational chart. The problem, of course, is that during a migration, information such as a user's title is the last thing the harried mind of the network administrator thinks about. To leverage the investment in Active Directory, you need to enter this type of information because it quickly becomes instrumental in the daily lives of users. This is where the power of ADSI and Microsoft Visual Basic, Scripting Edition (VBScript) really begins to shine. We can update hundreds or even thousands of records easily and efficiently using scripting. Such a task would be unthinkable using conventional point-and-click methods.

> **Just the Steps**   To modify user properties in Active Directory
>
> 1. Implement the appropriate protocol provider.
> 2. Perform binding to Active Directory.
> 3. Specify *ADsPath*.
> 4. Use the *Put* method to write selected properties to users.
> 5. Use the *SetInfo* method to commit changes to Active Directory.

General User Information

One of the more confusing issues when you use VBScript to modify information in Active Directory is that the field names displayed on the various tabs of the graphical administratative tools such as Active Directory Users And Computers (ADUC) do not correspond with the ADSI nomenclature. This was not done to make your life difficult; rather, the names you see in ADSI are derived from Lightweight Directory Access Protocol (LDAP) standard naming conventions. Although this naming convention makes traditional LDAP programmers happy, it does nothing for the network administrator who is a casual scripter. This is where the following script, ModifyUserProperties.vbs, comes in handy. The LDAP properties corresponding to each field in Figure 12-1 are used in this script. Some of the names make sense, but others appear to be rather obscure. Notice the series of *objUser.Put* statements. Each lines up with the corresponding fields in Figure 12-1. Use the values to see which display name maps to which LDAP attribute name.

ModifyUserProperties.vbs

```
Option Explicit
Dim provider 'defines how will talk to active directory
Dim ou 'path to where object resides
Dim domain 'name of domain connecting to
Dim oCN 'name of object are creating
```

```
Dim oUname 'user name
Dim objUser 'holds connection to adsi

provider = "LDAP://"
ou = "ou=mred,"
domain = "dc=nwtraders,dc=msft"
oCN = "CN="
oUname = "myNewUser,"

Set objUser = GetObject(provider & oCN & oUname & ou & domain)
WScript.echo provider & oCN & oUname & ou & domain ' debug info
objUser.put "SamaccountName", "myNewUser"
objUser.put "givenName", "My"
objUser.Put "initials", "f."
objUser.Put "sn", "User"
objUser.Put "DisplayName", "My New User"
objUser.Put "description" , "simple new user"
objUser.Put "physicalDeliveryOfficeName", "RQ2"
objUser.Put "telephoneNumber", "999-222-1111"
objUser.Put "mail", "fff@hotmail.com"
objUser.Put "wwwHomePage", "http://www.fred.msn.com"

objUser.SetInfo

If Err.Number = 0 then
WScript.Echo("User " & oUname & " was modified")
Else
WScript.echo "an error occurred. it was: " & Err.Number
End if
```

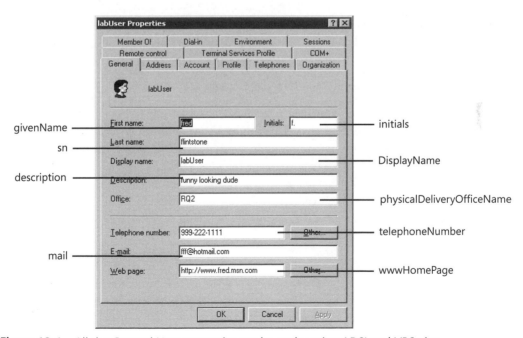

Figure 12-1   All the General User properties can be set by using ADSI and VBScript

> **On the CD**   Discussion of the Header information section of ModifyUserProperties.vbs has been omitted for clarity. This section does, however, exist in the original script on the companion CD.

Reference Information

The Reference information section of the script assigns values to the variables used in the script. Here you assign the LDAP provider to the provider variable. You then assign the entire *ou* path to the *ou* variable. The variable called *Domain* gets assigned both of the domain components that are used for constructing a fully qualified name. These domain components are the "*DC*=" sections of the code. You use *oCn* to hold the "cn=" string and you end the section by equating *oUname* to the user name you plan to modify. If you were using a text file to supply the variable, you could still use this variable. The Reference section follows:

```
provider = "LDAP://"
ou = "ou=lab22,"
domain = "dc=nwtraders,dc=msft"
oCn = "cn="
oUname = "labUser,"
```

Worker Information

The Worker information section of the ModifyUserProperties.vbs script contains a lot of code because it modifies all the properties contained on the General tab of the user properties in Microsoft Windows Server 2003. The first line in the Worker information section performs the binding to Active Directory. In this instance, you bind not to an OU but to a specific user, as shown here:

```
Set objUser = GetObject(provider & oCn & oUname & ou & domain)
```

You assign "*CN*" to the variable *oCn* to keep it separate from the user name portion. In this way, you can more easily make changes to multiple users. In our particular situation, you connect to the ou created in the previous chapter, and the Lab 22 ou is off the root in the Active Directory hierarchy. If the ou were nested, you could still use the script, and in the Reference section specify something like *ou = "ou=level1, ou=level2, ou=level3"* (or whatever the actual namespace consisted of). The domain variable holds the entire domain component. *CN*, *UserName*, *ou*, and *Domain* make up the *ADsPath* portion of the binding string.

Once you have the binding to Active Directory, you are ready to begin modifying user information. The nice part about using the *Put* method is that it overwrites any information already present in that property of the cached copy of the *User* object. You will see the effect only on the particular property being put until you call *SetInfo* to write the changes to Active Directory. If you don't specify a particular piece of information (that is, you leave the space between the quotation marks empty), you'll be greeted with an error message. Figure 12-2 shows this message.

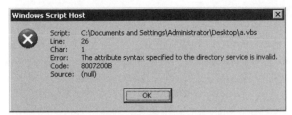

Figure 12-2 Error message received when a property value is left out of a *Put* command

To write information to a specific user property, use the *Put* method. This entails specifying both the ADSI field name and the desired value. The pertinent Worker information section of the ModifyUserProperties.vbs script follows:

```
objUser.Put "givenName", "fred"
objUser.Put "initials", "f."
objUser.Put "sn", "flintstone"
objUser.Put "DisplayName", "labUser"
objUser.Put "description" , "funny looking dude"
objUser.Put "physicalDeliveryOfficeName", "RQ2"
objUser.Put "telephoneNumber", "999-222-1111"
objUser.Put "mail", "fff@hotmail.com"

objUser.Put "wwwHomePage", "http://www.fred.msn.com"
```

The last item in the Worker information section is the *SetInfo* command. If *SetInfo* isn't called, the information isn't written to Active Directory. There will be no error message—merely an absence of data. The ModifyUserProperties.vbs script uses the following *SetInfo* line to ensure changes are written to Active Directory:

```
objUser.SetInfo
```

Output Information

Once all the changes are loaded into Active Directory, you include an output statement to let you know that the changes have been made to Active Directory. In the ModifyUserProperties.vbs script, you use a simple *WScript.Echo* statement. This echo statement is listed here:

```
WScript.Echo("User " & oUname & " was modified")
```

Quick Check

Q. In the ModifyUserProperties.vbs script, what is the field name for the user's first name?

A. The field for the user's first name is called "*givenName*". You can find field mapping information in the Platform SDK.

Q. Why do you need to do a *SetInfo* command?

A. Without a *SetInfo* command, all changes introduced during the script are lost because the changes are made to a cached set of attribute values for the object being modified. Nothing is committed to Active Directory until you call *SetInfo*.

Modifying the Address Tab Information

One of the more useful tasks you can perform with Active Directory is exposing address information. This ability is particularly important when a company has more than one location and more than a few hundred employees. I remember when one of the first uses for an intranet was to host a centralized list of employees. Such a project quickly paid for itself because companies no longer needed an administrative assistant to modify, copy, collate, and distribute hundreds of copies of the up-to-date employee directory—potentially a full-time job for one person. Once an intranet site was in place, personnel at each location were given rights to modify the list. With Active Directory, you avoid this duplication of work by keeping all information in a centralized location. The Address tab in Active Directory Users And Computers is shown in Figure 12-3.

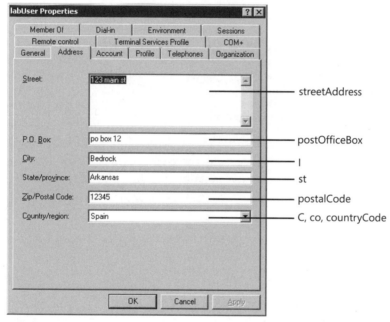

Figure 12-3   Every item on the Address tab in Active Directory Users And Computers can be filled in via ADSI and VBScript

In the ModifyUserAddressTab.vbs script, you use ADSI to set the street, post office box, city, state, zip code, c, co, and country values for the *User* object. Table 12-1 lists the Active Directory attribute names and their mappings to the Active Directory Users And Computers (ADUC) management tool "friendly" display names.

Table 12-1   Address Tab Mappings

Active Directory Users And Computers label	Active Directory attribute name
Street	*streetAddress*
P.O. Box	*postOfficeBox*

Table 12-1   Address Tab Mappings

Active Directory Users And Computers label	Active Directory attribute name
City	*l* (note that this is lowercase L)
State/Province	*st*
Zip/Postal Code	*postalCode*
Country/Region	*c,co,countryCode*

ModifyUserAddressTab.vbs

```
Option Explicit
On Error Resume Next
Dim strProvider 'defines how will talk
Dim strOU 'path to where new object will be created
Dim strDomain 'name of domain connecting to
Dim strOUName 'user name
Dim objUser 'holds connection to adsi

strProvider = "LDAP://"
strOU = "ou=mred,"
strDomain = "dc=nwtraders,dc=msft"
strOUName = "CN=myNewUser,"

Set objUser = GetObject(strProvider & strOUName & strOU & strDomain)
WScript.Echo strProvider & strOUName & strOU & strDomain ' debug info
objUser.Put "streetAddress", "123 main st"
objUser.Put "postOfficeBox", "po box 12"
objUser.Put "l", "Bedrock"
objUser.Put "st", "Arkansas"
objUser.Put "postalCode" , "12345"
objUser.Put "c", "US"
objUser.Put "co", "United States"
objUser.Put "countryCode", "840"
objUser.SetInfo

If Err.Number = 0 Then
WScript.Echo("User " & strOUName & " was modified")
Else
WScript.Echo "an error occurred. it was: " & Err.Number
End If
```

Reference Information

The Reference information section assigns values to the variables declared in the script. In this section, you assign the LDAP provider to the provider variable. You then build the entire OU path to the *ou* variable. The domain variable gets assigned both domain components and constructs a fully qualified name. You use *strOUName* to hold the user name you plan to modify.

Worker Information

The Worker information section begins by performing an Active Directory binding:

```
Set objUser = GetObject(strProvider & strOUName & strOU & strDomain)
```

The hardest part of the Worker information section of this script is figuring out how to make the country assignment show up in ADUC. I will admit that it took me a bit of time before I realized that the country codes have to be entered in accordance with International Organization for Standardization (ISO) standard 3166. If you use the *c* field, you use the two-letter country code. If you use ISO standard 3166-1, which contains two-letter country codes that have been officially assigned, you will be in fine shape. However, 3166-1 also contains country number assignments and short text names. The alternate forms of country codes do not work with the *c* field. ISO 3166 is actually divided into three different parts and is updated on a regular basis to keep up with global political changes. In compliance with ISO 3166, country codes can actually be entered in three different ways. The easiest to deal with uses the letter *c* as the field and a two-letter country code as the property.

Although ISO 3166-1 specifies all the country codes as uppercase letters, ADSI seems to be case-agnostic for this field, so *us* or *US* will both cause the field to display the name of United States. (One interesting thing about the ISO 3166-1 codes is that in most cases they are the same as the national top-level domain names.) A sample two-letter country code sheet based on ISO 3166-1 is listed in Table 12-2. The full table is available at *http://www.iso.org*.

Table 12-2 ISO 3166-1 Country Codes

Country code	Country name
AF	Afghanistan
AU	Australia
EG	Egypt
LV	Latvia
ES	Spain
US	United States

Staying Put

Filling out the Address tab of the Active Directory Users And Computers user address properties entails modifying a lot of fields. To do this, you use the *Put* command, as shown in the following code:

```
objUser.Put "streetAddress", "123 main st"
objUser.Put "postOfficeBox", "po box 12"
objUser.Put "l", "Bedrock"
objUser.Put "st", "Arkansas"
objUser.Put "postalCode" , "12345"
objUser.Put "c", "US"
objUser.Put "co", "United States"
objUser.Put "countryCode", "840"
```

Most of the fields are self-explanatory. The only two that do not make much sense are the small letter *l* for *city* and the country code, because of the way you fill it in, which you learned about earlier.

Warning   The three country fields are not linked in Active Directory. You could easily have a *c* code value of US, a *co* code value of Zimbabwe, and a *countryCode* value of 470 (Malta). This could occur if someone uses Active Directory Users And Computers to make a change to the country property. When ADUC is used, it updates all three fields. If someone later runs a script to only update the *countryCode* value, or the *co* code value, then Active Directory Users And Computers will still reflect the "translated value" of the *c* code. This could create havoc if your Enterprise Resource Planning (ERP) application uses the *co* or *countryCode* value, and not the *c* attribute. Best practice is to update all three fields via your script. Unfortunately, you're not always presented with an error; the script just does not seem to update, so you are left (or at least I am left) clicking the Refresh button in Active Directory Users And Computers as you wait for a replication event that never seems to take place.

Note   Do not forget to use the *SetInfo* method to commit your changes to Active Directory. If I seem to harp on this, it's because I've forgotten to do so on occasion, and I want to spare you the mental agony. This is one occasion when it is easy to commit. You just use this code: *objUser.SetInfo*.

Output Information

After creating all those lovely updates, I want to see something to let me know the script has completed running. Obviously, if you were running this in the scheduler, you wouldn't want to present a message box (although you might want to write something to the event log). In your script, you use a simple *WScript.Echo* box to let you know the script completed. The script evaluates the *Err* object to catch any errors. Note: In this case, we must have *On Error Resume Next* turned on (that is, not commented out) or a runtime error will cause the script to fail before it gets to the Output section of the script. If an error were to occur, we would want to see the actual error number (*Err.Number*). The output code follows:

```
If Err.Number = 0 Then
WScript.Echo("User " & strOUName & " was modified")
Else
WScript.Echo "An error occurred. it was: " & Err.Number
End If
```

Quick Check

Q.   **To set the country name on the Address tab for Active Directory Users And Computers, what is required?**

A.   To update the country name on the Address tab for Active Directory Users And Computers, you must specify the *c* field and feed it a two-letter code that is found in ISO publication 3166.

> **Q.**   **What field name in ADSI is used to specify the city information?**
>
> **A.**   You set the city information by assigning a value to the *l* (lowercase *L*) field after making the appropriate connection to Active Directory.
>
> **Q.**   **If you put an inappropriate letter code in the *c* field, what error message is displayed?**
>
> **A.**   No error message is displayed. The update simply fails to display in ADUC. If, however, you go into ADSI Edit, you will see the value stored there. The Active Directory Users And Computers tool is smart enough to not display codes it does not understand.

Modifying the user profile settings

1. Open Microsoft Notepad or some other script editor.

2. Open the \My Documents\Microsoft Press\VBScriptSBS\ch12\ModifyUserAddressTab.vbs script and save it as YourNameModifyUserProfile.vbs.

3. Delete all but four of the *Put* statements in the Worker section. Once deleted, the *Put* statements will look like the following:

```
objUser.Put "streetAddress", "123 main st"
objUser.Put "postOfficeBox", "po box 12"
objUser.Put "l", "Bedrock"
objUser.Put "st", "Arkansas"
```

4. We are going to assign values for the following four attributes: *profilePath, scriptPath, homeDirectory*, and *homeDrive*. Replace the "old" attributes with the user profile attributes and assign appropriate values to the attributes. Use folders and scripts accessible on your network, or you can use my values that are listed below:

```
Set objUser = GetObject(strProvider & strOUName & strOU & strDomain)
WScript.Echo strProvider & strOUName & strOU & strDomain 'debug info
objUser.put "profilePath", "\\London\profiles\myNewUser"
objUser.put "scriptPath", "logon.vbs"
objUser.Put "homeDirectory", "\\london\users\myNewUser"
objUser.Put "homeDrive", "H:"
objUser.SetInfo
```

5. Save and run the script. You should see the Profile tab filled out, as seen in Figure 12-4. If your script generates errors, compare it with the \My Documents\Microsoft Press\VBScriptSBS\ch12\ModifyUserProfile.vbs script.

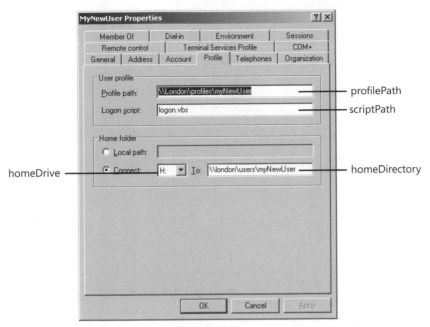

Figure 12-4   ADSI attributes used to fill out the Profile tab in Active Directory

Modifying the user telephone settings

1. Open Notepad or your favorite script editor.

2. Open the \My Documents\Microsoft Press\VBScriptSBS\ch12\ModifyUser
   AddressTab.vbs script and save it as YourNameModifyTelephoneAttributes.vbs.

3. Delete two of the *Put* statements in the Worker section of the script. After this deletion,
   the *Put* statements will look like the following:

```
objUser.Put "streetAddress", "123 main st"
objUser.Put "postOfficeBox", "po box 12"
objUser.Put "l", "Bedrock"
objUser.Put "st", "Arkansas"
objUser.Put "postalCode" , "12345"
objUser.Put "c", "US"
```

4. We are going to assign values for the six attributes used to configure the Telephone tab
   in the *User* object in Active Directory. These attributes are: *homePhone, pager, mobile,
   facsimileTelephoneNumber, ipPhone,* and *info*. Replace the existing attributes from the
   Address tab information with the attributes from the Telephone tab. Assign appropriate
   values to each attribute, as seen in the completed Worker section below:

```
Set objUser = GetObject(strProvider & strOUName & strOU & strDomain)
WScript.Echo strProvider & strOUName & strOU & strDomain ' debug info
objUser.put "homePhone", "(215)788-4312"
objUser.put "pager", "(215)788-0112"
objUser.Put "mobile", "(715)654-2341"
```

```
objUser.Put "facsimileTelephoneNumber", "(215)788-3456"
objUser.Put "ipPhone", "192.168.6.112"
objUser.Put "info", "All contact information is confidential, " &_
"and is for official use only."
objUser.SetInfo
```

5. Save and run your script. You should see the Telephone tab filled out, as seen in Figure 12-5. If not, compare your script with the \My Documents\Microsoft Press \VBScriptSBS\ch12\ModifyTelephoneAttributes.vbs script.

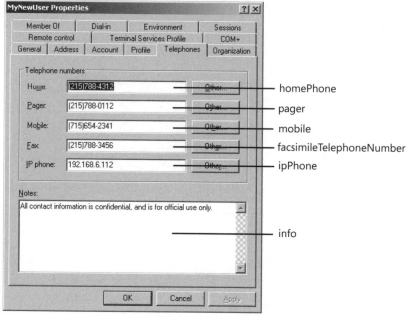

Figure 12-5 Telephone tab attributes found in Active Directory

Creating multiple users

1. Open Notepad or your favorite script editor.

2. Open the \My Documents\Microsoft Press\VBScriptSBS\ch12\CreateUser.vbs script and save it as YourNameCreateThreeUsers.vbs.

3. Declare two new variables in the Header section: *strUsers* (which will contain a string of three user names) and *aryUsers* (which will be an array of user names)—*aryUsers* will become an array once the *Split* function is used on *strUsers*. The two new variable declaration statements are seen below:

```
Dim strUsers 'a string of three users here
Dim aryUsers 'an array of users from SPLIT
```

4. In the Reference section, assign three user names to the *strUsers* variable: myBoss, myDirect1, and myDirect2. This is seen in the following code:

```
strUsers = "cn=MyBoss,cn=MyDirect1,cn=MyDirect2"
```

5. Assign *aryUsers* to hold the array that is created by using the *Split* function on the "strUsers" string when we break the string at the comma character. This is seen below:

```
aryUsers = Split(strUsers,",")
```

6. Instead of hardcoding the value of *strOUname*, we will assign values to it by using *For Each...Next* to walk through the array. Place this code directly under *strClass = "User"*. This is seen below.

```
For Each strOUname In aryUsers
```

7. Delete the *strOUname= "cn=MyNewUser"* line.

8. Add the *Next* statement after you call *objOU.SetInfo*.

9. Just above the *Next* statement and immediately following *objOU.SetInfo*, call the *subError* subroutine. The placement is seen here:

```
objOU.SetInfo
subError
Next
```

10. Turn the error handler into a subroutine called *subError*. To do this, use the *Sub* statement followed by the name *subError*. End your subroutine with the *End Sub* statement. This is seen here:

```
Sub subError
If Err.number = 0 Then
WScript.Echo(strOUname & " was created")
Else If Err.number = "-2147019886" Then
WScript.Echo strOUname & " already exists"
Else
WScript.Echo " error on the play " & Err.Number
End If
End If
End sub
```

11. Save and run your script. You should see three new users created in the *Mred* OU. If they are not, compare your script with CreateThreeUsers.vbs.

Modifying the organizational settings

1. Open Notepad or your favorite script editor.

2. Open the \My Documents\Microsoft Press\VBScriptSBS\ch12\ModifyUserAddressTab.vbs script and save it as YourNameModifyOrganizationPage.vbs.

3. Delete all but four of the *Put* statements in the Worker section of the script. After this deletion, the *Put* statements will look like the following:

```
objUser.Put "streetAddress", "123 main st"
objUser.Put "postOfficeBox", "po box 12"
objUser.Put "l", "Bedrock"
objUser.Put "st", "Arkansas"
```

4. We are going to assign values to the four attributes used to configure the Organization tab of the *User* object in Active Directory. These attributes are: *title, department, company,* and str*Manager*. Replace the existing attributes from the Address tab information with the attributes from the Worker section, as seen below:

```
Set objUser = GetObject(strProvider & strOUName & strOU & strDomain)
WScript.Echo strProvider & strOUName & strOU & strDomain 'debug info
objUser.Put "title", "Mid-Level Manager"
objUser.Put "department", "Sales"
objUser.Put "company", "North Wind Traders"
objUser.Put "manager", strManager & strOU & strdomain
objUser.SetInfo
```

5. In the Reference section of your script, assign a value for the *strManager* variable. MyNewUser's boss is named MyBoss and was created when we created the three users in the previous exercise.

```
strManager = "cn=MyBoss,"
```

6. Save and run your script. The Organization tab should be filled out and look like Figure 12-6. If it does not, then compare your script with the \My Documents\Microsoft Press\VBScriptSBS\ch12\ModifyOrganizationalPage.vbs script.

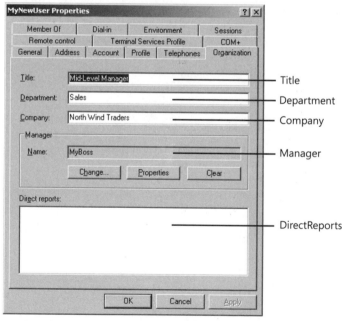

Figure 12-6   Organizational attributes in Active Directory

Modifying Terminal Server Settings

One of the big problems users of Microsoft Terminal Services faced in the Windows 2000 days was the inability to modify Terminal Server profile information via a script. This was particularly frustrating because the information appeared on a tab in Active Directory Users And Computers—causing many administrators to assume the information was "in Active Directory" and that it should be accessible through ADSI scripting. In Windows Server 2003, a new interface was introduced that enables ADSI scripting to edit Terminal Server settings. This interface is called the IADsTSUserEx, and it exposes the properties listed in Table 12-3.

Table 12-3   Terminal Server Setting Properties

Property	Meaning	Value
TerminalServicesProfilePath	Roaming or mandatory profile path to use when the user logs on to the Terminal Server	Disabled = 0, Enabled = 1
TerminalServicesHomeDirectory	Home directory for the user	UNC path to directory
TerminalServicesHomeDrive	Home drive for the user	Drive letter followed by colon
AllowLogon	Value that specifies whether the user is allowed to log on to the Terminal Server	Disabled = 0, Enabled = 1
EnableRemoteControl	Value that specifies whether to allow remote observation or remote control of the user's Terminal Services session	Disable = 0, EnableInputNotify = 1, EnableInputNoNotify = 2, EnableNoInputNotify = 3, EnableNoInputNoNotify = 4
MaxDisconnectionTime	Maximum amount of time a disconnected session remains viable	Time in minutes
MaxConnectionTime	Maximum duration of a connection	Time in minutes
MaxIdleTime	Maximum amount of time a session can remain idle	Time in minutes
ReconnectionAction	Value that specifies whether to allow reconnection to a disconnected Terminal Services session from any client computer	Any Client = 0, Originating client = 1
BrokenConnectionAction	Value that specifies the action to take when a Terminal Services session limit is reached	Disconnect = 0, End Session = 1
ConnectClientDrivesAtLogon	Value that specifies whether to reconnect to mapped client drives at logon	Disabled = 0, Enabled = 1

Table 12-3   Terminal Server Setting Properties

Property	Meaning	Value
ConnectClientPrintersAtLogon	Value that specifies whether to reconnect to mapped client printers at logon	Disabled = 0, Enabled = 1
DefaultToMainPrinter	Value that specifies whether to print automatically to the client's default printer	Disabled = 0, Enabled = 1
TerminalServicesWorkDirectory	Working directory path for the user	UNC path to directory
TerminalServicesInitialProgram	Path and file name of the application that the user wants to start automatically when the user logs on to the Terminal Server	UNC path to directory

The following script, ModifyTerminalServerProperties.vbs, will assign values to all of the available properties for a user Terminal Server profile. Please keep in mind, this script requires access to a Windows Server 2003 machine, and you will need to give the script the appropriate name for both the *User* object and the server itself. Also remember that under normal circumstances, one would not need to assign values to all of these properties, because many of them can be set server side, instead of user side. One reason, however, for assigning values on the user side of the equation is that under certain circumstances, a network administrator wants to allow the user settings to override the "default" server settings.

In the ModifyTerminalServerProperties.vbs script, all of the property values have been abstracted into constants that are assigned values in the Reference section of the script. This was done to facilitate modifying the script in the future, as well as to provide a better place for script documentation. In the version of this script in the \My Documents\Microsoft Press\VBScriptSBS\CD-ROM\ch12 folder, the script is fully commented (most comments in the script below have been removed for clarity).

ModifyTerminalServerProperties.vbs

```
Option Explicit
On Error Resume Next
Dim strProvider 'defines how will talk
Dim strOU 'path to where object is located
Dim strDomain 'name of domain connecting to
Dim strOUName 'user name
Dim objUser 'holds connection to ADSI

strProvider = "LDAP://"
strOU = "ou=mred,"
strDomain = "dc=nwtraders,dc=msft"
strOUName = "cn=myNewUser,"
Const blnENABLED = 1
Const blnBROKEN_CONNECTION = 1
Const blnRECONNECTION = 1
Const intREMOTE_CONTROL = 1
```

```
Const intMAX_CONNECTION=60
Const intMAX_DISCONNECT=6
Const intMAX_IDLE=10
Const strHOME_DIR = "\\London\Shared\"
Const strHOME_DRIVE = "t:"
Const strPROFILE_PATH = "\\London\Profiles\"
Const strINIT_PROG = "notepad.exe"
Const strWORK_DIR = "\\London\Profiles\"
Const strTEMP_DIR = "\tmp"

Set objUser = GetObject(strProvider & strOUName & strOU & strDomain)
'Terminal Services Profile tab
objUser.AllowLogon            = blnENABLED
objUser.TerminalServicesHomeDirectory = strHOME_DIR & funfix(strOUName)
objUser.TerminalServicesHomeDrive    = strHOME_DRIVE
objUser.TerminalServicesProfilePath  = strPROFILE_PATH & funfix(strOUname)
'Remote control tab. This property sets ALL 4 controls on the tab
objUser.EnableRemoteControl = intREMOTE_CONTROL
'Sessions tab
objUser.BrokenConnectionAction = blnBROKEN_CONNECTION
objUser.MaxConnectionTime    = intMAX_CONNECTION
objUser.MaxDisconnectionTime  = intMAX_DISCONNECT
objUser.MaxIdleTime          = intMAX_IDLE
objUser.ReconnectionAction    = blnRECONNECTION
'Environment tab
objUser.ConnectClientDrivesAtLogon   = blnENABLED
objUser.ConnectClientPrintersAtLogon = blnENABLED
objUser.DefaultToMainPrinter        = blnENABLED
objUser.TerminalServicesInitialProgram = strINIT_PROG
objUser.TerminalServicesWorkDirectory = strWORK_DIR & funfix(strOUname) & strTEMP_DIR
objUser.SetInfo

subError

'****************** Subs and Functions are below **************
Sub subError
If Err.Number = 0 Then
WScript.Echo("User " & funFix(strOUName) & " was modified")
Else
WScript.Echo "An error occurred. It was: " & Err.Number
End If
End sub

Function funfix (strin)
funFix = Mid(strin,4)
funfix = Mid(funFix,1,Len(funFix)-1)
End Function
```

Modifying the Terminal Server user profile settings

1. Open Notepad or some other script editor.

2. Open the \My Documents\Microsoft Press\VBScriptSBS\ch12\ModifyUserAddressTab.vbs script and save it as YourNameModifyTerminalServerProfile.vbs.

3. In the Reference section of your script, under the *strOUName= "CN=MyNewUser"* line, add a constant *blnENABLED* and set it equal to one.

4. On the next line, define a constant called *strHOME_DIR* and set it equal to "*London**Shared*\".

5. On the next line, define a constant called *strHOME_DRIVE* and set it equal to "*t:*".

6. On the next line, define a constant called *strPROFILE_PATH* and set it equal to "*London**Profiles*\".

7. The completed Reference section will look like the following:

```
strProvider = "LDAP://"
strOU = "ou=mred,"
strDomain = "dc=nwtraders,dc=msft"
strOUName = "cn=myNewUser,"
Const blnENABLED = 1
Const strHOME_DIR = "\\London\Shared\"
Const strHOME_DRIVE = "t:"
Const strPROFILE_PATH = "\\London\Profiles\"
```

8. Delete *WScript.Echo* and all the *objUser* commands except for the *objUser.SetInfo* command under the *Set objUser* line. Your revised Worker and Output section will now look like the following:

```
Set objUser = GetObject(strProvider & strOUName & strOU & strDomain)

objUser.SetInfo

If Err.Number = 0 Then
WScript.Echo("User " & strOUName & " was modified")
Else
WScript.Echo "An error occurred. it was: " & Err.Number
End If
```

9. Turn on allow logon by assigning the *blnENABLED* value to *objUser.AllowLogon*, as seen below:

```
objUser.AllowLogon = blnENABLED
```

10. Set the terminal server home directory by assigning the *strHOME_DIR* value to *objUser.TerminalServicesHomeDirectory*, as seen below. Use the *funfix* function to clean up the user name. (Note: We have not yet created the *funfix* function!)

```
objUser.TerminalServicesHomeDirectory = strHOME_DIR & funfix(strOUName)
```

11. Set the terminal server home drive letter by assigning the *strHOME_DRIVE* constant to *objUser.TerminalServicesHomeDrive*, as seen below:

```
objUser.TerminalServicesHomeDrive = strHOME_DRIVE
```

12. Set the profile path for the terminal server user by assigning the *strPROFILE_PATH* constant to *objUser.TerminalServicesProfilePath*. Use the *funfix* function to clean up the username.

```
objUser.TerminalServicesProfilePath  = strPROFILE_PATH & funfix(strOUname)
```

13. Turn the *If Err.Number* section of code into a subroutine. Do this by adding *Sub subError* above the section of code, and E*nd sub* at the bottom of the code. It will look like the following when completed.

```
Sub subError
If Err.Number = 0 Then
WScript.Echo("User " & funFix(strOUName) & " was modified")
Else
WScript.Echo "An error occurred. It was: " & Err.Number
End If
End sub
```

14. On the line following *objUser.SetInfo* call the *subError* subroutine. This is seen in the code below:

```
subError
```

15. Copy the *funfix* function from the \My Documents\Microsoft Press\VBScriptSBS\ Utilities\Funfix.vbs script to the bottom of your script. The *funfix* function looks like the following:

```
Function funfix (strin)
funFix = Mid(strin,4) 'removes cn= from strOUName to give username
funFix = Mid(funFix,1,Len(funFix)-1) 'removes "," from end of strOUName
End Function
```

16. Save and run your script. If there are problems, compare it with the ModifyTerminalServerProfile.vbs script in the Chapter 12 folder.

Deleting Users

There are times when you need to delete user accounts, and with ADSI you can very easily delete large numbers of users with a single click of the mouse. Some reasons for deleting user accounts are:

- To clean up a computer lab environment, that is, to return machines to a known state.

- To clean up accounts at the end of a school year. Many schools delete all student-related accounts and files at the end of each year. Scripting makes it easy to both create and delete the accounts.

- To clean up temporary accounts created for special projects. If the creation of accounts is scripted, their deletion can also be scripted, ensuring no temporary accounts are left lingering in the directory.

> **Just the Steps**   To delete users
>
> 1. Perform the binding to the appropriate OU.
> 2. Use *GetObject* to make a connection.
> 3. Specify the appropriate provider and *ADsPath*.
> 4. Call the *Delete* method.
> 5. Specify object class as *User*.
> 6. Specify the user to delete by *CN*.

To delete a user, call the *Delete* method after binding to the appropriate level in the Active Directory namespace. Then specify both the object class, which in this case is *User*, and the CN of the user to be deleted. This can actually be accomplished in only two lines of code:

```
Set objDomain = GetObject(provider & ou & domain)
objDomain.Delete oClass, oCn & oUname
```

If you modify the CreateUser.vbs script, you can easily transform it into the DeleteUser.vbs script, which follows. Notice that the Reference information section is basically the same. It holds the path to the OU and the path to the user in the variables, enabling you to modify the script more easily. The main change is in the Worker section of the script. The binding string is the same as seen earlier. However, you use the connection that was made in the binding string and call the *Delete* method. You specify the class of the object in the *oClass* variable in the Reference section of the script. You also list the *oUname* and *cn=* parts as well. The syntax is *Delete(Class, target)*. The deletion takes effect immediately. No *SetInfo* command is required.

DeleteUser.vbs

```
Option Explicit
'On Error Resume Next
Dim strProvider 'defines how will talk
Dim strOU 'path to where new object will be created
Dim strDomain 'name of strDomain connecting to
Dim strClass 'the class of object we are creating
Dim strOUname 'name of object are creating
Dim objDomain 'holds connection to adsi
Dim objOU 'holds handle to create method

strprovider = "LDAP://"
strOU = "OU=mred," 'when using is OU=mred, THE , would be required.
strDomain = "dc=nwtraders,dc=msft"
strClass = "User"
strOUname = "CN=MyNewUser"
```

```
Set objDomain = GetObject(strProvider & strOU & strDomain)
objDomain.Delete strClass, strOUname

If Err.number = 0 Then
WScript.Echo(strOUname & " was deleted")
Else If Err.number = "-2147016656" Then
WScript.echo strOUname & " does not exist"
Else
WScript.echo " error on the play " & Err.Number
End If
End If
```

Deleting Users Step-by-Step Exercises

In this section, you will practice deleting users. You begin with a starter file that is used to create the user. This is a good practice because you can ensure that all created users get deleted when the time comes. While working on your script, if you need to run the script several times, you can use the \My Documents\Microsoft Press\VBScriptSBS\ch12\Step-ByStep\sbsStarter.vbs file to create your user prior to deleting the user. If the user isn't present when you try deletion, you get an error.

1. Open Notepad or your favorite script editor.

2. Open sbsStarter.vbs and save it as YourNameDeleteUser.vbs.

3. Delete the declaration for the variable *objUser*.

4. Delete three of the four lines that call *objUser* in the Worker information section of the script. These lines look like the following:

   ```
   objUser.Put "sAMAccountName", oUname
   objUser.Put "DisplayName", oUname

   objUser.SetInfo
   ```

5. Locate the *Set objUser* line initially used to create the user so that the line now deletes the user instead. The original line looks like the following:

   ```
   Set objUser = objDomain.create(oClass, oCn & oUname)
   ```

6. Remove the *Set objUser* portion of the line. It will now look like the following:

   ```
   objDomain.create(oClass, oCn & oUname)
   ```

7. Change the method called in the preceding line from *Create* to *Delete*. The line will now look like the following:

   ```
   objDomain.Delete(oClass, oCn & oUname)
   ```

8. Save your work. If you try to run the script now, you'll get an error because you need to remove the parentheses. Once removed, the code looks like the following:

   ```
   objDomain.Delete oClass, oCn & oUname
   ```

9. Change the output message so that it says *deleted* instead of *created*. It looks like the following once the change is implemented:

    ```
    WScript.Echo("User " & oUname & " was deleted")
    ```

10. Save your work.

11. Open Active Directory Users And Computers to verify that *LabUser* was deleted.

12. Run the script. If it fails, run the starter script to ensure there is a user on the server. After this is done, run the script to see whether it works. When it does, run the sbsStarter.vbs script again, because you'll need the user for the next exercise. If it does not run correctly, compare your script with the DeleteUser.vbs script in the Chapter 12 Step-by-Step folder.

One Step Further: Using the Event Log

In this exercise, you modify the delete user script from the previous step-by-step exercise and write the resulting output to the event log instead of to a pop-up dialog box. This results in an enterprise type of solution because the script could be scheduled, or the script might delete a large number of users, in which case writing output to a dialog box or even to a command prompt would be impractical. The event log always exists, so it is a convenient place to log information. Only three lines of code are required to implement writing to the event log.

1. Open Notepad or your favorite script editor.

2. Open \My Documents\Microsoft Press\VBScriptSBS\ch12\OneStepFurther \DeleteUser.vbs file and save it as YourNameDeleteUserLogged.vbs. This will ensure you have a fresh working copy of the script and will give you a fallback option if required.

3. If *MyNewUser* does not exist in the *MrEd* OU, then run the CreateUser.vbs script to create the user you will be deleting.

4. Delete the *WScript.Echo* line that is at the bottom of the script. This line looks like the following:

    ```
    WScript.Echo("User " & oUname & " was deleted")
    ```

5. Add two new variables. The first variable is *objShell* and is used to hold the connection to the scripting shell object. The second variable is *oMessage* and holds the text of the message you write to the event log. These two declarations look like the following:

    ```
    Dim objShell 'holds connection to scripting shell
    Dim oMessage 'holds text of the message we write
    ```

6. Assign the value *oUname* & *"was deleted"* to the *oMessage* variable.

    ```
    oMessage = oUname & " was deleted"
    ```

7. Now define a constant called *EVENT_SUCCESS* and set it equal to *0*. The code to do this looks like the following:

```
Const EVENT_SUCCESS = 0
```

8. Save your work.

9. At the bottom of the script where the *WScript.Echo* command used to reside, use the *CreateObject* method to create an instance of the scripting shell. Set the handle equal to *objShell*. The code to do this looks like the following:

```
Set objShell = CreateObject("WScript.Shell")
```

10. Use the *LogEvent* method to write your message to the event log. You're interested in only a return code of *0*, which indicates a success. (Complete information on the *LogEvent* method is available in the WSH 5.6 help file, script56.chm, in \My Documents \Microsoft Press\VBScriptSBS\Resources.) The code looks like the following:

```
objShell.LogEvent EVENT_SUCCESS, oMessage
```

11. Save the script and run it.

12. Notice that there is no feedback. However, if you open the application log on the machine running the script, you see the event message. This is quite useful because the event message allows you to log updates as well as to audit them. The log looks like the one in Figure 12-7.

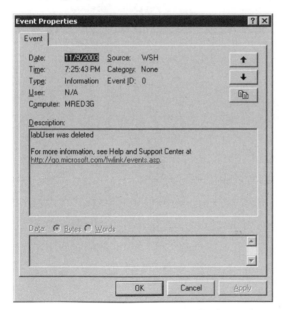

Figure 12-7   Use the *LogEvent* method to write scripts that provide notification and don't require user intervention

13. Open Active Directory Users And Computers to verify the user was deleted.

14. If your script does not perform as expected, compare your script with the DeleteUserLogged.vbs script in the Chapter 12 One Step Further folder.

Chapter 12 Quick Reference

To	Do This
Easily delete users	Modify the script you used to create the user and change the *Create* method to *Delete*
Commit changes to Active Directory when deleting a user	Nothing special is required; changes take place when deleted
Find country codes used in Active Directory Users And Computers	Use ISO 3166
Modify a user's first name via ADSI	Add a value to the *GivenName* attribute; use the *SetInfo* method to write the change to Active Directory
Overwrite a field that is already populated in Active Directory	Use the *Put* method
Modify terminal server profile settings in Active Directory	Use the *IADsTSUserEx* object
Assign a value to a terminal server profile attribute after making a connection into Active Directory	Assign the value to the property; no need to use the *Put* method
Delete the value of an attribute in Active Directory	Use the *Delete* method

Chapter 13

Using ADO to Perform Searches

Before You Begin

To work through the material presented in this chapter, you need to be familiar with the following concepts from earlier chapters:

- Active Directory Service Interfaces (ADSI) binding operations
- ADSI namespace
- Creating a dictionary object
- Implementing the *For Each...Next* construction
- Implementing the *Select Case* construction
- Implementing the *While Not Wend* construction

After completing this chapter, you will be able to:

- Connect to Microsoft Active Directory directory service to perform a search
- Control the way data is returned
- Use compound query filters
- Search Microsoft Excel, Access, and text files

Connecting to Active Directory to Perform a Search

In this section, you are going to use a special query technique to search Active Directory. You'll be able to use the results returned by that custom query to perform additional tasks. For example, you could search Active Directory for all users who don't have telephone numbers assigned to them. You could then send that list to the person in charge of maintaining the telephone numbers. Even better, you could modify the search so that it returns the users' names and their managers' names. You could then take the list of users with no phone numbers that is returned and send e-mail to the managers to get the phone list in Active Directory updated. The functionality incorporated in your scripts is primarily limited by your imagination. The following summarizes uses for search technology:

- Query Active Directory for a list of computers that meet a given search criterion
- Query Active Directory for a list of users who meet a given search criterion

- Query Active Directory for a list of printers that meet a given search criterion
- Use the data returned from the preceding three queries to perform additional operations

> **Just the Steps**   To search Active Directory
>
> 1. Create a connection to Active Directory by using Microsoft ActiveX Data Objects (ADO).
> 2. Use the *Open* method of the object to access Active Directory.
> 3. Create an ADO command object and assign the ActiveConnection property to the connection object.
> 4. Assign the query string to the CommandText property of the command object.
> 5. Use the *Execute* method to run the query and store the results in a *RecordSet* object.
> 6. Read information in the result set using properties of the *RecordSet* object.
> 7. Close the connection by using the *Close* method of the connection object.

The following script, BasicQuery.vbs, illustrates how to search using Active Directory. This script follows the steps detailed in the "Just the Steps: To search Active Directory" section.

BasicQuery.vbs

```
Option Explicit
On Error Resume Next
Dim strQuery
Dim objConnection
Dim objCommand
Dim objRecordSet

strQuery = "<LDAP://dc=Nwtraders,dc=msft;;name;subtree"

Set objConnection = CreateObject("ADODB.Connection")
Set objCommand = CreateObject("ADODB.Command")
objConnection.Open "Provider=ADsDSOObject;"
objCommand.ActiveConnection = objConnection
objCommand.CommandText = strQuery
Set objRecordSet = objCommand.Execute

While Not objRecordSet.EOF
  WScript.Echo objRecordSet.Fields("name")
  objRecordSet.MoveNext
Wend

objConnection.Close
```

In the BasicQuery.vbs script, you define your query after using the normal *Option Explicit* and *On Error Resume Next* commands. You then assign the query string to the variable called *strQuery*. The syntax of the query looks similar to the syntax you used to query Windows Management Instrumentation (WMI) in Chapter 9, "WMI Continued," and it follows a formula similar to that used with structured query language (SQL). The aspect of this syntax that is somewhat unusual is assigning a search string to a CommandText property If you envision the statement as stating that the command you want to execute is in the form of the query, perhaps the syntax will make a little more sense.

The query actually consists of two parts. The first part of the query is contained in angle brackets (< >) and specifies both the provider to use and the Lightweight Directory Access Protocol (LDAP) name of the container to which you want to connect. The second part of the query lists the fields you want to return in the result set.

> **Note**   The BasicQuery.vbs script query we're examining follows the same syntax you would use for an (ADO) search. ADO is a standard for connecting and querying different types of data sources. The basic syntax of an ADO connection is discussed in the "Creating More Effective Queries" section of this chapter, and it is highlighted in Table 13-1.

Header Information

The Header information section of the BasicQuery.vbs script contains the *Option Explicit* command as the first line and *On Error Resume Next* on the next line, which causes the script to continue executing lines after an error occurs. The following lines of the script detail all the variables that have been declared in the script:

```
Dim strQuery
Dim objConnection
Dim objCommand
Dim objRecordSet
```

Reference Information

The Reference information section of the script is used to define the LDAP query, as shown in the following code:

```
strQuery = "<LDAP://dc=Nwtraders,dc=msft>;;name;subtree"
```

The *strQuery* variable is used to define the query you will submit to Active Directory. In this instance, you're interested in the *Name* attribute, which is specified following two semicolons. The *subtree* part of the query tells Microsoft Visual Basic, Scripting Edition (VBScript) the scope of your query. The *subtree* modifier means that you want to search the subtree found under the target that you specified in the LDAP portion of the query. You define the starting point of your search by using angle brackets and the LDAP syntax. In this case, you start your search at the root of *nwtraders.msft*, and you're interested in returning the *Name* attribute from every object in the subtree—which means searching the entire hierarchy.

Worker and Output Information

Set objConnection creates a connection object that will be used to connect to Active Directory. Specifying *ADODB* means you will use the ActiveX Data Objects (ADO) technology to talk to Active Directory. The *CreateObject* method creates an instance of the ADO connection object in memory.

Now that you have a connection object resident in memory (named *ObjConnection*), you can create a command object that will be used to shuttle a query into Active Directory. You name this command object *objCommand* and set it equal to the object you get when you call *ADODB.Command*.

Having created the command object, you're now ready to open the connection to Active Directory. In this case, you use the ADsDSOObject provider. Because you can use ADO to talk to different data sources, you must specify which data provider to use when opening the connection. Here's an analogy to help you understand why you must specify a particular data provider when opening a connection. Think of opening a connection as being like opening a can of food in your kitchen. In most cases, the standard wheel type of can opener provides the needed leverage, such as removing the entire top of a can for a can of catfood. At times, however, you might need a different type of can opener, such as the kind that pokes holes in the top of the can to enable you to pour out liquid such as a can of orange juice. In the same way, depending on your data source, you might need to use a different provider. When talking to Active Directory, you will always use the *ADsDSOObject* provider.

Next, you need to define which connection to use for the command object. In this instance, you tell VBScript to use *objConnection* as the active connection. After telling VBScript to use *objConnection* as the active connection, specify the query to use by assigning the value of the *strQuery* variable to *commandText*.

Now you have a query, a connection, a command, a provider, an active connection, and command text. All that is left is to execute the command, which you do by using the following code:

```
Set objRecordSet = objCommand.Execute
```

You use the *Execute* method of the command object and set the data that comes back equal to the variable called *objRecordSet*.

The Worker information section of the BasicQuery.vbs script is used to iterate through the recordset that was returned when you used the *Execute* method of *objCommand*. In this instance, you use the *While Not Wend* construction to echo out the name field. The *While Not Wend* control structure enables you to know whether you've reached the end of the Recordset The recoredset has a property called *EOF*, that indicates the current record position is after the last record in the record set object.) If you haven't reached the *EOF* property you echo out the name retrieved by the initial query. After you echo out the name, you move to the next record in the record set. Here's the code that illustrates this process:

```
Set objConnection = CreateObject("ADODB.Connection")
Set objCommand = CreateObject("ADODB.Command")
objConnection.Open "Provider=ADsDSOObject;"
objCommand.ActiveConnection = objConnection
objCommand.CommandText = strQuery
Set objRecordSet = objCommand.Execute

While Not objRecordSet.EOF
  WScript.Echo objRecordSet.Fields("name")
  objRecordSet.MoveNext
Wend
objConnection.Close
```

The Output information section of BasicQuery.vbs does a very simple *WScript.Echo* output that indicates the result of the search. In more advanced scripts, you might want to write to a text file, a database, or even a Web page. After you produce output for all your information, you close the active connection by using *objConnection.Close*.

Quick Check

Q.   **What technology is used to search Active Directory?**

A.   ADO is used to search Active Directory.

Q.   **Which part of the script is used to perform the query?**

A.   The command portion of the script is used to perform the query.

Q.   **How are results returned from an ADO search of Active Directory?**

A.   The results are returned in a record set.

Creating More Effective Queries

Effective querying of Active Directory requires that you understand more about ADO searches. Table 13-1 lists the objects that are associated with searching Active Directory.

Table 13-1   Objects used to search Active Directory

Object	Description
Connection	An open connection to an OLE DB data source such as ADSI
Command	Defines a specific command to execute against the data source
Parameter	An optional collection used to supply parameters to the command object
RecordSet	A set of records from a table, a command object, or SQL syntax; can be created without any underlying *Connection* object
Field	A single column of data in a record set
Property	A collection of values supplied by the provider for ADO
Error	Contains details about data access errors; refreshed when an error occurs in a single operation

For ADO to talk with ADSI, two objects are required. The first object is the connection object, and the second object is the *RecordSet*. The command object is used to maintain the connection, pass along the query parameters, and perform such tasks as specifying the page size and search scope and executing the query. The *Connection* object is used to load the provider and to validate the user's credentials. By default, it uses the credentials of the currently logged-on user. If you need to specify alternative credentials, you can use the properties listed in Table 13-2.

Table 13-2   Authentication properties for the *Connection* object

Property	Description
User ID	A string that identifies the user whose security context is used when performing the search. (For more information about the format of the user name string, see IADsOpenDSObject::OpenDSObject in the Platform SDK.) If the value is not specified, the default is the logged-on user or the user impersonated by the calling process.
Password	A string that specifies the password of the user identified by "User ID."
Encrypt Password	A Boolean value that specifies whether the password is encrypted. The default is False.
ADSI Flag	A set of flags from the ADS_AUTHENTICATION_ENUM enumeration. The flag specifies the binding authentication options. The default is zero.

A number of search options are available to the network administrator. The use of these search options will have a large impact on the performance of your queries against Active Directory. It is imperative, therefore, that you learn to use the following options. Obviously, not all options need to be specified in each situation. In fact, in many situations, the defaults will perform just fine. However, if a query is taking a long time to complete, or you seem to be flooding the network with unexpected traffic, you might want to examine the search properties in Table 13-3.

Note that you should specify a page size. In Windows Server 2003, Active Directory is limited to returning 1,500 objects from the results of a query when no page size is specified. The Page Size property tells Active Directory how many objects to return at a time. When this property is specified, there is no limit on the number of returned objects Active Directory can provide. If you specify a size limit, the page size must be smaller.

Table 13-3   ADO search properties

Property	Description
Asynchronous	A Boolean value that specifies whether the search is synchronous or asynchronous. The default is False (synchronous). A synchronous search blocks until the server returns the entire result (or for a paged search, the entire page). An asynchronous search blocks until one row of the search results is available, or until the time specified by the Timeout property elapses.
Cache results	A Boolean value that specifies whether the result should be cached on the client side. The default is True; ADSI caches the result set. Turning off this option might be desirable for large result sets.

Table 13-3   **ADO search properties**

Property	Description
Chase referrals	A value from ADS_CHASE_REFERRALS_ENUM that specifies how the search chases referrals. The default is ADS_CHASE_REFERRALS_ EXTERNAL.
Column Names Only	A Boolean value that indicates that the search should retrieve only the name of attributes to which values have been assigned. The default is False.
Deref Aliases	A Boolean value that specifies whether aliases of found objects are resolved. The default is False.
Page size	An integer value that turns on paging and specifies the maximum number of objects to return in a result set. The default is no page size. (For more information, see PageSize in the Platform SDK.)
SearchScope	A value from the ADS_SCOPEENUM enumeration that specifies the search scope. The default is ADS_SCOPE_SUBTREE.
Size Limit	An integer value that specifies the size limit for the search. For Active Directory, the size limit specifies the maximum number of returned objects. The server stops searching once the size limit is reached and returns the results accumulated up to that point. The default is no limit.
Sort on	A string that specifies a comma-separated list of attributes to use as sort keys. This property works only for directory servers that support the LDAP control for server-side sorting. Active Directory supports the sort control, but this control can have an impact on server performance, particularly when the result set is large. Be aware that Active Directory supports only a single sort key. The default is no sorting.
Time Limit	An integer value that specifies the time limit, in seconds, for the search. When the time limit is reached, the server stops searching and returns the results accumulated to that point. The default is no time limit.
Timeout	An integer value that specifies the client-side timeout value, in seconds. This value indicates the time the client waits for results from the server before quitting the search. The default is no timeout.

Searching for Specific Types of Objects

One of the best ways to improve the performance of Active Directory searches is to limit the scope of the search operation. Fortunately, searching for a specific type of object is one of the easiest tasks to perform. For example, to perform a task on a group of computers, limit your search to the *Computer* class of objects. To work with only groups, users, computers, or printers, specify *objectClass* or *objectCategory* in the search filter. The *objectCategory* attribute is a single value that specifies the class from which the object in Active Directory is derived. Users are derived from an object category called *users*. All the classes you looked at in the last chapter (users, computers) are defined in the schema as values for the *objectCategory* attribute. When you create a new user, Active Directory identifies the attributes the *user* class contains. Then it uses those attributes when the new user is created. In this way, all users have the same attributes available to them. The attribute called *objectClass* is a multivalued attribute, and as you learned in the discussion of WMI, you have to use a *For...Next* statement to iterate all instances of values contained in the multivalued attribute.

> **Just the Steps**   To limit the Active Directory search
>
> 1. Create a connection to Active Directory by using ADO.
> 2. Use the *Open* method of the connection object to access Active Directory.
> 3. Create an ADO command object and assign it to the ActiveConnection property of the *Connection* object.
> 4. In the query string, specify the object category of the target query.
> 5. Choose specific fields of data to return in response to the query.
> 6. Assign the query string to the CommandText property of the *Command* object.
> 7. Use the *Execute* method to run the query and store the results in a *RecordSet* object.
> 8. Read information in the result set using properties of the *RecordSet* object.
> 9. Close the connection by using the *Close* method of the connection object.

In the FilterComputers.vbs script, you use ADO to query Active Directory with the goal of returning a record set containing selected properties from all the computers with accounts in the directory. The Header information and Worker information sections of the script are the same as in the previous script, so we won't discuss them.

FilterComputers.vbs

```
Option Explicit
On Error Resume Next
dim strQuery
dim objConnection
dim objCommand
dim objRecordSet

strQuery = "<LDAP://dc=nwtraders,dc=msft>;" & _
        "(objectCategory=computer);" &_
    "name,distinguishedName;subtree"

Set objConnection = CreateObject("ADODB.Connection")
Set objCommand = CreateObject("ADODB.Command")
objConnection.Open "Provider=ADsDSOObject;"
objCommand.ActiveConnection = objConnection
objCommand.CommandText = strQuery
Set objRecordSet = objCommand.Execute

Do until objRecordSet.EOF
WScript.Echo objRecordSet("name"), objRecordSet("distinguishedName")
objrecordset.MoveNext
loop

objConnection.Close
```

Reference Information

The Reference information section is basically the same as in the previous script, with the exception of the query. You call the query *strQuery* in this script, as shown here:

```
strQuery = "<LDAP://dc=nwtraders,dc=msft>;" & _
       "(objectCategory=computer);" &_
   "name,distinguishedName;subtree"
```

You can see the power of using the ADO connection to query Active Directory. You choose a couple of attributes from the dozens of available attributes associated with the *Computer* object in Active Directory. This makes an efficient query because you return only the desired information.

Output Information

The alert reader will realize that we've returned data on two attributes of the *Computer* object: the *distinguishedName* and the *name* of the computer. The Output information section of the script looks like the following:

```
WScript.Echo objRecordSet("name"), objRecordSet("distinguishedName")
```

At this point, it is sufficient to illustrate how to write data from the record set. You use the *Echo* command to send the data out, but the interesting part is you specify the field by name. It is perhaps confusing here that the field you are sending out is called *name*. To send out the *distinguishedName* field, put *distinguishedName* in quotation marks. We are actually specifying the Field property of the record set, but because it is the default property, we do not need to list it in our reference to *objRecordSet*. This also gives us the ability to specify two attributes at the same time, as seen in our output line.

Quick Check

Q. **What is one way to limit the amount of data returned by an ADO query of Active Directory?**

A. To limit the amount of data returned by an ADO query of Active Directory, you can specify *objectCategory*, which is easy to do. In this way, you can limit searches to just computers, users, printers, or other objects in Active Directory.

Q. **To specify an alternate set of credentials or to encrypt the password, what must be done in your script?**

A. To specify an alternate set of credentials or to encrypt the password, you must use the authentication properties of the connection object.

Q. **What two items must be specified for ADO to talk to Active Directory?**

A. The two items that must be specified for ADO to talk to Active Directory are the connection string and record set. All other fields are optional.

Querying multiple attributes

1. Open Microsoft Notepad or your favorite script editor.

2. Open \My Documents\Microsoft Press\VBScriptSBS\ch13\FilterComputers.vbs and save it as YourNameFilterComputersByName.vbs.

3. Edit the *strQuery* line to add an additional attribute to the filter. On the second line, add an extra set of parentheses around *(objectCategory=computer)* to hold the extra attribute. Your filter will now look like:

   ```
   ((objectCategory=computer))
   ```

4. Before *objectCategory=computer*, but between the new parentheses you added on the right side, add the new filter criteria: *(name=MyNewComputer)*. Make sure you use the name of a computer that will be present in Active Directory. This line will now look like the following:

   ```
   ((objectCategory=computer)(name=MyNewComputer))
   ```

5. To glue the two search attributes together, add an ampersand (&) character between the set of parentheses on the left side of the filter. It will look like the following:

   ```
   (&(objectCategory=computer)(name=MyNewComputer))
   ```

6. Add the *location* attribute to the list of properties you are selecting. This is seen below:

   ```
   ";name,location,distinguishedname;subtree"
   ```

7. Compare your complete search filter with the code below.

   ```
   strQuery = "<LDAP://dc=nwtraders,dc=msft>;" & _
           "(&(objectCategory=computer)(name=MyNewComputer))"&_
           ";name,location,distinguishedname;subtree"
   ```

8. Save and run your script. It should retrieve only the computer you specified in the *name=* portion of your search filter.

9. Modify the Output section of the script to print out the name of the computer for which you searched. This will be the first line in your Output section. Underline the name of the computer by using the *ForMatTxt* function.

   ```
   WScript.Echo ForMatTxt("Computer named: " & objRecordSet("name"))
   ```

10. Copy the *ForMatTxt* function from the ForMatTxt.vbs script in the Chapter 13 folder. Place it at the bottom of your script. This function is seen below:

    ```
    Function ForMatTxt(lineOfText)
    Dim numEQs
    Dim separator
    Dim i
    numEQs = Len(lineOfText)
    ```

```
        For i = 1 To numEQs
                separator = separator & "="
        Next
        ForMatTxt = lineOfText & vbcrlf &separator & vbcrlf
End Function
```

11. Remove the additional *WScript.Echo* statements in the Output section and add appropriate labels to each field when it is printed out. Use line continuation and concatenation as required. When done, the Output section will look similar to the one below.

```
WScript.Echo ForMatTxt("Computer named: " & objRecordSet("name")) &_
objRecordSet.Fields("name") & " is located: " & objRecordSet.Fields("location") &_
vbcrlf & "Distinguished name: " & objRecordSet.fields("distinguishedname")
```

12. Save and run your script. If it does not produce the expected output, compare it with \My Documents\Microsoft Press\VBScriptSBS\ch13\FilterComputersByName.vbs.

What Is Global Catalog?

As you become more proficient in writing your scripts, and as you begin to work with the enterprise on a global scale, you will begin to wonder why some queries seem to take forever and others run rather quickly. After configuring some of the parameters you looked at earlier, you might begin to wonder whether you're querying a Global Catalog server. A *Global Catalog server* is a server that contains all the objects and their associated attributes from your local domain. If all you have is a single domain, it doesn't matter whether you're connecting to a domain controller or a Global Catalog server, because the information would be the same. If, however, you are in a multiple domain forest, you might very well be interested in which Global Catalog server you are hitting. Depending on your network topology, you could be executing a query that is going across a slow wide area network (WAN) link. You can control replication of attributes by selecting the Global Catalog check box. You can find this option by opening the Active Directory Schema MMC, highlighting the Attributes container, and then double-clicking the attribute you want to modify. You will then be presented with the form shown in Figure 13-1.

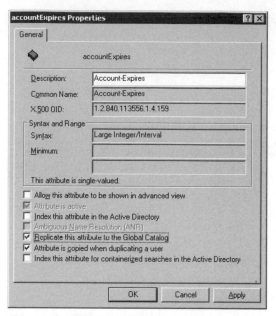

Figure 13-1   By indicating inclusion in the Global Catalog server, the industrious network administrator can improve query performance

In addition to controlling the replication of attributes, the administrator might also investigate attribute indexing. (See Figure 13-2.) Active Directory already has indexes built on certain objects.

> **Warning**   The Active Directory Schema MMC tool is not available by default. You must first register the schmmgmt.dll tool using Regsvr32. Changes made to the Active Directory Schema can only be made by members of the Schema Admins group in Active Directory. If you are a member of that group, then the Active Directory Schema MMC tool is much more dangerous than Regedit, because it will permit changes to the schema. Modifying the Active Directory Schema should only be undertaken when one is fully cognizant of the implications from both a performance and a security standpoint.

However, if an attribute is heavily searched on, you might consider an additional index. You should do this, however, with caution, because an improperly placed index is worse than no index at all. The reason for this is the time spent building and maintaining an index. Both of these operations use processor time and disk input/output (I/O).

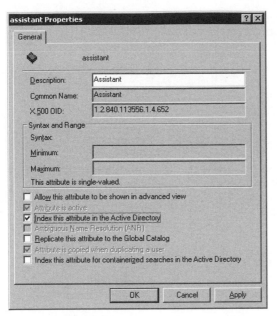

Figure 13-2   Indexing improves query performance in situations where the indexed attribute is part of the selection criteria

Suppose you create a custom attribute called *badgeNumber* in Active Directory. This attribute would be a small number with a high degree of cardinality. *Cardinality* is a database term that refers to the level of uniqueness of the data. High cardinality implies greater uniqueness. For example, in most cases, the *givenName* field in Active Directory will have a low level of cardinality because several users are likely to have the popular first names of Bob, Alice, Sally, Teresa, and Ed. On the other hand, only one user in Active Directory is associated with a particular employee number and therefore the *employeeNumber* field has a high level of cardinality. *EmployeeNumber*, then, would be a good candidate for indexing.

However, just because a field is a good candidate for indexing doesn't mean it should be indexed. It simply means it could be indexed. Before you decide to select the check box for the *badgeNumber* attribute, for example, decide how often you'll search on users by badge number. To help you figure this out, you could audit LDAP queries that are performed against Active Directory.

Querying a Global Catalog server

1. Launch Notepad or your favorite script editor and open \My Documents\Microsoft Press\VBScriptSBS\Utilities\BasicQueryTemplate.vbs. Save it as YourNameQueryGC.vbs.

2. At the bottom of the template, find the section of the *funfix* function that builds the connection string into Active Directory. It will look like the following:

```
If strOU <> vbempty Then
funfix = "<LDAP://" & strOU & "," & funfix & ">"
else
funfix = "<LDAP://" & funfix & ">"
End if
```

3. Change LDAP to GC in both places in the function. The modified code is seen below:

```
If strOU <> vbempty Then
funfix = "<GC://" & strOU & "," & funfix & ">"
else
funfix = "<GC://" & funfix & ">"
End if
```

4. Save and run the script. If the script does not run properly, compare you script with \My Documents\Microsoft Press\VBScriptSBS\ch13\QueryGC.vbs. Remember, you will want to run this script under Cscript and make sure it points to the appropriate domain on your network.

Querying a specific server

1. Open the ADOSearchTemplate.vbs in the Utilities folder and save the file as Your-NameSpecificSearchServer.vbs.

2. Identify the LDAP connection line, seen below:

```
strQuery = "<LDAP://ou=mred,dc=nwtraders,dc=msft>;" _
```

3. After *LDAP://* add the name of your server. Make sure it is before the *ou=* statement, and that it is followed by a trailing /. This is seen below:

```
strQuery = "<LDAP://London/ou=mred,dc=nwtraders,dc=msft>;" _
```

4. Compare your completed *strQuery* code with the one listed below:

```
strQuery = "<LDAP://London/ou=mred,dc=nwtraders,dc=msft>;" _
    & "(objectCategory=user);" _
    & "name;" _
    & "subtree"
```

5. Save and run your script. If it does not produce the expected results, compare your script with the \My Documents\Microsoft Press\VBScriptSBS\ch13\SpecificSearch-Server.vbs script.

Quick Check

Q. Why would a local Global Catalog server not be used in responding to a query?

A. One reason could be that the Global Catalog server does not contain the attribute for which you were searching. If it does not contain the attribute, it must refer the query to another server.

Q. What are the main questions a network administrator must answer prior to indexing an attribute in Active Directory?

A. A network administrator should look at the size of the data field, the level of cardinality, and the amount of use the attribute will generate as a search criterion.

Using ADO to query a Microsoft Office Excel spreadsheet

1. Launch Notepad or your favorite script editor and open the \My Documents\Microsoft Press\VBScriptSBS\Utilities\ADOSearchTemplate.vbs script. Save it as YourNameQueryExcelUsingADO.vbs.

2. In the Header section of the script, declare four new variables. These variables will hold the provider name, the data source statement, the extended attributes for Excel, and the name of the file. They are listed below:

```
Dim strProvider
Dim strDataSource
Dim strExtend
Dim strFileName
```

3. Specify the Jet provider to use to open Excel. It is the Microsoft.Jet.OLEDB.4.0, and you will assign it to the *strProvider* variable, as seen below:

```
strProvider = "Provider=Microsoft.Jet.OLEDB.4.0"
```

4. Tell the provider to use the extended properties for Microsoft Office Excel 8.0 (this is true even if you are using Microsoft Office Excel 2003) and assign the extended properties string to the *strExtend* variable.

```
strExtend = "Extended Properties=Excel 8.0"
```

5. Assign the spreadsheet name (in this case, wmiProvidersXP.xls in the Chapter 13 folder) to the *strFileName* variable. Use the *funfix* function to pad the file name with double quotation marks, as seen below:

```
strFileName = funfix("WMIprovidersXP.xls")
```

6. Assign the file name string contained in the *strFileName* variable to the *strDataSource* variable, as seen below:

```
strDataSource = "Data Source =" & strFileName
```

7.   Modify the current line to assign the query to the *strQuery* variable. Use a *Select* statement to do this. The sheet name must be surrounded with square brackets, and the name of the sheet is appended with a dollar sign, as seen below:

```
strQuery = "Select * from [CIMV2$]"
```

8.   In the Worker section of the script, modify the *objConnection.Open* statement so that it is using the provider specified in the *strProvider* variable, the data source from *strData-Source,* and the extended attributes contained in *strExtended*. Each of these will be concatenated with the other, and separated by semicolons, as seen below:

```
objConnection.Open strProvider & ";" & strDataSource &";" & strExtend
```

9.   Modify the Output section of the script by editing the field name to reflect the column of interest (class name) from the spreadsheet. This is seen below:

```
WScript.Echo objRecordSet.Fields("Class Name")
```

10. Create the *funfix* function at the bottom of the script. This function will simply accept an input parameter called *strIN* and append single quotation marks to the front and back of the value. This is seen below:

```
Function funfix (strIN)
funfix = "'" & strIN & "'"
End Function
```

11. Save and run the script. If it does not produce a list of WMI classes, compare the script to \My Documents\Microsoft Press\VBScriptSBS\ch13\QueryExcelUsingADO.vbs.

Using ADO to query a Microsoft Office Access database

1.   Open \My Documents\Microsoft Press\VBScriptSBS\ch13\QueryExcelUsingADO.vbs in Notepad or your favorite script editor. Save the file as YourNameQueryAccessUsing ADO.vbs.

2.   Delete the line that declares the *strExtend* variable that was used to hold the extended properties required for querying Excel. The line to delete is seen below.

```
Dim strExtend
```

3.   Delete the line that assigns the extended properties for Excel to the *strExtend* variable. This line is seen below.

```
strExtend = "Extended Properties=Excel 8.0"
```

4.   Type in the name of the Access database you want to query. In this case, you will use the EmployeesTest.mdb file included in the Chapter 13 folder. Assign the file name to the *strFileName* variable, but feed it into the *funfix* function that is already present on the line. This function will append and prepend the single quotation marks required by the Datasource property.

```
strFileName = funfix("EmployeesTest.mdb")
```

5. Modify the query contained in the *strQuery* variable so that you select everything from the Employees table. The code to do this is seen below:

```
strQuery = "Select * from Employees"
```

6. Modify the *objConnection.Open* line, as seen below:

```
objConnection.Open strProvider & ";" & strDataSource
```

7. Modify the *WScript.Echo* command in the Output section of the script so it will print out both the first name and the city of each employee in the database. Combine the two fields on a single line using a single echo command. This line will look like the following:

```
WScript.Echo objRecordSet.Fields("firstName"), objRecordSet.Fields("city")
```

8. Save and run the script. You should see an output similar to that listed below. If it does not appear, then compare your script with the \My Documents\Microsoft Press\VBScriptSBS\ch13\QueryAccessUsingADO.vbs script.

```
sam memphis
sally atlanta
sarah hollywood
jose charlotte
```

9. Modify the *output* command to remove the .Fields property. You do this by simply deleting the *.Fields* portion of the output. Naming this property in a record set is optional because it is the default property. This modification is seen below:

```
WScript.Echo objRecordSet("firstName"), objRecordSet("city")
```

10. Save and run the script. The output should be the same as the output from the previous time you ran the script. If it is not, then compare it with the \My Documents\Microsoft Press\VBScriptSBS\ch13\QueryAccessUsingADO.vbs script.

Using ADO to query a text file

1. Open the \My Documents\Microsoft Press\VBScriptSBS\ch13\QueryExcelUsing ADO.vbs script in Notepad or your favorite script editor and save it as YourNameQuery-TextFileUsingADO.vbs.

2. Declare a new variable called *strPath* that will contain the path to the text file to query.

```
Dim strPath
```

3. Modify the value of *strExtended* to provide the extended properties needed to query a text file. These attributes tell ADO that *datasource* is a text file, and we are specifying a header to the file that is delimited. This line of code is seen below:

```
strExtend = "Extended Properties=""text;HDR=YES;FMT=Delimited"""
```

4. After the *strExtend* line, add a line to hold the value of *strPath*. This is the folder that contains the text file to query. In this case, it is c:\fso, as seen below:

```
strPath = "c:\fso\"
```

5. Delete the *funfix* function from the bottom of the script. Also delete the reference to *funfix* from the *strFileName* variable in the Reference section of the script. The new file to query is called MyText.csv. This is the new value of *strFileName,* as seen below:

```
strFileName = "myText.csv"
```

6. The *strDataSource* variable will hold the path to the file, not the file name itself. Edit the assignment to *strDataSource* so it contains the *strPath* variable, as seen below:

```
strDataSource = "Data Source =" & strPath
```

7. To query a text file using ADO, we only need to use *Select ** from the name of the text file. Because the text file is contained in the *strFileName* variable, the query references *strFileName* instead of the square bracketed name of the Excel spreadsheet that was present in the original script. Edit the *strQuery* line to reflect this convention.

```
strQuery = "Select * from " & strFileName
```

8. Modify the Output section of the script. We are interested in printing out the name, address, and phone number of each employee. One of three methods for referring to these fields can be used: specify the field name as the item, specify the field directly, or refer directly to *objRecordSet*. This is illustrated in the code below. (Never do this in real life—choose one method for retrieving field names and use it consistently.) Use *vbTab* to space over the address and phone number lines for ease of reading.

```
WScript.Echo "Name: " & objRecordset.fields.item("Name")
WScript.Echo vbTab & "Address: " & objRecordset.fields("Address")
WScript.Echo vbTab & "PhoneNumber: " & objRecordset("PhoneNumber")
```

9. Save and run the script. You should see an output similar to the following:

```
Name: ed
   Address: charlotte
   PhoneNumber: 12345
Name: bob
   Address: atlanta
   PhoneNumber: 456787
Name: sally
   Address: Chicago
   PhoneNumber: 678345
Name: paul
   Address: cincinnati
   PhoneNumber: 245987
```

10. If your script does not produce the expected results, compare your code with \My Documents\Microsoft Press\VBScriptSBS\ch13\QueryTextFileUsingADO.vbs.

Creating an ADO Query into Active Directory Step-by-Step Exercises

In this section, you will practice creating an ADO query to Active Directory to pull out information about computer objects.

1. Open \My Documents\Microsoft Press\VBScriptSBS\Templates\BlankTemplate.vbs in Notepad or your favorite script editor and save your new script as YourNameStepBy StepADOquery.vbs.

2. Type **Option Explicit** on the first line to force the declaration of all variables.

3. Type **On Error Resume Next**.

4. Declare the following variables by using the *Dim* command: *qQuery*, *objConnection*, *objCommand*, and *objRecordSet*.

5. Create a query using the LDAP namespace that connects to your local domain controller. Specify that *objectCatagory* is equal to *computer*. Choose the following fields: *distinguishedName*, *name*, and *logonCount*. Set the search dimension to *subtree*. Assign this query to a variable called *qQuery*. Your code will look similar to the following (make sure you specify the actual name of your domain):

```
qQuery = "<LDAP://dc=nwtraders,dc=msft" & _
  "(objectCategory=computer)" & _
  ";distinguishedName,name" & _
  ",operatingSystem" & _
  ",logonCount" & _
  ";subtree"
```

6. Create a variable called *objConnection* and use it to hold an instance of the ADODB *connectionObject*. Your code will look like the following:

```
Set objConnection = CreateObject("ADODB.Connection")
```

7. Create an ADODB command object and assign it to a variable called *objCommand*. Your code will look like the following:

```
Set objCommand = CreateObject("ADODB.Command")
```

8. Open the connection using *connectionObject* and specify the ADsDSOObject provider. Your code will look like the following:

```
objConnection.Open "Provider=ADsDSOObject;"
```

9. Use the *ActiveConnection* method of the *objCommand* object to specify the connection held by *objConnection* as the active connection to Active Directory. Your code will look like the following:

```
objCommand.ActiveConnection = objConnection
```

10. Use the *commandText* method to set the query contained in the variable *qQuery* to be the command text for the command object. Your code will look like the following:

```
objCommand.CommandText = qQuery
```

11. Assign the record set returned by the *Execute* method of *commandObject* to the variable *objRecordSet*. Your code will look like the following:

```
Set objRecordSet = objCommand.Execute
```

12. Use a *While Not Wend* construction to iterate through the record set and echo out the following fields: *Name*, *distinguishedName*, *operatingSystem*, and *logonCount*.

13. Once you echo out these fields, use the *moveNext* method of the *objectRecordSet* object to advance to the next record. Your code will look like the following:

```
While Not objRecordSet.EOF
  WScript.Echo objRecordSet.Fields("name")
  WScript.Echo objRecordSet.Fields("distinguishedName")
  WScript.Echo objRecordSet.Fields("operatingSystem")
  WScript.Echo objRecordSet.Fields("logonCount")
  objRecordSet.MoveNext
Wend
```

14. Close the connection. Your code will look like the following:

```
objConnection.Close
```

15. Save and run the script by using CScript. If there are problems with your script, then compare it to \My Documents\Microsoft Press\VBScriptSBS\ch13\StepByStep\StepByStepADOQuery.vbs.

One Step Further: Controlling Script Execution While Querying Active Directory

In this section, you will modify the \My Documents\MicrosoftPress\VBScriptSBS\ch13\OneStepFurther\FilterMoreComputers.vbs script to control the way it executes while querying Active Directory.

1. Open the FilterMoreComputers.vbs script in Notepad or your favorite script editor and save the script as YourNameOSFcontrolScriptQuery.vbs.

2. On the line following the *objCommand.CommandText = qQuery* statement, add an *objCommand* property statement that will change the default asynchronous behavior from *false* to *true*. The amended script will look like the following:

```
Option Explicit
'On Error Resume Next

Dim qQuery
Dim objConnection
Dim objCommand
```

```
Dim objRecordSet

qQuery = "<LDAP://dc=nwtraders,dc=msft>;" & _
  "(objectCategory=computer)" & _
  ";distinguishedName,name;subtree"

Set objConnection = CreateObject("ADODB.Connection")
Set objCommand = CreateObject("ADODB.Command")
objConnection.Open "Provider=ADsDSOObject;"
objCommand.ActiveConnection = objConnection
objCommand.CommandText = qQuery
objCommand.properties("Asynchronous")=True
Set objRecordSet = objCommand.Execute

While Not objRecordSet.EOF
  WScript.Echo objRecordSet.Fields("name")
  WScript.Echo objRecordSet.Fields("distinguishedName")
  objRecordSet.MoveNext
Wend

objConnection.Close
```

3. Save the script.

4. Open a command prompt and run the script in CScript. You should see output coming from the script, but you will probably NOT notice any difference.

5. Turn off the caching of results by setting *Cache Results* to *false*. Do this under the *objCommand.properties("Asynchronous") = True* line you added in step 2. Your code for this command will look like the following:

```
objCommand.properties("cache results") = False
```

6. Save and run the script. Again you probably will not see any difference in the output.

7. Set a page size of *1* to tell Active Directory to return one object at a time. This line can go below the cache results setting specified in line 6. Your code will look like the following:

```
objCommand.properties("Page Size") = 1
```

8. Save and run the script.

9. Change the page size to *10* and set a size limit of *100* to limit the number of objects returned. The two lines of code will look like the following:

```
objCommand.properties("Page Size") = 10
objCommand.properties("Size limit") = 100
```

10. Set a query time limit that will limit how long the server is allowed to search for results. You will use the Time Limit property, as shown in the following code. Place this code below the size limit line.

```
objCommand.Properties("Time Limit") = 2
```

11. Save and run the script.

12. Set a timeout value that will limit how long the client machine waits for results from the server. This value should be smaller than the time limit value.

```
objCommand.Properties("Timeout") = 1
```

13. Save and run the script.

14. Close your work.

Chapter 13 Quick Reference

To	Do This
Make an ADO connection into Active Directory	Use the ADsDSOObject provider with ADO to talk to Active Directory
Modify an Active Directory query	Modify the search filter portion of the LDAP syntax query
Tell ADO search to cache results on the client side of the connection	Use the Cache results property
Directly query a Global Catalog server	Use *GC://* in your connection moniker, instead of using *LDAP://*
Directly query a specific server in Active Directory	Use *LDAP://* followed by the specific server name in your connection moniker, followed by a trailing /
Use ADO to query an Access database	Use the Microsoft.Jet.OLEDB.4.0 provider and specify the name of the database as the data source
Use ADO to query an Excel spreadsheet	Use the Microsoft.Jet.OLEDB.4.0 provider, specify Excel 8.0 as extended properties, and reference the spreadsheet by sheet name in square brackets with a trailing $
Query multiple attributes in an LDAP syntax query	Use a set of parentheses to surround each of the attributes, and place an ampersand at the beginning inside parenthesis to glue the two sets of attributes together

Chapter 14
Configuring Networking Components

Before You Begin

To work through the material presented in this chapter, you need to be familiar with the following concepts from earlier chapters:

- Creating text files
- Writing to text files
- Making a connection to WMI
- Making a connection to Microsoft Active Directory directory service
- Implementing the *For...Next* statement
- Implementing the *Select Case* statement

After completing this chapter, you will be able to:

- Use WMI to configure networking components
- Convert a text file from Active Directory into input for script
- Work with input text files

WMI and the Network

In this section, you use Windows Management Instrumentation (WMI) to configure networking components. However, instead of just dashing off a quick WMI script, you will take a step forward and begin combining several of the techniques presented earlier in this book, such as writing to text files and reading from Active Directory. This little bit of magic will track every step of your networked operations, enabling you to avoid dire consequences should an operation fail to properly complete. You can use this technique to:

- Import a list of computers from an organizational unit (OU) in Active Directory
- Import a list of users from an OU in Active Directory
- Import a list of users from a group that resides in Active Directory
- Read Active Directory and make changes on workstations

- Use a Lightweight Directory Access Protocol (LDAP) provider

- Make an ActiveX Data Objects (ADO) connection

- Execute an ADO command

- Use *While Not...Wend* to iterate through the record set

- Use WMI to make changes on desktop machines

Making the Connection

When creating a script with multiple parts or multiple actions, taking a systematic approach vastly simplifies the process. The script you will examine in this chapter has five major components. You will test each portion of the script after you write it to ensure it is working properly. Next, you will need to test the query syntax to ensure it is returning only the machines you want to modify. Once you have the query working properly, you will want to test the WMI portion of the script to ensure it works as planned. Finally, you will put the entire script together.

The following script is called ConnectToADOU.vbs, and it connects to Active Directory using the LDAP provider, makes an ADO connection, and executes an ADO command. Finally, it uses *While Not...Wend* to iterate through the returned record set. It does not use WMI at this point.

Note To run the ConnectToADOU.vbs script, you need to have access to an Active Directory controller. You also need to ensure that you modify the *oDom* and the *oOU* variables to accurately reflect your environment.

ConnectToADOU.vbs
```
Option Explicit
'On Error Resume Next

Dim qQuery
Dim oConnection
Dim oCommand
Dim oRecordSet
Dim oDom
Dim oProvider
Dim oOU

oProvider = "'LDAP://"
oDom = "dc=nwtraders, dc=msft'"
oOU = "ou=mred,"
qQuery = "Select Name from " & oProvider _
& oOU & oDom & "where objectClass='computer'"

Set oConnection = CreateObject("ADODB.Connection")
Set oCommand = CreateObject("ADODB.Command")
```

```
oConnection.Open "Provider=ADsDSOObject;"
oCommand.ActiveConnection = oConnection
oCommand.CommandText = qQuery
Set oRecordSet = oCommand.Execute

While Not oRecordSet.EOF
    Wscript.Echo oRecordSet.Fields("name")
    oRecordSet.MoveNext
Wend

oConnection.Close
```

Header Information

The Header information section of the script continues to be rather uninteresting. However, you shouldn't ignore it just because it is boring. Remember, when we use *Option Explicit*, we must declare all our variables. Because all the variables get listed out, *Option Explicit* provides a good place to document their use. By documenting the use of every variable, you perform two functions: provide a reference for future modifications and provide a reference for others who might read the script at a point later in time. I will admit that in the past, I did not document some scripts because at the time I understood what the script was doing. However, later, when I had to modify the script, I had to conduct a lot of additional research to figure out what I had done. The time to add documentation to a script is when you write it, not months later. Additionally, it makes sense to document the changes you make when you modify the script. This can take the form of comments with an associated date, and you can easily incorporate these comments into a script template, as shown in the following code section:

```
'================================================
'
' VBScript:  AUTHOR: Ed Wilson , MS,  11/09/2003
'
' NAME: <ConnectToADOU.vbs>
'
' COMMENT: Key concepts are listed below:
'1. making connection to AD
'2. Controlling results by using a filter
' REVISIONS:
' 11/10/2003 connection string - split into parts
' 11/11/2003 added computer filter to query
' 11/12/2003 changed names of vars from obj to o
'================================================
```

The standard header information is placed just below the template section, as shown here:

```
Option Explicit
On Error Resume Next

Dim qQuery
Dim oConnection
Dim oCommand
Dim oRecordSet
```

```
Dim oDom
Dim oProvider
Dim oOU
```

Reference Information

The Reference information section of the script is used to assign specific values to variables used in the script. One advantage of breaking the connection string into multiple parts is that the connection is easier to read and understand, and it also provides additional flexibility because of the ease of supplying different variables. The one issue to keep in mind when breaking up connection strings is that when the variables are concatenated back together, these variables must supply *exactly* what Microsoft Visual Basic, Scripting Edition (VBScript) is expecting.

> **Tip**   I often find myself having to use the *WScript.Echo* command to list out my connection string or my query after it has been put back together. More often than not, I find I've left out a semicolon, comma, or quotation mark that VBScript was expecting. This is where echoing out the query is invaluable. It takes one second to echo something out, whereas it could take hours of staring, visualizing, and imagining what the query or connection string looks like when put back together.

The variable *oProvider* is assigned to the string '*LDAP://*' and is used to tell VBScript you will be talking via LDAP to Active Directory. You use *oDom* to hold the domain components of the connection string. Using normal LDAP language, each part of the domain name is specified: *Dc=nwtraders, dc=msft*. In this example, you don't use a .com, .net, or .org upper-level domain name; you use the .msft imaginary name. The next variable you define is *oOU*, which you set equal to the workstations' OU. After assigning values to the provider, domain, and OU variables, you're ready to create the query. You use the *qQuery* variable to hold your constructed query. Notice that the syntax looks similar to a Structured Query Language (SQL) query. You are selecting the name field from '*LDAP://ou=mred, dc=nwtraders, dc=msft*', but you want only the name field if the object class is a computer. So you specify that in the *Where* clause of the query.

```
oProvider = "'LDAP://"
oDom = "dc=nwtraders, dc=msft'"
oOU = "ou=mred,"
qQuery = "Select Name from " & oProvider _
& oOU & oDom & "where objectClass='computer'"
```

Worker and Output Information

The next six lines of the script make an ADO connection to Active Directory. You use *oConnection* to hold the ADODB connection object that comes back from using the *CreateObject* command to give you an ADODB connection. Next, you use *oCommand* to hold the command object that comes back from using the *CreateObject* command to give us an ADODB command object. If the previous sentence seems redundant, that's because it is. This is one of the features of ADO, in fact! To reduce the learning curve, the developers tried very hard to make the syntax similar. Once you have the connection object and the command object, you can move forward with making the connection into Active Directory. You can think of building the ADO connection into Active Directory as connecting pipes. The provider is the kind of pipe you are going to run, the connection object is the path you are going to take while running the pipes, and the command is the valve that controls the flow of data through the pipes. Just as pipes are run one stick at a time, so too is each piece necessary to connect to Active Directory placed one at a time.

Now it's time to open the valve, but just like a water valve in your house, you need to know which valve to open and how far to turn the valve. With ADO, you specify the provider (that is, which pipe), which in this case is *ADsDSOObject*, and you specify which connection is the active connection. Next, you specify the command text, which is your *qQuery* (indicates how far you will open the valve). Once everything is lined up, you execute (open the valve). But wait! At home, you need a glass or a bucket to hold the water. With ADO, you need something to hold your data flow–in this script, you use the variable called *oRecordSet* to hold the data that comes back.

Iterate through the record set that comes back from the *qQuery*. To do this, you use a *While Not...Wend* statement. Because you don't know in advance how many computers are in the workstation OU, you return a set of records from Active Directory and work through each record in the set until you reach the end of the file, which is designated as *oRecordSet.EOF*. As long as the record set has records you haven't touched, you echo out the name of the record and then move to the next record in the set. If you come to the end of the record set, you end the *While Not...Wend* statement. You are using the *Echo* command right now as a test mechanism. In the script, right now, the *Echo* command is the Output section of the script. After you make sure the script works as planned, you replace the *Echo* command with some WMI code to change the Transmission Control Protocol/Internet Protocol (TCP/IP) address from static to dynamic.

```
Set oConnection = CreateObject("ADODB.Connection")
Set oCommand = CreateObject("ADODB.Command")
oConnection.Open "Provider=ADsDSOObject;"
oCommand.ActiveConnection = oConnection
oCommand.CommandText = qQuery
Set oRecordSet = oCommand.Execute

While Not oRecordSet.EOF
    WScript.Echo oRecordSet.Fields("name")
    oRecordSet.MoveNext
Wend

oConnection.Close
```

Quick Check

Q.   **What is an advantage of using *WScript.Echo* to display the text of a query?**

A.   An advantage of using *WScript.Echo* to display the text of a query is that it makes trouble-shooting a concatenated query string easy.

Q.   **Why do you need to use *While Not* in the Worker information section of the script?**

A.   *While Not* is used to iterate through the record set. It gives you the ability to work with an unknown number of computers.

Changing the TCP/IP Settings

After your script can connect to Active Directory and return a record set of computer names, you're ready to use WMI to convert the machines from static Internet Protocol (IP) addresses to Dynamic Host Configuration Protocol (DHCP)–assigned addresses. You scrounge around and come up with a script that uses WMI to turn on DHCP.

Caution   Please note this script will turn on DHCP on a computer. If you were to run it on a production server, it would turn on DHCP, and the server would request an IP address from your DHCP server. This could result in workstations not being able to communicate with your server. These scripts should be only used in a test environment until you configure them for your production environment.

The script to use to turn on DHCP, called EnableDHCP.vbs, is shown here:

EnableDHCP.vbs

```
Target = "."
Set oWMIService = GetObject("winmgmts:\\" & Target & "\root\cimv2")
Set colNetAdapters = oWMIService.ExecQuery _
 ("Select * from Win32_NetworkAdapterConfiguration where IPEnabled=TRUE")
For Each oNetAdapter In colNetAdapters
    errEnable = oNetAdapter.EnableDHCP()
     If errEnable = 0 Then
        WScript.Echo "DHCP has been enabled."
     Else
        WScript.Echo "DHCP could not be enabled."
     End If
Next
```

Just the Steps   To enable DHCP by using WMI

1.   Make a connection to *WinMgmts* on the target machine.

2.   Connect to the *root\cimv2* namespace in WMI.

3.   Create a collection to hold the result of the query.

4.   Use a query to choose network adapters that have TCP/IP bound and enabled.

> 5. Use a *For Each...Next* loop to iterate through the collection of network adapter configurations.
>
> 6. Use the *EnableDHCP* command on each network adapter configuration.

Header Information

The Header information section in this script is similar to the ConnectToADOU.vbs script. The variables are *Target*, *oWMIService*, *colNetAdapters*, *oNetAdapter*, and *errEnable*. When you merge the WMI script with Active Directory Service Interfaces (ADSI) script such as the ones examined in Chapters 11 and 12, you will need to declare new variables such as the ones mentioned here.

Reference Information

In the Reference information section, you assign values to the variables used in the script. The variable *oWMIService* is assigned to the hook that comes back from WMI when you use the *CreateObject* command. You attach to the *root\cimV2* namespace on the target machine. You use *colNetAdapters* to hold the hook that comes back from running a query against the WMI namespace. The query you run is designed to return all the network adapter configurations installed on the target computer that are IP-enabled. You do this because there is no point in trying to turn on DHCP on an Internetwork Packet Exchange/Sequenced Packet Exchange (IPX/SPX) or AppleTalk network adapter configuration.

Worker and Output Information

In the Worker information section of the script, you use the *oNetAadapter* variable as a placeholder by using the *For Each...Loop* to help you iterate through the collection of network adapter configurations. One nice thing you do here is use a variable called *errEnable*. You set *errEnable* to be equal to the value that is returned by VBScript when you try to turn on DHCP by using the *enableDHCP* command. If the operation is successful, the return code is 0. However, if the operation fails, you get a different return code. In this script, you're interested only in whether DHCP works. So if the return code is 0, everything is fine, and you echo out that DHCP was enabled. If DHCP enablement fails, you get a different error code as just mentioned, and so you use the *Else* part of the script and simply echo that DHCP failed.

> ### Quick Check
>
> **Q. To programmatically turn on DHCP, to which WMI namespace do you connect?**
>
> A. You need to connect to *root\cimV2*.
>
> **Q. In what fashion does WMI return the network adapter?**
>
> A. WMI returns the network adapter as a collection.
>
> **Q. What return code indicates a successful WMI operation?**
>
> A. A return code of 0 indicates a successful WMI operation.

Merging WMI and ADSI

Now that you know that both the ADSI script and the WMI script work as advertised, merging the two scripts is a rather easy task. By merging them, you will connect to Active Directory, perform a query of all computers in the *mred* OU, take the returned data into a record set, iterate through the record set, and enable DHCP on each workstation in the record set until you reach the end of the file. Along the way, echo out the results of the DHCP operation. The new script is called ADouWMIDHCP.vbs.

You need to assign a computer name to the variable *Target*. You do this inside the *While Not...Wend* loop by using *Target = oRecordSet.Fields("name")*, because as you walk through the record set, *Target* holds the name you get back. The variable *Target* will contain each computer name retrieved from ADSI during the execution of the script. Each name will then be used as a target of a WMI query. The rest of the WMI script is placed inside the *While Not...Wend* loop without additional alteration. Combining the two scripts enables you to leverage two different technologies to simplify a seemingly daunting desktop management problem. The only required changes to the ADSI script involved declaring the variables used by WMI in the Worker information section of the script. To make it obvious which variables were added with the merger, I added all new variables to two lines in the Header information section of the script. Although the only requirement for doing this is to place a comma between the variable names, I do not normally use this technique unless I have many variables that need to be declared.

ADouWMIDHCP.vbs

```
Option Explicit
'On Error Resume Next

Dim qQuery
Dim oConnection
Dim oCommand
Dim oRecordSet
Dim oDom
Dim oProvider
Dim oOU
Dim Target, oWMIService, colNetAdapters, oNetAdapter, errEnable


oProvider = "'LDAP://"
oDom = "dc=nwtraders, dc=msft'"
oOU = "ou=mred,"
qQuery = "Select Name from " & oProvider _
& oOU & oDom & "where objectClass='computer'"

Set oConnection = CreateObject("ADODB.Connection")
Set oCommand = CreateObject("ADODB.Command")
oConnection.Open "Provider=ADsDSOObject;"
oCommand.ActiveConnection = oConnection
oCommand.CommandText = qQuery
Set oRecordSet = oCommand.Execute
```

```
While Not oRecordSet.EOF
    Target= oRecordSet.Fields("name")

Set oWMIService = GetObject("winmgmts:\\" & Target & "\root\cimv2")
Set colNetAdapters = oWMIService.ExecQuery _
    ("Select * from Win32_NetworkAdapterConfiguration where IPEnabled=TRUE")
For Each oNetAdapter In colNetAdapters
    errEnable = oNetAdapter.EnableDHCP()
     If errEnable = 0 Then
        Wscript.Echo "DHCP has been enabled."
    Else
        Wscript.Echo "DHCP could not be enabled."
    End If
Next

    oRecordSet.MoveNext
Wend

oConnection.Close
```

> **Quick Check**
>
> **Q.** What is one technique for reducing the amount of space in a script that must declare a large number of variables?
>
> **A.** You can reduce the space that variables take up in a script by declaring multiple variables on the same line.
>
> **Q.** In the ADouWMIDHCP.vbs script just discussed, why was the WMI section of the script placed inside the *While Not...Wend* section?
>
> **A.** The WMI section of the script was placed inside the *While Not...Wend* section so it could gain access to the name field in the record set. The name then became the target of the WMI portion of the script.

Win32_NetworkAdapterConfiguration

The *Win32_NetworkAdapterConfiguration* WMI class has many properties and methods. The properties are elements containing information about the specific network adapter configuration, and the methods are used to perform a specific action on the network adapter configuration, such as enabling DHCP. Indeed, with 41 methods defined in Microsoft Windows Server 2003, it is hard to think of an operation that isn't covered. Some of the more common methods are listed in Table 14-1. You can find complete documentation by searching on *Win32_NetworkAdapterConfiguration* in the Platform Software Development Kit (SDK).

Table 14-1 *Win32_NetworkAdapterConfiguration* **Methods**

Method	Description
DisableIPSec	Disables IP security on this TCP/IP-enabled network adapter
EnableDHCP	Enables the DHCP for service with this network adapter

Table 14-1 *Win32_NetworkAdapterConfiguration* **Methods**

Method	Description
EnableDNS	Enables Domain Name System (DNS) name resolution on this TCP/IP-bound network adapter
EnableIPFilterSec	Enables IP security globally across all IP-bound network adapter configurations
EnableIPSec	Enables IP security on this specific TCP/IP-enabled network adapter
EnableStatic	Enables static TCP/IP addressing for the target network adapter
EnableWINS	Enables Windows Internet Naming Service (WINS) settings specific to TCP/IP but independent of the network adapter
ReleaseDHCPLease	Releases the IP address bound to a specific DHCP-enabled network adapter
ReleaseDHCPLeaseAll	Releases the IP addresses bound to all DHCP-enabled network adapter configurations
RenewDHCPLease	Renews the IP address on specific DHCP-enabled network adapter configurations
RenewDHCPLeaseAll	Renews the IP addresses on all DHCP-enabled network adapter configurations
SetDatabasePath	Sets the path to the standard Internet database files (Hosts, LMhosts, Networks, and Protocols)
SetDNSDomain	Sets the DNS domain
SetDNSServerSearchOrder	Sets the server search order as an array of elements
SetDNSSuffixSearchOrder	Sets the suffix search order as an array of elements
SetDynamicDNSRegistration	Indicates dynamic DNS registration of IP addresses for this IP-bound adapter
SetGateways	Specifies a list of gateways for routing packets destined for a different subnet than the one to which this adapter is connected
SetIPConnectionMetric	Sets the routing metric associated with this IP-bound adapter
SetKeepAliveInterval	Sets the interval separating Keep Alive Retransmissions until a response is received
SetKeepAliveTime	Sets how often TCP attempts to verify that an idle connection is still available by sending a Keep Alive packet
SetTcpipNetbios	Sets the default operation of network basic input/output system (NetBIOS) over TCP/IP
SetTcpMaxConnectRetransmissions	Sets the number of times TCP will retransmit a connect request before aborting
SetTcpMaxDataRetransmissions	Sets the number of times TCP will retransmit an individual data segment before aborting the connection
SetTcpNumConnections	Sets the maximum number of connections that TCP might have open simultaneously

Table 14-1   *Win32_NetworkAdapterConfiguration* Methods

Method	Description
SetTcpWindowSize	Sets the maximum TCP Receive Window size offered by the system
SetWINSServer	Sets the primary and secondary WINS servers on this TCP/IP-bound network adapter

Using WMI to Assign Network Settings Step-by-Step Exercises

Let's practice using WMI to set various networking configuration properties. The result of this will become the Worker information section for use in the One Step Further section.

> **Caution**   If this script were to be run in a production environment, it would turn on DHCP on the targeted machines. This could interrupt network communications. Please use this script in a practice environment first, and make the appropriate changes before ever running it in a production environment.

Instructions

1.   Open Microsoft Notepad or your favorite script editor.

2.   Open the \My Documents\Microsoft Press\VBScriptSBS\ch14\Step-ByStep\EnableDHCPStarter.vbs script and save it as YourNameEnableDHCP.vbs.

3.   On the first line, add the *Option Explicit* command.

4.   Change the variable *strComputer* to *Target* everywhere it is mentioned in the script. (The Find and Replace feature of Notepad is a good tool to use when renaming variables.)

5.   Change the variable *objWMIService* to *oWMIService* everywhere it is mentioned in the script.

6.   Change the variable *objNetAdapter* to *oNetAdapter* everywhere it is mentioned in the script.

7.   Declare all the variables used in the script by using the *Dim* command. You will need to declare seven variables: *Target*, *oWMIService*, *oNetAdapter*, *colNetAdapters*, *DNSDomainErr*, *DNSsearchErr*, and *DNSserver*.

8.   Modify the line *errEnable = oNetAdapter.EnableDHCP()* so that you can assign a DNS suffix for NWTraders.com. The line will look like the following:

```
DNSDomainErr = oNetAdapter.SetDNSDomain("NWTraders.com")
```

9.   Delete the Output section (the *If...Then...Else* section).

10. Add a couple of DNS servers to the DNS search list. To do this, use the *SetDNSsearch Order* method. However, because the DNS server is stored as an array, you will need to make a couple of entries in the script. On the line below the *Target = "."* line, add the following code:

```
DNSserver = Array("128.1.2.1", "129.1.2.2")
```

11. Add the *SetDNSsearchOrder* method under the *SetDNSDomain* line. Your code will look like the following:

```
DNSsearchErr=objNetAdapter.SetDNSServerSearchOrder(DNSserver)
```

12. Add a couple of lines of code so that you know the result of your operation. To do this, you echo out the value of both *DNSsearchErr* and *DNSDomainErr* along with appropriate remarks. The code for this looks like the following:

```
WScript.Echo "DNSDomain returned " & (DNSDomainErr)
WScript.Echo "DNSsearchOrder returned " & (DNSsearchErr)
```

13. Save your work as YourNameEnableDHCP.vbs. Run the script. You should see the IP address on your machine change to use a DHCP assigned address. If there is no DHCP server, then the machine will obtain an Automatic Private Internet Addressing (APIA) address. If this is not the case, then compare your script with the EnableDHCP.vbs script in the \My Documents\Microsoft Press\VBScriptSBS\ch14\StepByStep folder.

One Step Further: Combining WMI and ADSI in a Script

In this section, you combine the WMI script created in the previous exercise with an ADSI script. You can also use the \My Documents\Microsoft Press\VBScriptSBS\ch14\OneStep-Further\OSFch14Starter.vbs script.

> **Caution**   If this script were to be run in a production environment, it would turn on DHCP on the targeted machines. This could interrupt network communications. Please use this script in a practice environment first, and make the appropriate changes before ever running it in a production environment.

1. Open Notepad or your favorite script editor.

2. Open the OSFch14Starter.vbs file.

3. Open the \My Documents\Microsoft Press\VBScriptSBS\ch14\OneStepFurther\ConnectToADOU.vbs file.

4. Save the ConnectToADOU.vbs file as YourNameConnectToADOU_DHCP.vbs.

5. Copy the seven variable declarations from the OSFch14Starter.vbs file and paste them into the Header information section of your YourNameConnectToADOU_DHCP.vbs script. The seven variable declarations look like the following:

```
Dim target
Dim oWMIService
Dim colNetAdapters
Dim oNetAdapter
Dim DNSDomainErr
Dim DNSsearchErr
Dim DNSServer
```

6. In your YourNameConnectToADOU_DHCP.vbs file, locate the *While Not...Wend* section of the script. Remove the *WScript.Echo* portion of the *WScript.Echo oRecord-Set.Fields("name")* command.

7. Replace the *WScript.Echo* command with *Target =* so that the new command looks like the following:

```
Target = oRecordSet.Fields("name")
```

8. Copy the remaining portion of the OSFch14Starter.vbs script and paste it just below the new *Target = oRecordSet.Fields("name")* command. Make sure you do not include the *target="."* Section. The new *While Not...Wend* statement looks like the following:

```
While Not oRecordSet.EOF
    Target = oRecordSet.Fields("name")
    DNSserver=Array("128.1.2.1", "129.1.2.2")
    Set oWMIService = GetObject("winmgmts:\\" & target & "\root\cimv2")
    Set colNetAdapters = oWMIService.ExecQuery _
        ("Select * from Win32_NetworkAdapterConfiguration where IPEnabled=TRUE")
    For Each oNetAdapter In colNetAdapters
        DNSDomainErr = oNetAdapter.SetDNSDomain("NWTraders.com")
        DNSsearchErr=oNetAdapter.SetDNSServerSearchOrder(DNSserver)
        WScript.Echo "DNSDomain returned " & (DNSDomainErr)
        WScript.Echo "DNSsearchOrder returned " & (DNSsearchErr)
    Next
    oRecordSet.MoveNext
Wend
```

9. Save your work.

10. Test the script. If it works, remove the comment from the *On Error Resume Next* command. If it doesn't work, compare it with \My Documents\Microsoft Press\VBScriptSBS\ch14\OneStepFurther\ConnectToADOU_DHCP.vbs.

Chapter 14 Quick Reference

To	Do This
Control the behavior of NetBIOS over TCP/IP	Use the *WIN32_NetworkAdapterConfiguration* class
Disable NetBIOS over TCP/IP	Use the *SetTcpIpNetios* method of the *WIN32_NetworkAdapterConfiguration* class
Specify a unique domain name for a network connection	Use the *SetDNSDomain* method from the *WIN32_NetworkAdapterConfiguration* class
Specify a DNS server	Use the *SetDNSServerSearchOrder* method from the *WIN32_NetworkAdapterConfiguration* class
Obtain an up-to-date list of computers for performing WMI configuration operations	Use ADSI to query Active Directory for the computers; then call the appropriate WMI methods to perform the configuration

Using Subroutines and Functions

Before You Begin

To work through the material presented in this chapter, you need to be familiar with the following concepts from earlier chapters:

- Reading text files
- Writing to text files
- Creating files
- Creating folders
- Using the *For...Next* statement
- Creating the *Select Case* statement
- Connecting to Microsoft Active Directory directory service
- Reading information from WMI

After completing this chapter, you will be able to:

- Convert inline code into a subroutine
- Call subroutines
- Perform Active Directory user management

Working with Subroutines

In this section, you'll learn about how network administrators use subroutines. For many readers, the use of subroutines will be somewhat new territory and might even seem unnecessary, particularly when you can cut and paste sections of working code. But before we get into the *how-to*, let's go over the *what*.

A subroutine is a named section of code that gets run only when something in the script calls it by name. Nearly every script we've worked with thus far has been a group of commands, which have been processed from top to bottom in a consecutive fashion. Although this consecutive processing approach, which I call *linear scripting*, makes the code easy for the network administrator to work with, it does not always make his work very efficient. In addition, when you need to perform a similar activity from different parts of the script, using the inline cut-and-paste scripting approach quickly becomes inefficient and hard to understand. This is where subroutines come into play. A subroutine is not executed when its body is defined in the code; instead, it is executed only when it is called by name. If you define a subroutine, and use it only one time, you might make your script easier to read or easier to maintain, but you will not make the script shorter. If, however, you have something you want to do over and over, the subroutine does make the script shorter. The following summarizes uses for a subroutine in Microsoft Visual Basic, Scripting Edition (VBScript):

- Prevents needless duplication of code
- Makes code portable and reusable
- Makes code easier to troubleshoot and debug
- Makes code easier to read and maintain
- Makes code easier to modify

The following script (LinearScript.vbs) illustrates the problem with linear scripting. In this script are three variables: *a*, *b*, and *c*. Each of these is assigned a value, and you need to determine equality. The script uses a series of *If Then...Else* statements to perform the evaluative work. As you can see, the code gets a little redundant by repeating the same statements several times.

LinearScript.vbs

```
Option Explicit
Dim a
Dim b
Dim c

a=1
b=2
c=3

If a = b Then
WScript.Echo a & " and " & b & " are equal"
Else
WScript.Echo a & " and " & b & " are not equal"
End If

If b = c Then
WScript.Echo b & " and " & c & " are equal"
Else
WScript.Echo b & " and " & c & " are not equal"
End If

If a + b = c Then
WScript.Echo a+b & " and " & c & " are equal"
Else
WScript.Echo a+b & " and " & c & " are not equal"
End If
```

OK, so the script might be a little redundant, although if you're paid to write code by the line, this is a great script! Unfortunately, most network administrators are not paid by the line for the scripts they write. This being the case, clearly you need to come up with a better way to write code. (I am telegraphing the solution to you now...) That's right! You will use a subroutine to perform the evaluation. The modified script uses a subroutine to perform the evaluation of the two numbers. This results in saving two lines of code for each evaluation performed. In this example, however, the power is not in saving a few lines of code—it's in the fact that you use one section of code to perform the evaluation. Using one section makes the script easier to read and easier to write.

> **Note**   Business rules is a concept that comes up frequently in programming books. The idea is that many programs have concepts that are not technical requirements but still must be adhered to. These are nontechnical rules. For instance, a business rule might say that when a payment is not received within 30 days after the invoice is mailed, a follow-up notice must be sent out, and a 1 percent surcharge is added to the invoice amount. Because businesses sometimes change these nontechnical requirements, such rules would be better incorporated into a separate section of the code (a subroutine, for example) as opposed to sprinkling them throughout the entire program. If the business later decides to charge an additional 1 percent surcharge after 60 days, this requirement can be easily accommodated in the code.

In the script you are currently examining, your business rules are contained in a single code section, so you can easily modify the code to incorporate new ways of comparing the three numbers (to determine, for example, that they are not equal instead of equal). If conditions are likely to change or additional information might be required, creating a subroutine makes sense.

> Quick Check
>
> **Q.   To promote code reuse within a script, where is one place you can position the code?**
>
> A.   You can place the code within a subroutine.
>
> **Q.   To make changing business rules easier to update, where is a good place to position the rules?**
>
> A.   You can place business rules within a subroutine to make them easier to update.

Calling the Subroutine

In the next script you'll examine, SubRoutineScript.vbs, the comparison of *a*, *b*, and *c* is done by using a subroutine called *Compare*. To use a subroutine, you simply place its name on a line by itself. Notice that you don't need to declare the name of the subroutine because it isn't a variable. So, the script works even though you specified *Option Explicit* and did not declare the name used for the subroutine. In fact, you cannot declare the name of your subroutine. If you do, you will get a "name redefined" error.

Creating the Subroutine

Once you decide to use a subroutine, the code for creating it is very light. Indeed, all that is required is the word *Sub* followed by the name you will assign to the subroutine. In the SubRoutineScript.vbs script, the subroutine is assigned the name *Compare* by the following line: *Sub Compare*. That's all there is to it. You then write the code that performs the comparison and end the subroutine with the command *End Sub*. After you do all that, you have your subroutine.

SubRoutineScript.vbs

```
Option Explicit
Dim a, b, c
Dim num1, num2
a=1
b=2
c=3

num1 = a
num2 = b
compare

num1 = b
num2 = c
compare

num1 = a + b
num2 = c
compare

Sub Compare
If num1 = num2 Then
WScript.Echo (num1 & " and " & num2 & " are equal")
Else
WScript.Echo(num1 & " and " & num2 & " are not equal")
End If
End Sub
```

> **Just the Steps**   To create a subroutine
>
> 1. Begin the line of code with the word *Sub* followed by name of the subroutine.
> 2. Write the code that the subroutine will perform.
> 3. End the subroutine by using the *End Sub* command on a line by itself.

Creating Users and Logging Results

As your scripts become more powerful, they have a tendency to become longer and longer. The next script, CreateUsersLogAction.vbs, is nearly 80 lines long. The reason for this length is that you perform three distinct actions. First, you read a text file and parse the data into an array. Then you use this array to create new users and add the users into an existing group in Active Directory. As you create users and add them to groups, you want to create a log file and write the names of the created users. All the code to perform these actions begins to add up and can make a long script hard to read and understand. The subroutine becomes rather useful in such a situation. In fact, the subroutine used to create the log file is nearly 30 lines long itself because you need to check whether the folder exists or the log file exists. If the folder or file does not exist, you need to create it. If each is present, you need to open the file and append data to it. By placing this code into a subroutine, you are able to access it each time you loop through the input data you're using to create the users in the first place. After the user is created, you go to the subroutine, open the file, write to it, close the file, and then go back into *Do Until...Loop* to create the next user.

> **Note**   Holding the text file open might seem like an easier approach than closing the file, but I prefer to close the file after each loop so that I can guarantee the consistency of the file as a log of the accounts that are being created. Closing the file offers other benefits as well. It makes the operation more modular and therefore promotes portability. Making an open and a close part of the routine hides complexity that could arise.

If you kept the file open and wrote to the log file in an asynchronous manner, your log writer could get behind, and in the event of an anomaly, your log might not be an accurate reflection of the actual accounts created on the server. Here is the CreateUsersLogAction.vbs script.

CreateUsersLogAction.vbs

```
Option Explicit
On Error Resume Next
Dim objOU
Dim objUser
Dim objGroup
Dim objFSO
Dim objFile
Dim objFolder
Dim objTextFile
Dim TxtIn
Dim strNextLine
Dim i
Dim TxtFile
Dim LogFolder
Dim LogFile

TxtFile = "C:\UsersAndGroups.txt"
LogFolder = "C:\FSO"
LogFile = "C:\FSO\fso.txt"
Const ForReading = 1
Const ForWriting = 2
Const ForAppending = 8
Set objFSO = CreateObject("Scripting.FileSystemObject")
Set objTextFile = objFSO.OpenTextFile _
  (TxtFile, ForReading)
```

```
Do Until objTextFile.AtEndOfStream
  strNextLine = objTextFile.ReadLine
  TxtIn = Split(strNextLine , ",")
  Set objOU = GetObject("LDAP://OU=mred," _
    & "dc=nwtraders,dc=msft")
  Set objUser = objOU.Create("User", "cn="& TxtIn(0))
  objUser.Put "sAMAccountName", TxtIn(0)
  objUser.SetInfo

  Set objGroup = GetObject _
    ("LDAP://CN="& TxtIn(1) & ",cn=users," _
    & "dc=nwtraders,dc=msft")
  objGroup.add _
    "LDAP://cn="& TxtIn(0) & ",ou=Mred," _
    & "dc=nwtraders,dc=msft"
  Logging
Loop

Sub Logging
  If objFSO.FolderExists(LogFolder) Then
    If objFSO.FileExists(LogFile) Then
      Set objFile = objFSO.OpenTextFile _
        (LogFile, ForAppending)
      objFile.WriteBlankLines(1)
      objFile.Writeline "Creating User " & Now
      objFile.Writeline TxtIn(0)
      objFile.Close
    Else
      Set objFile = objFSO.CreateTextFile(LogFile)
      objFile.Close
      Set objFile = objFSO.OpenTextFile _
        (LogFile, ForWriting)
      objFile.WriteLine "Creating User " & Now
      objFile.WriteLine TxtIn(0)

      objFile.Close
    End If
  Else
    Set objFolder = objFSO.CreateFolder(LogFolder)
    Set objFile = objFSO.CreateTextFile(LogFile)
    objFile.Close
    Set objFile = objFSO.OpenTextFile _
      (LogFile, ForWriting)
    objfile.WriteLine "Creating User " & Now
    objFile.WriteLine TxtIn(0)
    objFile.Close
  End If
End Sub

WScript.Echo("all done")
```

Header Information

The Header information section of CreateUsersLogAction.vbs is used to declare all the variables used in the script. Thirteen variables are used in the script. The variable *i* is a simple counter and is not listed in Table 15-1 with the other variables.

Table 15-1   Variables Used in CreateUsersLogAction.vbs

Variable	Description
objOU	Holds connection to target OU in Active Directory.
objUser	Holds hook for *Create user* command; takes *TxtIn(0)* as input for user name.
objGroup	Holds hook for the *add* command; takes *TxtIn(1)* as input for name of group and *TxtIn(0)* as name of user to add.
objFSO	Holds hook that comes back from the *CreateObject* command used to create the *FileSystemObject*.
objFile	Holds hook that comes back from the *OpenTextFile* command issued to *objFSO*.
objFolder	Holds hook that comes back from the *CreateFolder* command issued to *objFSO* if the folder does not exist.
objTextFile	Holds the data stream that comes from the *OpenTextFile* command that is used to open the UsersAndGroups.txt file.
TxtIn	An array that is created from parsing *strNextLine*. Each field split by the comma becomes an element in the array. Holds user name to be created and the group that the user is to be added to.
strNextLine	Holds one line worth of data from the UsersAndGroups.txt file.
TxtFile	Holds path and name of text file to be parsed as input data.
LogFolder	Holds path and name of folder used to hold logging information.
LogFile	Holds path and name of text file to be used as the log file.

Reference Information

The Reference information section of the script is used to assign values to some of the variables in the script. In addition to the mundane items such as defining the path and title for the text file used to hold the users and groups, in this section, you create three constants that are used in working with text files.

> **Note**   If you create standard variable names, and you consistently use them in your scripts, you will make it easier to reuse your subroutines without any modification. For instance, if you use *objFSO* consistently for creating *FileSystemObject*, you minimize the work required to "rewire" your subroutine. Of course, using the Find and Replace feature of Microsoft Notepad, or any other script editor, makes it rather easy to rename variables.

These constants are *ForReading*, *ForWriting*, and *ForAppending*. The use of these constants was discussed in detail in Chapter 4, "Working with Arrays." The last two tasks done in the Reference information section of the script are creating an instance of the *FileSystemObject* and using the *OpenTextFile* command so that you can read it in the list of users that need to be created and the group to which each user will be assigned. Here is the Reference information section of the script:

```
TxtFile = "C:\UsersAndGroups.txt"
LogFolder = "C:\FSO"
LogFile = "C:\FSO\fso.txt"
Const ForReading = 1
Const ForWriting = 2
Const ForAppending = 8
Set objFSO = CreateObject("Scripting.FileSystemObject")
Set objTextFile = objFSO.OpenTextFile _
  (TxtFile, ForReading)
```

Worker Information

The Worker information section of the script is where the users are actually created and assigned to a group. To work through the UsersAndGroups.txt file, you need to make a connection to the file. This was done in a previous Reference information section of the script, in which we assigned *objTextFile* to be equal to the hook that came back once the connection into the file was made. Think back to the pipe analogy (in Chapter 5, "More Arrays"), in which you set up a pump and pulled the text, one line at a time, into a variable called *strNextLine*. As long as data is in the text file, you can continue to pump the information by using the *ReadLine* command. However, if you reach the end of the text stream, you exit the *Do Until...Loop* statement you created.

```
Do Until objTextFile.AtEndOfStream
  strNextLine = objTextFile.ReadLine
  TxtIn = Split(strNextLine , ",")
  Set objOU = GeCreateUsersLogAction.vbstObject("LDAP://OU=Mred," _
    & "dc=nwtraders,dc=msft")
  Set objUser = objOU.Create("User", "cn="& TxtIn(0))
  objUser.Put "sAMAccountName", TxtIn(0)
  objUser.SetInfo

  Set objGroup = GetObject _
    ("LDAP://CN="& TxtIn(1) & ",cn=users," _
    & "dc=nwtraders,dc=msft")
  objGroup.add _
    "LDAP://cn="& TxtIn(0) & ",ou=Mred," _
    & "dc=nwtraders,dc=msft"
  Logging
Loop
```

Output Information

Once you create a new user and assign that user to a group, you need to log the script changes. To do this, you call a subroutine (in our script, called *Logging*) that opens a log file and writes the name of the new user that was created as well as the time in which the creation occurred. The first task the *Logging* subroutine does is check for the existence of the logging folder that is defined by the variable *LogFolder*. To check for the presence of the folder, you use the *Folder-Exists* method. If the folder is present on the system, you next check for the existence of the logging file defined by the *LogFile* variable. To check for the presence of the logging file, you use the *FileExists* method. If both of these conditions are copasetic, you open the log file by using the *OpenTextFile* command and specify that you will append to the file instead of over-writing it (which is normally what you want a log file to do). In writing to the file, you use two different methods: *WriteBlankLines* to make the log a little easier to read, and *WriteLine* to write the user name and the time that user was created in the log.

If, on the other hand, the log folder exists but the log file does not exist, you need to create the log file prior to writing to it. This is the subject of the first *Else* command present in the sub-routine. You use the *CreateTextFile* command and the *LogFile* variable to create the log file. After the file is created, you must close the connection to the file; if you do not, you get an error message stating that the file is in use. After you close the connection to the log file, you reopen it by using the *OpenTextFile* command, and then you write your information to the file.

The other scenario our subroutine must deal with is if neither the folder nor the log file is in existence, in which case you have to create the folder (by using the *CreateFolder* method) and then create the file (by using the *CreateTextFile* method). It is necessary to use *objFile.Close* to close the connection to the newly created text file so that you can write your logging informa-tion to the file. Once you write to the log file, you exit the subroutine by using the *End Sub* command, and you enter *Do Until...Loop* again. The *Logging* subroutine is shown here:

```
Sub Logging
  If objFSO.FolderExists(LogFolder) Then
    If objFSO.FileExists(LogFile) Then
      Set objFile = objFSO.OpenTextFile _
        (LogFile, ForAppending)
      objFile.WriteBlankLines(1)
      objFile.WriteLine "Creating User " & Now
      objFile.WriteLine TxtIn(0)
      objFile.Close
    Else
      Set objFile = objFSO.CreateTextFile(LogFile)
      objFile.Close
      Set objFile = objFSO.OpenTextFile _
        (LogFile, ForWriting)
      objfile.WriteLine "Creating User " & Now
      objFile.WriteLine TxtIn(0)

      objFile.Close
    End If
  Else
    Set objFolder = objFSO.CreateFolder(LogFolder)
    Set objFile = objFSO.CreateTextFile(LogFile)
    objFile.Close
    Set objFile = objFSO.OpenTextFile _
      (LogFile, ForWriting)
    objfile.WriteLine "Creating User " & Now
    objFile.WriteLine TxtIn(0)
```

```
     objFile.Close
  End If
End Sub
```

```
WScript.Echo("all done")
```

Using a subroutine to retrieve service information from WMI

1. Open the \My Documents\Microsoft Press\VBScriptSBS\Templates\wmiTemplate.vbs script in Notepad or your favorite script editor and save it as YourNameListServicesIn-Processes.vbs.

2. Comment out *On Error Resume Next*.

3. Edit the *wmiQuery* line so that you are selecting only *processID* and the name from *win32_Process*. You want to, however, exclude the process ID that equals 0. This query will look like the following:

```
wmiQuery = "Select processID, name from win32_Process where processID <> 0"
```

4. In the Header section of the script, declare a new variable to hold the process ID. Call this variable *intPID*.

5. Inside the *For Each...Next* loop, delete all the *WScript.Echo* ": " & *objItem* lines except for one. The completed *For Each...Next* loop will look like the following:

```
For Each objItem in colItems
    WScript.Echo ": " & objItem.
Next
```

6. Modify the *WScript.Echo* line so that it prints out the name and the processed properties from the *win32_Process* class. Include labels with each property to identity each of the properties as belonging to a process. My code to do this looks like the following:

```
WScript.Echo "Process Name: " & objItem.Name & " ProcessID: " & objItem.ProcessID
```

7. Store the value of the process ID in the variable *intPID*. This is seen below:

```
intPID = objItem.ProcessID
```

8. Save and run YourNameListServicesInProcesses.vbs. There should be no errors at this point, and you should see an output similar to the following (of course your list of processes will be different). The process names and the process IDs seen in the output from your script will compare to the ones seen in Taskmanager.exe (refer to Figure 15-1).

```
Process Name: System ProcessID: 4
Process Name: smss.exe ProcessID: 776
Process Name: csrss.exe ProcessID: 868
Process Name: winlogon.exe ProcessID: 892
Process Name: services.exe ProcessID: 940
Process Name: lsass.exe ProcessID: 952
Process Name: svchost.exe ProcessID: 1136
```

```
Process Name: svchost.exe ProcessID: 1228
Process Name: svchost.exe ProcessID: 1352
Process Name: spoolsv.exe ProcessID: 1640
Process Name: explorer.exe ProcessID: 832
Process Name: wmiprvse.exe ProcessID: 632
Process Name: wmiprvse.exe ProcessID: 1436
Process Name: WINWORD.EXE ProcessID: 3764
Process Name: svchost.exe ProcessID: 2428
Process Name: PrimalScript.exe ProcessID: 2872
Process Name: cscript.exe ProcessID: 584
Process Name: wmiprvse.exe ProcessID: 3652
```

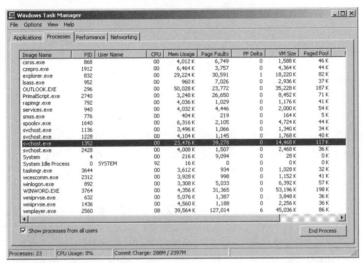

Figure 15-1   Taskmanager.exe view of processes and services; Svchost is comprised of several services.

9. Create a subroutine called *SubGetServices*. This is seen below:

```
' *** subs are below ***

Sub subGetServices

End Sub
```

10. Inside your new subroutine, declare three variables that will be used in the secondary Windows Management Instrumentation (WMI) query. One variable will contain the query, one will contain the collection returned by the query, and one will hold the individual service instances retrieved from the collection. The three variables you want to declare correspond to the variables used in the main body of the script: *wmiQuery1*, *collItems1*, *objItem1*.

```
Dim wmiQuery1
Dim colItems1
Dim objItem1
```

11. Under the new variables you declared in the subroutine, assign a new query to *wmiQuery1* that selects the name from WIN32_Service, where *processID* is the same as the one stored in *intPID*. This query will look like the following:

```
wmiQuery1 = "Select name from win32_Service where processID = " & intPID
```

12. On the line following *wmiQuery1*, use the *colItems1* variable to hold the collection that is returned by using the *execQuery* method to execute the query contained in *wmiQuery1*. This code will look like the following:

```
Set colItems1 = objWMIService.ExecQuery(wmiQuery1)
```

13. Use *For Each...Loop* to walk through *colItems1*. Use *WScript.Echo* to print out the name of each service that corresponds to the query defined in *wmiQuery1*. This is seen below:

```
For Each objItem1 In colItems1
  WScript.Echo vbTab, "Service Name: ", objItem1.Name
Next
```

14. In the main body of the script, after the line where the process ID is assigned to *intPID*, call the subroutine you just created. The placement of the call to *subGetServices* is seen below:

```
intPID = objItem.ProcessID
subGetServices
```

15. Save and run your script. You should see a printout that now lists services running inside processes. Compare your results with the listing below. If you do not see something like this (realizing the processes and services will be different), compare your script with \My Documents\Microsoft Press\VBScriptSBS\ch15\ListServicesIn Processes.vbs.

```
Process Name: System ProcessID: 4
Process Name: smss.exe ProcessID: 776
Process Name: csrss.exe ProcessID: 868
Process Name: winlogon.exe ProcessID: 892
Process Name: services.exe ProcessID: 940
 Service Name: Eventlog
 Service Name: PlugPlay
Process Name: lsass.exe ProcessID: 952
 Service Name: ProtectedStorage
 Service Name: SamSs
Process Name: svchost.exe ProcessID: 1136
 Service Name: DcomLaunch
Process Name: svchost.exe ProcessID: 1228
 Service Name: RpcSs
Process Name: svchost.exe ProcessID: 1352
 Service Name: AudioSrv
 Service Name: CryptSvc
 Service Name: EventSystem
 Service Name: Nla
 Service Name: RasMan
```

```
      Service Name: SENS
      Service Name: ShellHWDetection
      Service Name: TapiSrv
      Service Name: winmgmt
  Process Name: spoolsv.exe ProcessID: 1640
      Service Name: Spooler
  Process Name: explorer.exe ProcessID: 832
  Process Name: wmiprvse.exe ProcessID: 632
  Process Name: wmiprvse.exe ProcessID: 1436
  Process Name: WINWORD.EXE ProcessID: 3764
  Process Name: svchost.exe ProcessID: 2428
      Service Name: stisvc
  Process Name: wmplayer.exe ProcessID: 172
  Process Name: Dancer.exe ProcessID: 1180
  Process Name: PrimalScript.exe ProcessID: 1920
  Process Name: wmiprvse.exe ProcessID: 3156
  Process Name: cscript.exe ProcessID: 3468
```

Working with Functions

You have already used functions that are predefined in VBScript. These form the crux of most of the flexibility of VBScript. VBScript has more than 100 intrinsic functions, which provide the ability to perform string manipulation (*mid, len, instr, instrrev*), work with arrays (*array, ubound, lbound, split, join*), and control the way numbers are handled (*int, round, formatnumber*). With so much functionality, you might wonder why you need to create your own functions. Although you can write much code that does not require functions, there may be times when functions will make it easier to reuse your code. In addition, functions often make it easier to read and understand what the script is doing. In the VideoAdapterRam_Hard Coded.vbs script, video RAM is retrieved in bytes. To convert the number into something more manageable, we convert it into megabytes by dividing the number by 1,048,576. This causes a readability problem, as seen below.

VideoAdapterRAM_HardCoded.vbs
```
Option Explicit
'On Error Resume Next
Dim strComputer
Dim wmiNS
Dim wmiQuery
Dim objWMIService
Dim colItems
Dim objItem

strComputer = "."
wmiNS = "\root\cimv2"
wmiQuery = "Select AdapterRAM from win32_videoController"
Set objWMIService = GetObject("winmgmts:\\" & strComputer & wmiNS)
Set colItems = objWMIService.ExecQuery(wmiQuery)

For Each objItem in colItems
  WScript.Echo "AdapterRAM: " & objItem.AdapterRAM/1048576
Next
```

Add a function to convert to megabytes

1. Open the \My Documents\Microsoft Press\VBScriptSBS\ch15\VideoAdapter Ram_HardCoded.vbs script in Notepad or the script editor of your choice and save it as YourNameVideoAdapterRam_UseFunction.vbs.

2. At the bottom of the script, begin the function by using the command function call and name the function *convertToMeg*. Define a single input to the function as *intIn*. Close out the function by using the *End Function* command. This is seen below:

```
Function convertToMeg(intIN)
End Function
```

3. Between the *Function* and the *End Function* statements, divide *intIN* by 1,048,576 and assign the results to *convertToMeg,* as seen below:

```
convertToMeg = intIN/1048576
```

4. In the *WScript.Echo* line in the main script, call the *convertToMeg* function and supply *objItem.AdapterRAM* as the input parameter to the function. The modified output line is seen below:

```
WScript.Echo "AdapterRAM: " & convertToMeg(objItem.AdapterRAM)
```

5. Save and run the script. You should see the amount of video RAM reported in megabytes. If not, compare your script with \My Documents\Microsoft Press\VBScriptSBS \ch15\ VideoAdapterRam_UseFunction.vbs.

Comparing intrinsic function and user defined function

1. Open the \My Documents\Microsoft Press\VBScriptSBS\Templates\Blank Template.vbs script in Notepad or the script editor of your choice and save the script as YourNameFunString.vbs.

2. Add *Option Explicit* to the first noncommented line.

3. Use *WScript.Echo* to print out a line that calls the VBScript *String* intrinsic function. Tell the *String* function to repeat a dash character 15 times. This is seen below:

```
WScript.Echo "Intrinsic string function",VbCrLf,string(15,"-")
```

4. At the bottom of the script, create a function called *funString*. Have the function accept two input parameters called *intIN* and *strChar*. Close out the function by using *End Function*. This is seen below:

```
Function funString(intIN,strChar)

End Function
```

5. Inside the *funString* function, declare a variable to be used as a counter. Call this variable *j*.

6. Use a *For Each...Next* loop to build up the string of repeated characters. Use *j* to count from one to *intIN*.

```
For j = 1 To intIN

Next
```

7. Between *For j = 1* to *intIN* and *Next*, add *funString* to itself and to *strChar*, as seen below:

```
funString = funString & strChar
```

8. Copy the previous *WScript.Echo* line and replace the *String* function with the *funString* function, as seen below:

```
WScript.Echo "User string function",VbCrLf,funString(15,"-")
```

9. Save and run your script. The results from the two functions should be exactly the same. If they are not, compare your script with \My Documents\Microsoft Press\VBScriptSBS \ch15\FunString.vbs.

Using ADSI and Subs, and Creating Users Step-by-Step Exercises

In this section, you will expand the script used in this chapter. Instead of creating only a user, you will add information to the user. You will use a subroutine to perform logging.

1. Open Notepad or your favorite script editor.

2. Open the \My Documents\Microsoft Press\VBScriptSBS\ch15\StepByStep\Cre-ateUsers.vbs file and save it as YourNameCreateMultipleUsersSolution.vbs.

3. Make sure you have a file called C:\fso\UsersAndGroups.txt, and run the CreateUsers.vbs file. Go into Active Directory Users And Computers (ADUC) and delete the users that were created.

4. Cut the code used to open the text file that holds the names of users to add to Active Directory. It is under the variable declarations, in the Reference information section of the script. It is five lines long. This code looks like the following:

```
TxtFile = "C:\fso\UsersAndGroups.txt"
Const ForReading = 1
Set objFSO = CreateObject("Scripting.FileSystemObject")
Set objTextFile = objFSO.OpenTextFile _
  (TxtFile, ForReading)
```

5. Paste the code after the *WScript.Echo* command at the end of the script.

6. Under the declarations, where the *txtFile* code used to be, type **ReadUsers**. This is the name of the new subroutine you will create. It will look like the following:

```
Dim objOU
Dim objUser
Dim objGroup
Dim objFSO
Dim objTextFile
Dim TxtIn
Dim strNextLine
Dim i
Dim TxtFile
dim boundary


ReadUsers
```

7. On the line before the code that reads *TxtFile*, which you copied to the end of your script, use the *Sub* command to create a subroutine called *ReadUsers*.

8. At the end of the subroutine, add the *End Sub* command. The completed subroutine looks like the following:

```
Sub ReadUsers
  TxtFile = "c:\fso\UsersAndGroups.txt"
  Const ForReading = 1
  Set objFSO = CreateObject("Scripting.FileSystemObject")
  Set objTextFile = objFSO.OpenTextFile _
    (TxtFile, ForReading)
End Sub
```

9. Save your work. Run the script to make sure it still works. Open Active Directory Users And Computers and delete the users that were created by running the script.

10. Modify the subroutine so that it is reading a text file called MoreUsersAndGroups.txt. This file is located in the \My Documents\Microsoft Press\VBScriptSBS\ch15\Step ByStep folder.

> **Note**   If you do not add the full path to the MoreUsersAndGroups.txt file, you will need to ensure you are running the script from the same directory where the file is located.

11. In the Worker section of the script that creates the user, use the *Put* method to add the user's first name, last name, building, and phone number. The Active Directory attributes are called *givenName*, *sn*, *physicalDeliveryOfficeName*, and *telephoneNumber*. Each of these fields is in the array that gets created, so you need to increment the array field. The completed code will look like the following:

```
Set objUser = objOU.Create("User", "cn="& TxtIn(0))
objUser.Put "sAMAccountName", TxtIn(0)
objUser.Put "givenName", TxtIn(1)
objUser.Put "sn", TxtIn(2)
```

```
objUser.Put "physicalDeliveryOfficeName", TxtIn(3)
objUser.Put "telephoneNumber", TxtIn(4)
```

12. Because the group membership field is the last field and you added fields to the text file, you need to increment the array index that is used to point to the group field. The new index number is 5, and the code will look like the following:

```
Set objGroup = GetObject _
  ("LDAP://CN="& TxtIn(5) & ",cn=users,dc=nwtraders,dc=msft")
```

13. Save the script and run it. After you successfully run the script, delete the users created in Active Directory.

One Step Further: Adding a Logging Subroutine

In this section, you add logging capability to the script you finished in the Step-by-Step exercise.

1. Open Notepad or some other script editor.

2. Open \My Documents\Microsoft Press\VBScriptSBS\ch15\OneStepFurther\Create MultipleUsersStarter.vbs and save the file as YourNameCreateMultipleUsers Logged.vbs.

3. After the *objGroup.add* command statement but before the *Loop* command, add a call to the subroutine called *LogAction*. The modification to the script will look like the following:

```
Set objGroup = GetObject _
  ("LDAP://CN="& TxtIn(5) & ",cn=users,dc=nwtraders,dc=msft")
objGroup.Add _
  "LDAP://cn="& TxtIn(0) & ",ou=Mred,dc=nwtraders,dc=msft"
LogAction
Loop
```

4. Under the *ReadUsers* subroutine, add a subroutine called *LogAction*. This will consist of the *Sub* command and the *End Sub* command. Leave two blank lines between the two commands. The code will look like the following:

```
Sub LogAction


End Sub
```

5. Save your work.

6. Open the \My Documents\Microsoft Press\VBScriptSBS\ch15\OneStepFurther\ CreateLogFile.vbs file and copy all the variable declarations. Paste them under the variables in your script.

7. Delete the extra *objFSO* variable.

8. Copy the three reference lines from the CreateLogFile.vbs script and paste them under the variable declarations. This section of the script now looks like the following:

```
Dim objOU
Dim objUser
Dim objGroup
Dim objFSO
Dim objTextFile
Dim TxtIn
Dim strNextLine
Dim i
Dim TxtFile
Dim objFile        'holds hook to the file to be used
Dim message        'holds message to be written to file
Dim objData1       'holds data from source used to write to file
Dim objData2       'holds data from source used to write to file
Dim LogFolder
Dim LogFile
message="Reading computer info " & Now
objData1 = objRecordSet.Fields("name")
objData2 = objRecordSet.Fields("distinguishedName")
```

9. Modify the message so that it states that the code is creating a user, and use the element *TxtIn(0)* as the user name that gets created. This modified line will look like the following:

```
message="Creating user " & TxtIn(0) & Now
```

10. Move the message line to the line after you parse *strNextLine*. You do this because you are using an element of the array that must be an assigned value before it can be used.

```
strNextLine = objTextFile.ReadLine
TxtIn = Split(strNextLine , ",")
message="Creating user " & TxtIn(1) & Now
```

11. Modify the objData1 and objData2 data assignments. Use *TxtIn(0)* for the user field and *TxtIn(5)* for the group. The two lines will look like the following:

```
objData1 = TxtIn(0)
objData2 = TxtIn(5)
```

12. Copy the remainder of the script and paste it between the two lines used to create the subroutine. The completed section looks like the following:

```
Sub LogAction
  If objFSO.FolderExists(LogFolder) Then
    If objFSO.FileExists(LogFile) Then
      Set objFile = objFSO.OpenTextFile(LogFile, ForAppending)
      objFile.WriteBlankLines(1)
      objFile.Writeline message
      objFile.Writeline objData1
      objFile.Writeline objData2
      objFile.Close
    Else
      Set objFile = objFSO.CreateTextFile(LogFile)
      objFile.Close
```

```
      Set objFile = objFSO.OpenTextFile(LogFile, ForWriting)
      objfile.WriteLine message
      objFile.WriteLine objData1
      objFile.WriteLine objData2
      objFile.Close
   End If
 Else
   Set objFolder = objFSO.CreateFolder(LogFolder)
   Set objFile = objFSO.CreateTextFile(LogFile)
   objFile.Close
   Set objFile = objFSO.OpenTextFile(LogFile, ForWriting)
   objfile.writeline message
   objFile.WriteLine objData1
   objFile.WriteLine objData2
   objFile.Close
 End If
End Sub
```

13. Save and run the script.

Chapter 15 Quick Reference

To	Do This
Create a subroutine	Begin a line with the word *Sub* followed by the name of the subroutine. You end the subroutine by using the command *End Sub* on a line following your subroutine code.
Call a subroutine	Place the name of the subroutine on a line by itself at the place in your code where you want to use the subroutine.
Make code more portable and easier to read and troubleshoot, and to promote code reuse	Use a subroutine.

Chapter 16
Logon Scripts

Before You Begin

To work through the material presented in this chapter, you need to be familiar with the following concepts from earlier chapters:

- Using Windows Management Instrumentation (WMI)
- Using Active Directory Service Interfaces (ADSI)
- Using the *InStr* function
- Implementing the *For...Next* statement
- Implementing the *Select Case* statement
- Implementing file system objects

After completing this chapter, you will be able to:

- Use the *IADsADSystemInfo* interface
- Use *WshNetwork*
- Use the *Join* function
- Creat dynamic logon scripts
- Implement logging for logon scripts

Working with *IADsADSystemInfo*

In this section, you will use the *IADsADSystemInfo* interface to obtain data about the local computer. The *IADsADSystemInfo* interface is implemented to provide access to the *ADSystemInfo* class. Because this class resides in the Adsldp.dll file, which is part of ADSI, it is present on Microsoft Windows Server 2003, Windows XP, and even Windows 2000. To use *IADsADSystemInfo*, you need to create the object by creating an instance of the *ADSystemInfo* class. This process is actually simple—you use the *CreateObject* command. Table 16-1 summarizes the nine properties exposed by *IADsADSystemInfo*.

Table 16-1 Properties Exposed by *IADsADSystemInfo*

Property	Meaning
ComputerName	Retrieves the distinguished name of the local computer

Table 16-1   Properties Exposed by *IADsADSystemInfo*

Property	Meaning
DomainDNSName	Retrieves the Domain Name System (DNS) name of the local computer's domain
DomainShortName	Retrieves the short name of the local computer's domain (the network basic input/output system [NetBIOS] version of the name)
ForestDNSName	Retrieves the DNS name of the local computer's forest
IsNativeMode	Determines whether the local computer's domain is native or mixed mode
PDCRoleOwner	Retrieves the distinguished name of the domain controller (DC) that owns the primary domain controller (PDC) emulator role in the local computer's domain
SchemaRoleOwner	Retrieves the distinguished name of the Schema Master in the local computer's forest
SiteName	Retrieves the site name in which the local computer resides
UserName	Retrieves the distinguished name of the currently logged-on user

The advantage of using *IADsADSystemInfo* over other means of gaining user and computer information is that *IADsADSystemInfo* retrieves fully qualified domain names, which are immediately useful when working with Active Directory. In addition to the nine properties listed in Table 16-1, *IADsADSystemInfo* provides 13 methods. However, most of these methods duplicate the properties listed in Table 16-1, so Table 16-2 describes only the methods that provide additional information.

Table 16-2   *IADsADSystemInfo* Methods Providing Unique Information

Method	Description
GetAnyDCName	Retrieves the DNS name of a domain controller in the local computer's domain
RefreshSchemaCache	Refreshes ADSI's Active Directory schema cache on the local computer
GetTrees	Retrieves the DNS names of all the directory trees in the local computer's forest; returned as an array

The following script, called SysInfo.vbs, illustrates using the *IADsADSystemInfo* interface. In the first line, you use *objSysInfo* to hold the object that comes back when you use *CreateObject* to create an instance of *ADSystemInfo*. After you do this, you use the *RefreshSchemaCache* method to refresh the Active Directory schema cache that is resident on the local computer. Performing this step ensures that you are working with the most recent copy of the Active Directory schema. After refreshing the schema cache on the local machine, you echo out the pertinent information. The only step that is a little tricky is the use of *For Each...Next* to walk through the array that is returned when you use the *GetTrees* method. This step is required, even when only one domain is present in the forest.

SysInfo.vbs

```
Set objSysInfo = CreateObject("ADSystemInfo")
objSysInfo.RefreshSchemaCache
```

```
WScript.Echo "User name: " & objSysInfo.UserName
WScript.Echo "Computer name: " & objSysInfo.ComputerName
WScript.Echo "Site name: " & objSysInfo.SiteName
WScript.Echo "Domain short name: " & objSysInfo.DomainShortName
WScript.Echo "Domain DNS name: " & objSysInfo.DomainDNSName
WScript.Echo "Forest DNS name: " & objSysInfo.ForestDNSName
WScript.Echo "PDC role owner: " & objSysInfo.PDCRoleOwner
WScript.Echo "Schema role owner: " & objSysInfo.SchemaRoleOwner
WScript.Echo "Domain is in native mode: " & objSysInfo.IsNativeMode
WScript.Echo "Active Directory DomainController: " & objSysInfo.GetAnyDCName

For Each tree In objSysInfo.GetTrees
  WScript.Echo "Domain trees: " & tree
Next
```

Using Logon Scripts

In the old days, network administrators spent hours and hours trying to craft the perfect logon script. In the end, it was a fruitless effort, because needs were always changing and the capabilities of logon scripts were limited. Many networks today seem to run just fine without a logon script. With the widespread adoption of Group Policy, some people might question why we need logon scripts at all. However, when using Microsoft Visual Basic, Scripting Edition (VBScript) for your logon scripts, you can craft some very powerful solutions for configuring and maintaining your users' environments. In addition, because Group Policy is often handled by a separate department within enterprise networks, making a change to a logon script can be easier than talking another department into modifying its "perfect Group Policy." Logon scripts can be quickly called into service to perform several tasks:

- Mapping network drives
- Mapping printers
- Collecting system information
- Checking antivirus signatures
- Checking hotfix and security updates
- Checking security settings

Just the Steps   **To create powerful and flexible logon scripts**

1. Use *IADsADSystemInfo* to determine user information.
2. Use ADSI to query for group membership information.
3. Use Windows Scripting Host (WSH) to map network drives.
4. Use WSH to set default printers.

Deploying Logon Scripts

Perhaps the simplest way to implement a logon script is to modify the *Logon Script User* attribute. Although you can assign logon scripts to users by using the graphical user interface (GUI), you can also do this easily by using the *scriptpath* Active Directory attribute of the *User* object. I prefer, however, to use Group Policy to assign the logon script to users. However you choose to assign logon scripts to your users, once you write the script, this script will need to be saved in the Sysvol share in the Scripts directory as seen in Figure 16-1.

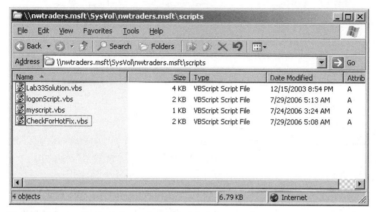

Figure 16-1   Sysvol share in Active Directory; logon scripts and accessory scripts

If you do this, you can link the script to multiple Group Policy Objects (GPOs). You could, of course, also save the logon script within the actual GPO itself. If you choose to save it in this way, you will not be able to reuse the script with other GPOs. In fact, you could end up deleting the script if you delete the GPO that is hosting the script. Linking a logon script to a GPO is illustrated in Figure 16-2.

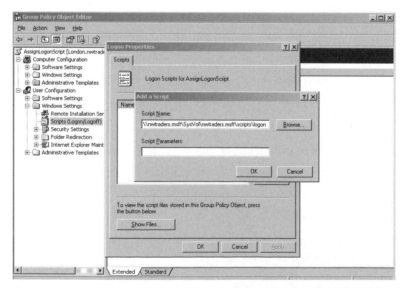

Figure 16-2   GPO logon script; assign the logon script to the *User* object in Group Policy

So what does a VBScript logon script look like? The following script, LogonScript.vbs, is similar to many logon scripts I've used with customers in the past. It has several advantages over the old-fashioned batch files that many of you grew up with. We'll discuss these advantages as we examine each section that makes up LogonScript.vbs.

> **Note**   The logon script below will fail if the user is a member of only one group. There are several ways to fix this problem ... the simplest is to simply use *On Error Resume Next*. Another way would be to use an error handler, and then if it fails the first time, come back and repeat the line without the *Join* function.

LogonScript.vbs

```
Option Explicit
Dim fServer
Dim pServer
Dim home
Dim wshNet
Dim ADSysInfo
Dim CurrentUser
Dim strGroups
Dim GroupMember
Dim a,b,c

Const HR = "cn=hrgroup"
Const MARKETING = "cn=marketinggroup"
Const SALES = "cn=salesgroup"

fServer = "\\london"
pServer = "\\london"
home = "\\london\users"
Set wshNet = CreateObject("WScript.Network")

Set ADSysInfo = CreateObject("ADSystemInfo")
Set CurrentUser = GetObject("LDAP://" & ADSysInfo.UserName)
strGroups = LCase(Join(CurrentUser.MemberOf))

wshNet.MapNetworkDrive "h:", fServer & "\Users\" & wshNet.UserName
WScript.Echo(wshNet.Username & " " & strgroups)

Select Case GroupMember
case a = InStr(strGroups, HR)
  HRsub
case b = InStr(strGroups, SALES)
SalesSub
case c = InStr(strGroups, MARKETING)
  MarketingSub
End Select

' *** departmental subs are below *****
Sub HRsub
wshNet.MapNetworkDrive "g:",fServer & "\Hr"
  wshNet.AddWindowsPrinterConnection pServer &"\HrPrinter"
```

```
   wshNet.SetDefaultPrinter pServer & "\HrPrinter"
   subRunScript
End Sub

Sub SalesSub
  wshNet.MapNetworkDrive "s:", fServer & "\Sales"
  wshNet.AddWindowsPrinterConnection pServer & "\SalesPrinter"
  wshNet.SetDefaultPrinter pServer & "\SalesPrinter"
End Sub

Sub MarketingSub
wshNet.MapNetworkDrive "m:", fServer & "\Marketing"
  wshNet.AddWindowsPrinterConnection pServer & "\MarketingPrinter"
  wshNet.SetDefaultPrinter pServer & "\MarketingPrinter"
End Sub

Sub subRunScript
Dim objShell
Set objShell = CreateObject("wscript.shell")
objShell.run ("CheckForHotFix.vbs")
End Sub
```

Header Information

The Header information section of LogonScript.vbs includes the *Option Explicit* command and the declaration of several variables.

> **Tip**   You don't use *On Error Resume Next* in logon scripts because if the logon script fails, you want to hear from your user community immediately. You don't want to suppress error messages or risk mapping only a few of the drives that the users need to be able to perform their work. I've seen situations in which the logon script messed up drive mappings for a group of users, and these users had no idea where their data was stored. We wound up having to reproduce the error in a lab to determine what drives had been mapped for which user so that we could find the work the users had "lost." Once this was done, we removed error suppression on the logon script, and although doing this might have resulted in a few more help desk calls, it vastly simplified the consequences when the logon script failed.

Eleven variables are used in LogonScript.vbs. They are listed in Table 16-3.

Table 16-3   LogonScript.vbs Variables

Variable	Use
fServer	Holds the name of the file server. Used when mapping home directory for the user.
pServer	Holds name of the print server. Used when mapping printers for the user.
Home	Holds the relative path of the users' home directory share. This variable also could be expanded by using site information to point the closed file server to the users.

Table 16-3   LogonScript.vbs Variables

Variable	Use
wshNet	Holds the object that comes back when you create an instance of *WScript.Network*. You use this to allow the mapping of drives and printers.
ADSysInfo	Holds the object that comes back when you create an instance of *ADSystemInfo*. This allows you to obtain current user information.
CurrentUser	Holds a connection into Active Directory using the Lightweight Directory Access Protocol (LDAP) provider.
strGroups	Holds a list of all the groups of which the user is a member.
GroupMember	Used by the *Select Case* statement to hold the value of the group membership.
a,b,c	Used with *Select Case* to determine case.

> **Tip**   Depending on how you decide to document your scripts, creating a table of variables can be a powerful reference tool. I know some Internet administrators who print out all their production scripts and store them in a binder along with their definitive software library (DSL). Others store backup copies of production scripts on a network share and use remarks to document the scripts. Even if you do not need a variable table for script documentation, you might find that creating one is sometimes helpful as a reference when writing the script—it forces you to think about the script flow, and in a long script, it is easier to work with a table than scrolling back up to the Header information section of the script. This is a good habit to develop if you program in C# or Microsoft Visual Basic .NET as well.

Reference Information

In addition to defining the variables listed in the Header information section of the script, you also define some constants. The three constants hold the name of the groups that are searched for by using the *InStr* command. In this example, the group memberships are *HrGroup*, *MarketingGroup*, and *SalesGroup*. You assign the "*cn=*" version of the name to the constants called *HR*, *Marketing*, and *Sales*. You do this because when you perform the query for the group memberships, the string of data returned will include the full LDAP name of the groups. However, to make the code easier to type and understand and thus easier to work with, you assign the longer names to constants. The resultant code looks like the following:

```
Const HR = "cn=hrgroup"
Const MARKETING = "cn=marketinggroup"
Const SALES = "cn=salesgroup"

fServer = "\\london"
pServer = "\\london"
home = "\\london\users"
```

The remainder of the Reference information section appears in the code that follows. You use a variable, *fServer*, to hold the name of the file server. This makes it easy to change the script if you move the shared directories to other servers. If you did not use this variable, the drive mappings would use the hardcoded Universal Naming Convention (UNC) path to a specific server share. This means that if the data got moved to a different server, the logon script would need to be modified in several places.

All the users' home directories are in a shared directory called *Users*. If you move the share to a different location, you will need to modify the *home* = "*london**users*" line in the script. Changing this line is easier than making a change in the Home Folder field on the Profile tab in Active Directory Users And Computers (ADUC). Change one line in the logon script, or make thousands of changes via the GUI in ADUC–it seems to be a relatively painless choice!

> ### Quick Check
>
> **Q.   What are three ways of assigning a logon script to a user?**
>
> A.   Three ways of assigning a logon script to a user are via the GUI interface by using Active Directory Users And Computers, via VBScript by using the ScriptPath property, or by using Group Policy.
>
> **Q.   What are three common activities performed by logon scripts?**
>
> A.   Three common activities performed by logon scripts are mapping to network shares, mapping to network printers, and setting default printers for users.

Using the *WshNetwork* Class

The next order of business is wiring up three connections to turn on the power of VBScript in our logon script. The first of these connections is used to hold the object that comes back from creating an instance of the *WScript.Network* class. You use *WScript.Network* to create an object that is called *WshNetwork*. *WshNetwork* enables you to connect to and disconnect from network shares and network printers. In addition, we can use *WshNetwork* to map or remove network shares or to access information about a user on a network. This said, you might be asking yourself why we decided to use *ADSystemInfo* to obtain the user name. The reason is that the user name coming from *WshNetwork* is a single-label name (for example, Bob). But to query Active Directory to obtain all your group memberships, you need the distinguished name (for example, a name like *cn=bob, ou=LabOU, dc=nwtraders, dc=msft.*) You can use the distinguished name to make an LDAP binding and then to query all the information you need to obtain for the logon script.

After you create an instance of *WshNetwork*, you are ready to connect to the *IADsADSystemInfo* interface so that you can get information about the local computer and local user.

After you have an object providing access to the *ADSystemInfo* interface, you use the *UserName* command to obtain the fully qualified local user name, and then combine that with the LDAP provider and make a connection into Active Directory. The object that comes back from Active Directory is called *CurrentUser*. You have now wired up all the connections necessary to get the logon script up and running.

You do need to define one more variable—a list of groups of which the current user is a member. To do this, you use the *MemberOf* command. The problem is that the *MemberOf* command will return with an array. In the following section, we will see how to address this problem.

Using the *Join* Function

Although arrays are useful, dealing with an array will make your script a bit more complicated—in fact, because you are interested only in the presence of a particular string sequence, you don't need an array at all. For assistance in dealing with the array, use the VBScript *Join* function. The *Join* function returns a string that is created by putting together (that is, joining) the data contained in the array elements. In this way, you can easily use the *InStr* command to search the string for the presence of your group membership items. You can see an example of using the *Join* function in the Join.vbs script, which you'll examine in a moment.

Notice that you begin the Join.vbs script by declaring a five-element array. You then assign a value to each element in the array. On the next-to-last line, you use the *Join* function to pull together all the elements of the array, which is called *MyArray*. The advantage here is using an intermediate variable to hold the array, and then using another variable to hold the string returned from the *Join* function. This adds a lot of flexibility to your script. You assign the string that is returned from the *Join* function to a variable called *MyString*. Because you now have a string that contains all the elements of the array, you can use *WScript.Echo* to display the value of *MyString*.

Join.vbs

```
Option Explicit
Dim MyString
Dim MyArray(4)
MyArray(0) = "Mr."
MyArray(1) = "Sam"
MyArray(2) = "Spade,"
MyArray(3) = "Private"
MyArray(4) = "Eye"
MyString = Join(MyArray)
WScript.Echo(MyString)
```

Worker Information

The Worker information section of LogonScript.vbs comprises a single *Select Case* statement. The *Select Case* statement is interesting because you are doing something new. *GroupMember* is a variable used to evaluate the group membership. In reality, this variable is just a placeholder, because you don't use it anywhere else in the script. Each case is evaluated by *InStr* and the corresponding subroutine is selected. The nice part of this *Select Case* statement happens on the other side of the equal signs. Instead of performing a simple match, you're adding a higher level of intelligence to the script and are requiring the *Select Case* statement to use the *InStr* function to search the string data contained in the variable *strGroups*. Each case is therefore tested to see whether the string represented by each constant is found in *strGroups*. When a match is found, the script jumps to the appropriate subroutine. This type of statement makes the Worker information section extremely easy to read and understand.

```
Select Case GroupMember
   case a = InStr(strGroups, HR)
  HRsub
   case b = InStr(strGroups, SALES)
        SalesSub
   case c = InStr(strGroups, MARKETING)
  MarketingSub
End Select
```

Output Information

Once you work through each case in the *Select Case* statement, you enter into a subroutine. Each subroutine is designed around the particular needs of various groups within your organization. The *WScript.Echo* commands let you know which subroutine is being run. These are primarily used for troubleshooting and can be either left in or deleted, depending on the type of customer experience your users are willing to put up with.

To map a network drive, you use the *MapNetworkDrive* method of a *WshNetwork* object. The important issue to keep in mind here is that assigning a drive letter requires a letter and a colon surrounded by double quotation marks. Next, a comma is required to separate the drive letter from the path statement.

When you use *WshNetwork* to map to a printer, you use the *AddWindowsPrinterConnection* method. (Although this command name is descriptive, it could have been shortened just a little.) The *AddWindowsPrinterConnection* method needs only a Universal Naming Convention (UNC) path to the print server and the share name. No commas are required here. (In fact, commas here will cause the command to fail.)

The last task our subroutine needs to perform is assigning the default Windows printer, so you use a method named *SetDefaultPrinter*. Again, the only work you need to do is include the UNC path to the print server and encase the share name in double quotation marks. Here are the subroutines for the Worker information section of the script:

```
Sub HRsub
wshNet.MapNetworkDrive "g:",fServer & "\Hr"
  wshNet.AddWindowsPrinterConnection pServer &"\HrPrinter"
  wshNet.SetDefaultPrinter pServer & "\HrPrinter"
  subRunScript
End Sub

Sub SalesSub
  wshNet.MapNetworkDrive "s:", fServer & "\Sales"
```

```
    wshNet.AddWindowsPrinterConnection pServer & "\SalesPrinter"
    wshNet.SetDefaultPrinter pServer & "\SalesPrinter"
End Sub

Sub MarketingSub
        wshNet.MapNetworkDrive "m:", fServer & "\Marketing"
    wshNet.AddWindowsPrinterConnection pServer & "\MarketingPrinter"
    wshNet.SetDefaultPrinter pServer & "\MarketingPrinter"
End Sub
```

> **Note**   To run the following script, you will need to have the following: AD configured; a server called London; several groups—HRGroup, SalesGroup, MarketingGroup; file shares; print shares; a set of users; and a set of home directories. Please edit the script below to match your own test environment.

Call an additional script during logon

1. Open \My Documents\Microsoft Press\VBScriptSBS\ch16\LogonScript.vbs in Notepad or the script editor of your choice and save it as YourNameLogonScriptCall ExternalScript.vbs.

2. At the bottom of your script, create a subroutine called *subRunScript*. This will look like the following:

    ```
    Sub subRunScript

    End Sub
    ```

3. Declare a variable, *objShell*, that will be used to hold the *wshShell* object. These are added into the *subRunScript* subroutine.

4. Create an instance of the *wshShell* object and assign it to the *objShell* variable. Use the *CreateObject* method to do this, as seen in the following code:

    ```
    Set objShell = CreateObject("WScript.Shell")
    ```

5. Use the *Run* method to launch the additional script. This is seen in the following code:

    ```
    objShell.run ("CheckForHotFix.vbs")
    ```

6. Save and run your script by logging in from a remote machine (because ordinary users do not have the ability to log on to the domain controller). If your script has problems, compare it with \My Documents\Microsoft Press\VBScriptSBS\ch16 \LogonScriptCallExternalScript.vbs.

Capture an error from calling an additional script during logon

1. Open the \My Documents\Microsoft Press\VBScriptSBS\ch16\LogonScriptCall ExternalScript.vbs script in Notepad or your script editor of choice and save it as YourNameLogonScriptCallExternalScriptCaptureError.vbs.

2. In the *subRunScript* subroutine, add a variable to hold the return code from the *Run* method. Call this variable *intRTN*.

3. On a new line after the *intRTN* variable, declare a constant called *HideWindow* and set it equal to 1.

4. On a new line after the *HideWindow* constant, create a new constant called *WaitForReturn* and set it equal to *True*. The completed Header and Reference section of the *subRunScript* subroutine now looks like the following:

```
Dim objShell
Dim intRTN
Const HideWindow = 0
Const WaitForReturn = True
```

5. Edit the *objShell.run* line of code, so that you use the *intRTN* variable to capture the return code. Add the *HideWindow* constant and the *WaitForReturn* constants as additional parameters to the *Run* method. The completed line now looks like the following:

```
intRTN = objShell.run ("CheckForHotFix.vbs",HideWindow,WaitForReturn)
```

6. Use an inline *If...Then* statement to evaluate *intRTN*. If *intRTN* is not equal to 0, then use *WScript.Echo* to print out the error. This is seen below:

```
If intRTN <> 0 Then WScript.Echo "Error",intRTN,"occurred"
```

7. Save and run your script by logging into the domain from a remote workstation. If your script does not work as expected, compare it with \My Documents\Microsoft Press \VBScriptSBS\ch16\ LogonScriptCallExternalScriptCaptureError.vbs.

Adding a Group to a Logon Script Step-by-Step Exercises

In this section, you will add a group to a logon script. To perform this exercise, you will need the following (you can modify the following exercise to match your existing test network as appropriate):

- Groups: hrGroup, MarketingGroup, ProductionGroup and SalesGroup
- A file server called London
- A User share called London\home
- Departmental shares called hr, sales, marketing, and production
- Printer shares called hrPrinter, marketingPrinter, productionPrinter, and salesPrinter
- An assortment of users who are members of the previously mentioned groups to test with
- A remote workstation that is a member of the NWTraders domain

1. Open Notepad or the script editor of your choice.

2. Open \My Documents\Microsoft Press\VBScriptSBS\ch16\StepByStep\AddGroup-ToLogonScriptStarter.vbs and save it as YourNameAddGroupToLogonScript.vbs.

3. Look over the script and add comments to each declared variable.

4. With the constants, declare a new constant called *Production*. Set it equal to *cn=productiongroup*. The completed constant section will look like the following:

```
Const HR = "cn=hrgroup"
Const MARKETING = "cn=marketinggroup"
Const SALES = "cn=salesgroup"
Const PRODUCTION = "cn=productiongroup"
```

5. Add a new *case d* to the *Select Case* statement. This new case is equal to finding the value assigned to the constant *Production* in the string assigned to *strGroups*. If the case is met, the script should jump to a subroutine called *ProductionSub*. The new *Select Case* statement looks like the following:

```
Select Case GroupMember
  Case a = InStr(strGroups, HR)
    HRSub
  Case b = InStr(strGroups, SALES)
    SalesSub
  Case c = InStr(strGroups, MARKETING)
    MarketingSub
  Case d = InStr (strGroups, PRODUCTION)
    ProductionSub
End Select
```

6. At the bottom of the various subroutines, add a new subroutine called *ProductionSub*. End the subroutine with the *End Sub* command. It will look like the following:

```
Sub ProductionSub

End Sub
```

7. For the first line of the *ProductionSub* subroutine, use *WScript.Echo* to inform the user that she is in the *Production* subroutine. Your line of text could look like the following:

```
WScript.Echo("made it to production")
```

8. Use the *MapNetworkDrive* method of the *WshNetwork* object to map the drive letter "*P:*" to the production share on the London server. This line of code will look like the following:

```
wshNet.MapNetworkDrive "P:","\\london\Production\"
```

9. Use the *AddWindowsPrinterConnection* method of *WshNetwork* to add a connection to the production printer that is set up on the London server. This line of code will look like the following:

```
wshNet.AddWindowsPrinterConnection "\\london\ProductionPrinter"
```

10. Set the new production printer to be the default printer for members of the production group. To do this, use the *SetDefaultPrinter* command of the *WshNetwork* object. This line of code will look like the following:

```
wshNet.SetDefaultPrinter "\\london\ProductionPrinter"
```

11. Save and test the script by logging into the domain as one of your test users from a remote machine. If there are problems with the script, compare it with \My Documents\Microsoft Press\VBScriptSBS\ch16\AddGroupToLogonScript.vbs.

One Step Further: Adding Logging to a Logon Script

In this section, you add logging to the AddGroupToLogonScript.

1. Open up the \My Documents\Microsoft Press\VBScriptSBS\ch16\OneStepFurther\LoggedLogonScriptStarter.vbs script in Notepad or your favorite script editor and save the file as YourNameLoggedLogonScript.vbs.

2. Copy the declared variables from the CreateLogFile.vbs file in the One Step Further folder and paste them into the Header information section of your script. The new Header information section of the script looks like the following:

```
Option Explicit
Dim fServer
Dim home
Dim wshNet
Dim ADSysInfo
Dim CurrentUser
Dim strGroups
Dim GroupMember
Dim objFSO        'holds connection to file system object
Dim objFile       'holds hook to the file to be used
Dim message       'holds message to be written to file
Dim objData1      'holds data from source used to write to file
Dim objData2      'holds data from source used to write to file
Dim LogFolder
Dim LogFile
```

3. Copy the entire Reference information section of the CreateLogFile.vbs file, including all the constants and variable assignments. Paste this under the constants in your script. The completed section looks like this:

```
Const HR = "cn=hrgroup"
Const MARKETING = "cn=marketinggroup"
Const SALES = "cn=salesgroup"
Const PRODUCTION = "cn=productiongroup"
Const ForWriting = 2
Const ForAppending = 8
LogFolder = "C:\fso"
LogFile = "C:\fso\logFile.txt"
Set objFSO = CreateObject("Scripting.FileSystemObject")
message="Reading computer info " & Now
```

```
objData1 = objRecordSet.Fields("name")
objData2 = objRecordSet.Fields("distinguishedName")
```

4. Change the message text so that it reads "Processing Logon Script".

5. Cut the *objData1* and *objData2* variables and paste them under the *strGroups = LCase* line. This section of the script now looks like the following:

```
Set ADSysInfo = CreateObject("ADSystemInfo")
Set CurrentUser = GetObject("LDAP://" & ADSysInfo.UserName)
strGroups = LCase(Join(CurrentUser.MemberOf))
objData1 = objRecordSet.Fields("name")
objData2 = objRecordSet.Fields("distinguishedName")
wshNet.MapNetworkDrive "h:", fServer & "\Users\" & wshNet.UserName
WScript.Echo(wshNet.Username & " " & strgroups)
```

6. Assign values to *objData1* and *objData2*. Make *objData1* equal to *ADSysInfo.UserName* and *objData2* equal to *strGroups*. The two modified *objData* lines now look like the following:

```
objData1 = ADSysInfo.UserName
objData2 = strGroups
```

7. At the bottom of the subroutines in your script, create a new empty subroutine called *LoggingSub*.

8. Inside the empty *LoggingSub* subroutine, paste the entire *If...Then...End If* section from the CreateLogFile.vbs file. The completed *LoggingSub* subroutine now looks like the following:

```
Sub LoggingSub
  If objFSO.FolderExists(LogFolder) Then
    If objFSO.FileExists(LogFile) Then
      Set objFile = objFSO.OpenTextFile(LogFile, ForAppending)
      objFile.WriteBlankLines(1)
      objFile.WriteLine message
      objFile.WriteLine objData1
      objFile.WriteLine objData2
      objFile.Close
    Else
      Set objFile = objFSO.CreateTextFile(LogFile)
      objFile.Close
      Set objFile = objFSO.OpenTextFile(LogFile, ForWriting)
      objFile.WriteLine message
      objFile.WriteLine objData1
      objFile.WriteLine objData2
      objFile.Close
    End If
  Else
  Set objFolder = objFSO.CreateFolder(LogFolder)
  Set objFile = objFSO.CreateTextFile(LogFile)
    objFile.Close
    Set objFile = objFSO.OpenTextFile(LogFile, ForWriting)
    objfile.WriteLine message
    objFile.WriteLine objData1
```

```
        objFile.WriteLine objData2
        objFile.Close
    End If
End Sub
```

9. Save your work.

10. In the *HRSub* subroutine, add a command to go to the *LoggingSub* subroutine after the *setDefaultPrinter* command. The new *HRSub* subroutine now looks like the following:

```
Sub HRsub
    WScript.Echo("made it to HR")
    wshNet.MapNetworkDrive "g:","\\london\Hr\"
    wshNet.AddWindowsPrinterConnection "\\london\HrPrinter"
    wshNet.SetDefaultPrinter "\\london\HrPrinter"
    LoggingSub
End Sub
```

11. Add the *LoggingSub* command to the end of the *salesSub*, *marketingSub*, and *production-Sub* subroutines as well. The completed subroutines look like the following:

```
Sub SalesSub
    WScript.Echo("made it to sales")
    wshNet.MapNetworkDrive "s:", "\\london\Sales"
    wshNet.AddWindowsPrinterConnection "\\london\SalesPrinter"
    wshNet.SetDefaultPrinter "\\london\SalesPrinter"
    Loggingsub
End Sub

Sub MarketingSub
WScript.Echo("made it to marketing")
    wshNet.MapNetworkDrive "m:","\\london\Marketing\"
    wshNet.AddWindowsPrinterConnection "\\london\MarketingPrinter"
    wshNet.SetDefaultPrinter "\\london\MarketingPrinter"
    Loggingsub
End Sub

Sub ProductionSub
    WScript.Echo("made it to production")
    wshNet.MapNetworkDrive "p:","\\london\Production\"
    wshNet.AddWindowsPrinterConnection "\\london\ProductionPrinter"
    wshNet.SetDefaultPrinter "\\london\ProductionPrinter"
    Loggingsub
End Sub
```

12. Save your work and test your script by logging on to the test domain from a remote machine. If you have problems with your script, compare it to \My Documents \Microsoft Press\VBScriptSBS\ch16\OneStepFurther\LoggedLogonScript Solution.vbs.

Chapter 16 Quick Reference

To	Do This
Obtain user and computer information that returns the distinguished user name, which can then bind to Active Directory and perform queries	Use *ADSysInfo* as opposed to *WshNetwork*
Put elements of an array together into a single string	Use the *Join* function
Map to network shares and network printers and remove network shares and network printers	Use *WshNetwork*
Refresh the local copy of the Active Directory schema on a computer	Use *RefreshSchemaCache*

Chapter 17
Working with the Registry

Before You Begin

To work through the material presented in this chapter, you need to be familiar with the following concepts from earlier chapters:

- Creating an instance of the *FileSystemObject* class
- Creating a connection into Microsoft Windows Management Instrumentation (WMI)
- Implementing the *For...Next* statement
- Implementing the *Select Case* statement

After completing this chapter, you will be able to:

- Implement the *WshShell* class
- Script Reg.exe
- Work with the *WMI StdRegProv* class
- Work with the *WshController* object

First You Back Up

In this section, you will use the Reg.exe program to back up the registry. Backing up is an important step, because you can make changes to the registry that would preclude Microsoft Windows Server 2003 from even loading. So before you ever make any change to the registry, you must have a backup.

> **Note** Don't be scared of working with the registry out of fear of "hosing" your machine. If you do not have a backup of the registry, and you suspect a registry change caused a problem, try booting your server and selecting "last known good" from the Startup menu. If this does not work, try booting into the recovery console off of the Microsoft Windows Server 2003 CD-ROM and using the command-line registry editor to undo the changes you previously made.

Numerous utilities can back up the registry; backing up using a script is convenient as well. By using the Reg.exe support tool via Microsoft Visual Basic, Scripting Edition (VBScript), you can perform the following operations:

- Back up a registry key prior to making modifications

- Back up a registry hive as part of maintenance
- Import a registry key as part of maintenance
- Import a registry key to restore a previous configuration

Just the Steps   To back up the registry using the Reg.exe command

1. Create an instance of the *WshShell* class.
2. Use the *Exec* method of *WshShell* to execute the *Reg.exe* command.
3. Use the Reg.exe *Save* command.
4. Specify the registry key to save and the file to save it into.

Creating the *WshShell* Object

To use the Reg.exe tool to back up the registry, it is necessary to create an instance of the *WshShell* class. This enables you to launch programs that are not part of Windows Scripting Host. The following program, RegBack.vbs, illustrates using the *WshShell* object.

RegBack.vbs
```
Option Explicit
Dim objShell

WScript.Echo("beginning " & Now)
Set objShell = CreateObject("WScript.Shell")
objShell.Exec "%comspec% /k reg.exe EXPORT HKLM c:\hklm.reg"
WScript.Echo("completed " & Now)
```

As you can see in RegBack.vbs, you declare a variable called *objShell* and use it to hold the *WshShell* object. After you have this object, you use the *Exec* method to launch a command-line interpreter with the */k* option.

Note   The */k* when used with the Cmd.exe program means to leave the command window open so that you can examine anything written to the window by using the program you are executing. However, it seems the behavior of */k* and */c* (which means to close the command window after the script is finished executing) is largely dependant upon the command being executed, and it therefore could seem to be erratic and unpredictable. As always, if something is important to you, test it in a lab.

Setting the *comspec* Variable

The way that you obtain the command interpreter in RegBack.vbs is by using a well-known system variable called *%comspec%*. If you are in doubt as to the value of *%comspec%* on your computer, open a system prompt and type the following:

```
Echo %comspec%
```

If you are running on a Windows Server 2003, Windows 2000, or Windows XP machine, the value returned is C:\WINDOWS\system32\cmd.exe.

Defining the Command

When you use the *Exec* method of *WshShell*, the command to be executed is placed inside the quotation marks. Because Reg.exe is a command-line program in the preceding code, there really was no need to include *%comspec%*. Our command line could have simply been the following:

```
objShell.Exec "reg.exe EXPORT HKLM c:\hklm.reg"
```

If, on the other hand, you need to use a command line for a command that is internal to the command processor (cmd.exe or command.com), such as the *dir* command, you need to launch a command shell interpreter, either by using the *%comspec%* system variable or by using Cmd.exe, as illustrated in the CmdDir.vbs script, which follows. If you run the Cmd-Dir.vbs script, keep in mind it could take a minute or two before it returns any information. The CmdDir.vbs script will find all files that end with the extension of .dat. Most likely, it will fine ntuser.dat, which is the current user profile setting. The issue of when to supply a command processor name and when not to can at times be a bit confusing.

CmdDir.vbs

```
Option Explicit
Dim objShell
Dim objExec
Dim strLine
Dim dirTxt
Dim dirFile

dirFile = "ntuser.dat"
WScript.Echo("beginning " & Now)
Set objShell = WScript.CreateObject("WScript.Shell")
Set objExec = objShell.Exec("%comspec% /c dir /aH c:\*.dat /s")

Do Until objExec.StdOut.AtEndOfStream
  strLine = objExec.StdOut.ReadLine()
  dirTxt = Instr(strLine,dirFile)
  If dirTxt <> 0 Then
    WScript.Echo strLine
  End If
Loop
WScript.Echo("all done " & Now)
```

> **Tip**   With the *WshShell Exec* method, everything inside the outer quotation marks is executed. One quick way to make sure that you are getting the results you want and that the code is running properly is to paste your executable code into a Start\Run dialog box. This approach will not work, however, if you are using embedded quotes in strings. In this case, it is better to use *WScript.Echo* to echo out the value of your variable, enabling you to ensure you are sending the correct commands to VBScript.

Connecting to the Registry

To work with the registry, you need to connect to it first. You can use the WMI *StdRegProv* class to make a connection and to read or write information into it. Although reading from the registry is a safe process, writing to the registry could have disastrous consequences if you don't take normal safety precautions such as making a backup of the key you intend to change and testing the script in a lab on machines that would be easily recoverable.

At times, just being able to read a listing of keys is sufficient for your needs. For instance, when the hotfix installer is run, it creates an entry under HKLM\SOFTWARE \Microsoft\Windows NT\CurrentVersion\HotFix. Realizing this, if you read this key, you can see what hotfixes have been applied to a particular machine. The following script, ReadHotFixes.vbs, does this very thing. By using the *EnumKey* method of the WMI *StdRegProv* class, you can rather easily create a listing of subkeys.

ReadHotFixes.vbs

```
Option Explicit
On Error Resume Next
Dim strKeyPath
Dim strComputer
Dim objReg
Dim subKey
Dim arrSubKeys

Const HKCR = &H80000000 'HKEY_CLASSES_ROOT
Const HKCU = &H80000001 'HKEY_CURRENT_USER
Const HKLM = &H80000002 'HKEY_LOCAL_MACHINE
Const HKU = &H80000003 'HKEY_USERS
Const HKCC = &H80000005 'HKEY_CURRENT_CONFIG

strKeyPath = "SOFTWARE\Microsoft\Windows NT" _
  & "\CurrentVersion\HotFix"
strComputer = "."

Set objReg=GetObject("winmgmts:\\" &_
  strComputer & "\root\default:StdRegProv")

objReg.EnumKey HKLM, strKeyPath, arrSubKeys

  WScript.Echo("Keys under " & strKeyPath)
For Each subKey In arrSubKeys
  WScript.Echo vbTab & subKey
Next
```

Header Information

The Header information section of ReadHotFixes.vbs consists of the *Option Explicit* and *On Error Resume Next* commands, as well as the declarations for five variables. The five variables are described in Table 17-1.

Table 17-1   Variables Used in ReadHotFixes.vbs

Variable	Use
strKeyPath	The main registry that defines the entry point for the script
strComputer	Holds the name of the computer that is targeted by WMI
objReg	Holds the *SWbemObjectEx* object that comes back from the WMI *StdRegProv* class
subKey	Holds the name of the registry key to be enumerated
arrSubKeys	Holds an array of registry keys found under the subKey

Reference Information

The Reference information section of the script is used to define constants and variables used in the operation of the script. Several tree values are defined in winreg.h that you can use to define constants and to shorten the length of your scripts. The default tree is HKEY_LOCAL_MACHINE, so in reality, specifying the tree is unnecessary. However, for clarity, and to ensure you hit the correct portion of the registry, I do not advocate relying on the default registry tree. All the hexadecimal (hex) numbers that represent the registry trees are listed in the Reference information section of this script. I normally include them in all registry scripts so that I don't have to look them up later. They don't take up too much space, and you can use them to form the basis of a nice registry script template.

The variable *strKeyPath* contains the registry key you want to look at. In this instance, because you're using the *EnumKey* method, you'll get back only a listing of key names that reside below *strKeyPath*. This is a useful method to use when you don't know what you'll find below a particular registry key.

You make your connection to the standard registry provider by using *GetObject* to make a connection into *winmgmts*. By default, *StdRegProv* resides in the root\default namespace—it is important to note, however, that software makers can compile the Regevent.mof file used to define the *StdRegProv* class into a different namespace for use in their applications. If you're working with such an application, you should connect to a different namespace.

```
Const HKCR = &H80000000 'HKEY_CLASSES_ROOT
Const HKCU = &H80000001 'HKEY_CURRENT_USER
Const HKLM = &H80000002 'HKEY_LOCAL_MACHINE
Const HKU = &H80000003 'HKEY_USERS
Const HKCC = &H80000005 'HKEY_CURRENT_CONFIG
strKeyPath = "SOFTWARE\Microsoft\Windows NT" _
  & "\CurrentVersion\HotFix"
strComputer = "."

Set objReg=GetObject("winmgmts:\\" &_
  strComputer & "\root\default:StdRegProv")
```

Worker and Output Information

The Worker and Output information section of the script is where you use the *SWbem ServicesEx* object provided by *StdRegProv* to perform some work. In the ReadHotFixes.vbs file, you use the *EnumKey* method of the *StdRegProv* WMI class to read a listing of subkeys. Because the hotfix installer documents hotfixes under the hotfix registry key, this is a useful application of the *EnumKey* method. Normally, however, you would use the *EnumKey* method to find out what subkeys existed prior to performing some other action on the registry. For instance, you could use *EnumKey* to find out whether a subkey existed, which in turn would enable you to determine whether a particular application had been installed on a computer. It would also be useful in finding certain types of viruses.

The *objReg.EnumKey* command uses the *HKLM* constant you defined in the Reference information section of the script as well as the *strKeyPath* variable. The information is written to a variable called *arrSubKeys*.

The subkeys are stored in an array, so you use a *For Each...Next* construction to iterate through each element in the array. You assign each new element to a variable called *subKey*. You use *WScript.Echo* to write the information, and you use the function *vbTab* to indent the results under the heading that was echoed out before entering the *For Each...Next* loop. The Worker and Output section of this script is listed below:

```
objReg.EnumKey HKLM, strKeyPath, arrSubKeys

WScript.Echo("Keys under " & strKeyPath)
For Each subKey In arrSubKeys
  WScript.Echo vbTab & subKey
Next
```

Unleashing the Power of the *StdRegProv* Class

The importance of the *StdRegProv* class is the power it brings to a script. In Chapter 1, "Starting from Scratch," our tutorial script illustrated using *RegRead*. You could follow the same methodology and use the *RegWrite* and *RegDelete* methods of *WshShell*, but there are limitations to using *WshShell* to work with the registry: You cannot work remotely, and there is no enumeration. However, all problems are resolved by using *StdRegProv*. It has 16 methods defined. These methods and a description of what they can do are listed in Table 17-2.

Table 17-2   *StdRegProv* Methods

Method	Description
CheckAccess	Verifies that the user has the specified access permissions
CreateKey	Creates a subkey
DeleteKey	Deletes a subkey
DeleteValue	Deletes a named value
EnumKey	Enumerates one or more subkeys

Table 17-2   *StdRegProv* Methods

Method	Description
EnumValues	Enumerates the named values of a key
GetBinaryValue	Gets the binary data value of a named value
GetDWORDValue	Gets the DWORD data value of a named value
GetExpandedStringValue	Gets the expanded string data value of a named value
GetMultiStringValue	Gets the multiple string data values of a named value
GetStringValue	Gets the string data value of a named value
SetBinaryValue	Sets the binary data value of a named value
SetDWORDValue	Sets the DWORD data value of a named value
SetExpandedStringValue	Sets the expanded string data value of a named value
SetMultiStringValue	Sets the multiple string values of a named value
SetStringValue	Sets the string value of a named value

One useful task you can perform as a network administrator is to create a key in the registry that you use to keep track of certain machines. This is similar to a trick I used to use with the Microsoft Systems Management Server product, where I placed a certain text file in the root drive of the workstation and used the presence of the file in creating ad hoc Systems Management Server (SMS) collections.

Just the Steps   To create a registry key

1. Create a constant for *HKLM* and assign it the value of *&H80000002*.
2. Define variables to hold the registry path you want to create.
3. Use *GetObject* to create an instance of the WMI *StdRegProvider* class.
4. Use the *CreateKey* method and feed it the *HKLM* constant and the registry path variable defined earlier.

Creating Registry Keys

To create keys and subkeys in the registry, you use the *CreateKey* method, as illustrated in the CreateRegKey.vbs script:

CreateRegKey.vbs
```
Option Explicit
On Error Resume Next
Dim strKeyPath 'the portion of registry to read
Dim strComputer 'the target computer
Dim objReg 'holds connection to registry provider
Dim subKey 'used to enumerate throught the array
Dim arrSubKeys 'holds the sub keys
Dim ParentKey
Const HKCR = &H80000000 'HKEY_CLASSES_ROOT
```

```
Const HKCU = &H80000001 'HKEY_CURRENT_USER
Const HKLM = &H80000002 'HKEY_LOCAL_MACHINE
Const HKU = &H80000003 'HKEY_USERS
Const HKCC = &H80000005 'HKEY_CURRENT_CONFIG

ParentKey = "SOFTWARE\EdWilson"
strKeyPath = "SOFTWARE\EdWilson\VBScriptBook"

strComputer = "."

Set objReg=GetObject("winmgmts:\\" & _
  strComputer & "\root\default:StdRegProv")


objReg.CreateKey HKLM, strKeyPath

  WScript.Echo("Created key :" & strKeyPath)
  WScript.Echo("New subkey under : " & ParentKey)

objReg.EnumKey HKLM, ParentKey, arrSubKeys
For Each subKey In arrSubKeys
  WScript.Echo vbTab & subKey
Next
```

Header Information

The Header information section is similar to that of ReadHotFixes.vbs. The only new variable is *ParentKey*, which is used to hold the path to the parent key that gets created.

Reference Information

The Reference information section is where you assign values to the variables defined in the Header information section. You assign a value to *ParentKey* of SOFTWARE\ EdWilson. You assign the value of SOFTWARE\EdWilson\VBScriptBook to *strKeyPath*. To create the registry key and subkey, you need only the *strKeyPath* variable. However, because you intend to use *EnumKey* to verify that you successfully created the new key and subkey, you defined *ParentKey* to simplify the use of *EnumKey*. The remaining items in the Reference information section of the script are the same as in the previous script. The beauty of the *StdRegProv* class is how similarly you use it through all the different methods. The Reference section of the script is seen below.

```
Const HKCR = &H80000000 'HKEY_CLASSES_ROOT
Const HKCU = &H80000001 'HKEY_CURRENT_USER
Const HKLM = &H80000002 'HKEY_LOCAL_MACHINE
Const HKU = &H80000003 'HKEY_USERS
Const HKCC = &H80000005 'HKEY_CURRENT_CONFIG

ParentKey = "SOFTWARE\EdWilson"
strKeyPath = "SOFTWARE\EdWilson\VBScriptBook"

strComputer = "."
```

```
Set objReg=GetObject("winmgmts:\\" &_
  strComputer & "\root\default:StdRegProv")
```

Worker and Output Information

In the Worker and Output information section of the script, you create the key and subkey and then use *EnumKey* to verify the existence of the new key. The only difference between using *CreateKey* and *EnumKey* is that *CreateKey* needs only two arguments: the registry tree constant and the key path to create. *EnumKey*, on the other hand, uses three arguments: the registry tree constant, the key path to enumerate, and the variable to hold the output. The Worker and Output section of the script is seen below.

```
objReg.CreateKey HKLM, strKeyPath

WScript.Echo("Created key :" & strKeyPath)
WScript.Echo("New subkey under : " & ParentKey)

objReg.EnumKey HKLM, ParentKey, arrSubKeys
For Each subKey In arrSubKeys
  WScript.Echo vbTab & subKey
Next
```

Writing to the Registry

I don't know about you, but I've always thought that writing to the registry would be really difficult. However, using the appropriate method of the *StdRegProv* WMI class makes it as easy as eating pineapple on the beach in Kauai, Hawaii—once you sink your teeth into it, it's sweet. In the script WriteToRegKey.vbs, you use the *SetStringValue* method to write information into a key called *bookReviews* that is stored under the SOFTWARE \EdWilson\VBScriptBook sub-key. When you execute the script, the key bookReviews does not exist. One nice aspect of *SetStringValue* is that it will create a key and set the value in one operation. Once you write your data, which is contained in a variable called *strData*, to the key, you use *GetStringValue* to read the information you just wrote. The syntax of *SetStringValue* needs several arguments: the registry tree (in this case, *HKLM*); the registry key path (held in *strKeyPath*); the registry key to modify (held in *strNamedValue*); and the data to write (held in *strData*).

To verify that your changes were made as expected, use *GetStringValue* to retrieve the data you just wrote to the registry. *GetStringValue* works much like *SetStringValue* except that the last argument is the variable name you want to use to hold the data returned from the registry. With *SetStringValue*, the fourth argument is the variable that holds the data you want to write to the registry. With *GetStringValue*, the fourth argument is the variable that will hold the data once you read it from the registry. Everything else about the two commands is the same.

WriteToRegKey.vbs
```
Option Explicit
On Error Resume Next
Dim strKeyPath 'the portion of registry
```

```
Dim strComputer 'the target computer
Dim objReg 'holds connection to registry provider
Dim subKey 'used to enumerate thought the array
Dim arrSubKeys 'holds the subkeys
Dim ParentKey
Dim strNamedValue
Dim strData
Dim strReturnValue
Const HKCR = &H80000000 'HKEY_CLASSES_ROOT
Const HKCU = &H80000001 'HKEY_CURRENT_USER
Const HKLM = &H80000002 'HKEY_LOCAL_MACHINE
Const HKU = &H80000003 'HKEY_USERS
Const HKCC = &H80000005 'HKEY_CURRENT_CONFIG

ParentKey = "SOFTWARE\EdWilson"
strKeyPath = "SOFTWARE\EdWilson\VBScriptBook"
strNamedvalue = "book reviews"
strData = "Awesome"

strComputer = "."

Set objReg = GetObject("winmgmts:\\" & _
  strComputer & "\root\default:StdRegProv")


objReg.SetStringValue HKLM, strKeyPath, strNamedValue, strData

WScript.Echo("value set")

objReg.GetStringValue HKLM, strKeyPath, strNamedValue, strReturnValue

WScript.Echo strNamedValue & " contains " & strReturnValue
```

Deleting Registry Information

If you need to delete a registry key, perhaps as a result of cleaning up after a virus, uninstalling software, or cleaning up after you're finished with the keys you created, you can use the *DeleteKey* method of *StdRegProv*. The next script, DeleteRegKey.vbs, illustrates how easy this is to do. Additional cautions about having a good backup and testing on other machines are applicable here! Be careful!

Though much of the script is similar to other registry provider scripts, a couple of items are important to note here. Notice in the Worker information section of the script that you have to delete the subkey before you can delete the parent key. The *DeleteKey* method deletes only keys. If you have a large section of the registry you need to lobotomize, you could use the *EnumKey* method and, as you iterate through the array, you could use *DeleteKey*.

DeleteRegKey.vbs
```
Option Explicit
On Error Resume Next
Dim strKeyPath 'the portion of registry to read
```

```
Dim strComputer 'the target computer
Dim objReg 'holds connection to registry provider
Dim subKey 'used to enumerate throught the array
Dim arrSubKeys 'holds the subkeys
Dim ParentKey
Const HKCR = &H80000000 'HKEY_CLASSES_ROOT
Const HKCU = &H80000001 'HKEY_CURRENT_USER
Const HKLM = &H80000002 'HKEY_LOCAL_MACHINE
Const HKU = &H80000003 'HKEY_USERS
Const HKCC = &H80000005 'HKEY_CURRENT_CONFIG

ParentKey = "SOFTWARE\EdWilson"
strKeyPath = "SOFTWARE\EdWilson\VbscriptBook"

strComputer = "."

Set objReg=GetObject("winmgmts:\\" & _
  strComputer & "\root\default:StdRegProv")


objReg.DeleteKey HKLM, strKeyPath
objReg.DeleteKey HKLM, ParentKey

If Err.Number = 0 Then
  wScript.Echo("Deleted key:" & strKeyPath)
  wScript.Echo("Deleted subKey: " & ParentKey)
Else
  wScript.Echo("Error number " & Err.Number & "occurred")
End If
```

Reading the Registry Using WMI Step-by-Step Exercises

In this section, let's practice reading the registry by using the WMI *StdRegProv* class.

1. Open \My Documents\Microsoft Press\VBScriptSBS\Templates\BlankTemplate.vbs in Microsoft Notepad or your favorite script editor. Save the script as Your-NameReadTheRegistry.vbs.

2. Add *Option Explicit* as the first line of your script.

3. Declare the following variables: *strKeyPath*, *strComputer*, *objReg*, *subKey*, and *arrSubKeys*. The Header information section of your script will look like the following:

    ```
    Option Explicit
    Dim strKeyPath
    Dim strComputer
    Dim objReg
    Dim subKey
    Dim arrSubKeys
    ```

4. Define a constant to be used for *HKLM*. Its hex value is *&H80000002*. Your code for this looks like the following:

    ```
    Const HKLM = &H80000002
    ```

5. Assign the Software\Microsoft path to the *strKeyPath* variable. It will look like the following:

```
strKeyPath = "SOFTWARE\Microsoft"
```

6. Assign the value of "." to the variable *strComputer*.

7. Use the *objReg* variable to hold the *SWbemServicesEx* object. Connect into the *root\default:stdRegProv* namespace on the local computer. Your code to do this looks like the following:

```
Set objReg=GetObject("winmgmts:\\" &_
  strComputer & "\root\default:StdRegProv")
```

8. Now use the *EnumKey* method to read the subkeys found under the Software\Microsoft key. The Software\Microsoft key is located in the *HKLM* tree. Feed the results out into a variable called *arrSubKeys*. The code for this looks like the following:

```
objReg.EnumKey HKLM, strKeyPath, arrSubKeys
```

9. Use *WScript.Echo* to echo out *strKeyPath*. This will be a header for the list of software contained in the Software\Microsoft key. You can use something like this:

```
WScript.Echo("Keys under " & strKeyPath)
```

10. Use a *For Each...Next* loop to iterate through the subkeys that are contained in the *arrSubKeys* variable. Use *WScript.Echo* to echo out the subkeys. Use the *subKey* variable as your placeholder. Your code will look like the following:

```
For Each subKey In arrSubKeys
  WScript.Echo vbTab & subKey
Next
```

11. Save and run the program under CScript.exe to avoid a plethora of dialog boxes.

One Step Further: Creating Registry Keys

In this section, you create a couple of registry keys that can be used to keep track of a software inventory of the workstation.

1. Open \My Documents\Microsoft Press\VBScriptSBS\Templates\BlankTemplate.vbs in Notepad or your favorite script editor.

2. On the first line, type **Option Explicit**. Save your script as YourNameCreateRegistryKeys.vbs.

3. Declare the following variables: *strKeyPath*, *strComputer*, *objReg*, *subKey*, *arrSubKeys*, and *ParentKey*. You code will look like the following:

```
Option Explicit
Dim strKeyPath
Dim strComputer
Dim objReg
```

```
Dim subKey
Dim arrSubKeys
Dim ParentKey
```

4. Define the constant for *HKLM* and set it equal to *&H80000002*. It will look like the following:

```
Const HKLM = &H80000002 'HKEY_LOCAL_MACHINE
```

5. Assign the value of *"SOFTWARE\INVENTORY"* to the *ParentKey* variable. It will look like the following:

```
ParentKey = "SOFTWARE\INVENTORY"
```

6. Assign the value of *"SOFTWARE\INVENTORY\Conducted"* to the *strKeyPath* variable. It looks like the following:

```
strKeyPath = "SOFTWARE\INVENTORY\Conducted"
```

7. Assign the value of "." to the *strComputer* variable. It looks like the following:

```
strComputer = "."
```

8. Use the *objReg* variable to hold the *SWbemServicesEx* object. Connect into the *root\default:stdRegProv* namespace on the local computer. Your code to do this looks like the following:

```
Set objReg=GetObject("winmgmts:\\" & _
   strComputer & "\root\default:StdRegProv")
```

9. Use the *createKey* method of *objReg* to create the new registry keys. The line will need both the *HKLM* constant and the *strKeyPath* for arguments. It will look like the following:

```
objReg.CreateKey HKLM, strKeyPath
```

10. Use *WScript.Echo* to provide feedback to the user that the key and the subkey were created. Your code could look like the following:

```
WScript.Echo("Created key :" & strKeyPath)
WScript.Echo("New subkey under : " & ParentKey)
```

11. Use *EnumKey* to verify the existence of the newly created registry keys. *EnumKey* will need *HKLM*, *ParentKey*, and *arrSubKeys* as arguments. Use a *For Each...Next* loop to walk through the *arrSubKeys* variable. Echo out each subkey. Your code will look like the following:

```
objReg.EnumKey HKLM, ParentKey, arrSubKeys
For Each subKey In arrSubKeys
   WScript.Echo vbTab & subKey
Next
```

12. Save and run the script.

Chapter 17 Quick Reference

To	Do This
Run an external program in VBScript	Use the *Run* method or the *Exec* method from the *WshShell* object
Use WMI to work with the registry	Use the *StdRegProv* WMI class
Write a string value to the registry using the *StdRegProv* WMI class	Use the *SetStringValue* method
Use the *DeleteKey* method of *StdRegProv* to delete a key and several subkeys from the registry	Delete the subkeys first, then delete the parent key

Chapter 18
Working with Printers

Before You Begin

To work through the material presented in this chapter, you need to be familiar with the following concepts from earlier chapters:

- Creating a connection into Microsoft Windows Management Instrumentation (WMI)
- Creating an instance of the *FileSystemObject* class
- Implementing the *For...Next* statement
- Implementing the *Select Case* statement

After completing this chapter, you will be able to:

- Work with the *Win32_Printer* WMI class
- Convert status codes into readable text
- Work with the *Win32_PrintJob* WMI class

Working with *Win32_Printer*

In this section, you are going to use the WMI *Win32_Printer* class. This particular WMI class is large and robust, defining more than 80 properties and implementing 7 methods. Some of its more useful properties are listed in Table 18-1.

Table 18-1   Useful *Win32_Printer* Properties

Property	Description
Attributes	Attributes of a Microsoft Windows printing device. Represented by a combination of flags.
Availability	Availability and status of the device. Return values are as follows: *2* = unknown, *3* = running or full power, *8* = offline.
AvailableJobSheets	Array of all job sheets available on a printer. Also used to describe the banner a printer might provide.
AveragePagesPerMinute	Print rate of the printer.
CharSetsSupported	Array of available character sets for output. Strings in this property are defined in Request for Comments (RFC) 2046 (Multipurpose Internet Mail Extensions [MIME] part 2) and in the Internet Assigned Numbers Authority (IANA) character-set registry. Examples: *utf-8*, *us-ascii*, and *iso-8859-1*.

Table 18-1   Useful *Win32_Printer* Properties

Property	Description
Comment	String that contains a comment for a print queue. Example: color printer.
CurrentLanguage	Printer language currently being used. Examples: *1* = other, *2* = unknown, *3* = PCL, *6* = PS.
Default	Boolean. If *true*, the printer is the default printer on the computer.
DefaultCopies	Number of copies that are produced for one job.
DetectedErrorState	Printer error information. Examples: *1* = unknown, *2* = other, *3* = no error, *5* = no paper, *6* = low toner, *9* = jammed, *10* = offline.
Direct	Boolean. If *true*, the print job is sent directly to the printer. If *false*, the print job is spooled.
DoCompleteFirst	Boolean. If *true*, the printer starts jobs that are finished spooling. If *false*, the printer starts jobs in the order they are received.
DriverName	String. Name of the Windows printer driver.
JobCountSinceLastReset	Number of print jobs since the printer was last reset.
KeepPrintedJobs	Boolean. If *true*, the print spooler does not delete completed jobs.
LastErrorCode	Last error code that the logical device reports.
Local	Boolean. If *true*, the printer is not attached to a network.
ServerName	String. Name of the server that controls the printer.
Shared	Boolean. If *true*, the printer is available as a shared network resource.
ShareName	String. Share name of the print device.
Status	String. Current status. Examples: ok, error, degraded, unknown, and stopping.
workOffLine	Boolean. If *true*, you can queue print jobs on the computer when the printer is offline.

> **Just the Steps**   To use the *Win32_Printer* class to manage a printer
>
> 1. Create a variable to hold a WMI connection.
> 2. Use *GetObject* and the WMI moniker to make a WMI connection.
> 3. Assign the object that comes back from the WMI connection to the variable in step 1.
> 4. Use the *ExecQuery* method to query *Win32_Printer*.
> 5. Use *For Each...Next* to iterate through the printer's collection.

Obtaining the Status of Printers

In your first printer management script, you'll use the *Win32_Printer* WMI class to obtain information about the status of printers defined on a computer. This particular script runs on Windows Server 2003 and on Windows XP, so it can run on a server to obtain the status of all the printers defined, or it can run as a diagnostic tool on a workstation. The MonitorPrinterStatus.vbs script follows:

MonitorPrinterStatus.vbs

```
Option Explicit
On Error Resume Next
Dim strComputer
Dim wmiNS
Dim wmiQuery
Dim objWMIService
Dim colItems
Dim objItem

strComputer = "."
wmiNS = "\root\cimv2"
wmiQuery = "Select * from win32_Printer"
Set objWMIService = GetObject("winmgmts:\\" _
& strComputer & wmiNS)
Set colItems = objWMIService.ExecQuery(wmiQuery)

For Each objItem in colItems
  WScript.Echo "Name: " & objItem.Name
  WScript.Echo "Location: " & objItem.Location
  WScript.Echo "Printer Status: " & funEvalStatus(objItem.PrinterStatus)
  WScript.Echo "Server Name: " & objItem.ServerName
  WScript.Echo "Share Name: " & objItem.ShareName
  WScript.Echo
Next

Function funEvalStatus(intIN)
Select Case intIN
    Case 1
      funEvalStatus = "Other"
    Case 2
      funEvalStatus = "Unknown"
    Case 3
      funEvalStatus = "Idle"
    Case 4
      funEvalStatus = "Printing"
    Case 5
      funEvalStatus = "Warmup"
    Case 6
    funEvalStatus = "Stopped Printing"
    Case 7
    funEvalStatus = "Offline"
  End Select
End Function
```

Header Information

The Header information section of the script does not perform any real magic. You begin with *Option Explicit* so that you're forced to keep track of your variables. Next you have *On Error Resume Next*, and then you have six variables. A description of the variables appears in Table 18-2.

Table 18-2   Variables for MonitorPrinterStatus.vbs

Variable	Use
strComputer	Holds the target computer
wmiNS	Holds the WMI namespace that will be connected to
wmiQuery	Holds the WMI query that will be executed
objWMIService	Holds the connection to WMI
colItems	Holds the collection that comes back as a result of the WMI query
objItem	Placeholder that allows us to iterate through the collection of items that was returned by the WMI query

Reference Information

The Reference information section of the script is used to assign values to some of the variables that were declared in the Header information section of the script. You use the period inside a set of double quotation marks to represent the local machine and assign it to *strComputer*. If you wanted to run the script against other computers, you could substitute their names for the period. The *root\cimv2* namespace is assigned to the variable *wmiNS*. You use "*Select * from Win32_Printer*" to return everything from the *Win32_Printer* class. Though easy to do, this is not the most efficient way to gather your information, which is somewhat of an issue when working with *Win32_Printer* because it is a rather large class. Your reference to the system's WMI service is *objWMIService*. You use the *winmgmts* moniker to simplify the connection process. The last reference information that needs to be set is using the *ExecQuery* method of *objWMIService* to execute the query represented by the variable *wmiQuery*. The Reference section is seen below.

```
strComputer = "."
wmiNS = "\root\cimv2"
wmiQuery = "Select * from Win32_Printer"
Set objWMIService = GetObject("winmgmts:\\" _
  & strComputer & wmiNS)
Set colItems = objWMIService.ExecQuery(wmiQuery)
```

Worker Information

The Worker information section of the MonitorPrinterStatus.vbs script consists of a single function called *funEvalStatus*. The *funEvalStatus* routine is used to translate the status code that is returned by the PrinterStatus property into a more meaningful message. To do the matching, you use a *Select Case* construction that looks for a match with one of the seven possible return status codes. The Worker section is seen below.

```
Function funEvalStatus(intIN)
Select Case intIN
   Case 1
     funEvalStatus = "Other"
   Case 2
     funEvalStatus = "Unknown"
   Case 3
     funEvalStatus = "Idle"
```

```
        Case 4
          funEvalStatus = "Printing"
        Case 5
          funEvalStatus = "Warmup"
        Case 6
        funEvalStatus = "Stopped Printing"
        Case 7
        funEvalStatus = "Offline"
      End Select
    End Function
```

Output Information

Once you work through matching the return status codes with a more meaningful status message, it is time to echo out the information. You use a *For Each...Next* construction to iterate through the collection of items that was returned by the WMI query. You use *WScript.Echo* to echo out a few of the more than 80 properties available via the *Win32_Printer* class. Because both the Name and the Location properties are simple string data, you can echo them out directly. However, to properly interpret the printer status code, you need to enter the *subEvalStatus* subroutine. You come out of that subroutine with a meaningful status message, and so you echo that out as well. Finally, you echo out the server name and the printer share name.

```
For Each objItem in colItems
  WScript.Echo "Name: " & objItem.Name
  WScript.Echo "Location: " & objItem.Location
  WScript.Echo "Printer Status: " & funEvalStatus(objItem.PrinterStatus)
  WScript.Echo "Server Name: " & objItem.ServerName
  WScript.Echo "Share Name: " & objItem.ShareName
  WScript.Echo
Next
```

> **Quick Check**
>
> Q. **What WMI class provides more than 80 properties for managing printers?**
>
> A. The *Win32_Printer* class provides more than 80 properties for managing printers.
>
> Q. **What is needed to obtain meaningful information from the PrinterStatus property?**
>
> A. To obtain meaningful information from the PrinterStatus property, you must interpret the status codes.
>
> Q. **When using the *Win32_Printer* class, how is the data returned?**
>
> A. When using the *Win32_Printer* class, the data is returned as a collection of printer objects.

Creating a Filtered Print Monitor

One cool thing you can do is filter out only the information you need prior to presenting it to the screen. A Windows Server 2003 print server commonly hosts a couple of hundred printers, so searching through all the print devices looking for one that is offline could take a long time. By making just a couple of changes to the MonitorPrinterStatus.vbs script, you can allow Microsoft Visual Basic, Scripting Edition (VBScript) to perform the weeding work for you.

> **Just the Steps**   To use a filter on the *Win32_Printer* class to manage a printer
>
> 1. Declare a variable to hold a connection into WMI.
> 2. Use *GetObject* and the WMI moniker to make a connection into WMI.
> 3. Assign the object that comes back from the WMI connection to the variable declared in step 1.
> 4. Use the *ExecQuery* method with a *Where* clause to query *Win32_Printer*. The *Where* clause should look for *1*, *2*, or *7* in the PrinterStatus property.
> 5. Use the Count property to determine the population of the collection of printers. If the collection of printers is empty, echo a message to that effect.
> 6. If the collection of printers is not empty, use *For Each...Next* to iterate through the collection.

The revised printer monitor script is called FilterPrinterStatus.vbs. Only a couple of changes were made to affect filtering. The addition of the *Where* clause to the WMI query takes place in the Reference information section. The use of *If...Then...Else* in conjunction with the Count property takes place in the Output information section. The FilterPrinterStatus.vbs script follows:

FilterPrinterStatus.vbs

```
Option Explicit
'On Error Resume Next
Dim strComputer
Dim wmiNS
Dim wmiQuery
Dim objWMIService
Dim colItems
Dim objItem

strComputer = "."
wmiNS = "\root\cimv2"
wmiQuery = "Select * from win32_Printer" _
    & " Where PrinterStatus = 1" _
    & " or PrinterStatus = 2" _
    & " or PrinterStatus = 7"
Set objWMIService = GetObject("winmgmts:\\" _
    & strComputer & wmiNS)
Set colItems = objWMIService.ExecQuery(wmiQuery)

If colItems.count = 0 Then
    WScript.Echo "All printers are fine"
Else
For Each objItem in colItems
  WScript.Echo "Name: " & objItem.Name
  WScript.Echo "Location: " & objItem.Location
```

```
    WScript.Echo "Printer Status: " & funEvalStatus(objItem.printerStatus)
    WScript.Echo "Server Name: " & objItem.ServerName
    WScript.Echo "Share Name: " & objItem.ShareName
    WScript.Echo
Next
End If

Function funEvalStatus(intIN)
Select Case intIN
    Case 1
      funEvalStatus = "Other"
    Case 2
      funEvalStatus = "Unknown"
    Case 3
      funEvalStatus = "Idle"
    Case 4
      funEvalStatus = "Printing"
    Case 5
      funEvalStatus = "Warmup"
    Case 6
    funEvalStatus = "Stopped Printing"
    Case 7
    funEvalStatus = "Offline"
  End Select
End Function
```

Reference Information

The Reference information section is where you modify your WMI query. The only change is adding a compound *Where* clause to the value you assigned to *wmiQuery*. You are interested in only those printers that have a status of *1*, *2*, or *7*. The Reference section of the script is seen below.

```
strComputer = "."
wmiNS = "\root\cimv2"
wmiQuery = "Select * from Win32_Printer" _
  & " where PrinterStatus = 1" _
  & " or PrinterStatus = 2" _
  & " or PrinterStatus = 7"
Set objWMIService = GetObject("winmgmts:\\" _
  & strComputer & wmiNS)
Set colItems = objWMIService.ExecQuery(wmiQuery)
```

Output Information

If you tried to iterate through a collection that had no members, you would not receive a meaningful message. To avoid this, you add an *If...Then...Else* construction around the Output information section that appeared in the earlier script. If there are no printers with an error condition, the Count property of *colItems* will be zero. You use *WScript.Echo* to send a message to the console that all printers are fine. If, however, the count is not zero, you echo out the information used in the MonitorPrinterStatus.vbs script. The revised section looks like the following code:

```
If colItems.count = 0 Then
WScript.Echo "All printers are fine"
Else
For Each objItem in colItems
  WScript.Echo "Name: " & objItem.Name
  WScript.Echo "Location: " & objItem.Location
  WScript.Echo "Printer Status: " & funEvalStatus(objItem.printerStatus)
  WScript.Echo "Server Name: " & objItem.ServerName
  WScript.Echo "Share Name: " & objItem.ShareName
  WScript.Echo
Next
End If
```

Quick Check

Q. **What was required in the FilterPrinterStatus.vbs script to return only selected records from the WMI query?**

A. To return selected records, a *Where* clause was added to the WMI query.

Q. **What is needed in the FilterPrinterStatus.vbs script to ensure you have printers in your collection?**

A. To ensure you have printers in your collection, you used the Count property of collected items in the FilterPrinterStatus.vbs script.

Q. **What does a *PrinterStatus* code of 7 mean?**

A. A *PrinterStatus* code of 7 means the printer is offline.

Monitoring Print Queues

To understand your print environment, it is necessary to examine the way the queues on the print servers are used. The MonitorPrintQueue.vbs script uses the *Win32_PrintJob* WMI class to obtain useful information about the load placed on your print servers. Because Monitor-PrintQueue.vbs is based on previous scripts, you will look only at the Worker and Output information section of the script. You assign *"Select * from Win32_PrintJob"* to the *wmiQuery* variable in the Reference section. That is the main change required in that section.

MonitorPrintQueue.vbs
```
Option Explicit
'On Error Resume Next
Dim strComputer
Dim wmiNS
Dim wmiQuery
Dim objWMIService
Dim colItems
Dim objItem
Dim intTotalJobs
Dim intTotalPages
```

```
Dim intMaxPrintJob

strComputer = '.'
wmiNS = '\root\cimv2'
wmiQuery = 'Select * from win32_PrintJob'
Set objWMIService = GetObject('winmgmts:\\' _
  & strComputer & wmiNS)
Set colItems = objWMIService.ExecQuery(wmiQuery)

If colItems.count = 0 Then
  WScript.Echo('There are no print jobs at this time')
Else
  For Each objItem In colItems
    intTotalJobs = intTotalJobs + 1
    intTotalPages = intTotalPages + objItem.TotalPages
    If objItem.TotalPages > intMaxPrintJob Then
      intMaxPrintJob = objItem.TotalPages
    End If
  Next
  WScript.Echo 'Total print jobs in queue: ' & intTotalJobs
  WScript.Echo 'Total pages in queue: ' & intTotalPages
  WScript.Echo 'Largest print job in queue: ' & intMaxPrintJob
End If
```

Worker and Output Information

To return meaningful information, you use the Count property of *colItems* just like you did in the previous script. If there are print jobs in the collection, iterate through them by using the *For Each...Next* construction. To get a count of the total number of print jobs in the queue, you use a counter called *intTotalJobs*, which gets incremented each time you loop through the collection of print jobs. For each print job in the collection, you get the TotalPages property and add it to the *intTotalPages* variable. By keeping a running total of pages, once you iterate through the collection, you will know the total pages left in the queue. To determine the largest print job in the queue, you use the variable called *intMaxPrintJob* and evaluate the size of each print job on the server. On each iteration through the collection of print jobs, we will list the print job size. Each time a larger print job is found, its value will be stored in *intMaxPrintJob*. At the end of the iteration, the largest print job will be stored in *intMaxPrintJob*, the total number of pages will be stored in the *intTotalPages* variable, and the total number of print jobs will be stored in the *intTotalJobs* variable.

Monitoring Print Jobs Step-by-Step Exercises

In this section, you will practice monitoring print jobs by using the *Win32_PrintJob* WMI class.

1. Open \My Documents\Microsoft Press\VBScriptSBS\Templates\BlankTemplate.vbs in Microsoft Notepad or your favorite script editor.

2. On the first line, type **Option Explicit**.

3. On the next line, type **On Error Resume Next** and then comment it out, so you can see the errors while working with the script.

4. Save your script as YourNameMonitorPrintJobs.vbs.

5. Declare the following variables: *strComputer*, *wmiNS*, *wmiQuery*, *objWMIService*, *colItems*, and *objItem*. Your Header information section will look like the following:

```
Option Explicit
'On Error Resume Next
Dim strComputer
Dim wmiNS
Dim wmiQuery
Dim objWMIService
Dim colItems
Dim objItem
```

6. Assign the value "." to the variable *strComputer,* as seen below

```
strComputer = <;$QD>.<;$QD>
```

7. Assign the value "*root**cimv2*" to the variable *wmiNS*, as seen below:

```
wmiNS = "\root\cimv2"
```

8. Assign the string "*Select * from Win32_PrintJob*" to the *wmiQuery* variable, as seen below:

```
wmiQuery = "Select * from win32_PrintJob"
```

9. Use *objWMIService* to hold the *SWbemServices* object that is returned by the *GetObject* command when we connect to the *root**cimv2* namespace on the local machine. Use the *winmgmts* moniker to make the connection. Specify the target computer as *strComputer*. Your code for this will look like the following:

```
Set objWMIService = GetObject("winmgmts:\\" _
  & strComputer & wmiNS)
```

10. Set the variable *colItems* equal to the object that is returned from the *ExecQuery* method of *objWMIService* when it executes the query contained in the variable *wmiQuery*. Your code will look like the following:

```
Set colItems = objWMIService.ExecQuery(wmiQuery)
```

11. Use the ColItems.Count property to ensure print jobs are in the collection. Implement an *If...Then...Else* construction to handle this. If there are no print jobs, echo a message to that effect. If there are print jobs, move into a *For...Each* loop. Your code for this part looks like the following:

```
If colItems.Count = 0 Then
WScript.Echo("There are no print jobs at this time")
else
```

12. Use a *For Each...Next* construction to iterate through the print jobs contained in the *colItems* collection. Use the variable *objItem* to hold each job as you walk through the collection. Echo out the JobId, JobStatus, Owner, and TotalPages properties. Your code for this looks like the following:

```
For Each objitem In colItems
  WScript.Echo("Print job: " & objItem.JobId)
```

```
    WScript.Echo("job status: " & objItem.JobStatus)
    WScript.Echo("Owner: " & objItem.Owner)
    WScript.Echo("Remaining pages: " & objItem.TotalPages)
Next
```

13. Close out the *If...Then...Else* construction by using *End If*.

14. Save your work and run the script under CScript. If it does not work as expected, compare it with \My Documents\Microsoft Press\VBScriptSBS\ch18\StepByStep\Monitor-PrintJobs.vbs.

One Step Further: Checking the Status of a Print Server

In this section, you will check the status of a print server, and if the server is not OK, you will cancel all print jobs on the box. This script is based on the FilterPrinterStatus.vbs script, so you use a starter file.

1. Open \My Documents\Microsoft Press\VBScriptSBS\ch18\OneStepFurther\Filter-PrinterStatus.vbs in Notepad or your favorite script editor. Save the script as Your NameCheckServerStatusCancelPrintJobs.vbs.

2. Delete the entire *subEvalstatus* subroutine from the bottom of the script. This subroutine looks like the following:

```
Sub subEvalStatus
  Select Case objItem.PrinterStatus
    Case 1
      strStatus = "Other"
    Case 2
      strStatus = "Unknown"
    Case 3
      strStatus = "Idle"
    Case 4
      strStatus = "Printing"
    Case 5
      strStatus = "Warmup"
    Case 6
      strStatus = "Stopped Printing"
    Case 7
      strStatus = "Offline"
  End Select
End sub
```

3. Locate the *For Each...Next* construction. Delete everything that is between the *For Each* and the *Next*. The *For Each...Next* statement is seen below. You will need to remove all the *WScript.Echo* commands and the *subEvalStatus* statement from the code below:

```
For Each objItem in colItems
  WScript.Echo "Name: " & objItem.Name
  WScript.Echo "Location: " & objItem.Location
  subEvalStatus
  WScript.Echo "Printer Status: " & strStatus
  WScript.Echo "Server Name: " & objItem.ServerName
```

```
WScript.Echo "Share Name: " & objItem.ShareName
WScript.Echo
Next
```

4. Inside the *For Each...Next* construction, echo out the objItem.Name property with an appropriate label. It will look like the following:

```
WScript.Echo "Name: " & objItem.Name
```

5. Under the *WScript* command, use the variable *canStatus* to hold the value contained in the objItem.CancelAllJobs property. The *CancelAllJobs* method has a return value that you want to capture with the *canStatus* variable. This line of code looks like the following:

```
canStatus = objItem.cancelAllJobs
```

6. Use *WScript.Echo* to echo out the value of *canStatus*. The completed *For Each...Next* construction now looks like the following:

```
For Each objItem In colItems
  WScript.Echo "Name: " & objItem.Name
  canStatus = objItem.CancelAllJobs
WScript.Echo(canStatus)
Next
```

7. Add the variable *canStatus* to the declarations section of the script.

8. Save and run the script. If it does not perform as expected, compare it to \My Documents\Microsoft Press\VBScriptSBS\ch18\OneStepFurther\CheckServerStatusCancelPrintJobs.vbs.

Chapter 18 Quick Reference

To	Do This
Use WMI to find comprehensive information about printers	Use the *WIN32_Printer* class
Find information about print jobs on either a workstation or on a server	Use the *WIN32_PrintJobs* class
Retrieve the number of items in a collection returned by the *ExecQuery* method of the *SWbemServices* object	Use the Count property of the *SWbemObjectSet* object
Reduce the number of records returned by a WMI query	Use a *Where* clause with the query

Part IV
Scripting Other Applications

In this part:

Chapter 19: Managing IIS 6.0 395

Chapter 20: Working with Exchange 2003 407

Chapter 21: Troubleshooting WMI Scripting 419

Chapter 19

Managing IIS 6.0

Before You Begin

To work through the material presented in this chapter, you need to be familiar with the following concepts from earlier chapters:

- Connecting to Microsoft Windows Management Instrumentation (WMI)
- Connecting to Microsoft Active Directory directory service
- Implementing the *For...Next* statement
- Implementing the *Select Case* statement
- Using the *ExecQuery* method

After completing this chapter, you will be able to:

- Connect to the *MicrosoftIISv2* namespace
- Use the Internet Information Server (IIS) WMI providers
- Work with the IIS metabase

Locating the WMI classes for IIS 6.0

All classes of the IIS 6.0 WMI provider are contained in a namespace called *MicrosoftIISv2*. This namespace is made up of five different classes discussed briefly in the next few sections.

CIM_ManagedSystemElement

The *CIM_ManagedSystemElement* class contains elements that relate to the IIS metabase schema. An example of one of these classes is *IISWebServer*, which maps to an instance of an IIS Web server. Another class is *IISWebVirtualDir*, which maps to an instance of a Web virtual directory. The elements in *CIM_ManagedSystemElement* are read-only. To set these types of settings, use the *CIM_Setting* class.

CIM_Setting

The elements in the *CIM_Setting* class map closely to the elements in the *CIM_ManagedSystem Element* class. This means that the elements correspond to nodes of the IIS 6.0 metabase schema. The *CIM_Setting* class contains methods that enable you to work with the properties that match the read-only elements of the *CIM_ManagedSystemElement* class.

> **Tip**   The *IIsWebServerSetting* element in the *CIM_Setting* element class enables you to make changes to your IIS Web server. To view data, you use the *IIsWebServer* element in the *CIM_ManagedSystemElement* class. It is important to remember that both of these elements refer to Web sites on your server. *IIsWebServer* is read-only, and *IIsWebServerSetting* enables you to make changes.

IIsStructuredDataClass

The *IIsStructuredDataClass* class presents information that is also accessible via Active Directory Service Interfaces (ADSI). However, the *IIsStructuredDataClass* information is structured in a way that is easier to work with than the ADSI data. For instance, the ServerBinding's property in ADSI is a string that consists of "IP:Port:Hostname". If the parts are out of order or are missing colons, an error occurs. By using *IIsStructuredDataClass*, you can take advantage of the element class called *ServerBinding*, whose properties are easier to set.

CIM_Component

CIM_Component is an association class that maps each element in the *CIM_ManagedSystem Element* class to other elements in the same class. It does this to mimic the way the data would be accessed via ADSI.

CIM_ElementSetting

The *CIM_ElementSetting* class is also an association class. As such, it maps elements in the *CIM_ManagedSystemElement* class to elements in the *CIM_Setting* class. The properties of the elements contained in the *CIM_ElementSetting* class are simply references to the two associated elements.

Using *MicrosoftIISv2*

To use the *MicrosoftIISv2* namespace, you need to understand the way the five classes represent the structure of the IIS 6.0 metabase schema. Instances of the elements in each of the classes contain current information that is viewable via the IIS Manager or the Metabase Configuration Editor.

On a default installation of IIS 6.0, the *IIsWebVirtualDir* element of the *Cim_ManagedSystem Element* class contains three instances of virtual directories: W3SVC/1/Root, W3SVC/1/Root /Scripts, and W3SVC/1/Root/Printers. These three virtual directories are also represented in the *IIsWebVirtualDirSetting* element of the *CIM_Setting* class. The only difference between the two is that you make changes to the virtual directories using only *IIsWebVirtualDirSetting*.

Just the Steps   To connect to the *MicrosoftIISv2* namespace

1. Define a variable to hold the object that comes back from the connection.
2. Specify the namespace as /root/*MicrosoftIISv2*.
3. Set your variable equal to the object that comes back from using the *GetObject* command to connect through *winmgmts* to the root/*MicrosoftIISv2* namespace on your machine.
4. Use the *ExecQuery* method to obtain information.

Making the Connection

To get an idea of the types of data accessible from the *CIM_Setting* element class, you can use the CIMSettingClass.vbs script. This script also illustrates connecting to the *MicrosoftIISv2* namespace and using WMI to query for IIS 6.0 configuration information.

Note   To run the scripts listed in this chapter, you will need to have IIS installed on your test server. If IIS is not installed and configured, then the scripts will not work.

CIMSettingClass.vbs

```
Option Explicit
On Error Resume Next
Dim strComputer
Dim wmiNS
Dim wmiQuery
Dim objWMIService
Dim colItems
Dim objItem

strComputer = "."
wmiNS = "/root/MicrosoftIISv2"
wmiQuery = "select * from CIM_Setting"
Set objWMIService = GetObject("winmgmts://" _
  & strComputer & wmiNS)
Set colItems = objWMIService.ExecQuery(wmiQuery)

For Each objItem In colItems
  WScript.Echo ": " & objItem.Name
Next
```

Header Information

The Header information section of CIMSettingClass.vbs, which follows, contains the normal *Option Explicit, On Error Resume Next*, and six variables. The advantage of splitting out the variables instead of including the data on the connection string is that doing so makes the script more portable and easier to modify. Use of the variables is detailed in Table 19-1.

```
Option Explicit
'On Error Resume Next
Dim strComputer
Dim wmiNS
Dim wmiQuery
Dim objWMIService
Dim colItems
Dim objItem
```

Table 19-1   Variables Used in CIMSettingClass.vbs

Variable	Use
strComputer	Holds assignment of target computer name
wmiNS	Holds the WMI namespace
wmiQuery	Holds the WMI query
objWMIService	Holds the connection into the target WMI namespace
colItems	Holds the collection of items that are returned from the WMI query
objItem	Used to iterate through the collection

Reference Information

The Reference information section of the script is used to assign values to the variables that are listed in the Header information section. *StrComputer* is the target computer—the one that is running IIS 6.0 and the one from which you are trying to obtain information. In this case, you are targeting the server called London. You next use the variable *wmiNS* to hold the namespace you want to connect into. When working with IIS 6.0, you will use the /root/ *MicrosoftIISv2* namespace.

You defined the target computer and the target WMI namespace. Next, you define your query. You use the generic "*Select* *" format and assign the query to the *wmiQuery* variable. The only tricky issue with querying WMI is how to know which class to target and what properties the class supports. For this information, the best tool is the Platform SDK, which is available at *http://www.msdn.microsoft.com*. You can download a copy of it and install it on your laptop. (It makes for great reading while you are sitting on the beach in Kauai. The only problem is keeping sand out of the keyboard.) Pursuant to our earlier discussions, you will query the *CIM_Setting* element class for names of all the read/write properties for the IIS 6.0 *admin* object.

The last task you need to complete in the Reference section is setting the *colItems* variable equal to the data returned from running the *ExecQuery* method when you feed it your WMI query. The Reference section of the script is seen below.

```
strComputer = "london"
wmiNS = "/root/MicrosoftIISv2"
wmiQuery = "select * from CIM_Setting"
Set objWMIService = GetObject("winmgmts://" _
  & strComputer & wmiNS)
Set colItems = objWMIService.ExecQuery(wmiQuery)
```

Worker and Output Information

The Worker and Output information section of the script is small because most of the real work was done in the Reference information section. Because you have a collection of items that comes back from the WMI query, you need to iterate through the collection to display the information. The easiest way to iterate through the collection is to use the *For Each...Next* construction. To represent the present record being worked with, *objItem* is used as a placeholder. Once you issue the next command, you move to the next record in the stream and assign it to the *objItem* variable. You then simply use *WScript.Echo* to echo out the name of the item in the collection. The Worker and Output section of the script is seen below.

```
For Each objItem In colItems
  WScript.Echo ": " & objItem.name
Next
```

Creating a Web Site

The advantage of using WMI to create Web sites is that it gives you a consistent product and vastly simplifies the creation process by automating dozens of minute details. For companies that create a lot of Web sites, scripting makes a lot of sense.

> **Just the Steps**   To use WMI to create a Web site
>
> 1. Define the appropriate variables.
> 2. Use *CreateObject* to create an instance of the *WbemScripting SWbemLocator* object.
> 3. Use the *locator* object so that you can use the *ConnectServer* method to connect to the *MicrosoftIISv2* namespace on the target computer.
> 4. Use the *service* object to get an instance of "*IIsWebService='W3SVC'*".
> 5. Use the *server* binding object to set your bindings.
> 6. Use the *createNewSite* method to create the Web site.

The following code is CreateSite.vbs. When run on a server that has IIS installed, it will create a Web site.

CreateSite.vbs
```
Option Explicit
'On Error Resume Next
Dim strComputer
Dim wmiNS
Dim siteName
Dim strSiteObjPath
Dim locatorObj
Dim providerObj
Dim objPath
Dim vDirObj
```

```
Dim serverObj
Dim serviceObj
Dim bindings
Dim strSitePath

strComputer = "."
wmiNS = "root/MicrosoftIISv2"
siteName = "LondonWebSite"

Set locatorObj = CreateObject("WbemScripting.SWbemLocator")
Set providerObj = locatorObj.ConnectServer _
  & (strComputer, wmiNS)
Set serviceObj = providerObj.Get _
  & ("IISWebService='W3SVC'")
Set objPath = CreateObject("WbemScripting.SWbemObjectPath")

Bindings = Array(0)
Set Bindings(0) = providerObj.Get("ServerBinding") _
  & .SpawnInstance_()
Bindings(0).IP = ""
Bindings(0).Port = "8383"
Bindings(0).Hostname = ""

strSiteObjPath = serviceObj.CreateNewSite _
  & (siteName, Bindings, "C:\Inetpub\wwwroot")
objPath.Path = strSiteObjPath
strSitePath = objPath.Keys.Item("")
  subCheckErrors

WScript.Echo "Created " & siteName
WScript.Echo "The path/ID is " & strSitePath

Sub subCheckErrors
  If Err Then
    WScript.Echo "Error: " & Hex(Err.Number) _
      & ": " & Err.Description
    WScript.Quit(1)
  End If
End Sub
```

Header Information

The Header information section of CreateSite.vbs includes a lot of variables. Understanding how to use these variables will further your understanding of the script. The variables used in this script are described in Table 19-2.

Table 19-2   Variables Used in CreateSite.vbs

Variable	Use
strComputer	Holds assignment of the target computer name
wmiNS	Holds the WMI namespace
siteName	Holds the name of the new Web site to create
strSiteObjPath	Holds the path to the new Web site

Table 19-2   Variables Used in CreateSite.vbs

Variable	Use
locatorObj	Holds the object that comes back from *SWbemLocator*
providerObj	Uses the object from *locatorObj* to make a connection to the server
objPath	Holds the object that comes back from *SWbemObjectPath*
serviceObj	Holds the object that comes back from the *providerObj* object to get an instance of *IIsWebService=<;$QS>W3SVC<;$QS>*
bindings	Holds the elements of the array that is used for *ServerBinding*
strSitePath	Holds the key items from *objPath*

Reference Information

The Reference information section in CreateSite.vbs is large. This section could be condensed somewhat by combining statements and pulling data directly into the script instead of first populating variables. However, reducing the code by a few lines would make a much less readable script. You begin the Reference information section of the script by assigning a value to *strComputer*. You then set the *wmiNS* variable to be equal to the root/*MicrosoftIISv2* namespace. Note that the *MicrosoftIISv2* namespace is under the root. It is not in root*cimv2*, as many of your WMI scripts have been. You now assign a name to the *siteName* variable, which is the name of the Web site you will be creating.

We set the variable *locatorObj* to be equal to the object that comes back when you use *CreateObject* to create an instance of the *SWbemLocator* object. You need to create an instance of the *SWbemLocator* object so that you can gain access to the *ConnectServer* method. You use *ConnectServer* to connect to the root/*MicrosoftIISv2* namespace on your target server. You use the variable *providerObj* to hold the object.

Quick Check

Q.   **Why is it necessary in the CreateSite.vbs script to use the *SWbemLocator* object?**

A.   The *SWbemLocator* object is necessary so that you can use the *ConnectServer* method that it exposes.

Q.   **Where does the *MicrosoftIISv2* namespace reside?**

A.   The *MicrosoftIISv2* namespace resides under the root WMI namespace.

You now set *serviceObj* equal to the object you get when you connect to the Web service on your London server. Once you make your connection to the Web service, you need to build a binding object. The binding object is a required parameter of the *CreateNewSite* method, and because it has multiple elements, it is stored as an array. *SpawnInstance* is the WMI method used because you're creating a new instance on an object. The Reference section is seen below.

```
strComputer = "."
wmiNS = "root/MicrosoftIISv2"
siteName = "LondonWebSite"
```

```
Set locatorObj = CreateObject("WbemScripting.SWbemLocator")
Set providerObj = locatorObj.ConnectServer _
  & (strComputer, wmiNS)
Set serviceObj = providerObj.Get _
  & ("IIsWebService='W3SVC'")
Set objPath = CreateObject("WbemScripting." _
  & "SWbemObjectPath")

Bindings = Array(0)
Set Bindings(0) = providerObj.Get("ServerBinding") _
  & .SpawnInstance_()
Bindings(0).IP = ""
Bindings(0).Port = "8383"
Bindings(0).Hostname = ""
```

Worker and Output Information

In the Worker and Output information section of the script, the Web site is created. The variable that holds the return information from using the *CreateNewSite* method of the *IIsWebService* object is *strSiteObjPath*. To call the *CreateNewSite* method, you have to specify the site name, the bindings, and the physical path for the files. The variable *strSiteObjPath* is in the format of *IIsWebServer='W3SVC/1180970907'*; therefore, to parse out the absolute path, you use the *SWbemObjectPath* WMI object.

After you complete parsing out the absolute path, you call the *subCheckErrors* subroutine. In the *subCheckErrors* subroutine, you check the *err* object and echo out both the number and description of the error.

The script ends by echoing out the completed site name as well as the path and the unique site ID number that was built by using the *strSitePath* variable. The Worker and Output section of the script is seen below.

```
strSiteObjPath = serviceObj.CreateNewSite _
  & (siteName, Bindings, "C:\Inetpub\Wwwroot")
objPath.Path = strSiteObjPath
strSitePath = objPath.Keys.Item("")
  subCheckErrors

WScript.Echo "Created " & siteName
WScript.Echo "The path/ID is " & strSitePath

Sub subCheckErrors
  If Err Then
    WScript.Echo "Error: " & Hex(Err.Number) _
      & ": " & Err.Description
    WScript.Quit(1)
  End If
End sub
```

Backing Up the Metabase Step-by-Step Exercises

In this section, we will develop a script that will back up the IIS metabase.

1. Open the \My Documents\Microsoft Press\VBScriptSBS\Templates\Blank Template.vbs script in Microsoft Notepad or some other script editor and save it as Your-NameBackUpIISMetaBase.vbs.

2. As the first non-commented line, type **Option Explicit**.

3. Declare the following variables: *strPassword*, *strFilePath*, *strMetabasePath*, *intFlags*, *locatorObj*, *providerObj*, and *computerObj*. Your completed Header information section will look like the following:

    ```
    Option Explicit
    Dim strPassword
    Dim strFilePath
    Dim strMetabasePath
    Dim intFlags
    Dim locatorObj
    Dim providerObj
    Dim computerObj
    ```

4. Define three constants to be used to control the export behavior: *EXPORT_CHILDREN = 0*, *EXPORT_INHERITED = 1*, and *EXPORT_NODE_ONLY = 2*. The *EXPORT_CHILDREN* constant is used to add the properties of child keys to the export file. The *EXPORT_INHERITED* constant is used to add inherited properties to the exported keys, and the *EXPORT_NODE_ONLY* constant does not add subkeys of the specified key to the export file. The constants section of the script will look like the following:

    ```
    Const EXPORT_CHILDREN = 0
    Const EXPORT_INHERITED = 1
    Const EXPORT_NODE_ONLY = 2
    ```

5. Assign the password *"ExportingPassw0rd"* to the *strPassword* variable.

6. Specify the physical path for the exported metabase. To do this, assign the value of *"C:\exported.xml"* to the *strFilePath* variable.

7. Set *strMetabasePath* to be equal to *"/lm/logging/custom logging"*. This is seen in the Metabase.xml file.

8. Set the *intFlags* variable equal to *EXPORT_NODE_ONLY OR EXPORT_INHERITED* constants. This will tell the export command to show only the node with inherited properties. This section of the script looks like the following:

    ```
    strPassword = "ExportingPassw0rd"
    strFilePath = "C:\exported.xml"
    strMetabasePath = "/lm/logging/custom logging"
    intFlags = EXPORT_NODE_ONLY OR EXPORT_INHERITED
    ```

9. Set the *locatorObj* variable equal to the object that comes back to the *SWbemLocator* object when you use the *CreateObject* command. This code looks like the following:

```
Set locatorObj = CreateObject("WbemScripting.SwbemLocator")
```

10. Set the *providerObj* variable equal to the object that comes back from using the *ConnectServer* method of *SWbemLocator*. At this point, the object will be used to connect into the London server *MicrosoftIISv2* namespace. This line of code looks like the following:

```
Set providerObj = locatorObj.ConnectServer _
  ("London", "root/MicrosoftIISv2")
```

11. Set the *computerObj* variable equal to the object into *IIsComputer = 'LM'* when you use the *Get* method of the *providerObj* object. This line of code looks like the following:

```
Set computerObj - providerObj.Get("IIsComputer = 'LM'")
```

12. Call the *Export* method from the computer object. The command needs the values that are contained in the *strPassword*, *strFilePath*, *strMetabasePath*, and *intFlags* variables. The code looks like the following:

```
computerObj.Export strPassword, strFilePath, strMetabasePath, intFlags
```

13. Print out the results by using the *WScript.Echo* command to echo out a message that includes the values contained in the variables *strMetabasePath* and *strFilePath*. Your code could look like the following:

```
WScript.Echo "Exported the node at " & strMetabasePath _
  & " to " & strFilePath
```

14. Save and run the script. If it does not perform as expected, compare your script with \My Documents\Microsoft Press\VBScriptSBS\ch19\StepByStep\BackUpIIS MetaBase.vbs.

One Step Further: Importing the Metabase

In this section, you will restore the metabase that was backed up in the previous section.

1. Open \My Documents\Microsoft Press\VBScriptSBS\Templates\BlankTemplate.vbs in Notepad or your favorite script editor and save it as YourNameImportIISMetaBase.vbs.

2. As the first non-commented line, type **Option Explicit**.

3. Declare the following variables: *strPassword*, *strFilePath*, *strSourceMetabasePath*, *strDestinationMetabasePath*, *intFlags*, *locatorObj*, *providerObj*, and *computerObj*. Your completed Header information section will look like the following:

```
Option Explicit
Dim strPassword
Dim strFilePath
Dim strSourceMetabasePath
Dim strDestinationMetabasePath
```

```
Dim intFlags
Dim locatorObj
Dim providerObj
Dim computerObj
```

4. Create four constants to control the import behavior. *CONST IMPORT_CHILDREN = 0* recursively imports the subkeys of the specified key; *CONST IMPORT_INHERITED = 1* imports the inherited properties of the keys; *CONSTANT IMPORT_NODE_ONLY = 2* does not import subkeys from the specified file. The last constant is *CONST IMPORT_MERGE = 4*, which merges the imported keys into the existing configuration instead of completely replacing what previously existed. The code for this looks like the following:

```
Const IMPORT_CHILDREN = 0
Const IMPORT_INHERITED = 1
Const IMPORT_NODE_ONLY = 2
Const IMPORT_MERGE = 4
```

5. Assign the password "*ExportingPassw0rd*" to the *strPassword* variable.

6. Specify the physical path for the exported metabase by assigning the value of "*C:\exported.xml*" to the *strFilePath* variable.

7. Set the *strSourceMetabasePath* variable to be equal to "*/lm/logging/custom logging*". This is represented in the Metabase.xml file.

8. Set the *strDestinationMetabasePath* variable to be equal to "*/lm/logging/custom logging*". This value can be different from the *strSourceMetabasePath* variable if required.

9. Set the *intFlags* to be equal to *IMPORT_NODE_ONLY OR IMPORT_INHERITED*. This will import only the node with the inherited properties. This section of code looks like the following:

```
strPassword = "ExportingPassw0rd"
strFilePath = "C:\exported.xml"
strSourceMetabasePath = "/lm/logging/custom logging"
strDestinationMetabasePath = "/lm/logging/custom logging"
intFlags = IMPORT_NODE_ONLY OR IMPORT_INHERITED
```

10. Set the *locatorObj* variable equal to the object that comes back to the *SWbemLocator* object when you use the *CreateObject* command. This code looks like the following:

```
Set locatorObj = CreateObject("WbemScripting.SWbemLocator")
```

11. Set the *providerObj* variable equal to the object that comes back from using the *ConnectServer* method of *SWbemLocator*. The *providerObj* variable is used to connect to the London server *MicrosoftIISv2* namespace. This line of code looks like the following:

```
Set providerObj = locatorObj.ConnectServer _
  ("London", "root/MicrosoftIISv2")
```

12. Set the *computerObj* variable equal to the object into *IIsComputer* = <;$QS>LM<;$QS> when you use the *Get* command of the *providerObj*. This line of code looks like the following:

```
Set computerObj = providerObj.Get("IIsComputer = 'LM'")
```

13. Call the *Import* method from the *Computer* object. The *Import* method requires the variables *strPassword*, *strFilePath*, *strSourceMetabasePath*, *strDestinationMetabasePath*, and *intFlags* to be set. This line of code looks like the following:

```
computerObj.Import strPassword, strFilePath, _
    strSourceMetabasePath, strDestinationMetabasePath, intFlags
```

14. Echo out the results. Include the *strFilePath* variable and the *strDestinationMetabasePath* variables as confirmation. Your code could look like the following:

```
WScript.Echo "Imported the node in " & strFilePath & " to " _
    & strDestinationMetabasePath
```

15. Save and test your file. If it does not perform as expected, compare it to \My Documents\Microsoft Press\VBScriptSBS\ch19\OneStepFurther\ImportIISMetaBase.vbs.

Chapter 19 Quick Reference

To	Do This
Manage IIS 6.0	Use the classes found in the *MicrosoftIISv2* WMI namespace
Locate the *MicrosoftIISv2* WMI namespace	Look directly under the \root namespace
Create a new IIS Web site using WMI	Use the *CreateNewSite* method of the *IISWebService* class

Chapter 20

Working with Exchange 2003

Before You Begin

To work through the material presented in this chapter, you need to be familiar with the following concepts from earlier chapters:

- Creating a connection into Microsoft Windows Management Instrumentation (WMI)
- Creating a WMI query
- Implementing the *For...Next* statement
- Implementing the *Select Case* statement

After completing this chapter, you will be able to:

- Connect to the *MicrosoftExchangeV2* namespace
- Query the *Exchange_Logon* class
- Query the *Exchange_Mailbox* class
- Query the *Exchange_PublicFolder* class
- Query the *Exchange_QueueSMTPVirtualServer* class

Working with the Exchange Provider

When Exchange 2003 is installed, it creates the *MicrosoftExchangeV2* namespace that resides under the root WMI namespace. This is a rich namespace that covers a wide range of resouce management and data management scenarios. Changes to the *MicrosoftExchangeV2* namespace for Exchange 2003 are detailed in Table 20-1.

Table 20-1 Changes to the Exchange WMI namespace

WMI class	Changes in Exchange 2003
ExchangeClusterResource	No changes.
ExchangeConnectorState	No changes.
ExchangeLink	No changes. Additional capabilities are provided in the new *Exchange_Link* class.
ExchangeQueue	No changes. Additional capabilities are provided in the new *Exchange_Queue* class.

Table 20-1   Changes to the Exchange WMI namespace

WMI class	Changes in Exchange 2003
ExchangeServerState	No changes. Additional capabilities are provided in the new Exchange_Server class.
Exchange_DSAccessDC	No changes.
Exchange_FolderTree	New class.
Exchange_Link	New class.
Exchange_Logon	New class.
Exchange_Mailbox	New class.
Exchange_MessageTrackingEntry	Additional message-tracking entry-type values were added to provide more detailed tracking of internal message-transfer events.
Exchange_PublicFolder	New class.
Exchange_Queue	New class.
Exchange_QueueCacheReloadEvent	New class.
Exchange_QueuedMessage	New class.
Exchange_QueuedSMTPMessage	New class.
Exchange_QueuedX400Message	New class.
Exchange_QueueSMTPVirtualServer	New class.
Exchange_QueueVirtualServer	New class.
Exchange_QueueX400VirtualServer	New class.
Exchange_ScheduleInterval	New class.
Exchange_Server	New class.
Exchange_SMTPLink	New class.
Exchange_SMTPQueue	New class.
Exchange_X400Link	New class.
Exchange_X400Queue	New class.

> **Just the Steps**   To query the *Exchange_QueueSMTPVirtualServer* class
>
> 1. Create a variable to hold the connection into the *root**MicrosoftExchangeV2* namespace.
> 2. Use the *ExecQuery* method to select * from *Exchange_QueueSMTPVirtualServer*.
> 3. Use *For Each...Next* to iterate through the returned collection.
> 4. Use *WScript.Echo* to echo out the important properties.

Connecting to *MicrosoftExchangeV2*

To use WMI to retrieve information from Exchange 2003, you need to make a connection into the *MicrosoftExchangeV2* namespace, which is even easier to work with than the Internet Information Server (IIS) namespace. As you will soon see, the *MicrosoftExchangeV2* namespace is very logically laid out, and the scripts will rapidly become redundant. The only trick to using the namespace is finding the data you want to retrieve.

The *Exchange_QueueSMTPVirtualServer* Class

For the first code sample (ExchangeSMTPQueue.vbs), consider the *Exchange_QueueSMTPVirtualServer* class, which returns properties for Simple Mail Transfer Protocol (SMTP) queue virtual servers. ExchangeSMTPQueue.vbs is shown here:

ExchangeSMTPQueue.vbs

```
Option Explicit
On Error Resume Next
Dim strComputer
Dim wmiNS
Dim wmiQuery
Dim objWMIService
Dim colItems
Dim objItem

strComputer = "."
wmiNS = "\root\MicrosoftExchangeV2"
wmiQuery = "Select * from Exchange_QueueSMTPVirtualServer"
Set objWMIService = GetObject("winmgmts:\\" & strComputer & wmiNS)
Set colItems = objWMIService.ExecQuery(wmiQuery)

For Each objItem In colItems
  WScript.Echo "Caption: " & objItem.Caption
  WScript.Echo "Description: " & objItem.Description
  WScript.Echo "GlobalActionsSupported: " _
    & objItem.GlobalActionsSupported
  WScript.Echo "GlobalStop: " & objItem.GlobalStop
  WScript.Echo "InstallDate: " & objItem.InstallDate
  WScript.Echo "Name: " & objItem.Name
  WScript.Echo "ProtocolName: " & objItem.ProtocolName
  WScript.Echo "Status: " & objItem.Status
  WScript.Echo "VirtualMachine: " & objItem.VirtualMachine
  WScript.Echo "VirtualServerName: " & objItem.VirtualServerName
  WScript.Echo "-=-"
Next
```

Header Information

The Header information section is going to look very similar in each of the Exchange 2003 WMI scripts, so this is the only place in this chapter you will look at it. You turn on *Option Explicit* and *On Error Resume Next*, and then you name several variables, which are described in Table 20-2.

Table 20-2   Variables used in ExchangeSMTPQueue.vbs

Variable	Use
strComputer	Holds the name of the target computer
wmiNS	Holds the target namespace
wmiQuery	Holds the WMI query text
objWMIService	Holds the connection into WMI
colItems	Holds the returned data
objItem	Used to iterate through the data

Reference Information

The Reference information section of the script is used to assign values to variables that were declared in the Header information section. The variable *strComputer* is set to a period, which means that the query will run against the local computer. The variable *wmiNS* is set to the "*root\MicrosoftExchangeV2*" namespace to enable you to work with Exchange 2003. In most of our scripts, the *strComputer*, *wmiNS*, and *wmiQuery* references will remain exactly the same. The only item needing modification in the Reference information section of the script is the class from which *Select ** is going to run. You set *objWMIService* to be equal to the object that comes back from using *GetObject* and the WMI moniker. This connection into WMI is targeted at *strComputer* and the namespace represented by *wmiNS*. The advantage of using variables to create the connection string is that the line of code will never need to be modified! Once you have the hook into WMI, you use that hook to cast your query. The query is contained in the *wmiQuery* variable, and as a result, you don't have to touch that line of code either. Here is the Reference information section:

```
strComputer = "."
wmiNS = "\root\MicrosoftExchangeV2"
wmiQuery = "Select * from Exchange_QueueSMTPVirtualServer"
Set objWMIService = GetObject("winmgmts:\\" & strComputer & wmiNS)
Set colItems = objWMIService.ExecQuery(wmiQuery)
```

Worker Information

The Worker information section of the script is a *For Each...Next* statement. You use the *objItem* variable to iterate through the data held in the *colItems* collection. This code does not need to be modified. This statement looks like the following:

```
For Each objItem In colItems

Next
```

Output Information

The Output information section of the script consists of a series of *WScript.Echo* statements. These statements are contained inside the *For Each...Next* statement in the Worker information section of the script. The Output information section will need to be customized for every WMI script you create using the *MicrosoftExchangeV2* namespace. For ExchangeSMTPQueue.vbs, the Output information section looks like the following:

```
WScript.Echo "Caption: " & objItem.Caption
WScript.Echo "Description: " & objItem.Description
WScript.Echo "GlobalActionsSupported: " _
   & objItem.GlobalActionsSupported
WScript.Echo "GlobalStop: " & objItem.GlobalStop
WScript.Echo "InstallDate: " & objItem.InstallDate
WScript.Echo "Name: " & objItem.Name
WScript.Echo "ProtocolName: " & objItem.ProtocolName
WScript.Echo "Status: " & objItem.Status
WScript.Echo "VirtualMachine: " _
   & objItem.VirtualMachine
WScript.Echo "VirtualServerName: " _
   & objItem.VirtualServerName
```

Exchange Public Folders

Working with public folders in Exchange 2003 is a lot better than working with them in earlier versions of Exchange, due to the enhancements of WMI. The addition of new and expanded WMI classes makes working with public folders especially easy. The script ExchangePublicFolders.vbs illustrates this point. As you can see from the code listing, much of the process of connecting to and accessing useful information about Exchange 2003 public folders via the *Exchange_PublicFolder* class is similar to this process in other WMI scripts. Indeed, the only changes are using the *Exchange_PublicFolder* class to select the statement you will use for the query and, of course, the Output information section of the script.

ExchangePublicFolders.vbs

```
Option Explicit
On Error Resume Next
Dim strComputer
Dim wmiNS
Dim wmiQuery
Dim objWMIService
Dim colItems
Dim objItem

strComputer = "."
wmiNS = "\root\MicrosoftExchangeV2"
wmiQuery = "Select * from Exchange_PublicFolder"
Set objWMIService = GetObject("winmgmts:\\" & strComputer & wmiNS)
Set colItems = objWMIService.ExecQuery(wmiQuery)

For Each objItem In colItems
  WScript.Echo "AddressBookName: " & objItem.AddressBookName
  WScript.Echo "AdministrativeNote: " & objItem.AdministrativeNote
  WScript.Echo "AdminSecurityDescriptor: " _
    & objItem.AdminSecurityDescriptor
  WScript.Echo "ADProxyPath: " & objItem.ADProxyPath
```

```
WScript.Echo "AssociatedMessageCount: " _
  & objItem.AssociatedMessageCount
WScript.Echo "AttachmentCount: " & objItem.AttachmentCount
WScript.Echo "Caption: " & objItem.Caption
WScript.Echo "CategorizationCount: " & _
  objItem.CategorizationCount
WScript.Echo "Comment: " & objItem.Comment
WScript.Echo "ContactCount: " & objItem.ContactCount
WScript.Echo "ContainsRules: " & objItem.ContainsRules
WScript.Echo "CreationTime: " & objItem.CreationTime
WScript.Echo "DeletedItemLifetime: " _
  & objItem.DeletedItemLifetime
WScript.Echo "Description: " & objItem.Description
WScript.Echo "FolderTree: " & objItem.FolderTree
WScript.Echo "FriendlyUrl: " & objItem.FriendlyUrl
WScript.Echo "HasChildren: " & objItem.HasChildren
WScript.Echo "HasLocalReplica: " & objItem.HasLocalReplica
WScript.Echo "InstallDate: " & objItem.InstallDate
WScript.Echo "IsMailEnabled: " & objItem.IsMailEnabled
WScript.Echo "IsNormalFolder: " & objItem.IsNormalFolder
WScript.Echo "IsPerUserReadDisabled: " _
  & objItem.IsPerUserReadDisabled
WScript.Echo "IsSearchFolder: " & objItem.IsSearchFolder
WScript.Echo "IsSecureInSite: " & objItem.IsSecureInSite
WScript.Echo "LastAccessTime: " & objItem.LastAccessTime
WScript.Echo "LastModificationTime: " _
  & objItem.LastModificationTime
WScript.Echo "MaximumItemSize: " & objItem.MaximumItemSize
WScript.Echo "MessageCount: " & objItem.MessageCount
WScript.Echo "MessageWithAttachmentsCount: " _
  & objItem.MessageWithAttachmentsCount
WScript.Echo "Name: " & objItem.Name
WScript.Echo "NormalMessageSize: " & objItem.NormalMessageSize
WScript.Echo "OwnerCount: " & objItem.OwnerCount
WScript.Echo "ParentFriendlyUrl: " & objItem.ParentFriendlyUrl
WScript.Echo "Path: " & objItem.Path
WScript.Echo "ProhibitPostLimit: " & objItem.ProhibitPostLimit
WScript.Echo "PublishInAddressBook: " _
  & objItem.PublishInAddressBook
WScript.Echo "RecipientCountOnAssociatedMessages: " _
  & objItem.RecipientCountOnAssociatedMessages
WScript.Echo "RecipientCountOnNormalMessages: " _
  & objItem.RecipientCountOnNormalMessages
WScript.Echo "ReplicaAgeLimit: " & objItem.ReplicaAgeLimit
WScript.Echo "ReplicaList: " & objItem.ReplicaList
WScript.Echo "ReplicationMessagePriority: " _
  & objItem.ReplicationMessagePriority
WScript.Echo "ReplicationSchedule: " _
  & objItem.ReplicationSchedule
WScript.Echo "ReplicationStyle: " & objItem.ReplicationStyle
WScript.Echo "RestrictionCount: " & objItem.RestrictionCount
WScript.Echo "SecurityDescriptor: " & objItem.SecurityDescriptor
WScript.Echo "Status: " & objItem.Status
WScript.Echo "StorageLimitStyle: " & objItem.StorageLimitStyle
WScript.Echo "TargetAddress: " & objItem.TargetAddress
```

```
    WScript.Echo "TotalMessageSize: " & objItem.TotalMessageSize
    WScript.Echo "Url: " & objItem.Url
    WScript.Echo "UsePublicStoreAgeLimits: " _
      & objItem.UsePublicStoreAgeLimits
    WScript.Echo "UsePublicStoreDeletedItemLifetime: " _
      & objItem.UsePublicStoreDeletedItemLifetime
    WScript.Echo "WarningLimit: " & objItem.WarningLimit
  WScript.Echo "-=-"
Next
```

Exchange_FolderTree

To look at the folder structure defined on an Exchange 2003 server, you can use the *Exchange_FolderTree* class. The only changes you must make to your script are the same changes you made to the other scripts—changing the class portion of *wmiQuery* to point to the *Exchange_FolderTree* class. Then you must modify the Output information section to echo out the properties you are interested in. The completed ExchangeFolderTree.vbs script is listed here:

ExchangeFolderTree.vbs

```
Option Explicit
On Error Resume Next
Dim strComputer
Dim wmiNS
Dim wmiQuery
Dim objWMIService
Dim colItems
Dim objItem

strComputer = "."
wmiNS = "\root\MicrosoftExchangeV2"
wmiQuery = "Select * from Exchange_FolderTree"
Set objWMIService = GetObject("winmgmts:\\" & strComputer & wmiNS)
Set colItems = objWMIService.ExecQuery(wmiQuery)

For Each objItem In colItems
  WScript.Echo "AdministrativeGroup: " _
    & objItem.AdministrativeGroup
  WScript.Echo "AdministrativeNote: " _
    & objItem.AdministrativeNote
  WScript.Echo "AssociatedPublicStores: " _
    & objItem.AssociatedPublicStores
  WScript.Echo "Caption: " & objItem.Caption
  WScript.Echo "CreationTime: " & objItem.CreationTime
  WScript.Echo "Description: " & objItem.Description
  WScript.Echo "GUID: " & objItem.GUID
  WScript.Echo "HasLocalPublicStore: " _
    & objItem.HasLocalPublicStore
  WScript.Echo "InstallDate: " & objItem.InstallDate
  WScript.Echo "LastModificationTime: " _
    & objItem.LastModificationTime
  WScript.Echo "MapiFolderTree: " & objItem.MapiFolderTree
```

```
WScript.Echo "Name: " & objItem.Name
WScript.Echo "RootFolderURL: " & objItem.RootFolderURL
WScript.Echo "Status: " & objItem.Status
WScript.Echo "-=-"

Next
```

Using the *Exchange_Logon* Class Step-by-Step Exercises

In this section, you use the *Exchange_Logon* class from the *MicrosoftExchangeV2* namespace.

1. Open the \My Documents\Microsoft Press\VBScriptSBS\Templates\Blank Template.vbs script in Microsoft Notepad or another script editor and save it as YourNameExchangeLogon.vbs.

2. As the first non-commented line of the script, type **Option Explicit**.

3. You need to declare six variables: *strComputer*, *wmiNS*, *wmiQuery*, *objWMIService*, *colItems*, and *objItem*. In addition, add *On Error Resume Next*, but comment out the line during development. The completed Header information section of your script will look like the following:

   ```
   Option Explicit
   'On Error Resume Next
   Dim strComputer
   Dim wmiNS
   Dim wmiQuery
   Dim objWMIService
   Dim colItems
   Dim objItem
   ```

4. Assign the variable *strComputer* to be equal to ".". This line of code will look like the following:

   ```
   strComputer = "."
   ```

5. Use the variable *wmiNS* to hold the string "\root\MicrosoftExchangeV2". This line of code looks like the following:

   ```
   wmiNS = "\root\MicrosoftExchangeV2"
   ```

6. Use the *wmiQuery* variable to be hold the string "*Select * from Exchange_Logon*". This line of code looks like the following:

   ```
   wmiQuery = "Select * from Exchange_Logon"
   ```

7. Set the variable *objWMIService* to be equal to the object that comes back from using the *GetObject* command into WMI. Use the *winmgmts* moniker, specify *strComputer* as the target computer, and specify *wmiNS* as the target namespace. This line of code looks like the following:

   ```
   Set objWMIService = GetObject("winmgmts:\\" & strComputer & wmiNS)
   ```

8. Set the *colItems* variable to hold the data that comes back from running the query contained in the variable *wmiQuery* when you use the *ExecQuery* method. This line of code looks like the following:

```
Set colItems = objWMIService.ExecQuery(wmiQuery)
```

9. Create an empty *For Each...Next* statement. Use *objItem* as your placeholder, and use *colItems* as the collection to be iterated through. This will look like the following:

```
For Each objItem In colItems

Next
```

10. Open the \My Documents\Microsoft Press\VBScriptSBS\ch20\ StepByStep\ StarterFileForExchangeLogon.txt file. This file contains the series of *WScript.Echo* commands that goes inside the empty *For Each...Next* statement that was created in step 9.

11. Copy all the *WScript.Echo* commands contained in \My Documents\Microsoft Press\VBScriptSBS\ch20\StepByStep\ StarterFileForExchangeLogon.txt and paste them into the *For Each...Next* statement. When completed, the script will look like the following:

```
For Each objItem In colItems
  WScript.Echo "AdapterSpeed: " & objItem.AdapterSpeed
  WScript.Echo "Caption: " & objItem.Caption
  WScript.Echo "ClientIP: " & objItem.ClientIP
  WScript.Echo "ClientMode: " & objItem.ClientMode
  WScript.Echo "ClientName: " & objItem.ClientName
  WScript.Echo "ClientVersion: " & objItem.ClientVersion
  WScript.Echo "CodePageID: " & objItem.CodePageID
  WScript.Echo "Description: " & objItem.Description
  WScript.Echo "FolderOperationRate: " _
    & objItem.FolderOperationRate
  WScript.Echo "HostAddress: " & objItem.HostAddress
  WScript.Echo "InstallDate: " & objItem.InstallDate
  WScript.Echo "LastOperationTime: " & objItem.LastOperationTime
  WScript.Echo "Latency: " & objItem.Latency
  WScript.Echo "LocaleID: " & objItem.LocaleID
  WScript.Echo "LoggedOnUserAccount: " _
    & objItem.LoggedOnUserAccount
  WScript.Echo "LoggedOnUsersMailboxLegacyDN: "    & objItem.LoggedOnUsersMailboxLegacy
DN
  WScript.Echo "LogonTime: " & objItem.LogonTime
  WScript.Echo "MacAddress: " & objItem.MacAddress
  WScript.Echo "MailboxDisplayName: " & objItem.MailboxDisplayName
  WScript.Echo "MailboxLegacyDN: " & objItem.MailboxLegacyDN
  WScript.Echo "MessagingOperationRate: " _
    & objItem.MessagingOperationRate
  WScript.Echo "Name: " & objItem.Name
  WScript.Echo "OpenAttachmentCount: " _
    & objItem.OpenAttachmentCount
  WScript.Echo "OpenFolderCount: " & objItem.OpenFolderCount
  WScript.Echo "OpenMessageCount: " & objItem.OpenMessageCount
```

```
          WScript.Echo "OtherOperationRate: " & objItem.OtherOperationRate
          WScript.Echo "ProgressOperationRate: " _
            & objItem.ProgressOperationRate
          WScript.Echo "RowID: " & objItem.RowID
          WScript.Echo "RPCSucceeded: " & objItem.RPCSucceeded
          WScript.Echo "ServerName: " & objItem.ServerName
          WScript.Echo "Status: " & objItem.Status
          WScript.Echo "StorageGroupName: " & objItem.StorageGroupName
          WScript.Echo "StoreName: " & objItem.StoreName
          WScript.Echo "StoreType: " & objItem.StoreType
          WScript.Echo "StreamOperationRate: " _
            & objItem.StreamOperationRate
          WScript.Echo "TableOperationRate: " & objItem.TableOperationRate
          WScript.Echo "TotalOperationRate: " & objItem.TotalOperationRate
          WScript.Echo "TransferOperationRate: " _
            & objItem.TransferOperationRate
    WScript.Echo "-=-"
    Next
```

12. Save and run the script by using CScript. If it does not appear to provide the information you expect, compare it with \My Documents\Microsoft Press\VBScriptSBS\ch20\ StepByStep\ExchangeLogon.vbs.

One Step Further: Using the *Exchange_Mailbox* Class

In this section, you create a script that connects to the *MicrosoftExchangeV2* namespace and queries the *Exchange_Mailbox* class.

1. Open \My Documents\Microsoft Press\VBScriptSBS\Templates\BlankTemplate.vbs in Notepad or some other script editor and save it as YourNameExchangeMailbox.vbs.

2. As the first non-commented line in the new file, type **Option Explicit**.

3. You need to declare six variables: *strComputer*, *wmiNS*, *wmiQuery*, *objWMIService*, *colItems*, and *objItem*. In addition, add *On Error Resume Next*, but comment out the line during development. The completed Header information section of your script will look like the following:

```
Option Explicit
'On Error Resume Next
Dim strComputer
Dim wmiNS
Dim wmiQuery
Dim objWMIService
Dim colItems
Dim objItem
```

4. Use the variable *strComputer* to hold the string ".". This line of code will look like the following:

```
strComputer = "."
```

5. Use the variable *wmiNS* to hold the string "*root\MicrosoftExchangeV2*". This line of code looks like the following:

```
wmiNS = "\root\MicrosoftExchangeV2"
```

6. Use the *wmiQuery* variable to hold the string "*Select * from Exchange_Mailbox*". This line of code looks like the following:

```
wmiQuery = "Select * from Exchange_Mailbox"
```

7. Set the variable *objWMIService* to be equal to the object that comes back from using the *GetObject* command into WMI. Use the *winmgmts* moniker, specify *strComputer* as the target computer, and specify *wmiNS* as the target namespace. This line of code looks like the following:

```
Set objWMIService = GetObject("winmgmts:\\" & strComputer & wmiNS)
```

8. Set the *colItems* variable to hold the data that comes back from running the query contained in the variable *wmiQuery* when you use the *ExecQuery* method. This line of code looks like the following:

```
Set colItems = objWMIService.ExecQuery(wmiQuery)
```

9. Create an empty *For Each...Next* statement. Use *objItem* as your placeholder and use *colItems* as the collection to be iterated through. This will look like the following:

```
For Each objItem In colItems

Next
```

10. Open the \My Documents\Microsoft Press\VBScriptSBS\ch20\OneStepFurther\StarterFileForExchangeMailBox.txtfile file. This file contains the series of *WScript.Echo* commands that goes inside the empty *For Each...Next* statement that was created in step 9.

11. Copy all the *WScript.Echo* commands contained in \My Documents\Microsoft Press\VBScriptSBS\ch20\OneStepFurther\ StarterFileForExchangeMailBox.txt and paste them into the *For Each...Next* statement. When completed, the script will look like the following:

```
For Each objItem In colItems
  WScript.Echo "AssocContentCount: " & objItem.AssocContentCount
  WScript.Echo "Caption: " & objItem.Caption
  WScript.Echo "DateDiscoveredAbsentInDS: " _
    & objItem.DateDiscoveredAbsentInDS
  WScript.Echo "DeletedMessageSizeExtended: " _
    & objItem.DeletedMessageSizeExtended
  WScript.Echo "Description: " & objItem.Description
  WScript.Echo "InstallDate: " & objItem.InstallDate
  WScript.Echo "LastLoggedOnUserAccount: " _
    & objItem.LastLoggedOnUserAccount
  WScript.Echo "LastLogoffTime: " & objItem.LastLogoffTime
  WScript.Echo "LastLogonTime: " & objItem.LastLogonTime
  WScript.Echo "LegacyDN: " & objItem.LegacyDN
  WScript.Echo "MailboxDisplayName: " & objItem.MailboxDisplayName
```

```
WScript.Echo "MailboxGUID: " & objItem.MailboxGUID
WScript.Echo "Name: " & objItem.Name
WScript.Echo "ServerName: " & objItem.ServerName
WScript.Echo "Size: " & objItem.Size
WScript.Echo "Status: " & objItem.Status
WScript.Echo "StorageGroupName: " & objItem.StorageGroupName
WScript.Echo "StorageLimitInfo: " & objItem.StorageLimitInfo
WScript.Echo "StoreName: " & objItem.StoreName
WScript.Echo "TotalItems: " & objItem.TotalItems
WScript.Echo "-=-"
Next
```

12. Save and run your script using CScript. If the script has problems, compare your script to \My Documents\Microsoft Press\VBScriptSBS\ch20\OneStepFurther\ ExchangeMailbox.vbs.

Chapter 20 Quick Reference

To	Do This
Manage and monitor Exchange 2003 using WMI	Use the classes found in the *MicrosoftExhangeV2* namespace
Connect to the *MicrosoftExchangeV2* namespace	Use *GetObject* and the WMI moniker; also specify the target computer and the *root\MicrosoftExchangeV2* namespace
Obtain information about Exchange 2003 public folders	Query the *Exchange_PublicFolder* class in the *root\MicrosoftExchangeV2* namespace

Troubleshooting WMI Scripting

Before You Begin

To work through the material presented in this chapter, you need to be familiar with the following concepts from earlier chapters:

- The basics of working with Microsoft Windows Management Instrumentation (WMI) namespaces
- The basics of writing a WMI script, connecting to namespaces, and retrieving class information

After completing this chapter, you will be able to:

- Understand the services involved in making WMI work
- Recognize dependencies that must be met for WMI to work
- Evaluate symptoms of a corrupt database
- Understand common methods of recovering from problems with WMI

Identifying the Problem

WMI is one of those services that simply work. Most people never have to troubleshoot WMI; in fact, many network administrators do not even know WMI exists, or that their sophisticated monitoring and tracking application relies heavily upon the services of WMI. For many, the only time they even begin to learn anything at all about WMI is when a critical application "all of a sudden quits." This is, unfortunately, the wrong time to begin to learn about WMI and more importantly how to troubleshoot WMI.

Spotting Common Sources of Errors

If you were going to see a WMI error, what kind of error would it be? Or put another way, what are some of the most common types of WMI errors? In general, problems with WMI end up in one of four categories. These four groups of errors are listed below:

- WMI database corruption
- Distributed Component Object Model (DCOM) security issues
- Provider security issues

■   Firewall issues

That is basically it. Those are 90 percent of all the WMI support calls that our Premier Support Services (PSS) support professionals work with. The other 10 percent are really strange, esoteric, downright exotic problems. We will therefore focus on the four issues that cause 90 percent of the problems.

Testing the Local WMI Service

The first thing that must be done when troubleshooting WMI is to test the local WMI service to see if it is in fact responding to requests. In fact, many problems that at first appear to be WMI-related are not WMI problems at all. It is important to see if WMI is actually working, or if it is corrupt, or the service is hung. The application that is using WMI could have a problem, or the script you are trying to run could have an issue. Two utilities can be used to easily, reliably, and effectively test WMI. These two utilities will not tell you specifically where you have a problem with WMI, but they will let you know whether WMI appears to be working. If these two tools do not work, you really do have a problem that bears further investigation. The first utility is the WMI Control tool. The second tool we may want to use to test WMI is the Windows Management Instrumentation Tester.

Using the WMI Control Tool

The most basic check you can make to see if WMI is working properly is to open the WMI Control tool and see if it will connect. If it will not connect to the local instance of WMI running on your machine, you have a symptom of some more serious problems with WMI. If it does connect, it does not mean no problem exists; rather, at least some things are working correctly. This is the easiest check to make, and it should be the first step in troubleshooting. If the WMI service does not have the appropriate configuration, the connection will fail.

If the connection with the WMI Control tool succeeds, the panel seen in Figure 21-1 will appear. On the General tab, you will see the operating system (OS) version build number, service pack version, and the WMI version. In Windows XP and in Windows Server 2003, the OS version number and the WMI version number should match. In Windows 2000, the version of WMI is 1085.0005. The other information that is important from this tab is the WMI location, which should be in *%systemroot%*\system32\WBEM (in most cases, *%systemroot%* will be reported as C:\WINDOWS, as seen in Figure 21-1).

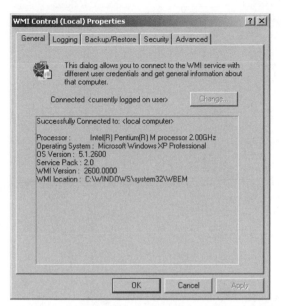

Figure 21-1   WMI general troubleshooting information

Paying Attention to Dependencies

By examining service dependencies, we can also obtain an indicator as to the health of the WMI service. This is important to the troubleshooting process. I have seen cases when someone thought they had a WMI problem and uninstalled the WMI service, or deleted the WMI database to rebuild it, and these actions did not solve the "WMI problem." Although not definitive, the state of a dependant service can provide a clue to the health of WMI.

If the WMI service is not running, several other services will not function either. The Security Center, System Management Software (SMS) Agent Host, and Windows Firewall are some of the services that depend on WMI. These service dependencies can be found in the Services tool, as seen in Figure 21-2. This means several errors should be in the Windows system event log, which indicates service failures.

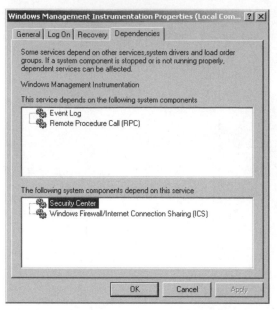

Figure 21-2   Many services depend on WMI

Using the Scriptomatic

The Scriptomatic is a tool created by the Microsoft Scripting Guys. It can be useful from a troubleshooting perspective. The Scriptomatic will connect to any WMI namespace and list all the classes in the namespace. (The Scriptomatic is available from \My Documents\Microsoft Press\VBScriptSBS\ Resources\ScriptomaticV2.hta.) When you choose the class, it will generate a Microsoft Visual Basic, Scripting Edition (VBScript) file listing all the properties of the class. You can then run the script from inside the ScriptoMatic. If properties are listed or if the script that is generated does not produce any output when run, you may have a problem with WMI.

Examining the Status of the WMI Service

If the WMI Control tool cannot make a local connection, you should check to see if the WMI service is running. The easy way to do this is:

1. Start a new instance of the command interpreter, Cmd.exe.

2. Type **net start**.

3. Near the bottom of the list, look for *Windows Management Instrumentation*.

If *Windows Management Instrumentation* appears in the list, it is started. If it does not appear, it is not running. This would be rather strange, because the WMI service should restart itself if it stops or is stopped. The recovery setting for WMI is set to restart the service on the first and on subsequent failures. The recovery interval is set to one minute. If the WMI service fails, Service Recover will attempt a restart of the service every minute.

The next step in looking at the WMI service is to examine the service settings. To do this, we will use the Services tool. The following steps will walk you through using this tool:

1. Click Start and then click Run.

2. In the Run dialog box, type **Services.msc** and press OK.

3. Scroll down the list until you find Windows Management Instrumentation. Double-click it.

4. Select the Log On tab. Under Log On As, Local System Account should be checked. Allow Service To Interact With Desktop should be unchecked.

5. Select the Recovery tab. Under Select The Computer's Response If This Service Fails, the first failure, second failure, and subsequent failures should all read Restart The Service. Reset Fail Count After should read 1 Days, and Restart Service After should read 1 Minutes. This is illustrated in Figure 21-3.

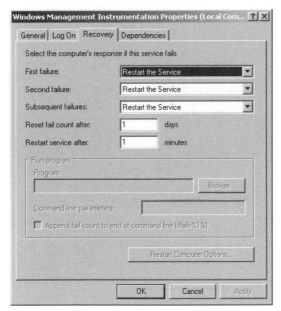

Figure 21-3   Use the Services tool to inspect and correct recovery settings

Using WBEMtest.exe

The Windows Management Instrumentation Tester can be used to troubleshoot WMI. In addition to just checking to see if WMI is actually running and accepting connections (as the WMI Control tool does), WBEMtest can be used to test the functionality of nearly every aspect of WMI, including security. One thing to keep in mind when using WBEMtest is that it cannot be used to specify alternate credentials for a local connection. To test alternate credentials, you must make a remote connection. In effect, WBEMtest is using the *SWbemLocator* method to supply alternate credentials, and SwbemLocator does not permit supplying alternate credentials for a local connection.

Quick Check

Q. **What is the easiest way to see if WMI is really broken?**

A. The easiest way to see if WMI is really broken is to open the WMI Control tool. If it makes a connection to WMI, then WMI is not totally broken—there may be other problems, but WMI is not completely broken. On the other hand, if the WMI Control tool is not able to connect, you have a problem.

Q. **Why is WBEMtest unable to permit you to make a local connection into WMI using alternative credentials?**

A. The reason WBEMtest will not permit you to make a local connection into WMI using alternative credentials is that WMI itself does not permit it.

Testing Remote WMI Service

WMI is already set up to run remotely. We use essentially the same procedures for testing the remote WMI service as we use when working locally. In the initial stages of testing the ability of WMI to respond to remote requests, the tools and the procedures are very similar.

Remotely Using the WMI Control Tool

The first tool to use will be the WMI Control tool. We must make sure we start it in the correct manner, or else the "remote" function of the tool will not be available. The following steps illustrate using the WMI Control tool to make a remote connection.

1. Click Start and then click Run.

2. Type **wmimgmt.msc** in the Run dialog box and click OK.

3. Right-click WMI Control (Local).

4. Select Connect To Another Computer... .

5. Select another computer and enter the remote computer name.

6. If needed, click Change to provide user credentials.

7. Click OK.

8. Right-click WMI Control (Remote System Name).

9. Select Properties.

If you are not able to make a remote connection with the WMI Control tool, then you need to ensure you have checked WMI locally on each machine. If you have checked both machines locally, the next steps you want to do are listed below:

1. Check connectivity.

2. Check firewall issues.

3. Check rights/permissions.

4. Check DCOM settings.

Testing Scripting Interface

After we have checked for local and for remote WMI functionality, we may need to test the scripting interface. To do this, we will need to check both the core WMI provider and the provider host interface. We can use a script to do this. In the RetrieveWMISettings.vbs script, we use the *connectServer* method from the *SWbemLocator* object. The reason for doing this is the *SWbemLocator* object is already set up for us to specify alternative connections on a remote computer. This will allow a fuller range of tests. We connect to the *WIN32_WMISetting* class. There is only one instance of the *WIN32_WMISetting* class. We can use the ampersand to enable us to get the one instance of the *WIN32_WMISetting* class that represents the WMI settings for the computer. After we have executed our query, we use the *GetObjectText_* method, which will retrieve all the properties in the class as well as the values assigned to those properties. The output text will be in Managed Object Format (MOF) format. The MOF format provides an easy way to create and register items into the WMI repository. We cannot specify any modifiers for this method. The input flag is optional. If you choose to specify the input flag, you must supply a zero, because 0 is the only allowed value for this flag. Specifying the input flag will not change the way the method operates, so we leave it off in the RetrieveWMISettings.vbs script. The Header information section of the script is left out for clarity purposes.

RetrieveWMISettings.vbs

```
strComputer = "."
wmiNS = "\root\cimv2"
wmiQuery = "Win32_WMISetting=@"
strUsr =""'Blank for current security. Domain\Username
strPWD = ""'Blank for current security.
strLocl = "MS_409" 'US English. Can leave blank for current language
strAuth = ""'If specify domain in strUsr this must be blank
iFlag = "0" 'Only two values allowed here: 0 (wait for connection) 128 (wait max two min)

Set objLocator = CreateObject("WbemScripting.SWbemLocator")
Set objWMIService = objLocator.ConnectServer(strComputer, _
 wmiNS, strUsr, strPWD, strLocl, strAuth, iFLag)
Set objItem = objWMIService.get(wmiQuery)

WScript.Echo objItem.GetObjectText_
```

If the RetrieveWMISettings.vbs script works, you have successfully tested the core WMI functionality. You have not, however, tested other WMI providers, only the WbemCore provider. The RetrieveComputerSystem.vbs script uses the *WIN32_ComputerSystem class*. The *WIN32_ComputerSystem* class relies on the CIMWin32 provider, and a query to this class will exercise an extremely important WMI provider. We specify the name of the computer in the *strComputer* variable, but because we want to use the *Get* method, we need to specify a particular instance of the *WIN32_ComputerSystem* class, which happens to be the local machine. When we use the WMI moniker to make a WMI connection, we do not supply the computer name in single quotation marks. We contain it in a variable called *strComputer,* which is delimited by double quotation marks. When we supply a computer name for the Key Name property of the *WIN32_ComputerSystem* class, WMI wants the computer name to be embedded inside single quotation marks. The use of quotation marks when supplying values to WMI is not consistent. At times numbers do not need quotation marks, but strings do. It is best to use quotation marks, and if it fails, then remove them. To use a single variable for these two uses, which have different requirements, we devised the simple *funFix* function and included it at the bottom of the script. All it does is take the string that is supplied to it, append a single quotation mark as both a prefix and as a suffix, and assign the resultant string to the function name. This allows dual use of the same variable name.

RetrieveComputerSystem.vbs

```
strComputer = "London" 'name of the target computer system
wmiNS = "\root\cimv2"
wmiQuery = "win32_ComputerSystem.name=" & funFix(strComputer)
Set objWMIService = GetObject("winmgmts:\\" & strComputer & wmiNS)
Set objItem = objWMIService.get(wmiQuery)

  Wscript.Echo myFun(wmiQuery) & objItem.getObjectText_

Function myFun(input)
Dim lstr
lstr = Len(input)
myFun = input & vbcrlf & string(lstr,"=")
End Function

Function funFix(strIN) 'computer name needs single '
funFix = "'" & strIN & "'"
End function
```

Obtaining Diagnostic Information

If the previously discussed checks do not point to an immediate solution, the next step is to obtain more information. To do this, you have several tools at your disposal. The primary source of troubleshooting information is WMI logging. By changing the logging level to Verbose, you will generate a diagnostic trace of WMI events in several WMI logs.

Enabling Verbose WMI Logging

WMI has three logging levels: Disabled, Errors Only, and Verbose. These logging levels are recorded in the registry at the following location:

HKEY_LOCAL_MACHINE\SOFTWARE\Microsoft\WBEM\CIMOM\Logging

A value of *0* disables all logging, a *1* will enable errors only logging, and a value of *2* will set the logging to Verbose.

These logging levels can be set using the WMI Control tool. As seen in Figure 21-4, the logging levels are displayed on the Logging tab—the same tool used to increase or decrease the logging level. After the WMI problem is solved, it is important that you reduce the logging level back to Errors Only, or the increased logging activity could cause performance problems for WMI and for all applications that rely upon its services. To increase the logging level, follow the steps listed below:

1.   Click Start and then click Run.

2.   In the Run dialog box, type **wmimgmt.msc** and click OK.

3.   Right-click WMI Control (Local).

4.   Select Properties.

5.   Select the Logging tab.

6.   Change Logging Level to Verbose.

7.   Increase the maximum log size to 256,000 or higher.

8.   Click OK and close the Microsoft Management Console (MMC).

Increasing the logging level will take effect immediately in Windows XP and on Windows Server 2003. Earlier versions of Windows will require a reboot.

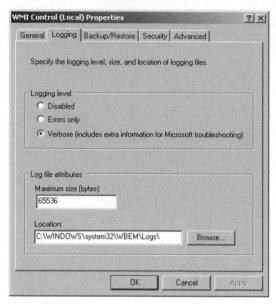

Figure 21-4   Verbose logging is a primary source of troubleshooting information

Examining the WMI Log Files

The WMI log files are stored in the *%systemroot%*\system32\WBEM\Logs\ directory by default. This is configurable from the Logging tab, as seen in Figure 21-4. In addition, the WMI log file directory is recorded in the registry at the following location:

HKEY_LOCAL_MACHINE\SOFTWARE\Microsoft\WBEM\CIMOM\Logging Directory

If you open the Logs directory, you will find a number of WMI logs. One of the challenges in troubleshooting WMI is to select the correct log file in which to look for the correct information that is needed to troubleshoot the problem at hand. Table 21-1 provides a quick listing of the most common WMI log files, as well as the purpose of each file.

Table 21-1   WMI log files and their usage

Log File	Purpose
Dsprovider.log	Traces information and error messages for the Directory Services provider
Framework.log	Traces information and error messages for the provider framework and the Win32 provider
MofComp.log	Compiles details from the MOF compiler, including MofComp failures during setup
Ntevt.log	Traces messages from the Event Log provider
Setup.log	Reports on MOF files that failed to load during the setup process
Viewprovider.log	Traces information from the View provider

Table 21-1   WMI log files and their usage

Log File	Purpose
WbemCore.log	Provides logging from the WbemCore provider
Wbemess.log	Logs entries related to events
Wbemprox.log	Traces information for the WMI proxy server; remote logons
Winmgmt.log	Traces information that is typically not used for diagnostics
Wmiadap.log	Provides error messages related to the AutoDiscoveryAutoPurge (ADAP) process
Wmiprov.log	Provides management data and events from WMI-enabled Windows Driver Model (WDM) drivers; hardware

Your computer system may or may not have all these log files. Some of the providers will have their own procedure for configuring logging levels. For example, the View provider requires adding a registry key to the following location:

```
HKEY_LOCAL_MACHINE \SOFTWARE\Microsoft\WBEM\
PROVIDERS\Logging\ViewProvider\Level
```

Once the registry key is added, you use the same *0, 1,* and *2* values to configure no logging, error only logging, or verbose logging respectively. This works in the same way as setting the overall WMI logging level.

The key WMI log files that you will probably use the most are listed below:

- WbemCore.log
- MofComp.log
- Wbemprox.log

> **Tip**   Use the date. When I am troubleshooting a WMI issue, once I bump up the diagnostic logging, the next thing I do is try to reproduce the problem. If I am successful in reproducing the problem, I will note the time, open the WMI logging directory, and sort by time. Sometimes, if I am lucky, I will find a log file with a time stamp that is very nearly the time I noted when I was able to reproduce the error. I also like to use the VBScript *Now* function in my script that is generating the error, because it will give me a time stamp I can refer back to when I am analyzing a diagnostic log file. If you follow this simple procedure, you can easily eliminate more than half of the WMI log files in your troubleshooting due to the fact they were not updated around the same time that you reproduced the error.

Using the Err Tool

As you look through the WMI log files, you will quickly see that they are filled with strange numbers. The Err.exe tool is sometimes called the Exchange Server Error Code Look-Up Tool, but it is much more than that. It pulls error codes from header files installed on your computer. On my Windows XP computer at home, it can supply information on nearly 20,000 error messages that come from more than 170 different sources–and I don't even have Microsoft's Exchange server installed at home! The Err.exe tool can be downloaded for free from the Microsoft Download center at *http://www.microsoft.com/downloads*. If you do a search for Exchange Server Error Code, the Err.exe tool will be the only item returned. We will use the Err tool in the Step-by-Step exercise while troubleshooting some WMI script problems. The Err tool is a single executable and does not need installation. This means it can easily be copied to any machine. To use the Err tool, type **err** at a command prompt (ensuring it is in the path) and supply an error number. An example of this is seen below:

```
C:\Utils>err 0x80041003
```

The tool will return every match it has for the error number. You may get only one item or you may get many, depending on the error number. You should always look for a source that is related to what you are troubleshooting. In the output below, we see there are two sources that generate an 0x80041003 error. But because we are troubleshooting a WMI problem, we choose the meaning Access Denied, because it is generated from wbemcli.h. We choose this meaning from the Err.exe output because wbemcli looks similar to wbem client–which sounds like an application that is using WMI.

```
# for hex 0x80041003 / decimal -2147217405 :
  REC_E_TOODIFFERENT              reconcil.h
  WBEM_E_ACCESS_DENIED            wbemcli.h
# 2 matches found for "0x80041003"
```

Using MofComp.exe

MofComp.exe is a tool that is used to compile MOF files. We will use MofComp in the One Step Further exercise. There are basically two times when you will need to use MofComp. If you have a MOF file you need in WMI, you will need to run MofComp to add the MOF to the repository. You would use MofComp in these situations to add additional functionality to WMI. Some applications do not register themselves with WMI for autorecovery, and if you ever delete the repository, you will need to recompile those MOFs back into WMI after rebuilding the repository. In either case, the syntax is the same. If we look at the number of switches available for MofComp, it looks like a rather complicated tool. This is seen below:

```
Microsoft (R) 32-bit MOF Compiler Version 5.1.2600.2180
Copyright (c) Microsoft Corp. 1997-2001. All rights reserved.

usage: mofcomp [-check] [-N:<Path>]
        [-class:updateonly|-class:createonly]
        [-instance:updateonly|-instance:createonly]
        [-B:<filename>] [-P:<Password>] [-U:<UserName>]
        [-A:<Authority>] [-WMI] [-AUTORECOVER]
        [-MOF:<path>] [-MFL:<path>] [-AMENDMENT:<Locale>]
        [-ER:<ResourceName>] [-L:<ResourceLocale>]
        <MOF filename>

  -check          Syntax check only
```

```
-N:<path>            Load into this namespace by default
-class:updateonly    Do not create new classes
-class:safeupdate    Update unless conflicts exist
-class:forceupdate   Update resolving conflicts if possible
-class:createonly    Do not change existing classes
-instance:updateonly  Do not create new instances
-instance:createonly  Do not change existing instances
-U:<UserName>        User Name
-P:<Password>        Login password
-A:<Authority>       Example: NTLMDOMAIN:Domain
-B:<destination filename> Creates a binary MOF file, does not add to DB
-WMI            Do Windows Driver Model (WDM) checks, requires -B switch
-AUTORECOVER        Adds MOF to list of files compiled during DB recovery
-Amendment:<LOCALE>     splits MOF into language neutral and specific versions
           where locale is of the form "MS_4??"
-MOF:<path>          name of the language neutral output
-MFL:<path>          name of the language specific output
-ER:<ResourceName>     extracts binary mof from named resource
-L:<ResourceLocale>     optional specific locale number when using -ER switch

Example c:>mofcomp -N:root\default yourmof.mof
```

Most of the time, you will not need any of these switches. In its most basic form, the MOF file tells WMI where to compile the class, namespace, or instance of an event provider. Using MofComp in this fashion only requires that you type **mofcomp mymof.mof** with no switches. Of course, mymof.mof would need to be the name of the MOF file you were trying to compile. The next most common MofComp command is one where you need to specify the namespace into which the MOF will be compiled. This is illustrated below:

```
C:\mofcomp -N:root\myNameSpace myMofFile.mof
```

Using WMIcheck

WMIcheck.exe is a tool that was developed by Microsoft Premier Support Services to aid in quickly gathering all the information needed to perform initial troubleshooting of WMI configuration problems. The amount of information supplied by this tool can save you hours of information gathering. It is included in the \My Documents\Microsoft Press\VBScriptSBS\Resources folder on the CD accompanying this book. To use the WMIcheck.exe tool, you open a command prompt and type the following command:

```
C:\>wmicheck >wmiCheck.txt
```

Open the WMIcheck.txt file that is produced by running the WMIcheck.exe program, in Microsoft Notepad. Some of the items reported by this program are listed below:

- Registry settings for WMI, including default namespace, logging levels, and log file sizes

- Operating system version and service pack level

- Software installed on the computer

- Services and processes running on the computer
- A listing of namespaces, providers, and event filters defined on the computer

General WMI Troubleshooting Steps

If you determine that WMI does in fact have a problem, you must consider several issues. These are detailed below:

- **DCOM security**   WMI uses DCOM. Changes in DCOM security settings will prevent WMI from working properly.

- **Service settings**   The Windows Management Instrumentation service must be running for WMI to work. If this service is disabled, WMI will not work. The Windows Management Instrumentation service must log on with local system privileges. If this account is changed, WMI will not have the permissions needed to operate properly.

- **Module registration**   The basic WMI service is robust. Due to the flexible nature of WMI, many software vendors use it to provide management of everything from applications to hardware monitoring. These classes often require special modules to be registered. The WMI Check tool can be used to report on the state of these modules. If the application is not working, and the modules are not registered, the application may need to be re-installed. At a minimum, the modules will need to be registered.

- **Rebuild WBEM repository**   Rebuilding the WMI repository should be the last step—not the first step—in troubleshooting WMI. It is easy to do so. You stop the WMI service, delete the database, and restart the database. But if it does not fix the problem, what do you do? Make sure you have a backup of the WMI database prior to deleting the database. If rebuilding does not solve the problem, and you have custom settings, you can always perform a restoration.

Quick Check

Q. **What are two tools you can use to see if WMI is accepting connections?**

A. The two tools you can use to see if WMI is accepting connections are the WMI Control tool and WBEMtest.exe.

Q. **If you want to produce a list of WMI classes in a namespace, choose a class, and see a sample WMI script produced that you can run to test WMI with, what tool would you use?**

A. If you need to produce a list of WMI classes in a namespace, choose a class, and see a sample WMI script produced that you can run to test WMI with, you would use the Scriptomatic.

Q. **If you want to test user credentials for a WMI connection on a remote computer, which tool can you use?**

A. If you need to test user credentials for a WMI connection on a remote computer, you can use WBEMtest.exe.

Q.   **If you receive a strange error number in the event log and you need to look up the meaning quickly and easily, what tool can you use?**

A.   If you receive a strange error number in the event log and you need to look up the meaning quickly and easily, you can use the Err.exe tool to translate the number into something more meaningful.

Q.   **If you need to compile a MOF file into the repository, what tool can you use?**

A.   If you need to compile a MOF file into the repository, use MofComp.exe.

Working with Logging Step-by-Step Exercises

In this section, we will use WMI logging capabilities to assist in troubleshooting a scripting problem. To do this, we will increase the logging level to Verbose and run two scripts that have a few problems in them. We will conclude the exercise by running a good script and comparing the information that is logged from this script with the results from the bad scripts.

1.   Increase the WMI logging level. Click Start and then click Run.

2.   In Open dialog box, type **wmimgmt.msc** and then click OK.

3.   Right-click WMI Control (Local).

4.   Select Properties.

5.   Select the Logging tab.

6.   Change the logging level to Verbose.

7.   Increase the maximum log size to 256,000 or more.

8.   Click OK and close the MMC.

9.   Open the WMI logging directory in Windows Explorer. The directory is listed below:

    `C:\WINDOWS\system32\wbem\Logs`

10.   Sort the file view by date. You can do this by clicking the Date Modified tab at the top of the Date column. Ensure that the most recent dates are on the top.

11.   Open the \My Documents\Microsoft Press\VBScriptSBS\ch21\StepByStep\ BadScript1.vbs script and run it. (Don't worry, it will not break anything.) Do not close the script output window. You will need the time stamp that is returned from the *Now* function.

12.   When the script completes, make a note of the exact date and time the script completed.

13.   Go to the WMI log file directory and press the F5 function key to refresh the view of the file dates. Examine the file dates closely. Do you see any that match (or are very close) to the time stamp that was produced by running BadScript1.vbs? You should see at least three files with time stamps very near the time indicated by the running of the

BadScript1.vbs file. The three files should be WinMgmt.log, Wbemprox.log, and WbemCore.log.

14. If you do not see any recent files with a recent date modified time stamp, you can refresh the folder view by pressing F5. If you still do not see any log files with a date modified time stamp close to the one resulting from running BadScript1.vbs, then go back and double-check to ensure the Verbose WMI logging level is properly set. If you are using an operating system earlier than Windows XP, you will need to restart the WMI service for the logging level change to take effect. Windows XP and Windows Server 2003 dynamically apply the changes.

15. Once you have found the log files, open WinMgmt.log with Notepad and scroll to the bottom of the file. Look for the time stamp that matches (or at least is within a few seconds of) the time produced by BadScript1.vbs. You will see some errors that look similar to the following:

```
(Sat Jul 30 06:41:16 2005.36668000) : Got a provider can unload event
(Sat Jul 30 06:41:46 2005.36698000) : Got a TIMEOUT work item
(Sat Jul 30 06:41:46 2005.36698000) : Got a FinalCoreShutdown work item
(Sat Jul 30 06:41:59 2005.36710921) : CForwardFactory::CreateInstance
(Sat Jul 30 06:42:01 2005.36713000) : Got a provider can unload event
```

16. Open the Wbemprox.log file with Notepad and scroll to the bottom of the file. Again look for the time stamp. You will see some errors that look like the following:

```
(Sat Jul 30 06:41:59 2005.36710921) : Using the principal -RPCSS/
Acapulco.NWTraders.MSFT-
(Sat Jul 30 06:41:59 2005.36710921) : ConnectViaDCOM, CoCreateInstanceEx resulted in h
r = 0x0
(Sat Jul 30 06:41:59 2005.36710921) : NTLMLogin resulted in hr = 0x8004100e
```

17. Once you find the *NTLMLogin resulted in* line, note that it says *hr = 0x8004100e*. This is the result code that is returned from trying to connect to WMI. If we look up the error 0x8004100e using the Err.exe tool, we might be able to find more information. The Err.exe tool does not provide answers to all error codes, but if the error is in the WMI files, the tool should find a match.

18. Open up a command prompt and change to the directory where you have the Err.exe tool installed. Type the following command:

```
Err 0x8004100e
```

19. Examine the output from the Err tool. The output looks like the following:

```
C:\Utils>err 0x8004100e
# for hex 0x8004100e / decimal -2147217394 :
  WBEM_E_INVALID_NAMESPACE                    wbemcli.h
# 1 matches found for "0x8004100e"
```

From the output we can see that part of the problem is related to an invalid namespace.

20. Open the WbemCore.log file and find the time stamp that is close in time to when you ran BadScript1.vbs. You will find an entry that looks similar to the one listed below:

```
Sat Jul 30 06:41:59 2005.36710921) : CALL ConnectionLogin::NTLMLogin
  wszNetworkResource = \\.\root\cimv1
  pPreferredLocale = (null)
  lFlags = 0x0
(Sat Jul 30 06:41:59 2005.36710921) : DCOM connection from NWtraders\LondonAdmin at au
thentiction level Privacy, AuthnSvc = 10, AuthzSvc = 0, Capabilities = 0
(Sat Jul 30 06:42:01 2005.36713000) : + DllCanUnloadNow()
(Sat Jul 30 06:42:01 2005.36713000) : - DllCanUnloadNow() S_FALSE
(Sat Jul 30 06:42:01 2005.36713000) : + DllCanUnloadNow()
(Sat Jul 30 06:42:01 2005.36713000) : - DllCanUnloadNow() S_FALSE
```

From examining the output, can you determine the problem with the script? Can you see the reason for the failed login reported in the Wbemprox.log file? Do you see why the error that was reported was invalid namespace? The namespace is specified as root\cimv1. WMI is unable to authenticate a user against a WMI namespace that does not exist.

21. Run the BadScript2.vbs script. Retain the time stamp from the script.

22. Open the WinMgmt.log file and locate the time that is closest to the time stamp retrieved from running BadScript2.vbs. The error messages should be near the bottom of the script. Compare the results from BadScript1.vbs in the WinMgmt.log file with the results from BadScript2.vbs. What is the difference between the two results? The BadScript2.vbs script should not record any errors in the WinMgmt.log file. The entry from BadScript2.vbs should look like the following:

```
(Sat Jul 30 07:39:35 2005.40167562) : CForwardFactory::CreateInstance
```

23. Open Wbemprox.log and locate the entries closest in time to the time stamp retrieved from BadScript2.vbs. The entries should be near the bottom of the file.

24. Do you find any errors listed in the Wbemprox.log file? No.

25. Compare the results in Wbemprox.log from BadScript2.vbs to the results generated by BadScript1.vbs. Are there any differences? Yes. The following line was generated by BadScript1.vbs, but not generated by BadScript2.vbs:

```
(Sat Jul 30 06:41:59 2005.36710921) : NTLMLogin resulted in hr = 0x8004100e
```

26. What does the absence of an error here mean? It indicates that the NTLMLogin operation succeeded. The connection to root\cimv2 was successful.

27. Open the WbemCore.log file and find the time stamp from the BadScript2.vbs run. It should be near the bottom. Compare the results from running BadScript2.vbs to the results from running BadScript1.vbs in the log file. Notice there are far more entries in the log file. You should find entries that look similar to the following:

```
(Sat Jul 30 07:39:35 2005.40167562) : CALL ConnectionLogin::NTLMLogin
  wszNetworkResource = \\.\root\cimv2
  pPreferredLocale = (null)
```

```
    lFlags = 0x0
(Sat Jul 30 07:39:35 2005.40167562) : DCOM connection from NWTRADERS\LondonAdmin at au
thentiction level Privacy, AuthnSvc = 10, AuthzSvc = 0, Capabilities = 0
(Sat Jul 30 07:39:35 2005.40167562) : CALL CWbemNamespace::ExecQuery
    BSTR QueryFormat = WQL
    BSTR Query = Select * from win32_Processer
    IEnumWbemClassObject **pEnum = 0x28FD0C8
(Sat Jul 30 07:39:35 2005.40167562) : CALL CWbemNamespace::ExecQueryAsync
    BSTR QueryFormat = WQL
    BSTR Query = Select * from win32_Processer
    IwbemObjectSink* pHandler = 0x0
(Sat Jul 30 07:39:35 2005.40167562) : STARTING a main queue thread 548 for a total of
1
(Sat Jul 30 07:39:35 2005.40167578) : CALL CWbemNamespace::ExecQuery
    BSTR QueryFormat = Wql
    BSTR Query = Select * from __ClassProviderRegistration
    IEnumWbemClassObject **pEnum = 0xF7F9C0
(Sat Jul 30 07:39:35 2005.40167578) : CALL CWbemNamespace::ExecQueryAsync
    BSTR QueryFormat = Wql
    BSTR Query = Select * from __ClassProviderRegistration
    IwbemObjectSink* pHandler = 0x0
(Sat Jul 30 07:39:35 2005.40167578) : STARTING a main queue thread 2032 for a total of
 2
(Sat Jul 30 07:39:47 2005.40179578) : STOPPING a main queue thread 548 for a total of
1
(Sat Jul 30 07:39:47 2005.40179578) : STOPPING a main queue thread 2032 for a total of
 0
```

In examining the log file, were we able to parse a WQL query? Yes. This is indicated by the following line in the log file:

```
(Sat Jul 30 07:39:35 2005.40167562) : CALL CWbemNamespace::ExecQuery
    BSTR QueryFormat = WQL
    BSTR Query = Select * from win32_Processer
    IEnumWbemClassObject **pEnum = 0x28FD0C8
```

28. Did BadScript1.vbs succeed in parsing a WQL query? No. There is no entry similar to the one above listed in WbemCore.log around the time the BadScript1.vbs script ran.

29. After the query is parsed, it now tries to find the class that is referenced in the query. Locate the entries that try to identify the class provider. The entries will look like the following:

```
(Sat Jul 30 07:39:35 2005.40167578) : CALL CWbemNamespace::ExecQuery
    BSTR QueryFormat = Wql
    BSTR Query = Select * from __ClassProviderRegistration
    IEnumWbemClassObject **pEnum = 0xF7F9C0
```

30. Examine the WbemCore.log file. Did the query for the class provider succeed? No. There is no indication in the log file that the query succeeded. The next entry in the log indicates the main thread queue stops, this is a normal log file entry, and it indicates WMI has finished processing the request. This is seen below:

```
(Sat Jul 30 07:39:47 2005.40179578) : STOPPING a main queue thread 548 for a total of
1
```

31. To compare our results from bad scripts with the results of a good script, run the GoodScript1.vbs script. Pay attention to the script complete time stamp.

32. Open Winmgmt.log and find the time stamp from running GoodScript1.vbs. Compare your results from running GoodScript1.vbs with the results from running BadScript2.vbs. They are similar.

33. Open Wbemprox.log and find the time stamp from running GoodScript1.vbs. Compare the results from running BadScript2.vbs. They are similar. This indicates that both BadScript2.vbs and GoodScript1.vbs were able to make a connection into WMI and have the query parsed.

34. Open WbemCore.log and compare the results from running BadScript2.vbs and the results from running GoodScript1.vbs. What do you notice? There are far more entries from GoodScript1.vbs. Why is this the case? The good script ran to completion. You may notice some errors in the log files, but these are not necessarily related to GoodScript1.vbs. WMI is used for many activities and there could be other processes logging at the same time. If you are having trouble locating the logging from your script, you can look at \My Documents\Microsoft Press\VBScriptSBS\ch21\StepByStep \GoodScript1Events.txt.

35. Can you identify the name of the provider that supplies WIN32_Processor? Yes. It is CIMWin32.

One Step Further: Compiling MOF files

In this section, we will use MofComp.exe to compile MOF files into the WBEM repository. We will first create a new namespace using MofComp.exe and a MOF file. We will then delete that namespace by using MofComp.exe and a MOF file. Next, we will create an instance of the *ActiveScriptEventConsumer* class. Following that, we will delete the instance of the active script consumer we create.

1. Copy the four MOF files in the \My Documents\Microsoft Press\VBScriptSBS\ch21\OneStepFurther folder to a directory you can easily access from a command prompt.

2. Open a command prompt.

3. At the command prompt, use MofComp to compile Createnamespace.mof. This will create a new namespace in WMI off the root namespace that is called *Mynamespace*. The syntax of the command will look something like the following:

```
C:\FSO>mofcomp createnamespace.mof
```

The output from this command will look like the following:

```
Microsoft (R) 32-bit MOF Compiler Version 5.1.2600.2180
Copyright (c) Microsoft Corp. 1997-2001. All rights reserved.
Parsing MOF file: createnamespace.mof
```

```
MOF file has been successfully parsed
Storing data in the repository...
Done!
```

4. Run the \My Documents\Microsoft Press\VBScriptSBS\ch21\
   OneStepFurther\ ListWMINamespace.vbs script to confirm the namespace was
   created.

5. Now we want to delete the namespace. At the command prompt, use MofComp to compile Deletenamespace.mof. The command will look like the following:

   ```
   C:\FSO>mofcomp deletenamespace.mof
   ```

   The output from the command will look like the following:

   ```
   Microsoft (R) 32-bit MOF Compiler Version 5.1.2600.2180
   Copyright (c) Microsoft Corp. 1997-2001. All rights reserved.
   Parsing MOF file: deletenamespace.mof
   MOF file has been successfully parsed
   Storing data in the repository...
   Done!
   ```

6. Now we want to create a new instance of the *ActiveScriptEventConsumer* class. We have a
   MOF file that will write to an event log when Calc.exe is closed out. It will require a
   reboot to take effect.

7. At the command prompt, use MofComp to compile the Asec.mof MOF file. This MOF
   file will take about a minute to compile, so do not get alarmed when it does not compile
   as quickly as the two previous files did. The command to do this will look like the following:

   ```
   C:\FSO>mofcomp asec.mof
   ```

   When it is completed compiling, the output will look like the following:

   ```
   Microsoft (R) 32-bit MOF Compiler Version 5.1.2600.2180
   Copyright (c) Microsoft Corp. 1997-2001. All rights reserved.
   Parsing MOF file: asec.mof
   MOF file has been successfully parsed
   Storing data in the repository...
   Done!
   ```

8. Reboot your computer and launch Calc.exe. Use it for a minute or so and perform some
   calculations with it. Exit the calculator.

9. Navigate to your C drive, where you should see a text file called Asec.log. Delete the log
   file. If you do not see a log file there within 5 to 10 seconds, then check the Windows
   Application event log for errors.

10. The last thing we need to do is to delete the instance of the active script event consumer.
    To do this, we will compile the DeleteAsec.mof file using MofComp. The command to
    do this will look like the following:

    ```
    C:FSO\>mofcomp deleteasec.mof
    ```

If the delete is successful, you will see an output similar to the following:

```
Microsoft (R) 32-bit MOF Compiler Version 5.1.2600.2180
Copyright (c) Microsoft Corp. 1997-2001. All rights reserved.
Parsing MOF file: deleteasec.mof
MOF file has been successfully parsed
Storing data in the repository...
Done!
```

Chapter 21 Quick Reference

To	Do This
Determine if WMI service is accepting new connections	Use WBEM Test
Test the scripting interface of WMI service	Use the Scriptomatic
Quickly diagnose the health of the WMI service	Open the WMI control tool
See if the WMI service is running	Use the Services tool

Part V
Appendices

In this part:

Appendix A: VBScript Documentation 443

Appendix B: ADSI Documentation 449

Appendix C: WMI Documentation 457

Appendix D: Documentation Standards 463

Appendix E: Special Folder Constants 467

Appendix A
VBScript Documentation

Constants

The constants in Tables A-1 through A-6 are built into Microsoft Visual Basic, Scripting Edition (VBScript) and therefore do not need to be defined prior to use. You can use them anywhere in your code to represent the values shown.

Table A-1 String constants

Constant	Value	Description
vbCr	Chr(13)	Carriage return
VbCrLf	Chr(13) and Chr(10)	Carriage return–linefeed combination
vbFormFeed	Chr(12)	Form feed; not useful in Microsoft Windows
vbLf	Chr(10)	Line feed
vbNewLine	Chr(13) and Chr(10) or Chr(10)	Platform-specific newline character; whatever is appropriate for the platform
vbNullChar	Chr(0)	Character having the value 0
vbNullString	String having value 0	Not the same as a zero-length string (""); used for calling external procedures
vbTab	Chr(9)	Horizontal tab
vbVerticalTab	Chr(11)	Vertical tab; not useful in Microsoft Windows

Table A-2 Comparison constants

Constant	Value	Description
vbBinaryCompare	0	Perform a binary comparison
vbTextCompare	1	Perform a textual comparison

Table A-3 Date and time constants

Constant	Value	Description
VbSunday	1	Sunday
VbMonday	2	Monday
vbTuesday	3	Tuesday

Table A-3   Date and time constants

Constant	Value	Description
vbWednesday	4	Wednesday
vbThursday	5	Thursday
VbFriday	6	Friday
vbSaturday	7	Saturday
VbUseSystemDayOfWeek	0	Use the day of the week specified in your system settings for the first day of the week
VbFirstJan1	1	Use the week in which January 1 occurs (default)
vbFirstFourDays	2	Use the first week that has at least four days in the new year
vbFirstFullWeek	3	Use the first full week of the year

Table A-4   Date formatting constants

Constant	Value	Description
vbGeneralDate	0	Display a date and/or time. For real numbers, display a date and time. If there is no fractional part, display only a date. If there is no integer part, display time only. Date and time display is determined by your system settings.
vbLongDate	1	Display a date using the long date format specified in your computer's regional settings.
vbShortDate	2	Display a date using the short date format specified in your computer's regional settings.
vbLongTime	3	Display a time using the long time format specified in your computer's regional settings.
vbShortTime	4	Display a time using the short time format specified in your computer's regional settings.

Table A-5   Tri-state constants

Constant	Value	Description
vbUseDefault	-2	Use default from your computer's regional settings
VbTrue	-1	True
VbFalse	0	False

Table A-6   Color constants

Constant	Value	Description
vbBlack	&h00	Black
vbRed	&hFF	Red
vbGreen	&hFF00	Green
vbYellow	&hFFFF	Yellow
vbBlue	&hFF0000	Blue
vbMagenta	&hFF00FF	Magenta

Table A-6   Color constants

Constant	Value	Description
vbCyan	&hFFFF00	Cyan
vbWhite	&hFFFFFF	White

VBScript Run-Time Errors

VBScript *run-time errors* result when your script attempts to perform an action that the system cannot execute. The errors are called run-time errors because they happen while your script is being executed. Run-time errors are listed in Table A-7.

Table A-7   Syntax error numbers and descriptions

Error Number	Description
429	Microsoft ActiveX component can't create object
507	An exception occurred
449	Argument not optional
17	Can't perform requested operation
430	Class doesn't support Automation
506	Class not defined
11	Division by zero
48	Error in loading the dynamic-link library (DLL)
5020	Expected ')' in regular expression
5019	Expected ']' in regular expression
432	File name or class name not found during Automation operation
92	*For* loop not initialized
5008	Illegal assignment
51	Internal error
505	Invalid or unqualified reference
481	Invalid picture
5	Invalid procedure call or argument
5021	Invalid range in character set
94	Invalid use of Null
448	Named argument not found
447	Object doesn't support current locale setting
445	Object doesn't support this action
438	Object doesn't support this property or method
451	Object not a collection
504	Object not safe for creating
503	Object not safe for initializing
502	Object not safe for scripting

Table A-7   Syntax error numbers and descriptions

Error Number	Description
424	Object required
91	Object variable not set
7	Out of memory
28	Out of stack space
14	Out of string space
6	Overflow
35	Sub or function not defined
9	Subscript out of range

VBScript Syntax Errors

VBScript *syntax errors* occur when the structure of one of your script statements violates one or more grammatical rules that govern the use of the scripting language. VBScript syntax errors occur during the program compilation stage, before the program has begun to be executed, and are therefore sometimes referred to as *compile time errors*. Syntax errors are listed in Table A-8.

Table A-8   Syntax error numbers and descriptions

Error Number	Description
1052	Cannot have multiple default properties/methods in a class
1044	Cannot use parentheses when calling a subroutine
1053	Class initialize or terminate does not have arguments
1058	*Default* specification can only be on property *Get*
1057	*Default* specification must also specify 'Public'
1005	Expected '('
1006	Expected ')'
1011	Expected '='
1021	Expected *Case*
1047	Expected *Class*
1025	Expected end of statement
1014	Expected *End*
1023	Expected expression
1015	Expected *Function*
1010	Expected identifier
1012	Expected *If*
1046	Expected *In*
1026	Expected integer constant
1049	Expected *Let*, *Set*, or *Get* in property declaration

Table A-8   Syntax error numbers and descriptions

Error Number	Description
1045	Expected literal constant
1019	Expected *Loop*
1020	Expected *Next*
1050	Expected *Property*
1022	Expected *Select*
1024	Expected statement
1016	Expected *Sub*
1017	Expected *Then*
1013	Expected *To.*
1018	Expected *Wend*
1027	Expected *While* or *Until*
1028	Expected *While, Until,* or end of statement
1029	Expected *With*
1030	Identifier too long
1014	Invalid character
1039	Invalid *Exit* statement
1040	Invalid *For* loop control variable
1013	Invalid number
1037	Invalid use of *Me* keyword
1038	*Loop* without *Do*
1048	Must be defined inside a class
1042	Must be first statement on the line
1041	Name redefined
1051	Number of arguments must be consistent across properties specification
1001	Out of memory
1054	Property *Set* or *Let* must have at least one argument
1002	Syntax error
1055	Unexpected *Next*
1015	Unterminated string constant

FileSystemObject Object Model

Figure A-1 details the VBScript *FileSystemObject* object model.

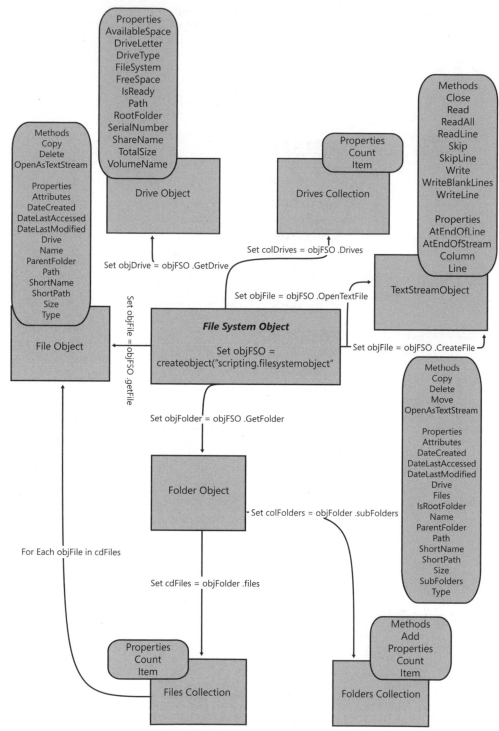

Figure A-1 *FileSystemObject* object model

Appendix B
ADSI Documentation

For network administrators, one of the most frustrating aspects of using Active Directory Service Interfaces (ADSI) is trying to match what is found in Active Directory Users And Computers with what is expected in a Microsoft Visual Basic, Scripting Edition (VBScript) script that uses ADSI to manipulate Microsoft Active Directory directory service. Although it is possible to use ADSI Edit to view the field names, reviewing Tables B-1 through B-20 in this appendix will lessen some of your learning curve.

Computer Object Mapping

Tables B-1 through B-4 show computer object names displayed in the Active Directory Users And Computers tool as they map to names available via ADSI scripting.

Table B-1 Computer Object General Property Tab

User Interface (UI) Label	Active Directory attribute	Comments
Computer Name (pre–Microsoft Windows 2000)	*sAMAccountName*	
Domain Name System (DNS) Name	*dNSHostName*	
Role	*userAccountControl*	Toggles a bit in the *userAccountControl* bitmask
Description	*description*	
Trust Computer For Delegation	*userAccountControl*	Toggles a bit in the *userAccountControl* bitmask

Table B-2 Computer Object Location Property Tab

UI Label	Active Directory Attribute
Location	*location*

Table B-3 Group Object Member of Property Tab

UI Label	Active Directory Attribute	Comments
Member Of	*memberOf*	The member attribute of each of the groups in this list contains the distinguished name of this computer object
Set Primary Group	*primaryGroupID*	

Table B-4 Computer Object Location Property Tab

UI Label	Active Directory Attribute
Name	*operatingSystem*
Version	*operatingSystemVersion*
Service Pack	*operatingSystemServicePack*

Domain Object User Interface Mapping

Table B-5 shows user object names displayed in the Active Directory Users And Computers tool as they map to names available via ADSI scripting.

Table B-5 Computer Object Location Property Tab

UI Label	Active Directory Attribute
Domain Name (pre–Windows 2000)	*DC*
Description	*description*

Group Object User Interface Mapping

Tables B-6 though B-8 show group object names displayed in the Active Directory Users And Computers tool as they map to names available via ADSI scripting.

Table B-6 Group Object General Property Tab

UI Label	Active Directory Attribute
Group Name (pre–Windows 2000)	*sAMAccountName*
Description	*description*
E-Mail	*mail*
Group Scope	*groupScope*
Group Type	*groupType*
Notes	*info*

Table B-7   Group Object Member of Property Tab

UI Label	Active Directory Attribute	Comments
Member Of	*memberOf*	Contains the distinguished names of the groups to which this group belongs. The member attribute of each of the groups in this list contains the distinguished name of this group object.
		The user interface does not directly modify the *memberOf* attribute. It modifies the *"member"* attribute on the group object of which this object is made a member. Active Directory maintains the *memberOf* attribute.

Table B-8   Group Object Member Members Property Tab

UI Label	Active Directory Attribute	Comments
Members	*member*	Contains the distinguished names of the members of this group object

Object Property Tab

Table B-9 shows object property names displayed in the Active Directory Users And Computers tool as they map to names available via ADSI scripting.

Table B-9   Group Object Member Members Property Tab

UI Label	Active Directory Attribute	Comments
Fully Qualified Domain Name of Object		This is the object's distinguished name in canonical form
Object Class	*objectClass*	
Created	*whenCreated*	
Modified	*whenChanged*	
Update Sequence Numbers: Current	*uSNChanged*	
Update Sequence Numbers: Original	*uSNChanged*	

Organizational Unit User Interface Mapping

Table B-10 and Table B-11 show organizational unit object names displayed in the Active Directory Users And Computers tool as they map to names available via ADSI scripting.

Table B-10   Organizational Unit (OU) General Property Tab

UI Label	Active Directory Attribute	Comments
Description	*description*	
Street	*street*	
City	*l*	The *l* attribute name is a lowercase *L*
State/Province	*st*	
Zip/Postal Code	*postalCode*	
Country/Region	*c*	This is a lowercase *c*

Table B-11   Organizational Unit (OU) General Property Tab

UI Label	Active Directory Attribute	Comments
Name	*managedBy*	
Manager Can Update Membership List	*n/a*	Changes the ownership to the person named in the name (managedBy) attribute
Office	*physicalDeliveryOfficeName*	
Street	*streetAddress*	
City	*l*	The l attribute name is a lowercase L.
State/Province	*st*	
Country/Region	*c*	This is a lowercase c.
Telephone Number	*telephoneNumber*	
Fax Number	*facsimileTelephoneNumber*	

Printer Object User Interface Mapping

Table B-12 shows printer object names displayed in the Active Directory Users and Computers tool as they map to names available via ADSI scripting.

Table B-12   Shared Folder Object General Property Tab

UI Label	Active Directory Attribute
Location	*location*
Model	*driverName*
Description	*description*
Color	*printColor*
Staple	*printStaplingSupported*
Double-Sided	*print DuplexSupported*
Printing Menu	*printRate*
Maximum Resolution	*printMaxResolutionSupported*

Shared Folder Object User Interface Mapping

Table B-13 shows shared folder object names displayed in the Active Directory Users And Computers tool as they map to names available via ADSI scripting.

Table B-13   Shared Folder Object General Property Tab

UI Label	Active Directory Attribute
Description	*description*
UNC Name	*uNCName*
Keywords	*keywords*

User Object User Interface Mapping

Tables B-14 through B-20 show user object names displayed in the Active Directory Users And Computers tool as they map to names available via ADSI scripting.

Table B-14   User Object General Property Tab

UI Label	Active Directory Attribute
First Name	*givenName*
Last Name	*sn*
Initials	*initials*
Description	*description*
Office	*physicalDeliveryOfficeName*
Telephone Number	*telephoneNumber*
Telephone: Other	*otherTelephone*

Table B-14   User Object General Property Tab

UI Label	Active Directory Attribute
E-Mail	*mail*
Web Page	*wwwHomePage*
Web Page: Other	*url*

Table B-15   User Object Account Property Tab

UI Label	Active Directory Attribute	Comments
User logon name	*userPrincipalName*	LDAP = logonPrincipalName, which prefixes the Logon Name drop-down list and adds the full text to the attribute
User logon name (pre–Windows 2000)	*sAMAccountname*	
Logon Hours	*logonHours*	
Log On To	*logonWorkstation*	
Account Is Locked Out	*userAccountControl*	Toggles a bit in the *userAccountControl* bitmask (flag: UF_ACCOUNTSDISABLE)
User Must Change Password At Next Logon	*pwdLastSet*	
User Cannot Change Password	*N/A*	This is the Change Password control in the ACL
Other Account Options	*userAccountControl*	The remaining items in Account Options toggle bits in the *userAccountControl* bitmask (flags in a DWORD)
Account Expires	*accountExpires*	

Table B-16   User Object Account Property Tab

UI Label	Active Directory Attribute	Comments
Street	*streetAddress*	
P.O. Box	*postOfficeBox*	
City	*l*	The l attribute name is a lowercase L as in Locale
State/Province	*st*	
Zip/Postal Code	*postalCode*	
Country/Region	*c, co, and countryCode*	

Table B-17   **User Object Account Property Tab**

UI Label	Active Directory Attribute	Comments
Member Of	*memberOf*	
Set Primary Group	*primaryGroupID*	LDAP: Linked to *primaryGroup Token* of the primary group

Table B-18   **User Object Account Property Tab**

UI Label	Active Directory Attribute	Comments
Title	*title*	
Department	*department*	
Company	*company*	
Manager: Name	*manager*	
Direct Reports	*directReports*	Back linked by Active Directory to directReports

Table B-19   **User Object Account Property Tab**

UI Label	Active Directory Attribute	Comments
Profile Path	*profilePath*	
Logon Script	*scriptPath*	
Home Folder: Local Path	*homeDirectory*	If Local Path is selected, the local path is stored in the homeDirectory attribute
Home Folder: Connect	*homeDrive*	If Connect is selected, the mapped drive is stored in the homeDrive attribute
Home Folder: To	*homeDirectory*	If Connect is selected, the path is stored in the homeDirectory attribute

Table B-20   User Object Account Property Tab

UI Label	Active Directory Attribute	Comments
Home	*telephoneNumber*	LDAP: homePhone
Home: Other	*otherTelephone*	LDAP: otherHomePhone
Pager	*pager*	
Pager: Other	*pagerOther*	LDAP: otherPager
Mobile	*mobile*	
Mobile: Other	*otherMobile*	
Fax	*facsimileTelephoneNumber*	
Fax: Other	*otherFacsimileTelephone Number*	
IP Phone	*ipPhone*	
IP phone: Other	*otherIpPhone*	
Notes	*info*	

WMI Documentation

Win32 Classes

Microsoft Windows classes give you the means to manipulate a variety of objects. Table C-1 identifies the categories of Windows classes.

Table C-1 WMI Log Files

File	Description
Computer system hardware	Classes that represent hardware-related objects
Operating system	Classes that represent operating system-related objects
Installed applications	Classes that represent software-related objects
Microsoft Windows Management Instrumentation (WMI) service management	Classes used to manage WMI
Performance counters	Classes that represent formatted and raw performance data

WMI Providers

The providers in Table C-2 can request information from and send instructions to WMI objects.

Table C-2 WMI providers

Provider	Description
Active Directory provider	The Active Directory provider maps Microsoft Active Directory directory service objects to WMI. By accessing the \Root \Directory\LDAP namespace in WMI, the Active Directory provider supplies WMI with access to information contained in Active Directory.
Cooked Counter provider	High-performance provider that is the preferred source of cooked (calculated) data. Cooked data is the same data displayed in the System Monitor. WMI supplies cooked classes such as Win32_PerfFormattedData_PerfOS_Cache, which enable applications to obtain cooked data for performance objects such as the cache.

Table C-2   **WMI providers**

Provider	Description
DFS provider	Supplies Distributed File System (DFS) functions that logically group shares on multiple servers and link them transparently to a tree-like structure in a single namespace.
Disk Quota provider	Enables administrators to control the amount of data that each user stores on a Microsoft Windows NT File System (NTFS) volume.
Event Log provider	Provides access to data from the event log service to notifications of events.
IP Route provider	Supplies network routing information.
Job Object provider	Provides access to data on named kernel job objects.
Performance Counter provider	High-performance provider that is the preferred source of raw performance data. WMI supplies raw classes such as *Win32_PerfRawData_PerfOS_Cache*, which enable applications to obtain raw performance data for performance objects such as the cache.
Performance Monitoring provider	Provider for cooked performance data.
Ping provider	Supplies WMI access to the status information provided by the standard *Ping* command.
Policy provider	Provides extensions to Group Policy and permits refinements in the application of policy.
Power Management Event provider	Supplies information to the *Win32_PowerManagementEvent* class to describe power management events that result from power state changes.
Security provider	Retrieves or changes security settings that control ownership, auditing, and access rights.
Session provider	Manages network sessions and connections.
SNMP provider	Maps Simple Network Management Protocol (SNMP) objects defined in Management Information Base (MIB) schema objects to WMI Common Information Model (CIM) classes. This provider is not preinstalled.
System Registry provider	Enables management applications to retrieve and modify data in the system registry and receive notifications when changes occur. This provider is not preinstalled.
Terminal Services provider	WMI classes that you can use for consistent server administration in a Terminal Services environment.
Trustmon provider	Provides access information about domain trusts.
View provider	Creates new instances and methods based on instances of other classes.
WDM provider	Provides access to the classes, instances, methods, and events of hardware drivers that conform to the Windows Driver Model (WDM).

Table C-2   WMI providers

Provider	Description
Win32 provider	Provides access to and updates data from Windows systems such as the current settings of environment variables and the attributes of a logical disk.
Windows Installer provider	Provides access to information collected from Windows Installer–compliant applications, and it makes Windows Installer procedures available remotely. On Windows Server 2003 this provider is not preinstalled.
Windows Product Activation provider	Supports Windows Product Activation (WPA) administration by using WMI interfaces, and it provides consistent server administration.

WMI Scripting API Objects

Table C-3 describes WMI scripting API objects and how they are used.

Table C-3   WMI scripting API objects

Object	Description
SWbemDateTime	Constructs and parses CIM date/time values.
SWbemEventSource	Retrieves events in conjunction with *SWbemServices.Exec NotificationQuery*.
SWbemLastError	Provides extended error information when an error occurs.
SWbemLocator	Obtains an *SWbemServices* object that can get access to WMI on a particular host computer.
SWbemMethod	Contains a single WMI method definition.
SWbemMethodSet	Gets a collection of *SWbemMethod* objects.
SWbemNamedValue	Contains a single named value.
SWbemNamedValueSet	Gets access to a collection of *SWbemNamedValue* objects.
SWbemObject	Contains and manipulates a single WMI object class or instance.
SWbemObjectEx	Extends the functionality of *SWbemObject*. This object adds the *Refresh* method for *SWbemRefresher* objects.
SWbemObjectPath	Generates and validates an object path.
SWbemObjectSet	Gets access to a collection of *SWbemObject* objects.
SWbemPrivilege	Sets or clears a privilege.
SWbemPrivilegeSet	Gets access to a collection of *SWbemPrivilege* objects.
SWbemProperty	Contains a single WMI property.
SWbemPropertySet	Gets access to a collection of *SWbemProperty* objects.
SWbemQualifier	Contains a single property qualifier.
SWbemQualifierSet	Gets access to a collection of *SWbemQualifier* objects.

Table C-3   WMI scripting API objects

Object	Description
SWbemRefresher	Collects and updates object property values in one operation.
SWbemRefreshableItem	Represents a single refreshable element in an *SWbemRefresher* object, such as a property.
SWbemSecurity	Manages security settings such as Component Object Model (COM) Privileges, *AuthenticationLevel*, and *ImpersonationLevel*.
SWbemServices	Creates, updates, and retrieves instances or classes.
SWbemServicesEx	Extends the functionality of *SWbemServices*. This object adds the *Put* and *PutAsync* methods to allow a class or instance to be saved to multiple namespaces.
SWbemSink	Receives the results of asynchronous operations and event notifications, which are used by client applications.

WMI Log Files

Table C-4 lists the log files created by WMI and the WMI providers.

Table C-4   WMI Log Files

File	Description
Dsprovider.log	Logs information and error messages for the Directory Services provider.
Framework.log	Traces information and error messages for the provider framework and the Win32 provider.
Mofcomp.log	Compiles details from the MOF compiler.
Ntevt.log	Traces messages from the Event Log provider. This provider requires that you set any bit value for the mask level in the system registry.
Setup.log	Reports MOF files that failed to load during the setup process. However, the error that caused the failure is not reported. You must review the Mofcomp.log file to determine the reason for the failure. After the error has been corrected, you can recompile the MOF file (using MofComp) with the autorecover switch.
Viewprovider.log	Traces information from the View provider based on the mask level you set in the registry.
Wbemcore.log	Reports wide spectrum of trace messages.
Wbemess.log	Logs entries related to events.
Wbemprox.log	Traces information for the WMI proxy server.
Wbemsnmp.log	Traces information from the Simple Network Management Protocol (SNMP) provider.
Winmgmt.log	Traces information that is typically not used for diagnostics.
Wmiadap.log	Reports error messages related to the AutoDiscoveryAutoPurge (ADAP) process.
Wmiprov.log	Manages data and events from WMI-enabled Windows Driver Model (WDM) drivers.

WMI Scripting Object Model

Figure C-1 illustrates the WMI Scripting Object Model.

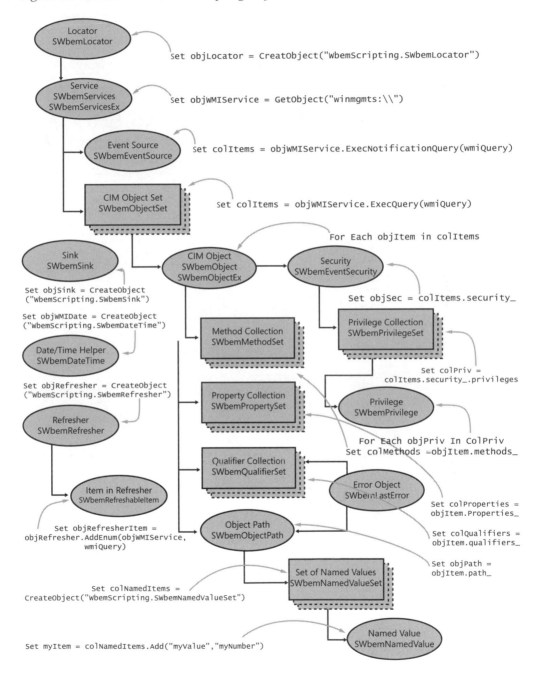

Figure C-1 WMI Scripting Object Model

Appendix D

Documentation Standards

As network administrators begin to write many scripts, a need for standards becomes rapidly apparent. Large companies commonly maintain a collection of *enterprise scripts* that have been tested and approved for use as network tools. To ensure these scripts can be readily maintained, modified, and debugged, proper documentation must be included with them. This appendix offers suggestions for what kind of information to include with these scripts.

Header Information Section

The following items should be considered for inclusion in the Header information section of a script:

- Script name
- Script writer
- Date the script was written
- Version information
- Description of the purpose of the script
- Special requirements for use of the script (for example, command-line arguments and access to Microsoft Active Directory directory service)

Reference Information Section

The following items should be documented in the Reference information section of the script:

- Use of all variables
- Use of all constants

Worker Information Section

The following items should be documented in the Worker information section of the script:

- Explanation of statements used to gather information
- Explanation of statements used to configure settings
- Explanation of any other statements used in the script

Output Information Section

The following items should be documented in the Output information section of the script:

- Explanation of where the data is coming from
- Explanation of how the data is built
- Explanation of where the calling procedure is
- Explanation of any worker elements used in formatting the output

Sample of Documentation Use

The following script illustrates how you might include the elements described in the previous sections of this appendix to fully "document" a script. Although documenting a script does add considerably to its length, it also makes the script easier to understand when you need to modify it at a later date.

```
'  ++++++++++++++++++++++++++++++++++++++++++++++++++++++
'  Written by Ed Wilson, 7/13/2006' version 1.0 basic script
'  version 1.1 -- added additional documention, 1/14/2006
'  Key concepts are listed below:

'  This script displays various Computer Names by reading
'  the registry
'  ++++++++++++++++++++++++++++++++++++++++++++++++++++++
Option Explicit
On Error Resume Next

Dim objShell 'holds connection to wscript.shell
Dim regActiveComputerName 'holds registry string for
             'active computer name
Dim regComputerName 'holds registry string for computer name
Dim regHostname 'holds registry string for hostname
Dim ActiveComputerName 'holds value found in registry
Dim ComputerName 'holds value found in registry
Dim Hostname 'holds value found in registry


regActiveComputerName = "HKLM\SYSTEM\CurrentControlSet" & _
  "\Control\ComputerName\ActiveComputerName\ComputerName"
```

```
regComputerName = "HKLM\SYSTEM\CurrentControlSet\Control" & _
  "\ComputerName\ComputerName\ComputerName"
regHostname = "HKLM\SYSTEM\CurrentControlSet\Services" & _
  "\Tcpip\Parameters\Hostname"


Set objShell = CreateObject("WScript.Shell") 'provides access to regRead
ActiveComputerName = objShell.RegRead(regActiveComputerName)
ComputerName = objShell.RegRead(regComputerName)
Hostname = objShell.RegRead(regHostname)

'WScript.Echo is simple output. The output variables are assigned value in
'the worker section due to the regRead method.
WScript.Echo activecomputername & " is active computer name"
WScript.Echo ComputerName & " is computer name"
WScript.Echo Hostname & " is host name"
```

Variable Naming Conventions

In most cases, you can name a variable whatever you wish. You can call it *a,b,c* or you can call it *myVariable* ... it really does not matter. This being the case, it makes good sense to use a variable that might actually help you to understand the code you have just written. If your code creates an object, then use a prefix that will let you know the variable contains an object. Then if you get a type violation, it will be easier to troubleshoot. See Table D-1 for variable naming standards.

Table D-1   Variable Naming Standards

Prefix	Sample	Use
obj	*objFSO*	Contains an object
int	*intCount*	Contains an integer
str	*strName*	Contains a string
bln	*blnEnabled*	Contains a Boolean value
ary	*aryUsers*	Contains an array
col	*colItems*	Contains a collection
sub	*subLoggging*	The name of a subroutine
fun	*funLine*	The name of a function
dtm	*dtmLastAccessed*	Contains a date

If we expand upon this naming convention, we can arrive at a select number of common variables that would be used in the vast majority of scripts we write for use in the enterprise. Doing so will greatly simplify the reading and the adapting of scripts produced in the same organization. Consider Table D-2:

Table D-2   Standard Variables

Variable	Meaning	How Created
objFSO	The file system object	*scripting.filesystemobject*
objFolder	*Folder* object	*objFSO.GetFolder*
colFiles	Collection of files	*objFolder.files*
objFile	*File* object	*For each objFile in colFiles*
objShell	*WshShell* object	*WScript.shell*
objNetwork	*WshNetwork* object	*WScript.network*
objWMIservice	*SwbemServices* object	*winmgmts:*
dtmTime	Date variant	Contains a time stamp

Appendix E
Special Folder Constants

The DisplayAdminTools.vbs script presented in Chapter 1, "Starting from Scratch," relies upon what are called shell special folder enumerated types. Although they are detailed in the Platform SDK, they can be a little hard to find in those documents. Due to the power of the DisplayAdminTools.vbs script, and its usefullness in the day-to-day life of network administrators (for both reporting purposes and for troubleshooting), I am including all the special folder constants in Table E-1.

Table E-1   Special folder constant values

Special Folder Name	Value In Hex	Value in Decimal
Admintools	0x30	48
Altstartup	0x1d	29
Appdata	0x1a	26
Bitbucket	0xa	10
Cdburn_area	0x3b	59
Common_admintools	0x2f	47
Common_altstartup	0x1e	30
Common_appdata	0x23	35
Common_desktopdirectory	0x19	25
Common_documents	0x2e	46
Common_favorites	0x1f	31
Common_music	0x35	53
Common_pictures	0x36	54
Common_programs	0x17	23
Common_startmenu	0x16	22
Common_startup	0x18	24
Common_templates	0x2d	45
Common_video	0x37	55
Controls	0x3	3
Cookies	0x21	33
Desktop	0x0	0

Table E-1 Special folder constant values

Special Folder Name	Value In Hex	Value in Decimal
Desktopdirectory	0x10	16
Drives	0x11	17
Favorites	0x6	6
Fonts	0x14	20
History	0x22	34
Internet	0x01	1
Internet_cache	0x20	32
Local_appdata	0x1c	28
Mydocuments	0x0c	12
Mymusic	0x0d	13
Mypictures	0x27	39
Myvideo	0x0e	14
Nethood	0x13	19
Network	0x12	18
Personal	0x5	5
Printers	0x4	4
Printhood	0x1b	27
Profile	0x28	40
Profiles	0x3e	62
Program_files	0x26	38
Program_files_common	0x2b	43
Programs	0x2	2
Recent	0x8	8
Sendto	0x9	9
Startmenu	0xb	11
Startup	0x7	7
System	0x25	37
Templates	0x15	21
Windows	0x24	36

Index

A

Access database, ADO to query, 308–309
Active Directory
  changes to, 257
  connect to, 252, 293–297
  control script execution while querying, 312–314
  create ADO query into, 311–312
  fill out profile tab in, 279
  limit search, 300
  modify user properties in, 270
  objects used to search, 297
  organizational attributes in, 282
  schema cache, 350
  search, 294
  Sysvol share in, 352
  telephone tab attributes in, 280
  in Windows Server 2003, 298
Active Directory Migration Tool (ADMT), 253
Active Directory Schema MMC, 303–304
Active Directory Service Interfaces (ADSI)
  binding, 256–257
  create computer account, 261–262
  create groups in, 260–261
  create multiple users, 280–281
  create users with, 258–262
  creating multi-valued users, 265–267
  delete users, 287–290
  Edit snap-in, 254
  event log, 290–291
  Flag property, 298
  general user information, 270–271
  IADsContainer, 256
  LDAP names, 255
  merge WMI and, 322–323
  modify organizational settings, 281–282
  modify terminal server settings, 283–287
  modifying address tab information, 274–282
  Output information, 257–258, 273
  provider, 253–254
  Reference information, 253–254, 272
  user profile settings, 278
  user telephone settings, 279–280
  Worker information, 255–256, 272–273
  working with, 251–257
  working with users, 269–273
  See also Active Directory
Active Directory Users and Computers (ADUC), 270, 274
ActiveX Data Objects (ADO)
  create effective queries, 297–299
  Global Catalog server, 303–311
  Header information, 295
  Output information, 296–297, 301–303
  Reference information, 295, 301
  search for specific types of objects, 299–303
  search properties, 298–299
  to query Access database, 308–309
  to query Excel spreadsheet, 307–308
  to query text file, 309–311
  WMI-network connection, 316–317
  Worker information, 296–297
Address tab
  mappings, 275
  modify information on, 274–282
  Output information, 277–282
  Reference information, 275
  Worker information, 275
ADO. *See* ActiveX Data Objects
ADouWMIDHCP.vbs, 322–323
ADsDSOObject provider, 296, 319
ADSI. *See* Active Directory Service Interfaces
Adsldp.dll file, 349
ADSystemInfo interface, 356
Ampersand (&), 5, 12, 68, 89
Angle brackets (<>), 295
appActivate method, 49
ArgComputerService.vbs, 87–88, 90
Arguments
  command-line, 81–83
  multiple, 86–89
  named, 85, 90–93
  passing, 81, 103–107
  "subscript out of range," 84
  supply value for missing, 85–86
  unnamed, 85–86
Array
  building, 107–111
  command-line arguments, 81–83
  create, 93
  defined, 93
  detecting properties, 210–211
  Join function and, 357
  moving past dull, 95–100
  passing arguments, 81, 103–107
  tell me your name, 89–93
  two-dimensional, 101–103
  using multiple arguments, 86–89
  working with, 93–95
ArrayReadTxtFileUBound.vbs, 98
ArrayReadTxtFile.vbs, 95–98
ASCII, 49
atEndOfStream, 59

Attribute indexing, 304–305
Attributes, query multiple, 302–303
Automatic cleanup, 172–174
Automation objects, 10

B

Backup window, 176
BasicArrayForEachNext.vbs, 94–95
BasicArrayForNext.vbs, 94
BasicQuery.vbs, 294–295
BindFolder.vbs, 175
Binding, 256–257
Binding string, 256–257
BIOSVersion property, 209–210
Business rules, 331

C

Capitalization, WMI properties and, 231
Capture error, 360
Carriage return, 61
Case sensitive, ADSI provider names as, 253
Change method, 200
CheckArgsPingMultipleComputers.vbs, 84–85
CheckNamedArgCS.vbs, 93
CheckServiceStatus.vbs, 99–100
CIM_Component class, 396
CIM_ElementSetting class, 396
CIM_LogicalDevice class, 200
CIM_ManagedSystemElement class, 395
CIM_Setting class, 395–396
CIMSettingClass.vbs, 397–398
Cleanup, automatic, 172–174
CmdDir.vbs, 369
CollectionOfDrivers.vbs, 26–27
Collections, 29–30
Command-line arguments
   create user error message, 84–86
   defined, 81–86
   implement, 82
   modify, 82–83
   no arguments, 84
   run from command prompt, 83
Command-line syntax, 90
Command object, 297
Command prompt, run command-line arguments from, 83
Comment, 13
Common classes, 194
Common name (cn), 259
Computer account, create, with ADSI, 261–262
ComputerRoles.vbs, 70–71, 76–79
comspec variable, 368–369
Concatenation, 5, 12, 68, 89
Connection object, 297–297

ConnectToADOU.vbs, 316–317
Constants
   benefits of, 28–29
   defining, 27
   vs. variables, 27–29
Consumers, WMI, 188
Continuation character, 89
CopyFolderExtended.vbs, 176–177
CopyFolder.vbs, 176
Core classes, 194
Count method, 94
Country codes, ISO 3166-1, 276
CPUTypeStarter.vbs, 74
CPUType.vbs script, 64–66, 74–79
CreateAddRemoveShortCut.vbs, 50
CreateBasicFolder_checkFirst.vbs, 175
CreateBasicFolder.vbs, 166
CreateMultiFolders.vbs, 166
   automatic cleanup, 172–174
   Header information, 167
   Output information, 167–168
   Reference information, 167
   Worker information, 167–168
CreateObject command, 165–167, 172, 296–297, 319
CreateOU.vbs, 252–253, 255–256
CreateRegKey.vbs, 373–374
CreateShortCut method, 49–50
CreateSite.vbs, 399–401
CreateUser.vbs, 258–259
CreateUsersLogAction.vbs, 332–334
Creating a literal, 27
CScript, 6, 12, 21–22, 41
Cscript.exe, 13
.csv file, 236

D

Database corruption, WMI, 419
Dataset, 201
DCOM security, 432
Defaults, accepting WMI, 208–214
Definitive software library (DSL), 355
DeleteBasicFolder.vbs, 172
DeleteMultiFolders.vbs, 173–174
DeleteRegKey.vbs, 377
DeleteUser.vbs, 288–289
Dependencies, 421
DHCP, 76
Diagnostic information, obtain, 426–432
Dim command, 6–7, 17–19, 27–28, 93–94, 108
   variables announced by, 32–33
DisplayAdminTool.vbs, 4
DisplayComputerNames.vbs, 5–6, 19, 59–61
DisplayComputerNameWithComments.vbs, 13–14
DisplayProcessInformation.vbs, 31–33
DisplayWPAStatus.vbs, 201–203

Distinguished names, 255–256
Distributed Component Object Model (DCOM) security
    issues, 419
DNS domain name of currently logged-on user, 15
Do...Loop command, 47
DoLoopMonitorForProcessDeletion.vbs, 47
Do Until...Loop, 333
Do Until loop, 97–98, 110
   defined, 43
   Header information, 44
   Reference information, 44
   worker and output information, 45–46
Do Until...Next command, 97–98
Do While...Loop command, 37–43
   difference between *Do Until* and, 46
   Header information, 38–39
   Output information, 40–43, 59, 61
   Reference information, 39–40
   Worker information, 40–43, 59, 61
Do While True, 41, 47
Domain components (DCs), 259
Domain name, 259
DSL. *See* Definitive software library
Dull arrays, 95–100
Dynamic classes, 194
Dynamic Host Configuration Protocol (DHCP), 320–
   321

E

Echo command, 12, 49, 176
EnableDHCP.vbs, 320–321
Encrypt Password property, 298
End If command, 46, 56, 61, 93
End Select, 74
End Sub command, 191
Err tool, 429–430
   output from, 434
Error handling process, 7
Error message, create useful, 84–86
Error object, 297
Errors, WMI, common sources of, 419–420
Event log, 290–291
Excel spreadsheet, ADO to query, 307–308
Exchange 2003, 407–418
   connect to *MicrosoftExchangeV2*, 408–409
   Exchange_FolderTree, 413–414
   Exchange_Logon, 414–416
   Exchange_Mailbox, 416–418
   Exchange_QueueSMTPVirtual
     Server, 409
   Header information, 409–410
   MicrosoftExchangeV2 namespace, 407
   Output information, 410–411
   public folders, 411–413
   Worker information, 410

Exchange WMI namespace, changes to, 407–408
ExchangeFolderTree.vbs, 413–414
ExchangePublicFolders.vbs, 411–413
ExchangeSMTPQueue.vbs, 409–410
Exec method, 49–50
Exists method, 92
Exit Do, 41
ExpandEnvironmentStrings method, 49

F

Field object, 297
FileSystemObject class, 44, 165, 167, 172
   CopyFolder method, 176
   folders and, 174–175
   MoveFolder method, 179
   OpenTextFile method, 171
Filter command, 108
FilterComputers.vbs, 300
Filtered print monitor, 386–388
FilterPrinterStatus.vbs, 386–387
Firewall issues, 420
Folders, 165–172
   binding to, 174–175
   check on existence of, 175
   copying, 176–179
   create, 182–183
   create basic, 165–166
   create multiple, 166
   create programmatically, 173
   delete, 172–174, 184
   listing sizes, 177–178
   moving, 178–181
For Each...Next, 72, 94
   defined, 26
   Header information, 27–30
   Reference information, 30
   step-by-step exercises, 51–52
   Worker information, 30–31
formatNumber function, 41–43, 62, 177
For...Next, 31–37, 94, 97–98, 102–103
   CreateObject code with, 168
   Header information, 32–33
   Reference information, 33–34
   worker and output information, 34–37
ForReading constant, 44, 57, 96, 110
ForWriting constant, 57
FSOTemplate.vbs, 177
funComputerRole function, 72–74
Functions
   add, to convert to megabytes, 342
   compare intrinsic and user defined, 342–343
   working with, 341–343
funfix function, 287

G

GetCommentsTimed.vbs, 60
GetComments.vbs, 56–57, 59
GetStringValue, 375
Global Catalog server, 303–311
   query, 305–306
Group
   add to logon script, 360–362
   create, with ADSI, 260–261
Group Policy Objects (GPOs), 352
Group Policy server, 15

H

Header information
   ADO, 295
   create users log, 335
   create Web sites, 400–401
   CreateMultiFolders.vbs, 167
   Do Until...Loop, 44
   Do While...Loop, 38–39
   EnableDHCP, 321
   Exchange 2003, 409–410
   For Each...Next, 27–30
   For...Next, 32–33
   If Then, 57
   If...Then...Elself, 64–65, 85
   IIS 6.0 connection, 397–398
   logon scripts, 354–355
   modify, 15–16
   monitor printer status, 383–384
   move past dull arrays, 96
   multiple arguments, 88
   reasons for, 5–6
   registry connection, 371
   registry key, 374
   script, 5–9, 16–18
   Select Case, 71
   two-dimensional arrays, 102
   WMI query, 228–229
   WMI script, 202
   WMI-network connection, 317–318
Hierarchical namespace, 188–191
Hotfix information, retrieving, 204–205

I

IADsADSystemInfo interface, 349–351
IADsContainer, 256
If...Then, 41, 46, 55–62, 93, 106
   Header information, 57
   Reference information, 57–58
   Worker and Output information, 58–62
If...Then...Else, 67–69
If...Then...Elself
   Header information, 64–65

Reference information, 65
   use, 62–63
   Worker and output information, 65–67
ifThenElse.vbs, 68
If...Then End if, 61–62
IfThen.vbs script, 55–56
IIS 6.0
   back up metabase, 403–404
   connection, 397–399
   create Web site, 399–402
   import metabase, 404–406
   locate WMI classes for, 395–397
IIsStructuredDataClass class, 396
Impersonation levels, 214–215
InformativeWMI.vbs, 245–247
Infrastructure, WMI, 188
Inputbox search, 197
InStr command, 45–46
InStr function, 60
Intelligence, adding, 55–79
Internet Protocol (IP) address, 51, 252
Intrinsic constants, 61
IP. *See* Internet Protocol (IP) address
ISO 3166, 276

J

Join function, 210, 357
JScript, 13

K

Key properties, 232–233

L

LBound, 97
LDAP names, 255
LDAP provider, 253–254, 316
Lightweight Directory Access Protocol (LDAP), 270
Linear scripting, 329
LinearScript.vbs, 330–331
Line concatenation, 5. *See also* Concatenation
Line continuation, 5, 89
Line feed, 61
ListClassMethods.vbs, 199–200
ListClassProperties.vbs, 198
ListName_Only_AllShares.vbs, 231
ListName_Path_Max_Shares.vbs, 232
ListShares.vbs, 228, 230–231
ListSpecificGreaterThanShares.vbs, 228–241
ListSpecificShares.vbs, 237–238
ListSpecificWhereVariableShares.vbs, 241–242
ListWMIClasses.vbs, 194–195
ListWMINamespaces.vbs, 189–191
ListWMIProviders.vbs, 192–193

Local computer, *IADsADSystemInfo* interface and, 349
LogEvent method, 49, 291
Logging
    add to logon script, 362–364
    service accounts, 239–241
    use subroutine to perform, 343–345
    verbose WMI, 427
    WMI, 433–437
Logging subroutine, 234–237, 336–338, 345–347
Logon script
    add group to, 360–362
    add logging to, 362–364
    deploy, 352–358
    Header information, 354–355
    IADsADSystemInfo interface, 349–351
    Output information, 358–360
    Reference information, 355–356
    use, 351
    Worker information, 357–358
    WshNetwork class, 356
LogonScript.vbs, 353–358
Loop counter, 103
Loop Until, 46

M
Machine boot configuration, WMI moniker to display,
        221–222
Managed Object Format (MOF) format, 425
Metabase
    back up IIS 6.0, 403–404
    import IIS 6.0, 404–406
Methods
    defined, 10–11
    WMI, 199–200
Microsoft Excel, 21
    .csv file opens, 236
Microsoft Exchange 2000 domain information, 15
Microsoft Management console (MMC), 254
Microsoft Windows Me, 15
Microsoft Windows 95, 15
Microsoft Windows 2000, 15
Microsoft Windows XP, 15
MicrosoftDNS namespace, 188
MicrosoftExchangeV2 namespace, 407
MicrosoftIISv2 namespace, 396–397
Millions of instructions per seconds (MIPS), 66
ModifyTerminalServerProperties.vbs, 284–285
ModifyUserAddressTab.vbs, 274–275
ModifyUserProperties.vbs, 270–273
MOF files, compiling, 437–439
MofComp.exe, 430–431, 437–439
Moniker, 190. See also WMI moniker
MonitorForChangedDiskSpace.vbs, 38, 47
MonitorPrinterStatus.vbs, 383–384
MonitorPrintQueue.vbs, 388–389

MoveFolder.vbs script, moving, 179
MrEd OU, 254
MsgBox, 12
msgBox function, 180
msgBox.vbs script, 63
Multiple users, create, 280–281

N
"Name redefined" error, 331
Named arguments, 85, 90–93
NamedArgCS.vbs, 91–92
Namespace
    default, 190
    defined, 189–191
    Exchange WMI, 407
    WMI, 189–191
Naming convention, Lightweight Directory Access Proto-
        col (LDAP), 270
NDS provider, 253
Networking components
    change TCP/IP settings, 320–321
    merge WMI and ADSI, 322–323, 326–327
    Win32_NetworkAdapterConfiguration, 323–325
    WMI and, 315–320, 325–326
Next command, 35
Notepad
    add, to SendTo menu, 22
    CScript, 21
    drag and drop .vbs file to, 21
    use, to speed script modification, 17
Now command, 35, 176–178
Null string, 46
numLoop, 103
NWCOMPAT provider, 253
nwtraders.msft, 254

O
Object
    create additional, 48–51
    defined, 10–11
    search for specific types of, with ADO, 299–303
    select specific properties from, 236
    WMI, 189–191
objectCategory attribute, 299
ObjTxtFile, 96–97
On Error Resume Next, 27–28
    benefit of, 229
    function of, 6–8
    If Then, 56
    with ListShares.vbs, 228
    logon script and, 353, 354
    turn off during development, 7, 32–33
Open command prompt, dragging and dropping .vbs
        file to, 21

OpenTextFile command, 59
Operator
    VBScript, 238–239
    WMI query using, 238–241
Option Explicit
    first line of script, 6–7, 27–28, 32–33, 38–39, 41, 44
    as spelling checker, 38–39
Organizational settings, modify, 281–282
Organizational unit (OU) structure, 251, 263–265
Output information
    ADO, 296–297, 301–303
    ADSI, 257–258, 273
    ADSI address tab script, 277–282
    create ADSI users, 260–262
    create users log, 336–341
    create Web sites, 402
    CreateMultiFolders.vbs, 168
    Do Until...Loop, 45–46
    Do While...Loop, 40–43, 61
    EnableDHCP, 321
    Exchange 2003, 410–411
    filtered print monitor, 387, 389
    For Each...Next, 102–103
    For...Next, 34–37
    If...Then, 58–62
    If...Then...Else, 68–69
    If...Then...Elseif, 65–67
    IIS 6.0 connection, 399
    logon scripts, 358–360
    modify, 19–22
    monitor printer status, 385
    move past dull arrays, 96–97
    registry connection, 371–372
    registry key, 374–375
    script, 12–13, 19–22
    Select Case, 72–74
    two-dimensional arrays, 102–103
    using multiple arguments, 88
    WMI moniker, 209
    WMI query, 229–230
    WMI script, 203
overwriteFiles constant, 176

P

Parameter object, 297
Pascal-cased, Windows NT as, 253
Passing arguments, 81, 103–107
Password property, 298
Ping script, modify, 52–53
PingMultipleComputers.vbs, 83
Ping.vbs script, 82–83
Platform SDK, defined privileges in, 215–216
PopUp method, 49

Printers
    check status of print server, 391–392
    create filtered print monitor, 386–388
    monitor print queues, 388–391
    obtain status of, 382–385
    Win32_Printer, 381–382
Privilege strings, 216
Processes, Taskmanager.exe view of, 338
Properties
    defined, 10–11
    detecting array, 210–211
    list running, 233–234
    select specific, from object, 236
    Terminal Server setting, 282–283
    Win32_Share, 229–230
    WMI, 197–199
Property object, 297
Provider, security issues, 419
Put command, 273, 276
Put method, 260

Q

Query
    Global Catalog server, 305–306
    security event log, 216–219
    WMI, 201–204
Quotation marks, WMI query in, 217

R

ReadHotFixes.vbs, 370–372
ReadTextFile.vbs, 43
RecordSet object, 297–297
Reference information, 39–40
    ADO, 295, 301
    ADSI, 253–254, 272
    ADSI address tab script, 275
    create ASDI users, 259
    create users log, 335–336
    create Web sites, 401–402
    CreateMultiFolders.vbs, 167
    Do Until...Loop, 44
    EnableDHCP, 321
    filtered print monitor, 387
    For Each...Next, 30
    For...Next, 33–34
    If Then, 57–58
    If...Then...Elseif, 65
    IIS 6.0 connection, 398–399
    logon scripts, 354–356
    modify, 16–18
    monitor printer status, 384
    move past dull arrays, 96
    purpose of, 9
    registry connection, 371–372

registry key, 374–375
script, 8–9, 16–18
Select Case, 71–72
two-dimensional arrays, 102
using multiple arguments, 88
WMI moniker, 208–209
WMI query, 229
WMI script, 202–203
WMI-network connection, 318

R

RegDelete method, 49
Registry
    back up of, 367–380
    connect to, 370–372
    create registry keys, 373–375
    create *WshShell* Object, 368–369
    creating keys, 378–379
    delete information, 376–377
    read using WMI, 377–378
    StdRegProv class, 372–373
    writing to, 375–376
Registry Editor, Copy Key Name feature, 9
Registry key, 7–9 12
RegRead method, 49
RegWrite method, 49
Relative distinguished names (RDNs), 255
Replace dialog box, 18–19
Resources, WMI, 188
Resultant Set of Policy information, 188
RetrieveComputerSystem.vbs, 426
RetrieveWMISEttings.vbs, 425–426
ROUND function, 60
RSOP namespace, 188
Run method, 48–49
RunNetStat.vbs script, 50–51
Running properties, list, 233–234
Runtime engines, 13

S

SBSQueryHotFix.vbs, 205
Script(s)
    add documentation to, 13–14
    add power to, 25–48
        Do...Loop, 47
        Do Until...Loop, 43–46
        Do While...Loop, 37–43
        For Each...Next, 26–31
        For...Next, 31–37
        While...Wend, 47–48
    defined, 4
    documenting, 355
    embedding, in Web pages, 21
    enhancing, 13–14

ensure correct path information for, 254
header information, 5–8, 15–16
how to run, 20–22
modify, 14–22
open existing, 4
output information, 12–13, 19–22
prevent choking, 13
promote code re-use within, 331
reference information, 8–9, 16–18
run, with named arguments, 92–93
run existing, 4
step-by-step exercises, 22–23
use Notepad to speed modification, 17
useful registry keys, 15
worker information, 9–11, 18–19
See also entries for individual scripts
Scripting interface, troubleshoot, 425
Scriptomatic, 422
Security event log, query, 216–219
Security issues
    Distributed Component Object Model (DCOM), 419
    provider, 419
Security permissions, modifying WMI moniker to
    include additional, 222–223
Security settings, WMI moniker, 214–220
Select Case statement, 69–74
    Header information, 71
    in logon script, 357–358
    modify CPUType.vbs, 74–77
    Output information, 72–74
    Reference information, 71–72
    Worker information, 72–74
sendKeys method, 49
SendTo menu, add Notepad to, 22
Server authenticated currently logged-on user, 15
ServersAndServices text file, 97–98
Service accounts
    identifying, 239
    logging, 239–241
Service dependencies, 421
Service information, 15
Services, Taskmanager.exe view of, 338
Set command, 58–59, 91
SetInfo command, 273
SetPowerState method, 200
SetStringValue, 375
Simple Mail Transfer Protocol (SMTP) address, 252
Single dimension array, 97
Sleep command, 36
SmallBIOS.vbs, 208
Space ( ) command, 35–36
Spacing, WMI properties and, 231
specialFolders method, 170
Spelling, 19, 38–39. *See also* Option Explicit
Split function, 106–107
SQL. *See* Structured Query Language (SQL)

StartTime function, 40
StdRegProv class, 372–373
StopService method, 46, 200
Structured Query Language (SQL), 210, 231
subCheckArgs subroutine, 86, 106
subLogging subroutine, 170–171
subRecursiveFolders subroutine, 180–181
Subroutine, 329–341
  defined, 48, 191
  call, 331–332
  create, 332
  create users and log results, 332–334
  defined, 329
  logging, 234–237, 345–347
  use to perform logging, 343–345
SubRoutineScript.vbs, 331–332
"Subscript out of range," 84
subtree modifier, 295
SysInfo.vbs, 350
Sysvol share, in Active Directory, 352

T

TCP. *See* Transmission Control Protocol (TCP)
TCP/IP. *See* Transmission Control Protocol/Internet Protocol (TCP/IP)
Telephone settings, user, 279–280
"Tell me everything about everything" script, 227
Terminal Server settings, modify, 282
Text file
  ADO to query, 309–311
  array, combine WMI and, 98
Time zone, echoing, 205
Timer function, 41–43, 60
TimeZoneSolution.vbs, 205
Transact-SQL (T-SQL), 210
Transmission Control Protocol (TCP), 51
Transmission Control Protocol/Internet Protocol (TCP/IP), 76
Transmission Control Protocol/Internet Protocol (TCP/IP) address, 319–321
Troubleshoot WMI scripting
  general steps, 432–433
  identify the problem, 419–420
  obtain diagnostic information, 426–432
    err tool, 429–430
    MofComp.exe, 430–431
    verbose WMI logging, 427–432
    WMI log files, 428–429
    WMIcheck, 431
  test local WMI service, 420–424
    dependencies, 421
    scriptomatic, 422
    service status, 422

    WBEMtest.exe, 423–424
    WMI Control tool, 420
  test remote service, 424–425
  test scripting interface, 425–426
Two-dimensional arrays, 101–103
Type mismatch error, 209

U

UBound, 94, 97–99
Underscore character, 89
Universal Naming convention (UNC) path, 176, 358
Unnamed arguments, 85–86
User ID property, 298
User name, used to log on to domain, 15
User profile settings
  ADSI, 278
  Terminal Server, 285–287
User telephone settings, 279–280
UserAccountControl, 262–263
Users, delete, using ADSI, 287–290
User's home directory, 15

V

Variable(s)
  benefits of, 28–29
  constants vs., 27–29
  declare, 6–7
  defined, 6
  standard names, 335
  tables of, 355
VB.NET, 7
vbNewLine command, 35–36
.vbs file, 21
VBScript, 6–7, 13
  double-check, 20
  to learn about WMI, 224
  logon script, 353–358
  operators, 238–239
  subroutines in, 330
Verbose WMI logging, enable, 427
VideoAdapterRAM_HardCoded.vbs, 341

W

WBEM repository, 432
WbemPrivilege, 215–220
WBEMtest.exe, 423
Web page, embedding script in, 21
Web sites, use WMI to create, 399–402
whenTest.exe utility, 65
Where clause, 241–244
While Not Wend construction, 296, 316, 319
While Not...Wend loop, 322
While...Wend, 47

WhileWendLoop.vbs script, 47–49
Win32_Environment, to learn about WMI, 224
Win32_NetworkAdapterConfiguration, 323–325
Win32_Printer, 381–382
Win32Printer class, use filter on, 386
WIN32Processor, SetPowerState method, 200
Win32_Share properties, 229–230
Win32WindowsProduct Activation, properties of, 203–204
Windows 2000, OS version build number, 420
Windows Management Instrumentation (WMI), 422
    accepting defaults, 208–214
    alternate ways to connect to, 212
    classes, 194–200
    combine text file and, 98
    connection string, 223
    consumers, 188
    create Web sites, 399–402
    DCOM security, 432
    Do Until...Loop, 45–46
    Do While...Loop, 40–43, 61
    echoing the time zone, 205
    enable DHCP using, 320–321
    For Each...Next, 26–27, 30–31, 102–103
    For...Next, 34–37
    If Then, 58–62
    If...Then...Elseif, 65–67
    infrastructure, 188
    Key property in, 232–233
    listing providers, 192–193
    merge ADSI and, 322–323
    methods, 199–200
    modify, 18–19
    module registration, 432
    moniker security settings, 214–220
    move past dull arrays, 96–94
    namespaces, 189–191
    network and. See WMI-network connection
    objects, 189–191
    properties, 197–199
    query, 201–204, 227–247. *See also* WMI query
    read registry using, 377–378
    resources, 188
    retrieving Hotfix information, 204–205
    script, 9–11
    Select Case statement and, 70–71
    service information, 198–199
    service settings, 432
    strComputer variable and, 64
    troubleshoot, 420–439
    two-dimensional arrays, 102–103
    understanding the model, 188
    use subroutine to retrieve service information from, 338–341
    using multiple arguments, 89

    using VBScript to learn about, 224
    using Win32_Environment to learn about, 224
    WBEM repository, 432
Windows NT, as Pascal-cased, 253
Windows Product Activation (WPA) information, 203–204
Windows Scripting Host (WSH), 12–13, 21, 84–86
Windows Server 2003
    Active Directory in, 298
    OS version build number, 420
    WMI in, 187–206
    WMI namespaces in, 190
Windows XP
    OS version build number, 420
    WMI namespaces in, 189
winmgmts, 202–203
WinNT provider, 253
WMI. *See* Windows Management Instrumentation (WMI)
WMI CIM Studio tool, 233
WMI classes, locate, for IIS 6.0, 395–397
WMI Control tool, 420, 424–425, 427
WMI database corruption, 419
WMI errors, common sources of, 419–420
WMI log files, 428–429
WMI logging, 433–437
WMI moniker
    additional security permissions, 222–223
    alternate ways of configuring, 207
    default, 220
    to display machine boot configuration, 221–222
    winmgmts as, 202–203
    See also Moniker
WMI namespace, changes to Exchange, 407
WMI object browser, 213
WMI Platform SDK, 73
WMI query
    choosing specific instances, 237–238
    Header information, 228–229
    obtaining more direct information, 245–247
    Output information, 229–230
    in quotation marks, 217
    Reference information, 229
    selecting multiple properties, 231–237
    selective data from all instances, 230–231
    "tell me everything about everything", 227
    using an operator, 238–241
    Where clause, 241–244
    Worker information, 229–230
WMI Query Language (WQL), 210, 231
WMI script, writing informative, 244
WMI service, test local, 420–424
WMIcheck, 431–432
WMI-network connection, 316–319
WmiTemplate.vbs template, 242

Worker information, 272–273
    ADO, 296–297
    ADSI, 255–256
    ADSI address tab script, 275–277
    create ADSI users, 259–260
    create users log, 336
    create Web sites, 402
    CreateMultiFolders.vbs, 167
    EnableDHCP, 321
    Exchange 2003, 410
    filtered print monitor, 389
    IIS 6.0 connection, 399
    logon scripts and, 357–358
    monitor printer status, 384–385
    registry connection, 371–372
    registry key, 374–375
    WMI moniker, 209
    WMI query, 229–230
    WMI script, 203
    WMI-network connection, 318–319
WorkWith2DArray.vbs, 101–102
WPA. *See* Windows Production Activation (WPA) infor-
    mation
WQL. *See* WMI Query Language (WQL)
Write command, 60
WriteToRegKey.vbs, 376
WScript, 10
WScript.Arguments, 87
WScript.Arguments.Count method, 84–85
WScript.Arguments.Named, 90–91
  to echo out value of strLine, 46
WScript.Echo command, 12, 20, 35, 36, 68, 84, 86, 97,
    168, 172, 209, 318
WScript.Echo line, 99
WScript.exe, 13, 20
WScript.quit, 67
Wscript.shell object, 48–49, 170–171
WSH. *See* Windows Scripting Host (WSH)
WshNetwork class, 356
WshShell object, 170–171, 368–369
  comspec variable, 368–369
  define command, 369

About the Author

Ed Wilson is a senior consultant with the Operational Consulting group at Microsoft, where he provides both consulting and training to global premier customers on the deployment and management of scripting and WMI solutions. As a former network administrator, he brings an infrastructure perspective to scripting solutions. Over the years, he has worked with customers in more than 35 different countries. He has written or contributed to 10 books and holds more than 20 industry certifications, including both the MCSE and the CISSP.

Additional Windows (R2) Resources for Administrators

Published and Forthcoming Titles from Microsoft Press

Microsoft® Windows Server™ 2003 Administrator's Pocket Consultant, Second Edition
William R. Stanek • ISBN 0-7356-2245-0

Here's the practical, pocket-sized reference for IT professionals supporting Microsoft Windows Server 2003—fully updated for Service Pack 1 and Release 2. Designed for quick referencing, this portable guide covers all the essentials for performing everyday system administration tasks. Topics include managing workstations and servers, using Active Directory® directory service, creating and administering user and group accounts, managing files and directories, performing data security and auditing tasks, handling data back-up and recovery, and administering networks using TCP/IP, WINS, and DNS, and more.

MCSE Self-Paced Training Kit (Exams 70-290, 70-291, 70-293, 70-294): Microsoft Windows Server 2003 Core Requirements, Second Edition
Holme, Thomas, Mackin, McLean, Zacker, Spealman, Hudson, and Craft • ISBN 0-7356-2290-6

The Microsoft Certified Systems Engineer (MCSE) credential is the premier certification for professionals who analyze the business requirements and design and implement the infrastructure for business solutions based on the Microsoft Windows Server 2003 platform and Microsoft Windows Server System—now updated for Windows Server 2003 Service Pack 1 and R2. This all-in-one set provides in-depth preparation for the four required networking system exams. Work at your own pace through the lessons, hands-on exercises, troubleshooting labs, and review questions. You get expert exam tips plus a full review section covering all objectives and sub-objectives in each study guide. Then use the Microsoft Practice Tests on the CD to challenge yourself with more than 1500 questions for self-assessment and practice!

Microsoft Windows® Small Business Server 2003 R2 Administrator's Companion
Charlie Russel, Sharon Crawford, and Jason Gerend • ISBN 0-7356-2280-9

Get your small-business network, messaging, and collaboration systems up and running quickly with the essential guide to administering Windows Small Business Server 2003 R2. This reference details the features, capabilities, and technologies for both the standard and premium editions—including Microsoft Windows Server 2003 R2, Exchange Server 2003 with Service Pack 1, Windows SharePoint® Services, SQL Server™ 2005 Workgroup Edition, and Internet Information Services. Discover how to install, upgrade, or migrate to Windows Small Business Server 2003 R2; plan and implement your network, Internet access, and security services; customize Microsoft Exchange Server for your e-mail needs; and administer user rights, shares, permissions, and Group Policy.

Microsoft Windows Small Business Server 2003 R2 Administrator's Companion
Charlie Russel, Sharon Crawford, and Jason Gerend • ISBN 0-7356-2280-9

Here's the ideal one-volume guide for the IT professional administering Windows Server 2003. Now fully updated for Windows Server 2003 Service Pack 1 and R2, this *Administrator's Companion* offers up-to-date information on core system administration topics for Microsoft Windows, including Active Directory services, security, scripting, disaster planning and recovery, and interoperability with UNIX. It also includes all-new sections on Service Pack 1 security updates and new features for R2. Featuring easy-to-use procedures and handy work-arounds, this book provides ready answers for on-the-job results.

MCSA/MCSE Self-Paced Training Kit (Exam 70-290): Managing and Maintaining a Microsoft Windows Server 2003 Environment, Second Edition
Dan Holme and Orin Thomas • ISBN 0-7356-2289-2

MCSA/MCSE Self-Paced Training Kit (Exam 70-291): Implementing, Managing, and Maintaining a Microsoft Windows Server 2003 Network Infrastructure, Second Edition
J.C. Mackin and Ian McLean • ISBN 0-7356-2288-4

MCSE Self-Paced Training Kit (Exam 70-293): Planning and Maintaining a Microsoft Windows Server 2003 Network Infrastructure, Second Edition
Craig Zacker • ISBN 0-7356-2287-6

MCSE Self-Paced Training Kit (Exam 70-294): Planning, Implementing, and Maintaining a Microsoft Windows Server 2003 Active Directory® Infrastructure, Second Ed.
Jill Spealman, Kurt Hudson, and Melissa Craft • ISBN 0-7356-2286-8

For more information about Microsoft Press® books and other learning products, visit: **www.microsoft.com/mspress** *and* **www.microsoft.com/learning**

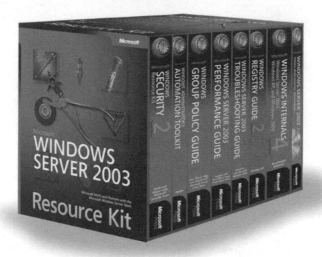

Additional SQL Server Resources for Administrators

Published and Forthcoming Titles from Microsoft Press

Microsoft® SQL Server™ 2005 Reporting Services *Step by Step*
Hitachi Consulting Services • ISBN 0-7356-2250-7

SQL Server Reporting Services (SRS) is Microsoft's customizable reporting solution for business data analysis. It is one of the key value features of SQL Server 2005: functionality more advanced and much less expensive than its competition. SRS is powerful, so an understanding of how to architect a report, as well as how to install and program SRS, is key to harnessing the full functionality of SQL

Server. This procedural tutorial shows how to use the Report Project Wizard, how to think about and access data, and how to build queries. It also walks the reader through the creation of charts and visual layouts to enable maximum visual understanding of the data analysis. Interactivity (enhanced in SQL Server 2005) and security are also covered in detail.

Microsoft SQL Server 2005 Administrator's Pocket Consultant
William R. Stanek • ISBN 0-7356-2107-1

Here's the utterly practical, pocket-sized reference for IT professionals who need to administer, optimize, and maintain SQL Server 2005 in their organizations. This unique guide provides essential details for using SQL Server 2005 to help protect and manage your company's data—whether automating tasks; creating indexes and views; performing backups and recovery; replicating transactions; tuning performance; managing server

activity; importing and exporting data; or performing other key tasks. Featuring quick-reference tables, lists, and step-by-step instructions, this handy, one-stop guide provides fast, accurate answers on the spot, whether you're at your desk or in the field!

Microsoft SQL Server 2005 Administrator's Companion
Marci Frohock Garcia, Edward Whalen, and Mitchell Schroeter • ISBN 0-7356-2198-5

Microsoft SQL Server 2005 Administrator's Companion is the comprehensive, in-depth guide that saves time by providing all the technical information you need to deploy, administer, optimize, and support SQL Server 2005. Using a hands-on, example-rich approach, this authoritative, one-volume reference book provides expert advice, product information, detailed solutions, procedures, and real-world troubleshooting tips from experienced SQL Server 2005 professionals. This expert guide shows you how to design high-availability database systems, prepare for installation, install and configure SQL Server 2005, administer services and features, and maintain and troubleshoot your database system. It covers how to configure your system for your I/O system and model and optimize system capacity. The expert authors provide details on how to create and use defaults, constraints, rules, indexes, views, functions, stored procedures, and triggers. This guide shows you how to administer reporting services, analysis services, notification services, and integration services. It also provides a wealth of information on replication and the specifics of snapshot, transactional, and merge replication. Finally, there is expansive coverage of how to manage and tune your SQL Server system, including automating tasks, backup and restoration of databases, and management of users and security.

Microsoft SQL Server 2005 Analysis Services *Step by Step*
Hitachi Consulting Services • ISBN 0-7356-2199-3

One of the key features of SQL Server 2005 is SQL Server Analysis Services—Microsoft's customizable analysis solution for business data modeling and interpretation. Just compare SQL Server Analysis Services to its competition to understand/grasp the great value of its enhanced features. One of the keys to harnessing the full functionality of SQL Server will be leveraging Analysis Services for the powerful tool that it is—including creating a cube, and deploying, customizing, and extending the basic calculations. This step-by-step tutorial discusses how to get started, how to build scalable analytical applications, and how to use and administer advanced features. Interactivity (which is enhanced in SQL Server 2005), data translation, and security are also covered in detail.

Microsoft SQL Server 2005 Express Edition
Step by Step
Jackie Goldstein • ISBN 0-7356-2184-5

Inside Microsoft SQL Server 2005:
The Storage Engine
Kalen Delaney • ISBN 0-7356-2105-5

Inside Microsoft SQL Server 2005:
T-SQL Programming
Itzik Ben-Gan • ISBN 0-7356-2197-7

Inside Microsoft SQL Server 2005:
Query Processing and Optimization
Kalen Delaney • ISBN 0-7356-2196-9

For more information about Microsoft Press® books and other learning products,
visit: **www.microsoft.com/mspress** *and* **www.microsoft.com/learning**

Microsoft®
Press

Prepare for Certification with Self-Paced Training Kits

Official Exam Prep Guides—
Plus Practice Tests

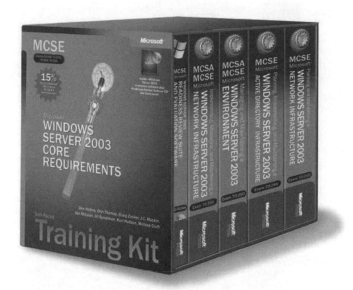

Ace your preparation for the skills measured by the MCP exams—and on the job. With official *Self-Paced Training Kits* from Microsoft, you'll work at your own pace through a system of lessons, hands-on exercises, troubleshooting labs, and review questions. Then test yourself with the Readiness Review Suite on CD, which provides hundreds of challenging questions for in-depth self-assessment and practice.

- **MCSE Self-Paced Training Kit (Exams 70-290, 70-291, 70-293, 70-294): Microsoft® Windows Server™ 2003 Core Requirements.** 4-Volume Boxed Set. ISBN: 0-7356-1953-0. (Individual volumes are available separately.)

- **MCSA/MCSE Self-Paced Training Kit (Exam 70-270): Installing, Configuring, and Administering Microsoft Windows® XP Professional, Second Edition.** ISBN: 0-7356-2152-7.

- **MCSE Self-Paced Training Kit (Exam 70-298): Designing Security for a Microsoft Windows Server 2003 Network.** ISBN: 0-7356-1969-7.

- **MCSA/MCSE Self-Paced Training Kit (Exam 70-350): Implementing Microsoft Internet Security and Acceleration Server 2004.** ISBN: 0-7356-2169-1.

- **MCSA/MCSE Self-Paced Training Kit (Exam 70-284): Implementing and Managing Microsoft Exchange Server 2003.** ISBN: 0-7356-1899-2.

For more information about Microsoft Press® books, visit: **www.microsoft.com/mspress**

For more information about learning tools such as online assessments, e-learning, and certification, visit: **www.microsoft.com/mspress** *and* **www.microsoft.com/learning**

What do you think of this book? We want to hear from you!

Do you have a few minutes to participate in a brief online survey? Microsoft is interested in hearing your feedback about this publication so that we can continually improve our books and learning resources for you.

To participate in our survey, please visit:
www.microsoft.com/learning/booksurvey

And enter this book's ISBN, 0-7356-2297-3. As a thank-you to survey participants in the United States and Canada, each month we'll randomly select five respondents to win one of five $100 gift certificates from a leading online merchant.* At the conclusion of the survey, you can enter the drawing by providing your e-mail address, which will be used for prize notification *only*.

Thanks in advance for your input. Your opinion counts!

Sincerely,

Microsoft Learning

Microsoft | Learning

Learn More. Go Further.